Life in Organizations

LIFE IN ORGANIZATIONS

Workplaces As People Experience Them

ROSABETH MOSS KANTER

AND

BARRY A. STEIN

EDITORS

Basic Books, Inc., Publishers   *New York*

Library of Congress Cataloging in Publication Data
Main entry under title:

Life in organizations.

  Bibliography: p. 429
  Includes index.
  1. Organizational behavior—Case studies.
2. Industrial sociology—Case studies. 3. Occupations—
Social aspects—Case studies. I. Kanter,
Rosabeth Moss. II. Stein, Barry A.
HD58.7.L53   301.18'32   77–20413
ISBN: 0–465–04040–3 cloth
ISBN: 0–465–04041–1 pbk.

For All of Us Who Live
a Significant Part of Our Lives
in Organizations

CONTENTS

f. 36
192
318

PART I
SLICES OF LIFE

PART II
LIFE TIMES

Contents

ACKNOWLEDGMENTS

WE are grateful for the assistance of Derick Brinkerhoff, Patricia Enright, Barbara Glas, Myron Kellner-Rogers, Wanda Koetz, Carolyn Wadhams, and Meg Wheatley, at various stages of conception and manuscript preparation.

ROSABETH MOSS KANTER
BARRY A. STEIN
*Cambridge, Massachusetts
and New Haven, Connecticut
April, 1978*

GENERAL INTRODUCTION

LIVES are lived in organizations. Few of us have the right to make decisions about how other people's organizational lives will be conducted, but all of us manage at least ourselves as we decide how to make a life out of the options presented to us by the organization. In that sense, we are all managers.

This book is about the human experiences of living in organizations and how to learn from them. We investigate the effects on people of being in various positions in organizations—effects not in any passive psychological sense of what is "done" to them but in an active sense of what becomes possible or impossible for them to do. The focus is on the potentials for behavior and action contained in various situations: the decisions people must make, the dilemmas that they must untangle or survive, the preoccupations and concerns that are likely to arise for them.

There are real people, real organizations, and real events represented here. Some of them are well-known: Henry Kissinger, Warren Bennis, the Planning Director of San Francisco and his dealings with Mayor Alioto, the Chairman of Continental Airlines, General Electric, the Lordstown auto plant strike, and the Gulf Oil political scandals. Others are more anonymous, but representative of the people and issues in familiar businesses, factories, offices, universities, and government agencies. A number of alternative workplaces trying to do things differently also appear.

There are tales of coping and tales of corruption. There is the excitement of newborn organizations and the trauma of dying organizations. We see leaders who are aware and those who are unaware; some who are power-sharing and some who are power-hungry; people who are "making it" and people who are not.

People's experiences are shaped by where they happen to be in the system at that moment and where the system happens to be. These situations are predictable and give rise to predictable kinds of issues and dilemmas. Organizations are internally differentiated, and there are different experiences in different positions. So first we take a cut through the organization and look at some of the slices of life by levels: the top, the middle, and the bottom. At the same time, the organization itself is moving through different states and is in different positions with respect to both its history and future and its environment. Each of these states also gives rise to different tensions, dilemmas, and experiences. We look at the times of birth and growth, the times of crisis and handling politicized environments, and the times of decay, decline, and even organizational death.

Issues of power and issues of relationships turn out to be a critical thread running through all of these differentiated experiences, but they take different form in each.

This book is about life in another sense, too. We try to breathe life into the theories, whether theories of organization or theories of management, theories about how to handle power or theories about how to get ahead. The stories of people and organizations that include events and details make it clear that there are few easy generalizations; life is rich and complex. The most practical "how to do it" guide is one that teaches people how to be aware of their own experiences—what it does to them to be in particular positions at particular times—and to understand the likely impact on others. With that kind of understanding of the meaning of being at the top or in the middle, in a growing or a decaying organization, the rules for "what to do" follow easily. And more importantly, people who read this book and reflect on its concepts and stories will be better able to create for themselves the rules on how to manage.

So, ultimately, we see this as a practical book, a book of advice. We ourselves straddle the worlds of academia and action. We believe in research and reflection, but we also believe in putting what we observe to work for the benefit of the people living in organizations. The practical "how to's" are contained in how people and organizations handled recurrent and predictable problems. The advice comes from the lessons we draw from these cases, the themes we extract, the theories and conclusions from research we review.

Leaders, policy-makers, or managers can take away a number of useful insights:

—what are the sources of real power to get things done;
—how to avoid powerlessness;

—how to handle leadership succession at the top;
—what motivates middle managers and middle professionals, and how to help them get along;
—the problems of professional women entering male domains for the first time;
—what makes people angriest at the bottom;
—how to improve the quality of work life for people in low level positions;
—what to be aware of as an organization grows, and how to manage growth;
—what are the real political factors to take into account in organizations;
—when face-to-face communication improves relationships, and the conditions that make participation work;
—why declining organizations frustrate their people and what *not* to do in such situations;
—how to manage transitions; moving from one state of an organization to others, the process of bringing new people in, the closing of a part of the organization (and how to handle terminations with dignity).

It is hard to look at these issues, however, without also raising some difficult questions of organizational policy and the human responsibilities of organizations. It is clear that many of the ways organizations are conventionally put together and managed have damaging consequences for some of their people, or even, in the case of two stories of corruption here, for the public. Corporate social responsibility is a matter getting considerable attention today. Thus, in various parts of the book, we also draw the attention of leaders and policy-makers to some hard questions about responsibility as well as efficiency.

For the larger number of people who are not leaders, many of these same lessons can help them cope. Furthermore, it is distressing to feel tensions without knowing why, or to be angry at someone without any idea of what is driving him or her. Insights help. It is comforting to know that other people have been through the same thing, that one is not alone. It is helpful to know what one's options are in a given situation, or even when a situation is hopeless. And for those who are not yet in the world of organizations—young people or returning housewives—it is useful to have some living pictures of the realities of the work world.

Finally, for students of organizations—professionals as well as students in the classroom—we hope that this book will help them decide *what* to study. Well-known theories and findings appear here, but there is also much that is new. Particularly as we move into an era where the people side of organizations will become increasingly important as an object of governmental and managerial attention, we urge our colleagues to study the human experience of organizational situations. This can be done in much the same way that we advise managers to do it: by asking the people themselves what they are doing and experiencing.

PART I

SLICES OF LIFE

SECTION ONE

~~~~~~

Life at the Top:
The Struggle for Power

EVERYONE KNOWS who is at the "top" of an organization, right? It's the big chiefs, the top leaders, the highest ranking executives, the people who set the terms and conditions for everyone else, and who symbolize and represent the organization to the rest of the world.

But what *is* the "top" of an organization, anyway? Organizations, after all, are abstractions rather than physical entities. Why, in our mobility-conscious and hierarchical Western way of drawing organization charts, do we use pyramidal images that require, by geometry if nothing else, a top, a pinnacle, a peak?

We could think about organizations and their leaders in a number of different ways, none of which see them at the "top." We could see leaders as being in the "center," occupying the center ring of a set of concentric circles and thus being closer to the action and accumulating information from the hinterlands. We could put them in "front," where they develop the ideas and plans that constitute marching orders for those standing behind. Other cultures, in fact, do visualize organizations and leaders differently and may carry this over into representations of the organization's design. In Yugoslavia, for example, organizations are described by overlapping circles.

Yet, the notion of a "top" *does* seem meaningful in the American and Western context, if we think about what "top" connotes. There are fewer positions and people at the top than else-where. (Indeed, many corporations are shaped more like the Eiffel Tower than a true pyramid, getting progressively narrower closer to the top, but with a large flat bottom.) Top positions supposedly look down over the entire organization and make decisions of wide scope. The places at the top repre-sent the highest achievement in the organization. In some com-panies, status is measured by distance from the top, not by rank up from the lowest level positions. For the people in the top jobs, there is no place to go in that organization without the implication of "demotion," of loss of status; it is, literally, all "downhill" from the vantage point of the "top." And those who occupy top positions also come to constitute a social elite. They are, in most conventional organizations, given the greatest lux-ury and privilege. They are accorded the most deference and may sometimes be considered socially superior human beings. They may even have other people to do for them what most people in the organization have to do for themselves: answer questions, talk to visitors, get food, drive a car. (One secretary to a top official in a small company said, "His wife does every-thing for him at home; I do everything for him here. The only thing he does for himself is . . . well, you know," she smiled, pointing toward the washroom.)

People at the top, in short, have come the furthest, are the fewest, and get the most. They are seen as the people with the power. But what is *not* clear is whether power always goes au-tomatically with top rank, with elite position, with defined au-thority to make decisions for the organization. In fact, it often does not. There is a striking difference between privileged posi-tion and the ability to make anything happen. This is the first and most central paradox of leadership in organizations.

Top executives experience this paradox themselves. The Pres-ident of a major city bank, frustrated by a Board of Directors he could not influence and a tradition-bound staff that seemed un-able to adopt new ideas, said to a group of students who won-dered why he didn't make major changes in the bank, *"Every-one has power—until they try to use it. Then you see how real the power is. I appear to have it, but it is impossible for me to act unilaterally."*

Despite official control of the largest number of resources, despite official leadership of the largest number of people, the capacity to mobilize those resources and people to get something done may not automatically follow. Responsibility and accountability can be formally defined and assigned to some people, but they do not automatically turn into *power*. If members of the upper organizational echelon are often aware that power may be elusive, they may also be aware of how hard it is to convince those further down in the organizations that they do *not* have much power. This in itself can be another source of feelings of impotence: the pressure from below for the top to do *something*, whether or not they can.

A simple game is sometimes used to simulate life in organizations and demonstrate what it means to be in different kinds of positions. In its typical form, the game begins by randomly assigning people to one of three categories—top managers, middle managers, and workers—and giving them a simple product to turn out, such as greeting cards or fortune cookie slogans. Top managers are given the pool of money to which all players have contributed and can make the decision about how it is to be distributed when the products are finished. Middle managers are the communication link between the top managers and the workers. Everytime we have run this game, we have seen the top people, who have the formal authority and the ability to reward or punish, end up feeling helpless rage toward the workers and middle managers whose decisions made the top managers essentially irrelevant. For example, while the top managers would be meeting to discuss what the workers should do, the workers would go ahead and turn out the product, or make up their own plans. In some cases, the top managers decided to keep all the money and turn *themselves* into the production line—in response to their inability to influence the workers, even with total control of the money supply.

Without doubt this is an imperfect picture of organizational reality. In most organizations, the fear of bosses or the desire to please them is strong, and people who work there need the money or the security enough to let themselves be ruled. Or they cannot do anything until resources float down from the top. But the game does drive home the point that having the rank and the resources means nothing by itself in terms of organizational goals or accomplishments at the other end. Some formally designated leaders are essentially powerless (Kanter, 1978a). Or they behave in ways that reduce, rather than increase, their power. As Warren Bennis put it in "Why Leaders Can't Lead" (chapter 2):

Leaders aren't leading. They're consulting, pleading, temporizing, martyrizing, trotting, putting out fire, either avoiding or taking the heat, and spending too much energy in doing both. They've got sweaty palms, and they're scared.

THE SEPARATION OF POWER AND AUTHORITY: SOME INSIGHTS FROM SOCIAL THEORY

Leaders of modern organizations are invested with authority, but they then need to use influence in order to accomplish what needs to be done and to motivate the people around them. But despite the milder words that can be used, still, much of life at the top consists of overt and covert issues of *power;* that is, translating formal authority and persuasive personal influence into real power to get things done, power which does not always rest unequivocally in the hands of those at the top.

One of the great insights of classical social and political theory was that power always involves a relationship, it always consists of interaction and, therefore, can never be one-sided or unilateral. For George Simmel (Wolff, 1950), in particular, there are always degrees of freedom in a relationship between a dominant and a subordinate. The sources of this freedom are of particular interest in contemporary organizations.

First, some orders require more consent than others because of the impossibility of anticipating every move that a subordinate might make or of the impossibility of total surveillance in order to insure that orders are carried out. Thus, the essential fact that organized social life depends on a certain degree of cooperation provides the subordinate with some degrees of freedom with respect to the top leaders.

Second, some relationships, particularly those in organizations, involve only a part of the person. Particularly in a pluralistic society, people often have other choices and can leave the organization rather than give in to orders they disapprove. Or there are limitations agreed on, such as court rulings about employment conditions, so that the power of the dominants is held in check.

Third, some threats cost the authority holder more than others, and therefore, the subordinate can count on their not being used. It is a good bet, for example, that modern leaders will not exhaust all their own resources just to get someone to obey an order; the leader is likely to retreat before depleting his or her own reserves. Nor is it likely that officials will punish subordinates needed to do a certain job so much that they are incapacitated. Only in the least skilled positions (and thus, those seen as most replaceable) are people considered so expendable that their own threats of withdrawal or inaction cannot counter the sanctions held by authorities. (This is a theme to which we return later, when we consider the nature of "life at the bottom.")

At the same time, top leaders are themselves controlled by a relationship of power. There are at least three ways in which authority figures themselves are bound by relationships of dominance and subordination.

First, they must give orders that will be obeyed: "I am their leader, therefore, I must follow them." *The Little Prince*, by Antoine Saint-Exupery (a children's classic read often by adults), tells the story of the "King of the Universe" who could make the sun rise and set, among other miracles. When the Little Prince asked him how he did it, he replied that it was all a matter of knowing what to ask for and when to ask for it. In our terms, the reactions of followers serve to control leaders; the willingness of subordinates to act, the degree to which the leader's orders, demands, or requests are congruent with the follower's expectations—both of these serve as a check on the arbitrary exercise of authority. The bank President quoted earlier felt that whatever power he had would disappear if he used it in a way that was incompatible with what others wanted and expected him to do.

A second check on power is the pressure to translate personal whim into something justifiable on more impersonal and collective grounds. (This pressure, of course, may not be universal; it reflects societies that value the rule of law, not individuals.) Even in relationships that begin as purely personal, as in the situation where an entrepreneur and his family begin an organization, the institutionalization and development or organization mean that dominants must always reach for justifying principles, for rationalizations, for laws that create regularity in the events and affairs of the organization. Thus, the purely personal and arbitrary exercise of will soon becomes translated into orderly principles and procedures for conducting the affairs of the organization. The justification becomes the "good of the organization," not the survival and power of its head. But this process may also bind the leader to the law he has made. The visionary who creates an empire may find himself threatened by the very people to whom he delegated control to help him run it—all in the name of the "good of the organization" he envisioned. There are many examples of entrepreneurs who seek their own immortality through organizations only to find their own presence seen by others as an obstacle to the organization's survival.

On a daily basis, too, authorities must translate their desires into more general principles if they are to carry any weight—and then find themselves subject to those same principles or rules. In modern Western organizations, what we would like from others is often the source of rules controlling ourselves as well. There are some exceptions, some twentieth-century entrepreneurs such as Charles Revson and Henry Ford who ruled personal organizational empires via whim and charisma as much as impersonal law. But it remains true that for most people at the top, the reaching for legitimizing principles also checks their own power. This is an interesting irony of social life. In fact, many founders of modern organizations could never be hired if they suddenly reappeared. Their behavior is now inappropriate.

Third, leaders must be willing to act on their promise of reward or threat of punishment. This then commits the leader himself or herself to a course of action to actually use whatever tools he or she has spoken about in attempting to direct the actions of subordinates. For some classical theorists, indeed, such as Vilfredo Pareto (Parsons, et al., 1961), the maintenance of power was inextricably bound up with the unambivalent exercise of power, with the willingness to use the most extreme tools at the leader's disposal. In milder form in contemporary organizations, we can see that those leaders who are reluctant to act authoritatively, who are often unwilling to act on threats or produce what has been promised, will quickly slip and lose the cooperation of those around them.

Thus, as Simmel pointed out (Wolff, 1950), leaders are always aware of controlling reactions from followers, and relationships of dominance and subordination are highly complex interactions of reciprocity, even if followers appear purely passive in the relationship. Even an unconditional ruler rules by some degree of mutual contract.

CAN LEADERS BE POWERLESS?

There is always, then, some degree of dependency on consent built into the exercise of power by those at the top of an organization. But what specific conditions might account for the degree of power or powerlessness a leader experiences—for how much capacity to take action?

Rosabeth Moss Kanter has shown that power in organizations often comes from doing the extraordinary: exercising discretion, creating, inventing, planning, and acting in non-routine ways (Kanter, 1977). But as Warren Bennis points out in "Why Leaders Can't Lead" (chapter 2), there is an "unconscious conspiracy" in organizations to bog down a leader in details. And since routine problems are easier, more manageable, require less change and consent on the part of anyone else, and lend themselves to instant solutions that can make a leader (temporarily) look good, routine work drives out non-routine work. As the ultimate recourse, the leader may get all the trivial problems dumped on his or her desk. A professor called President Bennis because the heat was down in a classroom; "I suppose he expects me to grab a wrench and fix it."

So people at the top need to insulate themselves from the routine operations of the organization in order to develop and exercise power. But this very insulation leads to a second source of powerlessness. In "How the Top Is Different," (Chapter 1) Kanter gives some examples of how top executives at "Industrial Supply Corporation" operate and are treated by others: sealed off in large distant offices; babied and flattered by aides; frustrated by their distance from the real action. There is often real loneliness mixed with the concern for secrecy at the top. President Bob Six (see chapter 4) could tell no one at Continental that he was thinking about the search. Some organizations are so accustomed to never seeing the top leaders that when a new senior vice president of a bank went to the branch offices to look around, the employees reacted with shock and horror as well as fear and concern. (By contrast, note the easy accessibility of the top in alternative organizations, such as the insurance company president in "At IGP, It's Not Business as Usual," chapter 18.

Bennis and Kanter both point to organizational phenomena which keep the top insulated: the tendency for leaders to create closed inner circles consisting of "doppelgangers"—people just like the leaders who look like them and tell them only what they want to know. In part, because the aides want to relieve the top of burdens, in part, because they think just like the top, and in part, to protect their own positions of power, these close assistants and key managers may prevent the top from getting any real information about what is going on in the organization. "A president," Bennis learned from his own experience, "is often lucky if he can find the buck at all, learn where it stopped, or discover who stopped it before it reached him." Bennis sees Nixon's downfall in Watergate in just such insulation.

Leaders can at least steer their own course between over-insulation and over-immersion in the routine. But two other issues are often beyond their control (perhaps giving rise to feelings of powerlessness): decisions in the environment and decisions by interest groups inside the organization.

The environment presses regardless of the top's grand plans for the organization. At the very least, things going on outside the organization can deflect a leader's attention and drain energy. At worst, however, decisions made elsewhere can have severe consequences for the organization and affect the top's sense of power and operating style inside. In the mid-1960s, for example, when the economy was booming and the student movement was not yet in full bloom, nearly every college administrator and corporation officer could look—and feel—highly successful and gain a great deal of credibility inside the organization for good leadership, which gave them the power, in turn, to put new things in motion. In the last few years, the environment has been strikingly different for many organizations—one of decline—and the capacity of many organizational leaders to do anything about it has been severely limited. Managing decline is quite a different matter from managing growth.

There are also pressures from inside organizations with

which people at the top are often incapable of dealing. When constituencies fragment, when special interest groups demand, when common purpose is lost, when "my vote cancels yours" (Bennis' bumper sticker example), then the system's own politics may reduce the top's capacity to act. Note the examples of politicized organizations in the second part of this book and see the ways in which fragmented special interest groups contribute to the top's inability to get the system moving. Just as managing decline seems to necessitate a much more passive and reactive stance than managing growth, so does mediating among conflicting interests. But many people at the top, because of what is happening outside and inside their organizations—and out of their control—are turned into decline-managers and dispute-mediators. Neither are particularly empowering roles (Kanter, 1978a).

Powerlessness has consequences for behavior and attitudes, as Kanter made clear in *Men and Women of the Corporation* (1977). Those with accountability for results but without the capacity to take action—to bring in the needed resources, to mobilize the needed people, to influence the wider environment—are essentially powerless, even though they might have formal authority of a wide scope. Powerlessness often engenders punitive behavior: the tendency to coerce and punish where moderate persuasion will not work; the tendency to become tight, detail-minded, rule-minded, and inflexible; and the tendency to control even more closely those aspects of the system over which the leader feels he or she does have some power.

Thus, if the people at the top feel out of control of the environment, for example, and if they are simultaneously insulated by the bureaucracy below from the direct capacity to make anything happen in the organization, they may respond with punitive acts of tyranny or dominance that are commonly called "power plays" but are better seen as "powerless plays." We have seen this scenario unfold in company after large company. The market goes bad, or a major supplier raises prices. The top needs to improve the corporation's financial picture. But the top is too remote from the rest of the organization and limited in its capacity to do anything about organizational operations anyway. So the top responds not by mobilizing people to produce more or to work more effectively but by *cutting*. One major American company's top leadership responded to their environmental powerlessness by reducing overhead—i.e., cutting the work force by a third, eliminating expense account lunches, and giving up the Christmas party. (Barry Stein describes how this felt to "Farmco's" people in chapter 20, "We're Going to Make Sure This Never Happens Again.")

It should not be assumed, then, that those at the top automatically *have* power. But we can still understand much of life at the top as centering around issues of power: getting it, wielding it, and holding onto it even beyond the tenure of any one person, by insuring appropriate institutionalization of policy or appropriate successors. All of these issues require attention to the fact that even those at the top are part of the system, and, as we have seen, the fact that an organization exists below is often a strong limitation on the power at the top.

THE PROBLEM OF PERSONALIZING LEADERSHIP

The top *is* different, as Kanter shows in chapter 1, in a variety of ways. One of these is that the top of an organization is much more personalized than the supposedly rational and impersonal bureaucracy below. The leader's self, his or her character, is more critical and is viewed more critically, just as Bob Six commissioned personal investigations of his possible organizational heirs. At the same time, people at the top may be guided by more personalistic and familistic principles, trying to operate as a closed social circle, trying to leave their personal mark on the system. In fact, as we see in Paul Ward's account of Henry Kissinger as State Department manager in chapter 3, there is often a tension between the desire of those at the top for personalized leadership and decision-making and the routine operations controlled by those below.

The Kissinger case is particularly interesting for students of power, for Kissinger, the intellectual, gave us advance indications of the principles Kissinger, the manager, would follow in office. In the 1960s, he documented his reflections on his own role model for leadership: Otto von Bismarck, Chancellor of Germany. Kissinger noted in Bismarck an intolerance for "the routine of a civil servant," an insistence on "identifying his will with the meaning of events," and a "matter-of-fact Machiavellianism" (1968: 322, 323, 335). Like Kissinger, who began his career in the Nixon Administration as National Security Adviser, Bismarck was in a relatively subordinate position in the state bureaucracy before rising to the visible power position at the top, and essentially as an adviser, his principal means of influencing public policy was through reports to his superiors. Thus, neither man climbed to power through the ranks—a key fact in assessing their problems in dealing with the "middle managers" responsible for the ongoing operations of the organization. Yet, Kissinger at least assumed that he could change the course of international relations merely as a policy decision from the top, without considering the institutional layers of the organization below.

But as Kissinger also saw in reflecting on Bismarck, no one person can run foreign affairs (or corporations or universities) by himself or herself, as a matter of personal power, for:

To be sure, while Bismarck governed, these dilemmas were obscured by a diplomatic tour de force based on a complicated system of pacts with Germany at their center. But the very complexity of these arrangements doomed them. A system which requires a great man in each generation sets itself an almost insurmountable challenge, if only because a great man tends to stunt the emergence of strong personalities. When the novelty of Bismarck's tactics had worn off and the originality of his conception came to be taken for granted, lesser men strove to operate his system while lacking his sure touch and almost artistic sensitivity. As a result, what had been the manipulation of factors in a fluid situation eventually led to the petrification of the international system which produced World War I. [Kissinger, 1968: 350]

In short, personal diplomacy is not enough. And Bismarck's downfall was also Kissinger's own "failure" as an organizational leader:

But the gods sometimes punish pride by fulfilling man's wishes too completely. Statesmen who build lastingly transform the personal act of creation into institutions that can be maintained by an average standard of performance. This Bismarck proved incapable of doing. His very success committed Germany to a permanent tour de force. It created conditions that could be dealt with only by extraordinary leaders. Their emergence in turn was thwarted by the colossus who dominated his country for nearly a generation. Bismarck's tragedy was that he left a heritage of unassimilated greatness. [Kissinger, 1968:319]

Was that also Kissinger's tragedy? What we see in Paul Von Ward's account from inside the State Department is the failure of Kissinger's outward orientation and personal diplomacy to penetrate very far down in the State Department as an organization; so that while Kissinger may have been effective as a foreign policy-formulator, he was unable to institutionalize his principles in an organization that would continue to carry them out after he had departed. He could not translate the personal into the organizational—a problem faced by many people who are inserted into positions at the tops of organizations they neither rose through nor created.

But contrast Kissinger's leadership style with that of Bob Six, President of Continental Airlines, whose long search for a successor is described by Rush Loving in chapter 4. While Kissinger was oriented upward and outward, Six was down in the organization itself and knew what was happening below him; the company cafeteria was the place everyone ate, so the troops could mingle. While Kissinger, true to the doppelganger principle, chose as assistants cronies without managerial experience, Six at least insured that his executive team (though a closed social—and familial—circle) had their leadership potential tested under fire in significant managerial assignments. Six's eight-year process of selecting the next president was in itself a response to the problem of how to institutionalize personal leadership: by passing the job on to a carefully groomed successor.

THE SUCCESSION QUESTION

Succession—continuity of leadership—is a particular problem for those at the top, if the top wishes to direct and control the organization and to continue to do so over time. An alternative, of course, is that top leaders come and go but real power resides lower down in the organization in the form of those groups with long-term involvements and entrenched interests who have better means of insuring their own succession, as in the Civil Service bureaucracies or the middle managers of some organization that are continually reshuffling positions at the top. Didn't the faculty, after all, really win at Bennington College in their resistance to young Gail Parker as president (Ephron, 1976), just as faculties often do in organizations as decentralized as universities?

It is an interesting question: the ease with which organizations of different kinds at different stages in their history can continue to function with ineffectual leadership at the top, or even function without a clear system of authority. Certainly, the success of some experiments in worker self-management shows that "bosses" are not always necessary, as some contemporary Marxists argue. Indeed, sometimes the function of those at the top is merely to symbolize organizational accountability, especially in dealing with outside authorities, but not to guide the actions of those within the organization. A vice president of a large insurance company remarked to us that "Presidents are powerless; no one needs them. They should all be sent off to do public relations for the company." While this is clearly a self-serving statement from someone next in line to command, it does give meaning to the expression "being kicked upstairs."

Thus, attention to the succession question may not be so much a matter of insuring continued efficient operation of the organization as it is of assuring the transfer of power in directions the current power-holders desire. It is their way of insuring their own grip on the future even as they pass out of organizational leadership. Small businesses give us examples of leaders-fathers unwilling to lose their grip on current power (Barnes and Hershon, 1976). Bob Six anticipated in advance the need for succession so that, in the course of choosing the successor, he could, in some ways, bind each of the four candidates to him and his ideas even closer.

The succession issue is tied to the question of how those at the top got there. Founding an organization is one thing; climbing up through an existing system or coming in over the heads of those already there is quite another. The entrepreneur-founding parent has an advantage in wielding power and in having the right to insure its continuity in hands he or she designates. The positions of all of those in the organization are to some extent, "children" of the founder's creation. The "top" invented the middle and bottom. However, this fact does not stop them—the employees, the managers, even other family members—from having strong interests of their own in the transfer of power (Barnes and Hershon, 1976). But it does provide one kind of entitlement allowing those at the top a major share in deciding how to pass on formal authority.

Those who arrive at the top by other processes—election by

an outside constituency, appointment by a governing body, movement up through the ranks—have different kinds of problems. They inherit an ongoing organization staffed by people who may wind up with much longer tenures than those at the top. For such leaders, the problem is developing power in the first place rather than passing it on, and managing to translate their authority into power with respect to those who feel they have more information and deserve the right to share in decisions.

This is a particular problem of highly decentralized and politicized organizations like universities, where special interest groups may engage in constant battle with those who presumably have centralized authority over the whole system. How a leader treats these groups makes all the difference in whether they will allow him or her to exercise power—that is, to move the system, to make anything new happen. Gail Parker, for example, when she became President of Bennington College, did not sufficiently listen to the faculty interest groups on campus, nor honor and respect their traditions (Ephron, 1976). In flaunting her sexual affair with a faculty colleague, something quite common at Bennington but punishable in her case, she also forgot that the person at the top is there as a *symbol* as much as a leader in most organizations and is therefore subject to different moral standards. While universities as organizations clearly pose special problems for their top people, and while the Bennington story is certainly unusual, there are lessons here for business and government leadership, too. If those at the top come in as outsiders, they may first have to put themselves in the paradoxical and somewhat anomalous position of honoring and obeying the system's existing culture before exercising any of their own authority with success.

The need to give homage to a system's traditions before attempting change is particularly true for those rare individuals who, through sheer talent and competence, break the "rule" that power tends to remain in closed social circles, and gain access to top positions. Such outsiders have to manage their acceptance with others at the top as well as their power downward, an extra problem that those "born" to leadership do not have.

The "talent" route to the top is much more difficult than the "old school tie" or "club member" route to the top. Ruling classes, traditional elites, always have a tendency to choose as trusted lieutenants talented members of outside groups; indeed, they would not often be able to function if they did not, for the elite group is generally unable to fill all the critical positions solely from within its own ranks (both because of the large number of key positions and because birth into the elite group guarantees only social, not intellectual, suitability). So talented outsiders are permitted to come close, take on major responsibilities, even run the show, but still as the "hired hands" of the ruling class. Great feats or miraculous rescues pulled off by the talented "employees" do not serve to bring such people into the inner circle; they merely confirm the judgment of the elite in using some of its resources to hire the rescuer. In fact, doing *too* well, showing too *much* talent, might sometimes work against the talented outsiders, by leading them to think that they have earned a claim to full membership and thus putting the traditional familial power group in the embarrassing position of having to make its boundaries clear.

In other ways, too, the embarrassment of the traditional elite is involved in understanding why the talented outsider's successes seem to get him nowhere or even, in extreme cases, cause him to seem to lose status. Traditional elites of all kinds—those who have inherited their positions, who had their positions bestowed upon them at an early age by virtue of appropriate background, or who have occupied them for a long time—have come to take them for granted. This has two consequences: (1) they forget (or never knew) what it is like to have less than full membership or to struggle to get in; and it seems rather "uncouth" or "pushy" of the talented outsider to be concerned about status, when the traditional occupants themselves find it in "bad taste" to mention the issue (as upper classes always do about wealth, consumption). (2) Whatever concerns they have about *deserving* their status may be forced into the open by the claim of the talented outsider—something most people in that position never like to think about.

After all, the talented outsider had to demonstrate *more* skill and ability than the traditional ruling group had shown in order to get into the "trusted lieutenant running the show" position in the first place. Why need someone to take over an operation at all if the traditional group was handling it well? Or, how would the outsider ever get into a place where he could make a legitimate claim for full membership if he weren't showing he had some greater talent than those who were members by virtue of birth, family, or "old school ties"? So it becomes threatening in a number of ways to even hear the talented outsider's claims or to admit that he has *that* much talent or to let on that his feats weren't really just part of the plan generated by the people who brought him in.

There is an interesting example of the tension between the outsider-manager and the ruling family in the case of Jack Yogman, ex-president of Seagram's. Edgar Bronfman, chairman of the board and head of the family owning the major portion of the stock, fired him, essentially on the grounds that, though Yogman did a great job, he wasn't a Bronfman, and "we want our company back." Thus, it can be argued that, in the face of organizations with a tradition of a rather closed inner circle at the top, talent rises to only a certain level and then finds increasing numbers of barriers to rising further. Even when talented outsiders are initially given an apparently high status position, some little hurdle is still left to be crossed, some little step still to be taken—the final promotion, the ultimate office arrangement, the last sign of inclusion and status. Often this retention of one hurdle, this not giving it all to the outsider right away, is quite unconscious on the part of the inner circle.

The limits on talent as a claim to increased power and status in organizations become clear. Continuing to count on talent requires *recognition* by the inner circle (with the difficulties already mentioned), which in turn requires *ingratiation* by the outsider, which can put the talented outsider in a one-down power position. Threatening to leave—a sign of how other outsiders recognize the talent as well as a legitimate set of alternatives—is also not an option, because (1) if the inner group hired one trusty lieutenant, they begin to think they can find another; and (2) as an "inner circle" or traditional elite, they are, almost by definition, unimpressed with groups other than themselves.

But the outsiders have their own ways to build power, and this is one way that ruling elites in organizations are gradually replaced by new kinds of people. They can develop a strong support base throughout the organization and get their own team in place. They can chip away at the things that the traditional inner circle retain as the preserves and perquisites of their status—e.g., getting them devalued, getting them distributed to everyone anyway, setting up other privileges and rewards. They can invent reorganizations that start to cut the ruling class out of the center, but that may be hard, by definition. They can develop a strong outside power base that can serve as a resource for work inside the organization. With *enough* recognition, money, visibility, prestige from the outside, the inner circle sometimes has to take notice.

And thus, power transforms itself. Particularly in modern organizations which must produce to survive, inner circles must at some point transfer power and must, if they are to function adequately, open doors to talented outsiders who change the very operation of power.

THE SELECTIONS

Power—and its rewards, its absence, its discontents, its dilemmas, and its transfer—is a major theme of the articles about "Life at the Top." We also see several different leadership styles and leadership philosophies in operation in different kinds of organizations—the corporation, the university, the government, small business—from the vantage point of some well-known public figures. And we learn something about the experience of living in the glass-walled room at the top, which, if it gives its occupants a view over the whole organization, also allows others to look in and puts those at the top on public display.

Rosabeth Moss Kanter describes some of the special characteristics of the top levels of a major American corporation, which she gave the fictional name of "Indsco" (Industrial Supply Corporation) in *Men and Women of the Corporation*. She studied Indsco as an "inside-outsider," collecting information during more than five years as a consultant to several operations. This discussion of "How the Top Is Different" considers both the extra benefits and the extra burdens of life at the top. It also brings some other key organizational characters into the picture, who bear a special relationship to the top: secretaries and wives. (It is no accident that these are both women, in a patrimonial relationship to those at the top, who are overwhelmingly men.) The similarities between Indsco and other organizations emerge in many of the other selections. In particular, the existence of closed social circles at the top is also a major theme in the next selection.

Warren Bennis, in "Why Leaders Can't Lead," speaks of the problems of leadership from both professional training (as a noted organizational psychologist) and from firsthand experience (as Provost of the University of Buffalo and then President of the University of Cincinnati). The article combines personal revelation and anecdote with lessons about the traps that contribute to powerlessness for the top. Bennis also demonstrates that university presidents have much to teach our political leaders.

Henry Kissinger is usually not thought of as a "former manager," but manager he was when he was secretary of state, especially from the vantage point of career foreign service officers like Paul Von Ward, who had the daily experience of "Kissinger as Department Manager." Ward not only shows the perils of personalized power in an organization with strong traditions below, but also gives us insight into how the middle may see the top.

In "Bob Six's Long Search for a Successor," we see a different kind of leader in operation, and from a different perspective: the journalist's narrative account. Bob Six founded Continental Airlines and guided it to a position of prominence. Then, the day inevitably came when he had to think about passing on his authority. In the careful way he went about the search and the selection, and in the details of his relationship to Continental, there are the keys to one eminently successful—and powerful— way of living at the top.

1 / How the Top Is Different

Rosabeth Moss Kanter

CORPORATE HEADQUARTERS of the company I have called Indsco, occupied many floors in a glass and steel office building in a large city. The surroundings were luxurious. At ground

Excerpted from *Men and Women of the Corporation*, by Rosabeth Moss Kanter, © 1977 by Rosabeth Moss Kanter, Basic Books, Inc., Publishers, New York. Pp. 34–36, 48–49, 52–54, 68, 75, 118–22, and additions.

level was a changing art exhibit in glass cases with displays of awards to Indsco executives for meritorious public service or newspaper clippings about the corporation. There might be piles of company newspapers on a nearby table or special publications like the report by foreign students who spent the summer with Indsco families. Such public displays almost always stressed Indsco's contributions to the welfare of the larger community. Across from gleaming chrome elevators and a watchman's post were doors leading into the employees' dining room. In the morning a long table with coffee, sweet rolls, and bagels for sale was set up outside the dining room; during the day coffee carts were available on each floor. Inside, the dining room was divided into two parts: a large cafeteria for everyone and a small area with already set tables, hostess seating, menus, and waitress service. Those tables were usually occupied by groups of men; the largely female clerical work force tended to eat in the cafeteria. Special luncheon meetings arranged by managers were held in the individual executive dining rooms and conference areas on the top floor; to use these rooms, reservations had to be made well in advance by someone with executive status.

Indsco executives were also likely to go out for lunch, especially if they were entertaining an outside visitor, to any of the numerous posh restaurants in the neighborhood. At these lunches a drink was a must; at one time it was two extra-dry martinis, but more recently it became a few glasses of wine. However, despite the fact that moderate social drinking was common, heavy drinking was frowned upon. A person's career could be ruined by the casual comment that he or she had alcoholic tendencies. Stories told about men who cavorted and caroused in bars, staying up all night, were told with the attitude that "that was really crazy."

The office floors were quietly elegant, dominated by modern design, white walls, and beige tones. At one end, just off the elevators, sat a receptionist who calls on a company telephone line to announce visitors. A secretary would then appear to escort a visitor to his or her appointment. Offices with windows were for higher-status managers, and their secretaries were often proud of having drapes. Corner offices were reserved for the top. They were likely to be larger in size, with room for coffee tables and couches, and reached through a reception area where a private secretary sat. Inside offices went to assistants and other lower-status salaried personnel; conference rooms were also found along the inside rim. Secretaries and other hourly workers occupied rows of desks with banks of cabinets and files in the public spaces between. There were few signs of personal occupancy of space, except around the secretaries' desks. Managers might put up a painting or poster on the wall, and they usually had a small set of photographs of their families somewhere on or near their desk. Rarely would more than a few books or reports be visible, and the overall impression was one of tidiness, order, and uniformity from office to office. In fact, it was often true that the higher the status of an executive, the less cluttered was his desk. Office furnishings themselves reflected status rather than personality. There was a clear system of stratification. As status increased, desks went from a wood top with steel frame through solid wood to the culmination in a marble-top desk. Type of ashtray was also determined by the status system; and a former executive secretary, promoted into a management position herself, reported that her former peers were upset that she took her stainless steel file trays with her because a secretary working for her would not be entitled to such luxurious equipment. The rational distribution of furniture and supplies was thought to make the system more equitable and to avoid competition for symbols of status. . . .

The secretary also contributed in minor ways to the boss' status. Some people have argued that secretaries function as "status symbol" for executives, holding that the traditional secretarial role is developed and preserved because of its impact on managerial egos, not its contribution to organizational efficiency. Robert Townsend, iconoclastic former president of Avis, claimed in *Up the Organization* that the existence of private secretaries was organizationally inefficient, as proven by his experience in gaining half a day's time by giving up what he called "standard executive equipment." One writer was quite explicit about the meaning of a secretary: "In many companies a secretary outside your door is the most visible sign that you have become an executive; a secretary is automatically assigned to each executive, whether or not his work load requires one. . . . When you reach the vice-presidential level, your secretary may have an office of her own, with her name on the door. At the top, the president may have two secretaries. . . ." A woman professional at Indsco agreed with the idea that secretaries were doled out as rewards rather than in response to job needs, as she talked about her own problems in getting enough secretarial help.

At Indsco, the secretary's function as a status symbol increased up the ranks as she became more and more bound to a specific boss. "It's his image, his status, sitting out in front," a personnel administrator said. "She's the sign of how important he is." . . .

Physical height corresponded to social height at Indsco, like other major corporations. Corporate officers resided at the very top on the forty-fifth floor, which was characterized by many people in Indsco as "a hospital ward." The silence was deafening. The offices were huge. According to one young executive who had served as an assistant to an officer, "One or two guys are sitting there; there's not much going on. It's the brain center, but there is no activity. It's like an old folks' home. You can see the cobwebs growing. A secretary every quarter mile. It's very sterile." An executive secretary told the story of her officer boss's first reaction to moving onto the forty-fifth floor. "He was the one human being," she said, "who was uncomfortable with the trappings of status. When he moved up, he had to pick an office." She wouldn't let him take anything but a corner—it was the secretary who had to tell him that. Finally he agreed for the sake of the corporate image, but he was rarely there, and he set up the office so that everything was in one corner and the rest was useless space.

Some people felt that the physical insulation of top executives also had its counterpart in social insulation. Said a former officer's assistant, "There are courtiers around the top guys, telling them what they want to hear, flattering them. For example, there was a luncheon with some board members. The vice-chairman mentioned that he was looking for a car for his daughter. A courtier thought, 'We'll take care of it.' He went down the line, and someone in purchasing had to spend half a day doing this. The guy who had to do it resented it, so he became antagonistic to the top. The vice-chairman had no idea this was going on, and if he had known, he would probably have stopped it; but you can't say anything at the top without having it be seen as an order. Even ambiguous remarks may get translated into action. At the top you have to figure out the impact of all of your words in advance because an innocent expression can have a major effect. A division president says, 'It might be a good idea to _____.' He's just ruminating, but that gets sent down to the organization as an ultimatum, and everyone scrambles around to make sure it gets done. He looks down and says, 'What the hell is happening?'"

At the same time, officers could also be frustrated by their distance from any real action. One remarked, "You get into a position like mine, and you think you can get anything done, but I shout down an order, and I have to wait years for any action. The guy in the plant turns a valve and sees the reaction, or the salesman offers a price, but I may never live to see the impact of my decisions." For this reason, it was known that once in a while officers could be expected to leave their protected environment and try to get involved in routine company activities. Some would go down and try to do something on the shop floor. Once in a while one would make a sales call at a very high level or make an appearance at a customer golf outing. It was also a legend that an early president had his own private laboratory outside of his office—his own tinkering room. As a manager put it, "He would close the door and go play. It was almost as though he was babied. He was given a playroom." . . .

CONFORMITY PRESSURES AT THE TOP: UNCERTAINTY
AND THE GROWTH OF INNER CIRCLES

Leaders who already have power seek as new recruits those they can rely upon and trust. They demand that the newcomers to top positions be loyal, that they accept authority, and that they conform to a prescribed pattern of behavior.

Unlike a more communal environment, where eccentrics can be lovingly tolerated because trust is based on mutual commitments and deep personal knowledge, those who run the bureaucratic corporation often rely on outward manifestations to determine who is the "right sort of person." Managers tend to carefully guard power and privilege for those who fit in, for those they see as "their kind." Wilbert Moore was commenting on this phenomenon when he used the metaphor of a "bureaucratic kinship system" to describe the corporation—but a kinship system based on homo-social reproduction in which men reproduce themselves in their own image. The metaphor is apt. Because of the *situation* in which managers function, because of the position of managers in the corporate structure, social similarity tends to become extremely important to them. The structure sets in motion forces leading to the replication of managers as the same kind of social individuals. And people at the top reproduce themselves in kind.

Conformity pressures and the development of exclusive management circles closed to "outsiders" stem from the degree of uncertainty surrounding managerial positions. Bureaucracies are social inventions that supposedly reduce the uncertain to the predictable and routine. Yet much uncertainty remains— many situations in which individual people rather than impersonal procedures must be trusted. "Uncertainty," James Thompson wrote in a recent major statement on organizations, "appears as the fundamental problem for complex organizations, and coping with uncertainty as the essence of the administrative process." Thompson identified three sources of uncertainty in even the most perfect of machine-like bureaucracies: a lack of cause-effect understanding in the culture at large (limiting the possibility for advance planning); contingencies caused by the fact that the bureaucracy is not alone, so that outcomes of organizational action are in part determined by action of other elements in the environment; and the interdependence of parts, the human interconnections inside the organization itself, which can never fully be reduced to predictable action. The requirements for a perfectly technically "rational" bureaucracy that never has to rely on the personal discretion of a single individual can never be met: complete knowledge of all cause-effect relationships plus control over all of the relevant variables. Thus, sources of uncertainty that are inherent in human institutions mean that some degree of reliance on individual persons must always be present.

It is ironic that in those most impersonal of institutions the essential communal problem of trust remains. For wherever there is uncertainty, *someone* (or some group) must decide, and thus, there must be personal discretion. And discretion raises not technical but human, social, and even communal questions: trust, and its origins in loyalty, commitment, and mutual understanding based on the sharing of values. It is the uncertainty quotient in managerial work, as it has come to be defined in the large modern corporation, that causes management to become so socially restricting: to develop tight inner circles excluding social strangers; to keep control in the hands of socially homogeneous peers; to stress conformity and insist upon a diffuse, unbounded loyalty; and to prefer ease of communication and thus social certainty over the strains of dealing with people who are "different."

If conditions of uncertainty mean that people have to be relied on, then people fall back on social bases for trust. The greater the uncertainty, the greater the pressures for those who have to trust each other to form a homogeneous group. At different times in an organization's history, and at different places in its structure, a higher degree of uncertainty brings with it more drive for social similarity. . . .

Uncertainty can stem from either the time-span of decisions and the amount of information that must be collected, or from the frequency with which non-routine events occur and must be handled. The impossibility of specifying contingencies in advance, operating procedures for all possible events, leaves an organization to rely on personal discretion. (It is also this pressure that partly accounts for the desire to centralize responsibility in a few people who can be held accountable for discretionary decisions.) Commented a sales manager at Indsco, "The need for flexibility is primary in my job. The situation changes from minute to minute. One minute it's a tank truck that collapsed. Another it's a guy whose wife just had a hysterectomy and is going to die. . . . I'm dealing with such different problems all the time."

The importance of discretion increases with closeness to the top of a hierarchical organization. Despite the institutionalization and routinization of much of the work of large organizations and despite the proliferation of management experts, uncertainty remains a generic condition, increasing with rank. Jobs are relatively unstructured, tasks are non-routine, and decisions must be made about a variety of unknown elements. Issues such as "direction" and "purpose" cannot be reduced to rational formulae. Organizational improvement, or even maintenance, is not a simple matter that can be summarized in statements about "the ten functions of managers" or techniques of operation. If the "big picture" can be viewed from the top, it also looks bigger and fuzzier. Computers have not necessarily reduced the uncertainty of decisions at the top; in some cases, they have merely increased the amount of information that decision-makers must take into account. A major executive of Indsco confessed in a meeting that "we don't know how to manage these giant structures; and I suspect no one does. They are like dinosaurs, lumbering on of their own accord, even if they are no longer functional."

Criteria for "good decisions" or good management performance also get less certain closer to the top. The connection between an upper management decision and a factor such as production efficiency several layers below or gross sales is indirect, if it is even apparent. (An Indsco division president said, "In the 1960s we thought we were really terrific. We patted ourselves on the back a lot because every decision was so successful. Business kept on expanding. Then came the recession, and we couldn't do anything to stop it. We had been lucky before. Everything turned to gold in the 1960s. But it became clear that we don't know the first thing about how to make this enterprise work.")

Financial measures of performance are sometimes even artifactual because of the juggling of figures; for example, when and how a loss is recorded. The are also a variety of dilemmas in trying to evaluate the success of managers: qualitative versus quantitative measures, short-run versus long-run outcomes. Decisions that look good in the short-term might be long-term disasters, but by that time the failure can be blamed on other factors, and those responsible for the decisions might be so entrenched in power that they now call the shots anyway. A former public relations manager at DuPont formulated what he called the Law of Inverse Certainty: "The more important the management decision, the less precise the tools to deal with it . . . and the longer it will take before anyone knows it was right." One example was a rigid cost cutter who helped increase profits by eliminating certain functions; by the time the company began to feel the loss of those functions, he had been promoted and was part of the inner power group. Someone else picked up the pieces.

The uncertainty up the ranks, like the uncertainty of beginnings, also puts trust and homogeneity at a premium. The personal loyalty normally demanded of subordinates by officials is most intense at the highest levels of organizations, as others have also noted. The lack of structure in top jobs makes it very important for decision-makers to work together closely in at least the harmony of shared understanding and a degree of mutual trust. Since for an organization to function at all requires that, to some extent, people will pull together around decisions, the solidarity that can be mustered through common membership in social networks, and the social control this provides, is a helpful supplement for decision-makers. Indeed, homogeneity of class and ethnic background and prior social experiences is one important "commitment mechanism" found to build a feeling of communion among members of viable utopian communities. Situational pressures, then, place a great emphasis on personal relations and social homogeneity as functional elements in the carrying out of managerial tasks. And privilege is also kept within a small circle.

The social homogeneity of big business leaders from the early-to-middle twentieth century has been noted frequently by critics such as C. Wright Mills as well as business historians. Their class background and social characteristics tended to be similar: largely white, Protestant men from elite schools. Much attention has also been paid to the homogeneity of type within any particular company. In one industrial organization, managers who moved ahead needed to be members of the Masonic Order and the local yacht club; not Roman Catholic; Anglo-Saxon or Germanic in origin; and Republican.

At Indsco, until ten years ago, top executives in the corporation were traceable to the founders of the company or its subsidiaries—people who held stock or were married to people who did. There was a difference between who did well in the divisions, where performance tended to account for more, and who got into top positions in the corporation itself. To get ahead in the corporation, social connections were known to be very important. Indeed, corporate staff positions became a place to put people who were nonmovers, whose performance was not outstanding, but were part of the "family." The social homogeneity of corporate executives was duly noted by other managers. One asked a consultant, "Do all companies have an ethnic flavor? Our top men all seem to be Scotch-Irish." (But as management has become more rationalized, and the corporation has involved itself more heavily in divisional operations, there has also been a trend, over the past five years, toward more "objective" criteria for high-level corporate positions.)

We expect a direct correlation, then, between the degree of

uncertainty in a position—the extent to which organizations must rely on personal discretion—and a reliance on "trust" through "homosocial reproduction"—selection of incumbents on the basis of social similarity. . . .

Management becomes a closed circle in the absence of better, less exclusionary responses to uncertainty and communication pressures. Forces stemming from organizational situations help foster social homogeneity as a selection criterion for managers and promote social conformity as a standard for conduct. Concerned about giving up control and broadening discretion in the organization, managers choose others that can be "trusted." And thus they reproduce themselves in kind. Women are occasionally included in the inner circle when they are part of an organization's ruling family, but more usually this system leaves women out, along with a range of other people with discrepant social characteristics. Forces insisting that trust means total dedication and non-diffuse loyalty also serve to exclude those, like women, who are seen as incapable of such a single-minded attachment.

There is a self-fulfilling prophecy buried in all of this. The more closed the circle, the more difficult it is for "outsiders" to break in. Their very difficulty in entering may be taken as a sign of incompetence, a sign that the insiders were right to close their ranks. The more closed the circle, the more difficult it is to share power when the time comes, as it inevitably must, that others challenge the control by just one kind. And the greater the tendency for a group of people to try to reproduce themselves, the more constraining becomes the emphasis on conformity. It would seem a shame, indeed, if the only way out of such binds lay in increasing bureaucratization—that is, in a growth in routinization and rationalization of areas of uncertainty and a concomitant decline in personal discretion. But somehow corporations must grapple with the problem of how to reduce pressures for social conformity in their top jobs. . . .

CONFORMITY REACHES HOME

It is one of the prevailing ironies of modern corporate life that the closer to the top of the organization, the more traditional and non-"modern" does the system look. As Max Weber noted, at this point more charismatic, symbolic, and "non-rational" elements come into play. At the top—and especially in interaction with its environment—the organization is most likely to show strong elements of a personal, familistic system imbued with ritual, drawing on traditional behavior modes, and overlaid with symbolism. The irony stems from the fact that it is the top level that prescribes routine and impersonality—the absence of particularism and familism—for the rest of the organization. The modern organization formally excludes the family from participation in organizational life and excludes family ties as a basis for organizational position, even to the extent of anti-nepotism rules. Yet, at the top the wife may come into the picture as a visible member of the husband's "team"; she may be given a position and functions (and, in some cases, may even jump over qualified employees in taking on an official, paid, executive position). The wife who is excluded below may be included at the top, as part of the diplomatic apparatus of the corporation. And she has little freedom to refuse participation.

The dilemma that can confront people at this level is the issue of publicness/privateness. Both husband and wife can be made into public figures, with no area of life remaining untinged with responsibilities for the company. Here, as Wilbert Moore said, "The man, and his wife, simply cannot divest themselves of corporate identification. Their every activity with persons outside the immediate family is likely to be tinged with a recognition of the man's position. He represents the company willy-nilly. His area of privacy, and that of his wife, is very narrowly restricted." One rising young Indsco executive felt that the following had to be considered the "modern risks" of corporate vice presidential and presidential jobs: traveling 80 percent of the time, getting shot at or kidnapped by radicals, prostituting yourself to customers, and opening your private life to scrutiny.

The higher executive's work spills over far beyond the limits of a working day. There may be no distinction between work and leisure. Activities well out of the purview of the organization's goals and defined as pleasure for other people (golf club memberships, symphony attendance, party-giving) are allowable as business expenses on income tax returns because the definition of what is "business" becomes so broad and nonspecific. People entertain one another on yachts or over long, lavish lunches—all in an attempt to mutually obligate, to create personal relations that will give someone an inside track when it comes to more formal negotiations. Whenever "selling" is a part of the organization's relations with its environment and sufficient sums of money rest on each deal, those who sell tend to offer gifts (tickets to a sports event, dinners at fancy restaurants, expensive pen and pencil sets) to those who buy, trying to bind the others beyond the limits of a rational contractual relationship. Entertaining in the home with the wife as hostess is especially binding, since it appears to be a more personal offering not given to all, sets up a social obligation, implicates others, and also calls on ancient and traditional feelings about the need to reward hospitality.

Fusion of business and private life also occurs around longer-term relationships. At the top, all friendships may have business meaning. Business relations can be made because of social connections. (One unlikely merger between two companies in very different fields was officially said to result from one company's need for a stock exchange listing held by the other, but off the record it was known to have been brought about by the friendship of the two presidents and their wives.) Charitable and community service activities, where the wife's role is especially pivotal, may generate useful business and political connections. Wives may meet each other through volunteer work and bring their husbands into contact, with useful business results. Stratification of the volunteer world paralleling class and ethnic differentiation in the society ensures that husbands and wives can pinpoint the population with which they desire connections by an appropriate choice of activity. As one chief executive wife wrote, "Any public relations man worth his salt will recognize the corporate wife as an instrument of communication with the community far more sincere and believable than all the booze poured down the press to gain their favor."

The importance of the wife stems not only from her own skills and activities (which could be, and are, performed by paid employees) but also from the testimony her behavior provides, its clue to the character and personal side of her husband. The usefulness of this testimony, in turn, is derived from unique aspects of top leadership. Image, appearance, background, and likability are all commodities traded at the top of the system, where actors are visible and where they put pressure on one another to demonstrate trustworthiness. . . . Farther down a hierarchy, jobs can be broken down into component skills and decisions about people and jobs made on the basis of ability to demonstrate those skills. At the top, decisions about people are not so easy or mechanical; they rest on personal factors to a degree perhaps much greater than systems themselves officially admit. The situations that a corporation president or a president of a country face are not routine and predictable; indeed, constituents are less interested in their handling of routine matters than in their capacities for the unexpected. So there is no test except a vague one: Is this person trustworthy? Even questions about philosophy and intelligence are proxies for trust.

Furthermore, the capacities of an organization itself are unknown and cannot be reduced precisely either to history or to a set of facts and figures. Thus, the character of its leaders can become a critical guide to making a decision about a future relationship with it: whether to invest, to donate funds, to allow it into the community, to provide some leeway in the regulation of its activities. Indsco was always concerned about character in its managers. Company newspapers from field locations routinely stressed church leadership in articles about individual managers, and "integrity" and "acceptance of accountability" appeared on the list of eleven traits that must be possessed by candidates for officer level jobs. Disclosures of corrupt practices by other companies in the mid-1970s enhanced Indsco's concerns about public respectability. Whereas, at lower levels of the organization, there was a tendency to formalize demands, to create routinized job descriptions, to ensure continuity of functioning by seeing to it that the occupant did not make over the job in his own image, and to exclude as much as possible of the personal and emotional life of the worker, close to the top, opposite pressure prevailed. Those with whom leaders entered into relationships looked for the private person behind the role and for the qualities and capacities that could not be encompassed by a job description but on which they must bet when deciding to trust the leader or the organization. Here's where the wives are important.

One way leaders can offer glimpses of their private beings is by bringing along their wives, by inviting others into their homes, and by making sure that their wives confirm the impression of themselves they are trying to give. By meeting in social circumstances, by throwing open pieces of private life for inspection, leaders try to convey their taste and their humanity. Wives, especially, are the carriers of this humanity and the shapers of the image of the private person. Of course, to the extent that social events and "informal" occasions are known to communicate an image for the purposes of making appropriate relationships, they may come to be as carefully managed and rationally calculated as any production task within the organization. The public relations department might even stage-manage the performance of the leader and his wife; when Dollie Ann Cole, wife of a General Motors president, wrote that p.r. departments no longer tell the wife what to wear and what to say, she made it explicit that they once did: ". . . a new day has dawned. Corporate wives no longer ask the public relations office what charity they should work with or whether they can debate for a cause on a local or national radio or television show—or even who is coming for dinner."

The wife is thus faced with an added task at the boundary of the public and the private: to make an event seem personal that is instead highly ritualized and contrived. She must recognize also the meanings conveyed by small acts (who sits next to whom, how much time she and her husband spend with each person, the taste implied by objects in the home, how much she drinks, who seem to be the family friends) and manage even small gestures with extreme self-consciousness, as one high-level wife at Indsco recalled she did at managers' meetings: "I had to be very careful to be invariably cordial, friendly, to remember everyone's names—and then to stay away. If I was too involved with someone, it would look like I was playing favorites; that would set up waves in highly inappropriate ways. Some of the young wives were terrified, but there was only so much I could do because I had other things to worry about."

Private life thus becomes penetrable and not very private at the top. Wives face the demand to suppress private beliefs and self-knowledge in the interest of public appearance. As an instrument of diplomacy and a critical part of her husband's image, the corporate wife must often hide her own opinions in order to preserve a united front, play down her own abilities to keep him looking like the winner and the star. The women's intelligence and superior education—assets when the men looked for wives—give way to other, more social traits, such as gregari- ousness, adaptability, attractiveness, discretion, listening abil- ity, and social graces.

Thus, unless serving as a surrogate for the husband, voicing opinions was not easily allowed of corporate wives at Indsco, like those political wives who must beware of outshining their husbands. An aide to Eleanor McGovern spoke of the contra- dictory pressures on a candidate's wife: to be able to give the speech when he can't make it but to shut her mouth and listen adoringly when he is there. Indeed, Eleanor was told to stop looking so good when she started getting better press notices than George. Abigail McCarthy recalled the anxiety she felt about how words would affect her husband's prospects: "After every interview, I lay awake in a black nightmare of anxiety, fearful that I had said something which would do Gene irrepa- rable harm." Betty Ford became an object of controversy (and of admiration) precisely because she violated these rules of the game and refused to distort her private life. Yet, wives of upper management at Indsco felt they did not have that luxury, even though they characterized the pressure to suppress indepen- dent opinions as "nonsense" and "frustrating." Not everyone complained. One wife reported that she was proud of never having unburdened herself, even to a confidante, and never having forgotten her public role throughout her husband's ca- reer.

Stresses, choices, and dilemmas in the top leadership phase, then, center around the tension between the public and the private. If men and their wives at the top gained public recog- nition, they also lost private freedoms. The emotional pressure this entailed was too much for some wives, as literature in the corporate-wives-as-victims tradition made clear; but it should be pointed out, too, that emotional breakdowns and secret de- viances could also reflect defiant independence, unobtainable in any other way under constraining role definitions. The wishes expressed by wives in this position were of two kinds. Some women said that if they were going to be used by the company anyway, they would like the opportunity to do a real job, exercise real skills—by which they meant take on official areas of responsibility. Others wanted merely to be able to carve out more areas of privacy and independence in an other- wise public existence.

POWER AND ITS PRICES

The top leadership of an organization has all of the privileges of office: the signs of status, the benefits and perquisites, the material advantages their position is seen to warrant. They play ball in a large field, and the scope of their decisions is vast and far-reaching. They have, on occasion, gigantic power which does not even have to be used; a mere wish on their part is translated into action, with full cooperation and without the show of force.

But such power exists in a vise of checks and constraints; it comes out of a system, and the system, in turn, exacts its price. What if a top leader tries to exercise power that violates the expectations of other top leaders and organization members—if he or she steps out of line, out of character, or out of role? Would obedience be so easily forthcoming? Power at the top is contingent on conformity. Pressures to "fit in" also mean restraints on the unbridled exercise of power.

Furthermore, power which in some respects is contingent on trust for its effective exercise also, ironically, breeds suspicion: Can people at the top trust what they hear? Can they trust each other? What beyond social appearance, can they use as keys to trust? Sometimes cut off from the "real action," they are seen by the organization's rank and file as remote from the daily events which truly constitute the organization—as once potent actors who now make whimsical decisions with little real understanding of organizational operations. And, as the final price of power, top leaders have to acknowledge the organization's ownership of that ultimate piece of property, their own private lives and beings. Life at the top is life in a goldfish bowl, an existence in which all the boundaries can be rendered transparent at the twitch of the public's curiosity.

The room at the top is all windows.

2 / Why Leaders Can't Lead

Warren Bennis

BEFORE Clark Kerr went through the revolving presidential door at Berkeley, he defined the modern multiversity president's job. It was, he said, to provide "sex for the students, football for the alumni, and parking for the faculty." Twelve years later, after four years as president of the University of Cincinnati—whose 36,104 students make it the largest urban multiversity in the country after New York City's—I can report:

- The parking problem is worse.
- College football is being energetically chased by man-eating tigers (in our case the Bengals).
- Sex is so taken for granted as to rate no priority.

If the problems change, however, they grow no fewer. All of them, whether from outside the university or from within it, no matter how trivial or irrelevant, wind up on the president's desk. Throughout my first year, the mere job of clearing it often kept me there until the small hours—far longer than what I accomplished seemed to justify. I appreciated more than ever the pertinence of Herman B. Wells's observation, after leaving Indiana's presidency, that a college president should be born with "the physical stamina of a Greek athlete, the cunning of a Machiavelli, the wisdom of a Solomon, the courage of a lion if possible," but, above all, "the stomach of a goat."

As, goatlike, I chew the ruminative cud of that first year's academic detritus, I think I begin to understand why so many first-class men, often the finest and the best, decide to quit the presidential chair before they have scarcely warmed it, staying in some cases less time than it took the search committee to find them.

My moment of truth came toward the end of my first ten months. It was one of those nights in the office. The clock was moving toward four in the morning, and I was still not through with the incredible mass of paper stacked before me. I was borne-weary and soul-weary, and I found myself muttering, "Either I can't manage this place, or it's unmanageable." I reached for my calendar and ran my eyes down each hour, half-hour, quarter-hour, to see where my time had gone that day, the day before, the month before.

Nobel laureate James Franck has said he always recognizes a moment of discovery by "the feeling of terror that seizes me." I felt a trace of it that morning. My discovery was this: *I had become the victim of a vast, amorphous, unwitting, unconscious conspiracy to prevent me from doing anything whatever to change the university's status quo.* Even those of my associates who fully shared my hopes to set new goals, new directions, to work toward creative change were unconsciously often doing the most to make sure that I would never find the time to begin. I found myself thinking of a friend and former colleague who had taken over one of our top universities with goals and plans that fired up all those around him and who said when he left a few years later: "I never could get around to doing the things I wanted to do."

This discovery, or rediscovery, has led me to formulate what might be called Bennis's First Law of Academic Pseudodynamics, to wit: Routine work drives out nonroutine work, or: how to smother to death all creative planning, all fundamental change in the university—or *any* institution.

This insight also gave me the strength I needed to get through the year. All my academic training and a great deal of its practical application as a consultant to business and other organizations had concerned the rational development of managerial strengths and the tactics and strategy for their optimal use. Now I was being confronted with the acid test: whether I, as a "leading theorist" of the principles of creative leadership, actually could prove myself a leader. I resolved that in the year ahead I would either do so or confess that I had better go back to the classroom to develop some better theory.

But, first, some illustrations of the First Law. To start, there are 150 letters in the day's mail that require a response. About 50 of them concern our young dean of the School of Education,

Hendrik Gideonse. Gideonse's job is to bring about change in the teaching of teachers, in our university's relationship to the public schools and to students in the deprived and deteriorating neighborhood around us. Out of these urban schools will come the bulk of our students of the future—as good or as bad as the schools have shaped them.

But the letters. They're not about education—they're about a baby, the dean's ten-week-old son. Gideonse feels very strongly about certain basic values. He feels especially so about sex roles, about equality for his wife, about making sure she has the time and freedom to develop her own potentials fully. So he's been carrying the baby into his office two days a week in a little bassinet, keeping him on his desk while he does his work. The daily *Enquirer* heard about all this, took a picture of Hendrik, baby, and bassinet, and played it on page one. TV splashed it across the nation—and my "in" basket has been overflowing ever since with letters that urge his arrest or merely his immediate dismissal. My only public comment has been that we're a tax-supported institution and, if Hendrik can engage in this form of applied humanism and still accomplish the things we both want done in education, then, like Lincoln with Grant's whiskey, I'd gladly send him several new babies for adoption. Nevertheless, Hendrik's baby is eating up quite a bit of my time.

Here's a note from a professor, complaining that his classroom temperature is down to 65 degrees: I suppose he expects me to grab a wrench and fix it. A student complains we won't give him course credit for acting as assistant to a city councilman. Another was unable to get into the student health center. The teacher at my child's day school, who goes to UC, is dissatisfied with her grades. A parent complains about four-letter words in a Philip Roth book being used in an English class. The track coach wants me to come over to see for myself how bad the track is. An alumnus couldn't get the football seat he wanted. Another wants a coach fired. A teacher just called to tell me the squash court was closed at 7 P.M., when he wanted to use it.

Last year perhaps 20 percent of my time was taken up by a problem at the General Hospital. It is city-owned but is administered by the University and serves as the teaching hospital of our medical school. Some terminal-cancer patients, with their consent, had been subjected to whole-body radiation as possibly beneficial therapy. Since the Pentagon saw this as a convenient way to gather data that might help protect civilian population in nuclear warfare, it provided a series of subsidies for the work.

When this story broke and was pursued in such a way as to call up comparisons with the Nazis' experiments on human guinea pigs, it became almost impossible for me or anybody else to separate the essential facts from the fantasized distortions. The problem, I hope, has subsided (after a blue-ribbon task force recommended significant changes in the experiment's design). But I have also invested endless time in a matter only vaguely related to the prime purposes of our university—and wound up being accused by some of interfering with academic freedom. Together with the story of Hendrik's baby, the episode illustrates how the media, particularly TV, make the academic cloister a global village in a goldfish bowl. By focusing on the lurid or the superficial, they can disrupt a president's proper activities while contributing nothing to the advancement of knowledge.

This leads me to Bennis's Second Law of Academic Pseudodynamics: Make whatever grand plans you will, you may be sure the unexpected or the trivial will disturb and disrupt them. . . .

Our overgrown universities are confronted with a sharp decline in the number of customers (high school graduates), and the rate of decline will sharpen. The public increasingly demands that higher education earn its future support by proving that its products have some direct relation to the job needs of the society. Where formerly six new faculty members were hired for every one who died or retired, now the ratio is only one to one and may grow less. In the next decade scores of small, private colleges may go under for lack of funds. Others, stifled by a tenure system, watch their faculties grow older and less flexible while angry, frustrated, younger teachers find themselves the captives of dwindling mobility, fewer job offerings, and less chance for advancement on merit.

All our major institutions, particularly but not exclusively the university, are afflicted with a threefold sense of loss: loss of community, loss of purpose, and loss of power.

Perhaps there was never a true "university community" any

more than a Camelot. But the image does suggest a time when professors recognized their colleagues on sight and could even remember the name of a senior who asked for a recommendation to a graduate school. Today the faculty, once unified by a common definition of the nature and purposes of scholarship, is fragmented into competing professional citadels. Many have shifted their concern from the intellectual and moral content of education to privilege and ritual.

Students in the multiversity find very little real personal contact or summoning call of the spirit. The real enemy is not anarchy but apathy. Alumni, too, are estranged; many of the older ones are outraged by the weird sea of changes on the campus they remember, while the younger feel no affectionate bond for the institution. And the greatest loss of community, the greatest estrangement, is among the general public—the citizens and parents and their mirror images in legislatures and Congress—on whom the very life of public institutions depends and who are no longer at all sure it is a life worth saving.

With the loss of community has come the loss of power. For example, at Cincinnati we have not only a faculty senate and a student senate but sixty-nine other committees that are involved, in one way or another, in university governance—including a junior faculty committee, a black faculty committee, and a Jewish faculty council. (In all fairness I must note that despite the difficulties in touching base with all these groups they all have tried to cooperate with, and be supportive of, my administration.) Vast splintering and fragmentation arise from the new populism of those who felt denied in the past and who, rightly, want to be consulted in those decisions that affect them. All this is supposed to add up to "participatory democracy" but adds up, instead, to a cave of the winds where the most that can usually be agreed upon is to do nothing (like the bumper sticker "My Vote Cancels Yours").

As for the purposes of higher education, they became blurred indeed in the quarter-century of postwar expansion. As long as the money poured in and the sky was the limit, there was no visible need to choose between and among programs. One inevitable result was that each university and college began to resemble all the others, becoming a sort of service station from which a student could pluck what he wanted. Now, as the flow of resources and students dries up, colleges and universities are forced for the first time to determine what is essential and what is expendable. A tangle of commitments that were none too purposefully acquired now demands what I call "creative retraction"—a task made all the more difficult and painful by the haphazard, heedless way that Topsy grew.

Unquestionably, universities are among the worst-managed institutions in the country. Hospitals and some state and city administrations may be as bad; no business or industry except Penn Central can possibly be. One reason, incredibly enough, is that universities—which have studied everything from government to Persian mirrors and the number "7"—have never deeply studied their own administration.

The University of Cincinnati, with a staff of 6,000 is the second-largest employer (after General Electric) in Greater Cincinnati. It is in the hotel business (high-rise dorms housing 4,000 students), the restaurant business (ten, all told), and the investment business (a $53-million endowment portfolio), and it must manage a total plant bigger than many utilities.

Its situation is complicated because it is extremely labor-intensive (instructional compensation is 84 percent of the budget) and extremely vulnerable to inflation. And, unlike industry, it has not increased "productivity" (only the construction industry matches education's failure to increase its productivity in twenty-five years). It is complicated further by being almost uniquely "flat" in its managerial structure. That structure is not "transitive," as it is in business, where executives can expect an orderly rise from step one to step two as their experience and abilities merit. In the university the final locus of power is really the individual professor, who can be "transitive" only to the extent of heading his department; he advances along a *competence* hierarchy, not a *power* hierarchy—one that confers influence and status but not the ability to issue orders or to confer emoluments. In sum, it is society's closest realization of the pure model of anarchy; i.e., the locus of decision making is the individual.

This is the cat's cradle in which university presidents are presently enmeshed. The crisis calls for leadership, but leaders aren't leading. They're consulting, pleading, temporizing, martyrizing, trotting, putting out fires, either avoiding or taking the heat, and spending too much energy in doing both. They've got sweaty palms, and they're scared. One reason is that many of them don't have the faintest concept of what leadership is all about. Like Auden's captain, they are studying navigation while the ship is sinking.

In my moment of truth, that weary 4 A.M. in my trivia-cluttered office, and in the reflective hours of the following summer, I began trying to straighten out in my own mind what the university president should be doing and not doing, what his true priorities should be, how he must lead. I daresay they apply to *all* presidents, *all* leaders, in whatever type of institution.

Lead, not *manage*. There is an important difference. Many an institution is very well managed and very poorly led. It may excel in the ability to handle each day all the routine inputs— yet may never ask whether the routine should be done at all.

Frequently, as I have noted, my best, most enthusiastic deputies unwittingly keep me from working any fundamental change. One, for example, was wheedling me into a personal "liaison" visit to the manager of a huge, new government complex scheduled to be our neighbor. I was about to accept this suggestion, but the lesson from my moment of truth intervened. "Look," I said. "If I go, all I'll hear is things the manager is going to want from the provost, the librarian, and so on. I'll have to come back and relay these things to them. I may not do so nearly as clearly or persuasively as he would firsthand; furthermore, they might be less cooperative."

All of us find ourselves acting on routine problems because they are the easiest things to handle; we hesitate to get involved too early in the bigger ones—we collude, as it were, in the unconscious conspiracy to immerse us in routine. In the past year I have talked with many new presidents of widely ranging enterprises, and each one has told me the biggest mistake he made was to take on too much, as if proving oneself depended on providing instant solutions and success were dependent on immediate achievements.

My entrapment in routine made me realize another thing: People were following the old army game. They did not want to take the responsibility, or bear the consequences, of decisions they properly should make. The motto was "Let's push up the tough ones." The consequence was that everybody and anybody was dumping his "wet babies" (as the old State Department hands call them) on my desk, when I had neither the diapers nor the information to take care of them.

So I have decided the president's first priority—the sine qua non of effective leadership—is to create around him an "executive constellation" to run the office of the president. It can be a mixed bag—some vice-presidents, some presidential assistants. All of the group must be compatible in the sense that they can work together but neither uniform nor conformist in the sense of yes men—they will be individuals who know *more* than the president does about everything within their areas of competency and can attend to it without dropping their wet babies on his desk. They must be people who take very seriously the functions of the office of the president. They ask what those functions are now and what they should be. They ask what various individuals want to do, are motivated to do, and are competent to do. And they try to work out the "fit."

What should the president himself do? He should be a *conceptualist*. That's something more than being just an "idea man." It means a leader with entrepreneurial vision and the time to spend thinking about the forces that will affect the destiny of his institution. He must educate his board members so that they not only understand the necessity of distinguishing between leadership and management but also can protect the chief executive from getting enmeshed in routine machinery. If he fails to do this, the directors or trustees will collude with the other constituencies to enmesh him—be more concerned about putting out fires than considering whether the building is worth saving.

The leader must create for his institution clear-cut and measurable goals based on advice from all elements of the community. He must be allowed to proceed toward those goals without being crippled by bureaucratic machinery that saps his strength, energy, and initiative. He must be allowed to take risks, to embrace error, to use his creativity to the hilt and encourage faculty and students to use theirs.

Man on a white horse? Some would say so. But consider the situation of the President of the United States, as Richard Neustadt portrays it: "Underneath our images of Presidents-in-boots, astride decisions, are the half-observed realities of Presidents-in-sneakers, stirrups in hand, trying to induce particular department heads, or Congressmen, or Senators, to climb aboard."

I don't want to ride a white horse. I'll settle for a dray horse, even one ready for the glue works. All I want to do is to get one foot in the stirrup. . . .

"ALL THE PRESIDENT'S MEN"

The really striking impression one gained during the Watergate hearings was the most obvious one: how much all the Nixon aides looked alike. I had trouble telling Dean from Magruder, Porter from Sloan, Strachan from Haldeman. All seemed cast in the same plastic mold—young, cleancut, narrow-tie, radiating both a humorless purposefulness and a numbness of moral sensibilities. In appearance, they were almost mirror images of the younger Nixon of the 1940s, as if they were that spiritual or ghostly double called *doppelgänger.*

This doppelgänger phenomenon is by no means accidental, and by no means confined to the White House. If Watergate-type cameras could zoom in on the headquarters of any huge bureaucracy-government, corporation, university, hospital— we would see it repeated more often than we should like to imagine. By and large, people at the top of massive organizations tend to select as key assistants people who resemble them. . . .

Of course, the desire for a congenial and closely knit management group is perfectly human and, up to a point, understandable. The huge size of such organizations and the enormous overload burdening every top leader make it impossible for him to verify all his own information, analyze all his own problems, or always decide who should or should not have his ear or time. Since he must rely for much of this upon his key assistants, he would not feel comfortable in so close and vital a relationship with men who were not at least of kindred minds and of compatible personalities.

This means, inevitably, that the leader is likely to see only that highly selective information, or those carefully screened people, his key assistants decide he should see. In a very crucial situation, he may discover only too late that he has acted on information that was inadequate or inaccurate, or that he has been shielded from "troublesome" visitors who had something to tell him he should have known, or that he has been protected from some problem that should have been his primary concern.

The corollary danger is that doppelgängers anxious to be more royal than the king may take actions they-feel-sure-he-wants-but-must-keep-from-him lest they either burden or, possibly, embarrass him.

The assistant is the inevitable product of the growth and scale and size of our institutions. He seems to be indispensable, although in a recent seminar with the new chairman and new president of a large life insurance company, I was fascinated to learn that, while each had come to the top as "assistants to" the leader, each was now determined to get along without any and so restructure his staff and line as not to need this right-hand winnowing. I will watch with great interest to see if they can do it. For me, assistants are very useful; I cannot do without them . . . It is incongruous and may be seen as pretentious to compare the problems of a university or an insurance company president to those of the President of the country. But, except for scale and magnitude, they are in many ways the same. And, if one leaves aside the questions of bugging, burglary, and the President's complicity, it can be said that we all have our doppelgängers and our Watergates. I speak, not only from experience as a consultant to organizations, but as president of the University of Cincinnati, which, with its $115 million budget, daily must meet problems comparable to those of a small city or of a sizable corporation.

Both experiences have taught me that the biggest problem of a president—any president—is getting the truth. Pierre du Pont said it well in a long-ago note to his brother Irenée: "One cannot expect to know what will happen, one can only consider himself fortunate if he can learn what *has* happened." To learn that, I must depend to a very large extent upon my vice-presidents, assistants, and staff. They are very good men and women, honest and truthful. Even so, it is not an easy matter to get full and objective truth from them.

I've always tried to be a very open person and to encourage the utmost openness and candor from all those around me. Yet time and again, after the most protracted and exhaustive meetings and discussions with these men and women, I have run into one or another of them later only to learn that some crucial question or important disagreement was not even raised.

"Why on earth didn't you talk up?" I ask. The answers I get are along these lines:

- "I didn't want to be calling you wrong in public."
- "You've got your areas, and this is one where you get very defensive."
- "I thought I'd catch you alone outside last week, but I never got around to it."
- "I didn't think I would win the argument against you, despite the fact that I felt you were making a mistake."
- "I didn't want to burden you by dropping another load on your shoulders."

Yet it may be precisely a burden that *should* be on my shoulders.

Much is made of that final responsibility "The buck stops here." However, a president is often lucky if he can find the buck at all, learn where it stopped, or discover who stopped it before it reached him. I wish I could get more genuine "bucks" on my desk, rather than the myriad of frittering detail that does get dumped there so that (what I have phrased as Bennis's law) routine work drives out the important.

People in power have to work very hard on getting people to tell them the truth. The right people will, and the right bosses will hear it. . . .

The staff around a president develops stereotypes about people: "The boss wouldn't want to see him—he's the fellow who went to the wedding in tennis shoes." The president himself may say, "Jesus, did you see what So-and-So told the *Post?*" and down through assistant through secretary to people taking down phone calls, go reverberations felt miles away even when they're quite unreal. So suddenly a very few people are implicitly skewing, selecting information that gives you an inaccurate picture on which decisions may be based. Such skewedness can affect history: Barbara Tuchman in her book on China tells how, in the 1940s, Mao Tse-tung wanted very much to visit Roosevelt, but Roosevelt canceled the proposed meeting on the basis of incredibly biased information from Ambassador Pat Hurley. It was nearly 30 years later that another President sought out the meeting with Mao which, had it taken place earlier, conceivably could have averted many subsequent disasters.

I have chosen, for my own principal assistants, people who have faculty tenure—for the simple reason that, since they have something to go back to if either of us doesn't like the relationship or find its results satisfactory, they are much freer to be outspoken and to try to give me the objective truth. At the same time, since they come from a constituency—the faculty—they know what is practical and possible in dealing with its problems, but being away from that constituency also enables them to approach these problems more objectively. I tell them I plan to rotate them frequently—so that no one will spend more than one or two years as an assistant—both to keep them fresh and to preclude their becoming preoccupied with a personal vested position.

This objectivity is imperative because everyone else who reports to you—deans in my case or Cabinet officers in the case of the President—does represent a constituency and simply because of this cannot give you objective, unbiased advice.

A beautiful example of this happened when I promoted one of my ablest assistants to a top academic post. Only a month before, he had argued with me most persuasively that my notion of using a faculty member as a half-time assistant just would not work. Now, when I told him I had in mind choosing an academic department head as his replacement, he urged that the man act as my assistant only half-time while continuing to head his department. He gave very good and cogent reasons as to why his views on half-time work had shifted 180 degrees in a single month, but what had really changed was that he was now speaking from a constituency, and with very different concerns.

A president's assistant should give him complete loyalty. The problem is that if he is your person, and *only* your person, he has a personal stake in his continuation in that role and for that reason he may, unconsciously, not tell you the whole truth. It is the vulnerability that comes from being totally dependent on one person.

If it is not absurd to transpose the lessons of my own experience to former President Nixon's much-debated problems, these latter seem to me to have stemmed in considerable part from the fact that his Orange County doppelgängers were in precisely that position of vulnerability. None had ever been elected to any office and thus had little or no concept of what was politically realistic and what was politically dangerous, perhaps even mortally so. Having no previous constituency, none had anything to fall back upon, and all were completely dependent on the approval or disapproval of one man. As we have seen, this skewed, not only the information they got and gave, but also their personal concepts of what was ethically, morally, or legally permissible. Whatever responsibility the President may have had for the mess he ended in, there is no question that his own doppelgängers helped put him there. As a French saying has it, "It was worse than a crime; it was a blunder."

How can future Presidents avoid such humiliation and entrapment by overeager "spiritual and ghostly doubles"? To this end I would urge:

1. *As much as possible, he should put his key assistants on temporary duty,* at most for two years, with the advance knowledge that they will be rotated. This will make them less likely to overreach in the effort to consolidate their own power positions. . . .

2. *He should see that some, not all, of his assistants have at some time had relationships with some important constituency.* . . .

3. *He should run, not walk, from the doppelgänger syndrome.* . . . [and] seek to surround himself with the utmost diversity of view still capable of being orchestrated harmoniously. . . .

4. *He ought to read at least one daily newspaper.* . . . A President who hears only what he wants to hear, and finds only what he wants to find, will find himself in trouble.

5. *Finally—to make one thing perfectly clear—he cannot rely exclusively on his palace guard for information.* Hard as it is to do so, he must remain accessible, despite the fact that accessibility in modern times seems one of the most underrated of political virtues. . . .

The Romans, who were the greatest politicians of antiquity, and probably also the busiest men, valued the quality of accessibility highly in their leaders. Cicero, in praising Pompey, commented on his ready availability, not only to his subordinates, but to the ordinary soldiers in his command. . . .

I would offer much the same suggestions to the president of any large organization. Today we are *all* organization men and women. Where 75 years ago, only 10 percent of our people worked for what Berle and Means called an organization and 90 percent were self-employed, today the ratio is just the reverse. Every pebble dropped in Watergate has had its ripples throughout our complex organizational society, and by the same token it is the excesses, the concealments, the arrogances and half-truths of a thousand faceless doppelgängers, in innumerable large organizations, that make a Watergate possible.

3 / Henry Kissinger as Department Manager

Paul Von Ward

FOR FOUR YEARS NOW, by virtue of my formal assignments and my own inclinations, I have been concerned with the problem of enhancing the institutional effectiveness of the Department of State. This period has included a year of intensive academic study of organizational theory and change, a year heading an analytic unit in the personnel system, a year on the Bureau of Personnel's policy staff, and almost a year working on department organizational and management questions from the perspective of the American Foreign Service Association (while assigned to a departmental policy office in the bureau dealing with U.S. cultural exchange programs).

This paper represents a view from the inside, with no claim to being unbiased, but I am hopeful that it flows from a systematic survey of significant events and depicts more than a single personalized perspective. While I have used the commentary of many colleagues, I am solely responsible for the way it is reflected here. I neither suffered personal trauma nor was I singularly blessed by Kissinger's three and a half years in the State Department and to that extent it should be a relatively objective view.

Today we look at an era which was dominated by Henry A. Kissinger, an articulate, forceful personality who viewed himself as a pattern-maker. We attempt to assess the long-term impact of his perspective and decisions. In so doing, we raise a question that has become more important both to students of

Prepared for the 18th Annual Convention of the International Studies Association, St. Louis, Missouri, March 16–20, 1977. This represents the personal views of the author and in no way reflects the official position of the Department of State or any other organization. It is based on the public record and the author's personal interpretation of that data. Reprinted with the permission of the author.

public policy and to elected and appointed officials as the size
and complexity of the government sector has increased;
namely, *how does a senior manager impact on the course of public policy and leave an enduring imprint?* In the context of the
Kissinger era, the question is what are the future policy implications of such a virtuoso performance? . . .

One can achieve immortality, or institutionalization if you
prefer, by either or both of two ways—which are not completely separable except in a theoretical sense: One can make
and get implemented a decision that sets in train a course of
events that assumes a life of its own and becomes difficult or undesirable to change. An example is the 1971 opening to the People's Republic of China. The second method is to influence an
institution in such a way that one's perspective or approach
lives on. In this paper I wish to focus on the second method.

A secretary of state can cope personally with only a small
fraction of the issues in any given day. He or she has a responsibility to influence the way the department handles, or fails to
handle, the remainder. In fact the composite of all the problems being attacked or ignored by the bureaucracy probably
has a greater cumulative impact on the future course of events
than a few highly visible crisis points that occupy the Secretary's attention. It is the bulk of the organization, then, and the
manner in which the Secretary influences the way it does its
work that needs much greater attention from scholars.

Three general questions are: How do leaders of institutions,
including cabinet secretaries, shape those institutions' processes and substantive outcomes? How can that impact endure
beyond the tenure of the incumbent? What effect do they have
on the career bureaucracy they inherit, or does the bureaucracy manage to outlive them and maintain its traditional
ways? More specific questions arise in a Kissinger/Department
of State analysis: Did he make progress in resolving some of the
longstanding organizational problems in the department? If so,
which ones? If not, what are the likely implications?

Kissinger, with the support of two presidents, personified the
top-down approach, in which the chief executive makes all the
decisions; yet he talked often of the need to "institutionalize
foreign policy"—that is, to create an organization capable of
carrying out his ideas about foreign affairs even after he had
left the office. He had also written profoundly on the problems

of bureaucracy prior to his entry into government service: In 1966, he demonstrated a clear recognition of (1) the inevitability of institutional influences on foreign policy decision making in the nuclear age; (2) the stultifying influence of bureaucratic processes on problem solving; (3) the importance of career experiences in shaping the conceptual patterns of leading officials; and (4) the rigid, backward-looking, and mediocre orientation of bureaucratic behavioral norms. His critique gave a good description of the symptoms, but demonstrated no clear understanding of the causes and offered no prescription for change. Events suggest that he was more able at diagnosis than prescription, better as critic than manager.

Perhaps Kissinger himself came to recognize this disparity since by January 10 of 1977, he was apparently discounting the institutional or bureaucratic role in the formulation of his foreign policy. He told the National Press Club that U.S. "policy emerged from an amalgam of factors: objective circumstances, domestic pressures, the values of our society, and the decisions of individual leaders."

This contrast between the early awareness of institutional deficiencies and subsequent difficulties coping with them has its parallels: Flora Lewis, *New York Times* diplomatic correspondent in Europe, noted such a paradox in the case of Charles De Gaulle. De Gaulle, she pointed out, the man who spoke most of the need to create institutions and maintain them, left only the shadow of an institutional policy for posterity.

In his first statement as secretary to the employees of the Department of State Kissinger signaled his concern for institutionalization and called for better assessment of the implications of foreign events and greater emphasis on policy making and advising the President of concrete policy options. He stressed the need to be thoughtful about world problems instead of blindly trying to overwhelm them. He called for the movement of able younger people into key positions as rapidly as possible.

At the end of a year on the job he was apparently actively considering how to implement such concepts. Several draft statements on institutionalization were prepared by a speech writer, Lawrence M. Mead, and others in the department in late 1974 and early 1975 in anticipation of a secretarial announcement of strategy for organizational change. Finally a speech was made by Kissinger on the subject of the department's organization and personnel system in June, 1975, before a newly sworn in class of Foreign Service Officers (FSOs). It was based on a Bureau of Personnel study which attempted to address the whole, but in terms of prescriptions represented a patchwork of ideas that touched on separate bits of the problem. Nevertheless, it was a recognition that something had to be done with the organization if a Kissinger perspective was to endure.

This paper looks at some of the events that fall between that September, 1973 speech given on his accession to State Department leadership, and the expression of January, 1977 and attempts to assess efforts at "institutionalization" and their implications for U.S. global policy.

A manager has various levers with which to influence an institution. Specifically, a secretary of state can have impact on the department through the following five different channels.

a. *Personal Decisions.* The manager decides on certain institutional questions personally, but the ability to exert direct and personal influence has its limitation; the impact is most often only short-term. In addition, the way substantive matters are personally handled by the manager has direct influence on the institution.

b. *Selecting People.* The most important indirect way of exerting influence on institutions is the placement of people in roles which control crucial policy or organizational decisions.

c. *Modification of Formal Structure.* An organizational manager's changes in the formal structures and procedures change the character of policy actions by altering the relations of the various actors and the flow of data among them. In addition to changing the communication and decision-making processes, the alterations affect the reinforcement patterns that reward or punish certain kinds of policy-oriented behavior.

d. *Developing and Training.* A manager's decisions on the personnel and training functions of the organization affect policy outcomes by having an effect on the kinds of personalities the system develops.

e. *Reshaping Conceptual Patterns.* The most indirect path of institutional influence is the introduction of new basic concepts or assumptions that take hold among individuals in the organization, alter their world-view, reshape their perceptions and analyses, and affect institutional processes; all of which have policy ramifications.

Using these five elements, I try to look at what Kissinger said and did, describe something of its institutional impact, speculate as to its subsequent influence on policy, and sketch out implications for future managers *qua* policy-makers.

Personalized secretarial decision making was preordained by the views set forth in his subsequently widely publicized and analyzed *Daedalus* article on foreign policy in 1966. He saw the bureaucracy as an obstacle to policy innovation, particularly when it involved questions of changing strategy for the future. He expressed his view, which he has since often repeated, that the institutional decision-making process was so complicated and disgorging a policy, so painful, that little energy was left to later revise it when change was called for. It is clear that he saw bureaucracy as backward-looking, rewarding mediocrity, and inhospitable to innovation; yet he believed it was an inevitable and necessary reality given the risks of the nuclear age.

Given this view of bureaucracy, a view reinforced by the managerial philosophy of the Nixon administration, it is not surprising that his approach to foreign policy did not include a profound role for the established institutions. His inclination was to go it alone instead of risking the perils of ineffective organizations.

What he did in both the White House and the department is well known and needs only illustrative examples here: (1) First trip to the People's Republic of China in July 1971 without the knowledge of the State Department. (2) On-the-spot, shuttle diplomacy decisions without reference to the bureaucracy. (3) Back-channel communications during the SALT negotiations. (4) Decision-making team in southern Africa leaving the department out.

Decision making in the department came to a halt when he was away, and only papers from the trunk on his plane or telegrams to the department could result in action approvals. The sheer volume of decisions reserved to him insured that they could only get limited attention. Very few subordinates could speak for him, and then only on limited occasions. Seeming to believe the bureaucracy was not attuned to him, he tried to keep as much action as close to his personal signature as possible. While a logical short-run tactic from his perspective, it may prove to have been the most significant hindrance to his effort to leave an institutional legacy.

Kissinger's personnel selection practices went through an interesting metamorphosis. His early appointees in the National Security Council were bright, young, energetic men of conviction (including FSOs) who gave him the capability to run circles around the State Department, yet by the time he left the department eight years later, most of his top advisors were disciplined, reliable FSOs.

The extent of his evolution from the outside to the key insider was reflected in a January 18, 1977 comment: "we will never have a professional service if it is not used for all of the positions of the department."

In the department he appointed career FSOs in the highest number ever to top jobs. This action initially brought forth applause from the career service, but as the appointees were held in close check, with private and public reprimands, some began to characterize it as a mixed blessing. The pattern of Kissinger's reassignments indicated that to maintain the newly achieved status, officers had to be overly concerned about deviating from his line.

Instead of such appointments energizing the career service, most officers at lower levels felt themselves cut off from their few colleagues in the inner circle. The appointments were not always seen as constructive examples for a service that perceived itself as professional. There was frequently not a perception that merit had been rewarded and that models had been established for emulation.

The individuals so chosen considered themselves to be either explicitly or implicitly charged with the responsiblity only of carrying out the secretary's wishes. Frequently they seemed to act because he had ordered it, not because of personal commitment of the type that stems from participating in a decision. The period reinforced the narrow concept of disciplined "professionals" who can, and should, just as easily, carry out a different policy in the future. This was incongruent with a growing belief that such a role for the foreign affairs profession would be inadequate to the challenges ahead. Kissinger himself seemed to have mixed feelings about it; at times he called for individualism and dissent and yet his behavior often negated what he said.

In two decisions of organizational significance, Kissinger, after over a year on the job, appointed new people to the positions of Deputy Under Secretary for Management and Director General of the Foreign Service. He appointed people he knew and had worked with: Lawrence Eagleburger, who worked with him at the National Security Council and was his executive assistant in the department, and Carol Laise, the first women appointed as director general, who, as assistant secretary in the Bureau of Public Affairs, had led a very successful program that put Kissinger before key audiences in the U.S. They were given the mandate to revitalize the general management and personnel functions respectively. Eagleburger maintained control over any policy or significant program changes recommended by the Bureau of Personnel.

Both came to their new positions with considerable Foreign Service and Washington experience, but with no significant management expertise. They were both highly motivated and desirous of bringing about improvements in the system, but they failed to put together the type of staff required to develop an effective action program. The few well-qualified career personnel management professions in the department were not used, and appropriate outsiders were not called on either. The task of conceiving, designing, and implementing constructive organizational change strategies fell to persons with limited training, experience, and capabilities in the requisite fields. Consequently, the overall organizational response to Kissinger's challenge was very limited.

Close ties with the secretary in the case of Eagleburger also proved, ironically, to be a hindrance in the development of significant managerial innovations. As the secretary's "right hand" for substantive matters, Eagleburger found it impossible to devote more than a small portion of his day to the institutional side of the department. He was intensely interested in change proposals presented to him for review, but was unable to give them the continuing profound attention required to develop and sustain a comprehensive organizational strategy.

Modification of formal organizational relationships was relatively limited during Kissinger's three and one-half years as secretary. No reorganization as such was attempted.

Despite a widespread judgment that dramatic changes were required in the government's mechanism for dealing with international relations, and his own statements to that effect, Kissinger failed to pay much attention to larger organizational questions. He ignored a large scale study (the Commission on the Organization of Government for the Conduct of Foreign Policy, known as "The Murphy Commission") that recommended significant changes. That he might feel he lacked time to devote much attention to institutional matters is understandable, but given his pronouncements on the subject, it is surprising that he did not select a management or organizational expert and delegate the task. A likely plausible explanation seems to be his own limited understanding of organizational and behavioral theory and the absence of anyone with those competencies close enough to him to be able to recommend attention to process in a non-threatening way.

An interesting framework for a different explanation is David McClelland's concept of the need for personalized power, contrasted with the social power motive.

Kissinger in the *Daedalus* article lamented that planning staffs always desired to be "useful" to the leadership and therefore has a "bias against novel conceptions . . . [always] projecting the present into the future." Ironically his planning staff, for the most part, fulfilled his old prophecy. He moved the Policy Planning Staff to the center of the action—operationally involved in policy making and implementation. This had unintended side effects. The future got little innovative attention and operational units were weakened.

The secretary set up a Policy Priorities Group (PPG), including the deputy under secretary for management and other top central figures, such as the director general of the Foreign Service, and the assistant secretary for administration. Its responsiblity is to review the allocation of funds and positions and relate resource use to global policy priorities. It has developed a Policy Analysis and Resource Management System (PARM), which is being tried out worldwide this year and replaces earlier instruments designed for similar purposes.

The inspector general and his staff have been given a role in the assessment of the relationship between staffing and policy priorities; they are actively involved in the newly developed annual PARM process.

In addition, Kissinger talked of revitalizing the Bureau of Intelligence and Research's role in policy formulation, but action has been limited to placing his personal choices in the bureau director's job.

In sum, very little was done to adjust the organization structure to the changing nature of the environment that Kissinger's speeches so well described: the increasing inter-relatedness of problems, the merging of domestic and foreign issues, the new agenda of diplomacy, and the changing nature of public expectations.

Use of the formal personnel system was apparently seen by Kissinger as a way to have some institutional impact. He asked both director generals who served under him, Nathaniel Davis and Carol Laise, to prepare reports for him on what could be done in the formal personnel system to carry out his aspirations for revitalizing the department. The first report, prepared in 1974, was classified, made few recommendations, and given little attention. When Carol Laise assumed the office, a considerably broader study was prepared under her direction and presented to the secretary. On the basis of that report, and the advice of his career advisors, Kissinger decided to make some changes in the personnel system. Although he billed them as "reforms," they could hardly be characterized as anything but minor adjustments to the system. Consequently, they have had little impact on the substantive performance of the department.

In a speech to a new FSO Class in June, 1975 he announced the changed that would (1) require all FSO candidates to take the same test (to select only the best) regardless of their backgrounds, thereby eliminating advance self-selection of functional specialties; (2) establish standards and competitive process for hiring non-FSOs; (3) increase employment of women and minorities; (4) strengthen the promotion system by adding screening thresholds at both junior and senior levels; (5) improve the assignment process; (6) improve the departmental training program; and (7) give greater outside experience to FSOs.

In the first annual FSO written examination following the speech, the announced changes were implemented, but with little discernible impact on the types of new officers selected. More information was made available to Foreign Service employees on up-coming job vacancies in an effort to make the assignment process more open and at the same time more centrally controlled, but the informal network still remains the

primary channel for most assignments. The number of assignments to other governmental entities and private institutions
has increased and will undoubtedly in the long-run reduce the
parochial nature of employees' perceptions of themselves and
the outside world.

But the career service has not been able to develop fully ac-
tionable plans for all the promised changes and almost two
years later no significant improvements of the promotion process and training programs have been made. Less than 25 percent of the minority and women goals have been met, and standards for non-FSO hirings have not been developed.

The cumulative impact of these so-called reforms is not unlike that of an earlier Kissinger initiative to improve one aspect
of the department's performance: foreign assessment. In one of
the first institutional interventions, he cabled an exhortation to
improvement to overseas posts on October 24, 1973, calling for
more analysis and conceptual writing. He assigned responsibility for follow-up to the under secretary for political affairs,
William J. Porter, who canvassed officers for ideas and then set
forth bureau and post reporting guidelines. With Porter's appointment as U.S. ambassador to Canada in early 1974, the effort faded away. . . . There had been some improvement for a
short period following the Porter effort, but at the time of the
inspection things were as bad as they had been before. No one
ever seriously addressed the myriad and inter-related managerial, training, and reward factors that would require modification to effect a change in the general quality of overseas analysis and reporting.

This one-dimensional approach to corrective action was evident in another intervention: an attempt to enhance the ability
of officers to recognize the inter-relationship of events and
place them in a global context. Kissinger recognized the weak-
ness, but thought it was caused by too many tours in one area.
The result was GLOP (Global Outlook Program), which was enforced by setting a percentage formula to ensure that officers
would move around the globe in a series of assignments.
Whether in fact the assignment pattern was the real underlying
cause of myopia is a question that was never analyzed.

*In the introduction of conceptual patterns into the discussion
of global issues Kissinger was extremely articulate and prolific.*
His years as Secretary, in his "virtuoso" role and not as "man-

ager," were filled with statements that contained views on the world and how the United States and its government should relate to it. On January 10, 1977 at the National Press Club, he said "I . . . hold the view that the real essence of our foreign policy was to be found in the series of speeches I have given around the country."

And, indeed, I believe it can be said that certain of his themes, whether they be seen as parts of a whole or isolated strands, were reiterated often enough and have such implications for our basic frame of reference in thinking about international relations and the U.S. role in the world, that they may have a significant long-term impact on the conceptual and analytic process of the institution, and consequently, influence future policy. . . . It is not possible to predict the impact of Kissinger's actions on specific issues of future policy, but it is possible to identify certain elements of institutional life that were directly affected by him and project some of their general policy implications.

The level in the organization at which decisions were made was raised even higher than is normal for a bureaucratic hierarchy. Raising the approval level had two negative effects on decisions quite apart from their specific content: they were slower in getting made and all the alternatives were worn off in the compromising clearance process. By drawing so much to himself, Kissinger reinforced two facets of the bureaucracy that he had so often criticized: the cumbersome process and the cautious outcomes of decision making.

The closeness with which much information was held reduced the ability of lower levels to effectively implement and give support through their day-to-day actions. One could not expect the Public Affairs Bureau and the Office of Congressional Relations to use their resources effectively in building public understanding and support for policy-choices when they didn't know what choices were being made. A desk officer or officer in the field could not adequately forecast the course of events in the Middle East without knowing what arrangements had been made in Israel.

As State Department officers came to understand that Kissinger wanted his personal imprint on all policy, *it became more and more productive from a bureaucratic point of view, to give him what he seemed to want the first time, thereby reducing the consideration given to alternatives.* In these areas, his manage-rial style had a direct impact on the substance of policy. But perhaps of more importance was the impact of Kissinger's style on the attitudes and motivations of employees, and on the amount of energy and dedication they would devote to a task.

By selecting and rewarding the "disciplined" FSOs for sec-ond echelon policy jobs, Kissinger cut down on the new thoughts that would be advanced.

Not only was his direct impact on the institution often coun-terproductive, but his personnel placements were also not con-structive. This is not a criticism of the abilities and motivations of the individuals chosen by him for policy jobs. It was a func-tion of personal style; they were individual performers who had served him well, but were not skilled in effective organizational management. In addition they were hampered by his continual demands on them, leaving little time for institution building. He used them as individuals and not as managers of institu-tions. . . .

The personnel system of the department, which is widely de-scribed as inappropriate to today's challenges, remained unim-proved during Kissinger's tenure despite the public fanfare. The few changes proved to be more dysfunctional than con-structive. Inasmuch as they did not bring about visible im-provement, they tended to decrease employees' faith in the sys-tem and its ability to facilitate their work.

The reasons for this failure are legion, but the lack of a clear picture of the challenge is not one of them; Kissinger articu-lated it very well.

His many speeches on the new agenda of diplomacy and the convergence of foreign and domestic policy have widespread institutional implications. Kissinger appeared to vaguely un-derstand them and relate them to the need for a redefinition of the department's role or mission. He called such a redefinition "the first phase of institutionalization." He characterized the new institutional challenge as nothing less then "reconciling the increasingly complex and interrelated domestic and foreign policy issues." Although he articulated the need well, forcefully, and repeatedly, he did not develop a useful prescrip-tion for dealing with it. Neither has the career leadership been able to define its implications for operational institutional changes. Thus far it has been unable to relate such a new conception of need to the real world of workable and appropriate plans for organizational change. Reactions have been simplistic and superficial, taking the grafting or incremental approach instead of a strategy of profound reshaping of the organization.

Kissinger accurately perceived the problems, but did not devote much time to analysis of their underlying causes. *He also failed to do the next best thing: give the mandate to a trusted person competent to the task and provide adequate staff support.* He asked the system to correct itself, an impossible demand given the existing specialized foreign service perspective of most career officers and the dearth of innovative personnel management professionals.

Throughout Kissinger's approach to the institution, we saw an inconsistency between words and deeds. On the one hand he called for interpretative reporting, independent analysis, conceptual innovation, clarification of options rather than bureaucratic compromise, and the expression of dissent. But, his behavior frequently signaled that he wanted something else.

This bifurcation made it impossible to develop a comprehensive effort at institutional change of the magnitude that would have been required to bring about the performance he called for. It would have demanded widespread involvement at all levels in a process of rethinking the department's vision of the world and the Foreign Service's role in it. The openness necessary to such a process was antithetical to the way he apparently believed he had to operate when handling critical policy issues. To open the door to institutional debate must have appeared too threatening.

It is a great irony that a leader who understood the weaknesses of modern bureaucracies and the need for institutional change found it impossible to bring about the necessary changes when placed in charge. In his attempt to avoid getting mired in the bureaucracy, he left it to its own fate and, by his style, discouraged those on the inside from rising to the challenge and trying renewal from within. The opportunity costs have been considerable.

With his substantive tactical skills, Kissinger left the U.S. in a period of potentially creative quiescence, but his managerial acts perpetuated the reactive mode in which U.S. foreign policy has previously been constructed and left the institution incapable of taking advantage of the lull. The institution was left inadequate to meet the immediate challenges posed by burgeoning populations, shrinking resources, and proliferation of nuclear and conventional weapons.

Little has been added to the functional competence of the work force, and the few new experts who have been hired are not included in the central policy process in the regional bureaus, the policy planning staff, nor the offices of the 7th floor principals. Even if additional specialists were brought into the more technical areas of the department, such as the political-military, economic and business, and oceans and international environmental and scientific bureaus, they would be unable to impact effectively on broader policy considerations.

This continuing lack of expertise in the State Department means that the functional departments, such as Treasury, Agriculture, Defense, will continue to act in the international arena according to their individual visions of what our global policy ought to be. And nowhere in Washington is there an institution which can put it all together in a global perspective that permits the U.S. Government to act in a timely fashion in the nation's long-term interests.

SOME IMPLICATIONS FOR FUTURE MANAGERS OF STATE

The first thing that is required in order for any secretary to significantly increase the capacity of the department is a comprehensive and coherent managerial strategy. Such a strategy must encompass planned action with reference to all the following elements: basic assumptions about the global environment and the department's role in it, the attitudes, behaviors and processes which facilitate and reward the desired performance; organizational structures and systems which support the desired outcomes; and an explicit evaluation and renewal element.

Such a strategy would have to include consideration of the kinds of people required in key positions and an understanding of the series of action steps required to move the organization toward the new model, including how to involve people in changing themselves. To be effective, the principles of the change strategy would have to be congruent with the nature of its desired objectives; i.e., such innovation cannot be ordered by an authoritarian system.

Kissinger himself indicated what was required to institutionalize the new global policy perspective and approach: a reshaping of the traditional overseas perspective of career officers; the development of a senior corps of advisors to the President on global policy; increased Washington inter-agency experience and new functional expertise in the career staff; and increased dialogue between the public and department personnel. . . .

The traditional concept of diplomacy as primarily secret—formal government-to-government relations—would have to be replaced by a more open process, involving the public to a much greater degree. This implies entirely new concepts of organizational processes and structures. And it requires a person at the top who is not himself a secretive, personal diplomat, who will not closely guard decision making for himself and his chosen aides. No organization—even the U.S. Department of State—functions without the support and cooperation of the people below, the people who have to carry out decisions and implement policy.

4 / Bob Six's Long Search for a Successor

Rush Loving, Jr.

DURING HIS TENURE as chief executive, the head of a large corporation makes decisions that shape the lives of thousands. He decides whether people are hired, promoted, or fired. His policies may generate profits in the millions, or bring about

Reprinted from the June 1965 issue of *Fortune Magazine* by special permission; © 1965 Time Inc. Pp. 93–97, 175–78.

huge losses. But no decision is more critical to the future of the enterprise than his selection of a successor. That decision is irrevocable, like the writing of a will bequeathing all corporate powers to a sole survivor.

When the chief executive is the man who built the company, he can be racked by great emotion. Some pioneers have chosen their successors well. But at least three founders of major U.S. airlines have chosen unwisely. At United, at Pan Am, and at American, the successors of Pat Patterson, Juan Trippe, and C. R. Smith foundered and were eventually removed by the directors.

This hard fact has haunted one of the last of the airline pioneers, Robert F. Six, head of Continental Air Lines, who presented a plan for his own succession to the company's board last month. Six was determined that what had happened at United, Pan Am, and American would not happen at Continental, and to ensure that it would not, he spent eight years seeking the right man. The search was as thoughtful and incisive as it was deliberate. Its length and depth were especially surprising, because it was conducted personally by Six himself, a man who has acquired a reputation as a hipshooter.

THE DROPOUT WHO MADE GOOD

As it happens, that reputation is undeserved, but it has been fostered by Six's colorful past. Fifteen years ago, Six literally did shoot from the hip. Traveling around Colorado with a group of quick-draw artists, he gave exhibitions with handguns, hitting a bulls's-eye in a fraction of a second.

As a businessman, he talks bluntly and moves fast. The men he has been able to choose among in selecting a successor all know more about running an airline than he did when he became president thirty-seven years ago. "I just started off and learned the hard way," he says. "There wasn't any criteria for it."

A six-foot-four-inch outdoorsman, son of a doctor in Stockton, California, Six was a high-school dropout who worked as a factory hand and a merchant seaman (retaining a vocabulary to match). He got hooked on airplanes in the Twenties, and barnstormed throughout California for two years. He tried to become an airline pilot, but because he had already made three crash landings, he was turned away.

Finally, in 1936, Six borrowed $90,000 from his father-in-law and bought into Varney Air Transport Inc., a tiny El Paso mail-plane operator. First as operations manager, then as president, Six built Varney into the present-day Continental. Today his airline flies 22,657 miles of routes from Miami and Chicago to the West Coast and Hawaii.

Continental bears the vivid imprint of Six's flamboyant personality. He has an instinct for what the customers want, and he has sold the airline so well that some passengers revere it with the ardor of a cult. Many Westerners will fly no airliners but Six's golden-tailed 727's and DC-10's. Edward E. Carlson, chairman of United Air Lines, Continental's biggest and toughest competitor, says: "Continental is a great success story, and Continental is Bob Six. What the public perceives of Continental is Bob Six's imagination, personality, and willingness to do the unusual."

Six has played on the fact that Continental is a little company battling competitors who are mammoth and impersonal (Continental's operating revenues of $457 million were only one-fifth of United's last year). By casting his company in the role of David, Six has created a remarkable esprit de corps and a feisty and innovative operating style. Says Joseph A. Daley, Six's vice president for public relations and one of Continental's brightest marketing minds: "We've got to be different. Six is operating a delicatessen next to a supermarket. We've got to carry the bagels and the Danish beer and deliver." Among other things, Continental delivered the first hot meals and wide seats in coach, the first economy class, and a management representative on every airplane to take care of passengers' problems.

Continental's compactness makes the airline relatively easy to manage. Everyone seems to know everyone else. All flight crews based in Los Angeles check in at the operations room on the second floor of the company's general offices, where they frequently run into Continental's senior officers, and even the c.e.o. himself. Six insists that the officers take their lunch in the company cafeteria, where everyone from Six on down rubs elbows with mechanics, secretaries, and pilots. "Here the officers are human beings," says one Continental newcomer. "In some companies they go out to '21' and you never see them."

Six has instilled quality and consistency in the airline by treating his employees with the affection of a father while applying the tough discipline of a Puritan schoolmaster. At the same time, he has kept the company from bankruptcy by watching costs like an Ebenezer Scrooge reincarnate.

He charms his people into putting out for Continental, largely by knowing as many as he can personally. While clipping a twenty-five-year pin on a terminal supervisor, Six interrupted the proceedings to recall how the man had been first officer on a DC-3 that had iced up one night over Lubbock, Texas. The event took place more than two decades ago.

By touring the system and prowling the hallways at headquarters with a cold eye for detail, Six keeps acquainted with just about every facet of his company. He knows that there's been a low-pressure area over the Pacific for the past week, or that the cargo business is up from San Antonio to Alaska, or that National flies its DC-10's at lower cost than Continental.

And wherever he goes, Six reminds his people that what they do reflects on them, because *they* are Continental. When he finds that the airline is falling below his standards of quality, he is outraged—and the quality soon goes up. On a recent flight to Houston, he noticed that the tenderloin steaks were being served wrapped in strips of bacon that were nearly raw. Six asked the hostess if the dinners were being prepared this way for all flights.

"I haven't seen that on your airplanes before, sir," she said.

"What do you mean, my airplanes? This is *your* airplane!" he roared.

When Six returned to Los Angeles, he ordered the bacon taken off and the savings used to buy bigger steaks.

Although Continental has always been highly leveraged and sparse with cash, it has managed to report a profit every year but one since Six became president. The company has one of the lowest records of customer complaints in the industry. Its on-time performance last year was second (to Western) among all the nation's trunk lines. And on six of its nine most competitive routes, Continental fills more seats per plane than its competitors.

ADVICE FROM A HEADHUNTER

To find a man who can sustain that record is a difficult task. In the early Sixties, Six thought he had such a man in Harding Lawrence, Continental's executive vice president and general manager. Six planned to retire in 1972, when he would reach sixty-five, and he intended to promote Lawrence to president, but Lawrence quit in 1964 to run Braniff. Lawrence's departure left Six with no really qualified, well-identified successor, and in 1967 he asked the advice of Henry O. Golightly, president of Golightly & Co. International Inc., a New York consulting firm. . . .

On April 21, 1967, Golightly sent Six a twenty-three-page outline of their plan. Using the outline as a guide, R. Randall Irwin, Golightly's expert on selecting and evaluating executives, interviewed every officer in Continental's top management who showed any measure of presidential potential. To keep their intentions secret, the interviews were conducted under cover of "a special program for assisting in the developing of executives."

By the end of June, Golightly and Irwin had singled out and profiled nine vice presidents, including former White House Press Secretary Pierre Salinger, who was then vice president, international (he later quit to return to politics). Each profile was ten to twelve pages long and included an appraisal by Irwin and an independent evaluation by Golightly, who knew each man personally. They bound each report in a black cover and sent them to Six. The black books described each man's character, background, education, management experience, and personal aspirations.

They also provided an insight into each officer's home life, sports, social graces, and his wife, including comments on whether she would be an asset if he became president. They even explored his relationship with his children and how well he had raised them.

At the same time, Irwin wrote Six a confidential letter telling him that out of the nine, he and Golightly had selected four potential candidates. "We are greatly impressed with their caliber," Irwin wrote. "They all have high intelligence; are highly motivated; and are completely dedicated to Continental."

After reading the nine black books, marking key phrases with a red felt-tipped pen, and putting the books away in his office safe, Six told Golightly he readily concurred with their conclusions.

By both their positions in the company and the initials of their last names, the four candidates composed the A, B, C, and D of Continental Air Lines.

RICHARD M. ADAMS, now fifty-six, senior vice president, operating and technical services, is a quiet engineer who enjoys good music and photography. The son of a New Jersey patent attorney, Adams has a warmth and an air of ability that have won him a staunch following among his subordinates. He moved over from Pan Am in 1962 to head Continental's maintenance division. Six soon moved Adams up, putting him in charge of flight operations as well as maintenance. Under him Continental has achieved the best records in the industry for aircraft utilization and jet safety.

CHARLES A. BUCKS, forty-seven, senior vice president, marketing, quit college after World War II to become a baggage handler in his home town of Lubbock at an airline that was later acquired by Continental. Showing a natural talent for salesmanship, he rapidly moved up through the marketing division until, at thirty-four, he became the air-transport industry's youngest vice president. (United now has a president ten years his junior, a fact that galls Bucks no little.)

Bucks has been the brain behind some of Continental's most outlandish marketing gimmicks. In 1959, to promote flights from Chicago, he dropped a helicopter onto Wrigley Field in the middle of a game and had a crew of midgets "kidnap" the Cubs' centerfielder. Six-foot-four, silver-maned, handsome, and an outdoorsman like Six, Bucks is second only to Six in popularity among Continental's rank and file. "Mr. Bucks knows he's a sex symbol," says a hostess on the ramp at Burbank, adding emphatically: "And he has the right to know it."

G. EDWARD COTTER, fifty-seven, is senior vice president, legal and diversification, and the company secretary. Disarmingly frank and ambitious, cool and well ordered, Cotter was born in the China mission field, the son of an Episcopal minister. He worked for a New York law firm and was secretary of Freeport Sulphur Co. before taking over Continental's legal division in 1965. Cotter has an extraordinary conceptual grasp of such broad issues as the airline's needs for long-term growth. And he articulates these ideas with the self-confidence and orderly flow of a seasoned barrister. "I'm a goddam good lawyer," he says. "I'm a very capable guy and this company is goddam lucky to have me."

Cotter has indeed been valuable to Continental, though most employees are unaware of his achievements. Yet everyone is aware of another fact of Cotter's life: he is Six's brother-in-law. His sister, actress Audrey Meadows, has been married to Six for fourteen years.

ALEXANDER DAMM, fifty-nine, senior vice president and general manager, is Continental's moneyman. Damm (rhymes with palm) came from T.W.A. in 1959 to bolster the company's lackluster financial division. He installed tight budget controls and a monthly head count that allows Six to veto the most minute addition to the payroll. Damm and Six are opposites in personality and complement one another, but they have never forged a close personal bond.

Born in Nebraska, the son of a Burlington railroad roundhouse foreman, Damm is a serious, no-nonsense taskmaster. He lives by the memo, often to Six's exasperation, and insists that written communication is the best way for an executive to keep informed. Nevertheless, Damm's rigid system of controls has kept Continental out of the red. Like many good general managers, he is not well liked by employees, largely because over the years he has had to execute the austerity programs that have laid off hundreds of men and women.

Six watched each man's performance for two years. Then, in August, 1969, Golightly and Irwin presented him with an updated profile of each man. They also uncovered a fifth candidate, Dominic P. Renda, who had come to Continental eighteen months earlier as senior vice president, international. Renda, sixty-one, a tall, swarthy man who is married to a former Miss Maryland, had been senior vice president, legal, of Western Air Lines. At this point, Golightly told Six that Damm, Renda, and Adams—in that order—were the best qualified candidates, and that in an emergency Continental could turn to any one of them as a new president.

A TIME FOR GROOMING

So far as the other candidates were concerned, Cotter had shown surprising growth in the two years, tightening his grasp of the airline business and toning down his competitive spirit, though he was sometimes still abrasive. Bucks, however, was a real comer. Golightly told Six that, for the long haul, Bucks was probably the strongest presidential prospect in the entire industry. But Golightly and Six calculated that he would require five to eight more years of grooming.

For all their strengths, each of the five candidates needed more experience. Accordingly, Six decided to put off his retirement until 1976, when he would be sixty-nine. Meanwhile, he decided to broaden the younger men's duties and see how they developed. "It's been great fun," he says proudly. "I enjoy watching these guys come up."

Bucks, for instance, had headed only the sales end of the marketing division. Six exposed him to the rigors of top-level decision making by placing him in charge of the entire division. To expand Cotter's responsibilities beyond legal affairs and into operations, Six put him in charge of a small chain of hotels in the Pacific and Continental Air Services, a contract carrier serving the government and private companies in Southeast Asia.

As Six watched eagerly through the early 1970s, each of the candidates made noticeable progress. Bucks became a practiced witness at regulatory hearings and drew on his native traits of showmanship to strengthen his following among employees around the Continental system. When the women's liberation movement attacked Continental's ad slogan—"We Really Move Our Tail For You!"—Bucks turned the dispute to his advantage by getting on a TV talk show and, waving a copy of the ad in front of the camera, stealing the show—and valuable publicity.

Under Cotter's guidance, Continental Air Services outperformed its competitor, Air America, the Central Intelligence Agency's own air-transport arm. Cotter, the missionary's son, even showed a hidden marketing flair. When he opened a new hotel on Saipan for the Japanese tourist trade, he flew in three Shinto priests to bless the place.

Gaining experience as general manager, Damm extended his knowledge beyond his financial specialty and into operations. He became a tough inspector, and he soon recognized the untapped potential of air cargo, pestering Six and Bucks for a better, more comprehensive and competitive freight program.

Damm also was turning into a hard bargainer. As head of a Continental negotiating team, he used eleventh-hour brinksmanship to win very favorable contracts for new airplanes from McDonnell Douglas and Boeing. And while his demeanor remained very serious, he was becoming more relaxed with people.

But the most important accomplishment during the early Seventies belonged to Adams, who persuaded Damm and Six to go against all the sacrosanct dogma of the industry and sell off Continental's brand-new fleet of four 747's. Indisputably the most popular airplane now flying, the 747 can also be a money eater. While it carries twice as many passengers as the DC-10, it costs more than four times as much to maintain.

With one notable exception, the five candidates worked well together, even though it was slowly dawning on all of them that they were in a race for the top. Any temptations to jockey for position were dampened by the knowledge that Six disliked office politics. The race did affect Six's relationship with Bucks, however. Since both men shared a fondness for the outdoors, they had gone off together over the years on week-long hunting trips. But, as the search for a president continued, their close companionship set off rumors that Six had anointed Bucks his heir. When Six heard the rumors, he abruptly ended their camaraderie. Unfortunately, he never explained why, and Bucks, who regards Six as something of a father, felt hurt long afterwards. He believed he must have inadvertently done something that annoyed the boss.

The one major friction among the contenders was between Cotter and Renda, both lawyers and men of strong personality. "He's very amiable," Cotter says of Renda. "A lot of people like him. I didn't like him personally. We were not compatible." The two barraged Six with a cross fire of memos, each disputing the other on some minor matter. "It was all nickel-and-dime stuff," says Six, who talked to both men and tried to make peace. Finally Six lost patience and told them he wasn't having any more to do with their bickering, but the memos kept coming in. The fight ended in 1972, when Renda left Continental to go back to Western as its executive vice president.

By May of last year, Six was beginning to realize that even though the four remaining contenders had developed, not one of them had perfected all the attributes he wanted in his successor. Adams understood financing as well as operations, but he was short on marketing expertise. Long a staff man, Cotter still lacked experience as a line officer. Damm had little of Cotter's conceptual ability, but he had developed an eye for detail and a general knowledge of marketing, operations, and scheduling. Bucks had been so busy untangling the structural intricacies of the marketing division and selling seats on Continental's highly competitive new runs to Hawaii that he still lacked experience in finance and route planning. Besides, Six complained, Bucks was too reluctant to fire those subordinates who failed to measure up, declaring in exasperation: "Jesus, Charlie, you're the Billy Graham of the air-transport industry!"

Since there was no single candidate with all the qualifications, Six decided to select a team of two successors. In the near term, he would move from president to chairman, a post that was vacant. One candidate would become vice chairman and another would be named president and chief operating officer. A year later, when Six stepped down, the best man would become chief executive.

To prepare for the final selection, Six and Golightly agreed they should compile an accurate measurement of the candidates' traits and have each man prepare an analysis of himself, though that would obviously be subject to some bias. "You'd do a perfect self-evaluation," said Golightly. "I'd write a glowing one," Six declared, grinning. "S——! It'd be half wrong." By last February all the evaluations were in, and Six put them away with the black books in his safe.

In the middle of last winter, Bucks's standing was enhanced by one further event. A number of rulings by the Civil Aeronautics Board had restricted Continental's use of some highly promotional sales gimmicks. Bucks's employees in the marketing division felt so hamstrung that they lost some of their enthusiasm, and the airline's distinctive individualism and feistiness was beginning to evaporate. For a year and a half, Six had been agitating for a return to the good old ways, and Bucks had picked up the call. The CAB had ordered Continental either to take the popular cocktail lounges out of its DC-10's or to charge extra for them. Continental had taken the ruling to court and, last December, the board was ordered to reconsider.

Even before the legal dust had settled, Bucks sold Six on a strategy to restore the airline's old-time pizzazz. Continental would reinstall the lounges and, going a step further, would put in electronic Ping-Pong games, show free movies—old newsreels, cartoons, and Saturday afternoon serials—and sell hot dogs, hot beef sandwiches, and Coors beer. The entire venture would cost $546,000, but Bucks estimated it would generate more than $1.3 million in extra revenues this year alone. If there had been any questions about Bucks's ability to burnish Continental's image, the new lounges swept those doubts away.

HE DIDN'T WANT PATSIES

Early this year, Six organized a selection committee including himself and three outside directors—Jay A. Pritzker, a Chicago investor whose family controls Hyatt Corp. and Cerro; Thomas D. Finney Jr., a Washington lawyer who is a partner of former Defense Secretary Clark Clifford; and David J. Mahoney, chairman and president of Norton Simon Inc., a former Continental director who is now one of its two advisory directors (the other is Audrey Six). Six chose the outsiders with care because, as he later explained, "I didn't want a patsy f—— committee." He was to get what he bargained for. The three men were to have a major impact on the final selection.

Six wanted to stick with his decision to name a vice chairman and a president, but now he worried about the two losers. He believed all four candidates would be valuable assets to any airline, and other carriers obviously shared that belief. In recent months Damm had been mentioned for the general manager's post of Pan Am, and Bucks had rejected the top marketing job at American. Six wanted to keep his team together, and to do that he planned to restructure the company's upper echelons and give the losing candidates additional powers.

Golightly urged Six to make his selection by using a scoring grid the consultant had set up for American Airlines:

TRAITS	MAXIMUM POINTS
Leadership	30
Technical ability	
airline experience	30
non-airline experience	15
Performance	20
Growth potential	10
Age: over 55	5
45–55	10
40–45	8
under 40	5

Though Golightly pressed the suggestion, Six rejected it. "Each of these guys I personally hired," he explained. "I just can't do it that way. My heart's not in it."

Six decided that his criteria had to be based on which man could best fulfill the particular goals and future needs of Continental. Now that the company had bought and financed its new airplanes, knowledge of operations and financing would be of secondary importance for the intermediate future. The company's main challenge would be to maintain its marketing edge and sustain its esprit de corps, while wringing as near perfect a performance as possible from its crews and terminal workers.

The unions had become more militant in recent years, and dealing with them would require personal leadership and insight into the art of handling people. While Damm had more general experience and Adams knew how to deal with flight crews, in Six's mind the candidate who fitted all those requirements best was Bucks.

But Six was also aware that Continental faced a serious and less noticeable challenge stemming from its own expansion. If the airline grew much larger, it might become impersonal and difficult for one or two men to control, a problem that had overwhelmed other airlines and railroads. Only one of the four candidates grasped the strategies needed to deal with this problem. That man was Cotter.

AUDREY KEEPS HER MOUTH SHUT

By late February the tension was gnawing at Six. Normally he can keep up with three conversations at one, but when Audrey broke the evening's silence to chat about some domestic subject, Six would answer absent-mindedly with a comment about the airline. Cotter's being his brother-in-law nagged at him terribly, perhaps more than he realized.

Except for attending traditional Christmas Eve family get-togethers, Six had made it a point to avoid seeing Cotter socially. For the past year Audrey had not discussed the four candidates with Six, knowing that he was aware of her preferences. "I'm not going to jeopardize anybody's chances by opening my big mouth," she told a friend. But once or twice she did pass on her observations to Golightly, who steadfastly refrained from repeating them to Six.

The candidates had their own opinions about who ought to get Six's job. Cotter believed himself both capable and worthy of it. "I have good judgment," he told a visitor one afternoon. "There are all sorts of extremely able people, fine sales types, accounting people. But they lack the basic element called common sense."

For his part, Damm had never doubted that his position as general manager put him next in line, but neither could he believe he would actually get the promotion. Adams and Bucks, on the other hand, took a rather unpretentious stance. Although both harbored the desire to run a major airline, they believed Damm to be the best choice. They were loyal to a senior executive who had worked hard and contributed greatly to the company's success.

Early this spring, Six privately reached his own decision. He favored Cotter as vice chairman because he understood the concepts needed to run an expanding company. He wanted Damm to be president and chief operating officer because of his vast experience in finance and administration. Six left open the decision as to which of the two would become chief executive upon his own retirement.

The trouble with the choices was that neither man was particularly popular with rank-and-file employees. When asked his opinion of Cotter, for instance, a passenger-service supervisor in

Phoenix replied: "Cotter? He's in charge of ramp facilities, isn't he?" But Six believed he could persuade Continental employees that his decision was the right one. "I've been selling these kids all my life," he said. "There's no reason I can't sell them on this."

Six planned to reveal his decision to the selection committee, which had agreed to meet on April 2 in New York. He decided to send each member copies of the candidates' self-analyses, his own critique of these, and an outline of each man's career drawn up by Golightly. In order to avoid any possible leaks Six flew from Los Angeles on March 23 to Continental's former headquarters at Denver's Stapleton field, where he still keeps an office. The following day he dictated his own critiques to a trusted former secretary, Judy L. Lawrence, who once worked for the FBI and holds a government security clearance. She typed copies for each committee member, and a little after five o'clock, Six stuffed the self-analyses and his critiques into three manila envelopes. Miss Lawrence handed the extra carbons and her stenographer's notebook over to Six and watched as he tore out her notes. He then drove to his apartment near downtown Denver and burned the notes in the kitchen sink.

"IF YOU GOT RUN OVER TOMORROW"

The committee (Six, Pritzker, Finney, and Mahoney) gathered at the Waldorf Towers at 6:30 on the evening of April 2, a Wednesday, in the living room of Suite 31-H, a warm and tasteful private apartment that Norton Simon Inc. keeps for private meetings and important visitors. Six sipped a vodka and Fresca, and the others, except for the teetotaling Mahoney, nursed scotches while they spread their papers on the carpet in front of their chairs and began talking. It soon became obvious that the outside members had studied the evaluations and come to some strong conclusions.

The committee seemed impressed by the fact that the evaluations and Six's critiques had shown incontrovertibly that none of the four candidates was totally equipped for the top job at Continental. Finney suggested that Six should postpone his retirement, and Mahoney asked him if he would extend his contract for two additional years. This proposition surprised Six, but the idea of remaining until he could bring Continental's earnings—and its stock price—closer to the levels the company had enjoyed in the mid-1960's greatly appealed to him. "Under today's conditions and with the stock options I've got," he replied, "the answer is yes."

Now that he was staying on, the Cotter-Damm tandem appointment he had in mind no longer made any sense. What Continental now needed was a president and a chief operating officer who could take over if something happened to Six. Mahoney asked: "Who would you name today if you got run over tomorrow?" Surprisingly, Six had not considered the question, but he did not hesitate in replying. The committee unanimously agreed that Al Damm would be recommended to the full board as president and chief operating officer after the annual meeting in Denver on May 7.

But Damm could not be expected to run the company for long. He will be sixty-two in 1978, when Six is to step down. With that in mind, the committee set about selecting a long-term heir. As one member said later: "Our discussion was not in the context of three years; our discussion was in the context of the next fifteen years." Nearly three hours later they came to a unanimous agreement and pledged themselves to secrecy. Some of the matters they had discussed were not to appear in the minutes of their meeting and not to be reported to the full board.

A week or so after the meeting, Mahoney called to ask sympathetically if Six had told Audrey about his decision. The answer was no. That was the worst part, not being able to talk about it. One day he had happened to sit with Bucks at lunch in the company cafeteria. "Charlie," he said, "I'm going to have to have lunch with all you fellows. I don't want to show any favorites in the cafeteria." And in the next few days he ate with Damm, Adams, and Cotter.

As May approached, Six found it harder to sleep; he woke up night after night, thinking about the decision. There still was no one to talk to about it. By this time, Mahoney was in Paris, Pritzker was involved with a troublesome acquisition, Finney was busy with his law practice, and Golightly was in London.

On the weekend before the annual meeting, Six flew to Denver, and the candidates followed a few days later. They seemed relaxed enough. Bucks sat up most of the night before the meeting playing poker. Six was asleep by 10:30 and slept well, waking only to get a drink of water and let out the dog.

The next morning Six presided over a rather uneventful annual meeting in the ballroom of the Brown Palace Hotel. After a brief luncheon he and the board filed into a small paneled meeting room on the hotel's second floor. The pine shutters were drawn against the noise of passing cars below, and a coffeepot and soft drinks were spread on a table along one wall.

After spending thirty minutes on routine business, Six excused the four candidates, who were all members of the board, and launched into his report. When he finished, Finney began reading the minutes of the Waldorf meeting. As Finney droned on, smoke from Six's cigar curled into the air and the green cloth that covered the board table began to be blanketed by a clutter of papers and empty Fresca bottles. At one point Six got up and walked out the door. "I'm just going to the boys' room, nothing big," he told two of the candidates who were waiting outside with Golightly and a half dozen vice presidents.

Without much discussion, the board voted unanimously to accept the committee's recommendations. Out in the hallway, the executives had formed a pool on how long the board would take to reach a decision. After one hour and thirty-eight minutes, Six ushered the candidates back in and Golightly pocketed $8 in winnings. Cotter pulled back his shoulders and stiffened as he walked into the room; Adams and Bucks were relaxed, but Damm was so tense he steadily avoided looking Six in the eyes. Six opened up with a bit of lightness, saying: "Sit down. I've got bad news. You guys are not going to like it. You're not rid of me yet." Damm could not seem to manage a smile. Then Six told them the board's decision: Damm was to be president, the others were elected executive vice presidents with added responsibilities, and all were named to a new profit-planning committee, which would give them experience in making top-level financial decisions. Damm was so shocked and happy he could hardly find words.

The selection committee is to continue until 1978, when it will formally choose a new chief executive. As Six explained the executives' additional duties, it was obvious that Bucks was well in the lead. He acquired control of scheduling, which Six considers the most important function of an airline executive.

Essential to maintaining a competitive edge, good scheduling requires an ability to sniff out trends and plan capacity well in advance of the market.

But what Six did not tell either the candidates or the board was that the committee already had its eye on Bucks, as that committee member said, "in the context of the next fifteen years." For one thing, at forty-seven, Bucks is by far the youngest candidate. And during the Waldorf meeting, Mahoney, joined at times by Pritzker, had urged that the top job ultimately go to a line officer. Mahoney sprinkled his argument with examples of successful line executives who had been promoted at Norton Simon, and after thirty minutes of discussion, Six was convinced. Cotter, a staff man, was virtually eliminated from contention. Adams, a line officer like Bucks, remains a backup candidate, should Bucks stumble.

Much to Six's relief, Audrey declared at the board meeting that the decision was a good one. And even Cotter seemed content. "We're a team," he told the board. "We're going to make it work together."

SECTION TWO

*Life in the Middle:
Getting In, Getting Up,
and Getting Along*

THE MIDDLE is by far the largest part of any organization. Indeed, it *is* the quintessential organization, for it includes all those between the people at the bottom, whose responsibilities are solely to follow orders and procedures, and the few at the top, who can set overall policy, strategy, and direction without concern for their detailed implementation. It is "the people in the middle" who provide the essential links between these two levels and assure their appropriate relationship. If an organization were a car, the top would be the driver, the bottom would be the engine and the drive train, while the middle would constitute all of the electrical and mechanical connections between them.

The middle is thus composed of a long stretch reaching from those with bare supervisory responsibilities over lowest-level workers to those just below top policy-makers. Broadly speaking, there are two sorts of such people. First are those with responsibility for the work of others, but without the power of top decision-makers—line managers. Their "middleness" lies in being caught between those below, whose cooperation they need, and those above, who give them the authority to implement stated policy. Second are the professionals in organizations, those with authority over their own work, but subject to organizational rules and constraints. Their "middleness" lies in their position between freedom and independence because of their expertise in their job, which only they control, and the terms and conditions of their work, set by the formal authority and structure of the organization. In terms of the automotive analogy, the line managers are the actual links between the driver's action and the car's response—steering wheel, accelerator, brake, and gear shift. The professionals are the instrumentation, maps, lighting, and other paraphernalia serving to advise the driver and assure his safety and direction.

Thus, although the middle is very broad, many characteristics tend to be held in common, and it is exactly these features that create the dilemmas for those in the middle. In a narrower sense, most people in the middle are also on top so far as some other people and tasks are concerned, and on the bottom in terms of others. But the present focus is not on the simpler issues of being boss or bossed, but on the dilemmas that need continuing resolution by the nature of "middleness." It is those that determine, define, and bound "life in the middle." People in the middle are simultaneously big fish in a small pond and small fish in a very large pond, just as Mr. Hoffman, one of the *Wall Street Journal's* "Managers," (Chapter 7) is a "big gun" at an explosive's factory, but has very little say in the decisions of the company of which the plant is a part. The situation is similar for John A. Armbruster (also in Chapter 7), whose contributions are characterized by TRW's president as "very real and very large, but also diffuse and subtle." As a professional, Mr. Armbruster is plainly "the boss" in his area of expertise—forecasting the effect of alternative corporate decisions—but he has no voice in the decisions actually made.

GETTING IN

The three issues of life in the middle of an organization are getting in, getting up, and getting along.

It is particularly the middle where getting in is problematic, for people in middle positions are those eligible for advancement in the organization, while those at the bottom, recruited in more machine-like interchangeable fashion, are expected to do only the routine. Because people at the bottom are rarely eligible for growth, it is less critical that they be selected carefully, and thus, they have an easier time getting in. They need not meet the organization's social tests. They need not be viewed as a potential part of the team. The organization is often not promising them too many privileges or (more-or-less) lifelong tenure. On the other hand, people in the middle are becoming part of the organization's family, perhaps for life, and they are the ones to whom daily responsibility is delegated. People at the top are dealing with larger issues and are not concerned with day-to-day management. Moreover, if people enter at the top—a not infrequent event in many organizations—they tend to have to satisfy a relatively smaller group and to be selected in part *because* they offer something unlike existing people and experience. Thus, their very difference may be a virtue, whereas for middle-managers, difference is anathema.

People who do enter the middle ranks laterally are therefore confronted with extra struggles, for they start as organizational outsiders. This is relatively easily overcome for those who arrive by the "normal" route and are more-or-less like others in the organization. For those outsiders drawn from any group whose members usually don't enter that organization, much greater difficulties arise. The difference can be derived from a variety of dimensions: race, sex, religion, ethnic background, educational background, or even physical appearance. Since they are not expected to be where they are, they may have more difficulty commanding respect in wielding authority, just as Mrs. Lowe's customers (as we see in Chapter 7) take her for a secretary and do not imagine that she is manager of the branch.

Outsiders often have to work harder to demonstrate their loyalty to the mainstream group that runs the organization, as Kanter (1977) has demonstrated. And sponsorship, which is often a necessity for mobility in organizations too large for all the decision makers to have personal knowledge of all the candidates, is often based on identification between the sponsor and the person being sponsored, such that the sponsor tends to choose people resembling himself to recommend for further movement. Again, outsiders are placed at a disadvantage.

This frequently is compounded by the fact that under such circumstances, outsiders, especially when very scarce (as they are likely to be), are forced into roles that place further barriers on their effectiveness. Everett Hughes (1945) for example, described the tendency of blacks to be forced into stereotypical roles (e.g., jokers) when they are isolated in white work groups. Kanter (1977) has extended this framework to women and other outsiders.

In a sense, such people are the victims of multiple middleness. They are not only in the middle in the formal sense within the organization; they are also caught in the middle between two informal social worlds: that of their new organizational peers, and that of the group to which they belong and which is usually not included in that component of the organization. Such organizational outsiders often have to pass special tests or wait a longer time before they are accepted and included in the organization. The saleswomen described in "The Gender Pioneers" (Chapter 8) are forced, over and over again, to respond to situations clearly illuminating their "difference" and confronting them with the continuing need to satisfy the men that their "difference" is safe, limited, and not threatening.

Thus there can be great frustration in middleness. It often comes from the bureaucratic squeeze: having to administer rules one did not make, having to mobilize others for tasks one did not design and may not even support.

GETTING UP

But there is also great promise in middleness. It comes from the hope of moving up the ladder, of attaining even more autonomy and status. Very few of those in the middle *know* that they have a shot at the top, though many sustain themselves by the belief that they do, so that most people in the middle concentrate on accumulating bits of status and privilege, and on enough movement to feel that they are recognized for making a contribution to the organization. In most organizations, however, opportunity has a structure; that is, there are clear patterns and paths for growth and advancement (Kanter, 1977). One's position in the structure of opportunity therefore has a major impact on the way one views oneself and one's job. The case of Wheeler Stanley by Studs Terkel (Chapter 5) is a good illustration. He is literally already sitting in his boss' chair. In a phenomenon that social scientists have called "anticipatory socialization," he has already adopted an orientation toward the world of those above him because he knows he will be moving up. This involves taking what he calls "a management attitude," reading the *Wall Street Journal,* and planning to buy stocks. Like many people, as research demonstrates, his aspirations to rise were a function of the opportunities he received, so that he stopped thinking about becoming a utility man when he was given a crack at a foreman's job, and now that he is considered successful at that job, he is already planning his next moves.

But the hope is only a hope for some people in the middle, for the pyramidal nature of most modern organizations means that as one moves up the ladder, other people are increasingly left behind, and for all those who move, it is likely that many more become stuck. James Rosenbaum (1978) has used the metaphor of a tournament to describe the mobility pattern in large organizations: there are a series of contests which a person must win if he is to move on. Winning an early contest is a prerequisite for moving into the next round, but it is by itself no guarantee that the next round will be won. An organization needs to let many people win in the early rounds in order to supply labor for the large number of positions that constitute the middle ranks, but the top jobs are scarcer, and therefore, fewer people win.

Of course, if the managerial "span of control" (the number of subordinates directly reporting to a manager) was identical, exactly the same proportion of such candidates would win at every level. Though this is often roughly true in organizations, contests at lower levels can be "won" by more people for two reasons. First, there are many lateral or temporary moves within lower and middle management, the net effect of which is to increase the likelihood that junior people can move somewhere (and it is often very difficult to unequivocally characterize a move as "only" lateral). Second, more people leave or retire from middle management than from the top (partly as a direct reflection of the fact that many more people get "stuck" at those levels than advance) and organizations tend to encourage early retirement—or what is euphemistically called "outplacement" of such people.

The contests are different at lower- and upper-middle levels. In the former case, they are impersonal, like racing the clock, and therefore relatively easy to work on or study for. In the latter case, the situation is quite different: one is generally quite aware of one's competition; the case is more like a race among runners. Those who lose the former often keep "studying" for the next chance; those who lose the latter often turn bitter.

In general, people get stuck in one of three ways. First, they may be in a job that has a low ceiling attached to it to begin with; that is, that characteristically involves very few moves on the part of people in it, that has few ladder steps associated with it, and that does not have clear access to other jobs in the organization (Kanter, 1977). Professional positions are often like this. They involve little ladder climbing because people are attached to the content of the work and they are assumed to be content to continue to do it for a rather long time. (Indeed, they often are). Such people often develop a comfortable niche—in a sort of organizational backwater—where they can pursue these narrow interests. Walt Comfort at the Crystal Palace (chapter 6) is such a person. Other people, those more traditionally oriented to line management, find themselves in dead end pockets of an organization and are prevented from further growth because of their job and their position.

The second way people get stuck is that they get into a position that usually carries growth and advancement potential, but because of their own characteristics or their background, or the route they take to that position, they are considered "different," and thus are not seen as candidates for other positions (Kanter 1977). For these people, getting along is often the problem, rather than getting up, for further growth may be closed to them. Hughes (1945) pointed out the plight of some of these people in a classic article on dilemmas and contraditions of status. The one black in a white work group has entered the organization by a route not typically taken by people in the middle ranks, and thus, in addition to the stigma of the "outsider," is added the stigma of a person from a non-traditional background.

The third way people get stuck is that they lose out in the competition for mobility in the organization; they are eliminated in rounds of the tournament. Sometimes this occurs because there simply are not enough top jobs to go around, and at each level, only a few can advance. But other times it happens because the organization is cutting back, or because it promised or appeared to promise more advancement to people than it can handle when the time comes. Many business organizations had this problem in the early 1970s because during the "go-go" years of the 1960s they filled entry-level and lower-middle management jobs with people who expected continued growth because companies were operating in what was widely assumed to be a permanently expanding economy; when the recessions of the late 1960s and early 1970s hit, companies were forced to renege on the implied or explicit promises. Universities in the 1970s similarly became crowded with assistant professors who expected tenure, but promotion freezes and budget cutbacks meant that they would either have to leave or remain stuck at their current level.

People who get stuck in such ways are often quite high up in their organizattion and responsible for day-to-day operations. This situation tends to generate tremendous frustration and anger, and even a desire to retaliate and punish the company for what it has done to them. Thus, three men who are not "making it," described in the last part of "The Managers," (chapter 7) are all suing their former employers for preventing them from further movement up the corporate ladder, in part because all were moving up fairly rapidly at some earlier period.

The notion of the tournament and the stories of three disaffected managers' lawsuits, both raise an important question. How fair are decisions about promotions for those in the middle levels of an organization? Many organizations pride themselves on the fairness and rationality of their systems, with elaborate measurement and data collection devices, such as routine performance appraisals against stated objectives, career development schemes, and lately, extensive assessment centers, results of which resemble the report cards we are used to getting in school. They not only indicate who can pass on to the next grade, but also indicate relative rank and stature within a given class.

But any evaluation *always* includes a large measure of less rational, subjective human decision. And there is ample evidence, (Stein, 1976; Silverman and Jones, 1971) that decisions about who will move in or move up are often made on the basis of social characteristics and personal acceptance rather than any direct measure of competence in the position or the job. There is a tendency for managers to reward and evaluate more highly those who are socially similar to them than those who are different. Indeed, this can be quite rational for higher positions, as Kanter has shown (1977), and as we saw in section one when we looked at the tendency of those at the top to develop closed inner circles. But organizational outsiders, again, are thus handicapped in getting up as well as getting in, as "The Gender Pioneers" (chapter 8) illustrates.

GETTING ALONG

There is, finally, an essential task for all middle managers—getting along. Effectiveness depends critically on one's ability to influence others, and more broadly, to gain access to the resources needed to carry out any task. These resources, whether in the nature of capital, equipment or supplies, information and ideas, or legitimacy, support, and contact, are never fully accessible by formal position or authority alone. If this is true at the top, it is doubly true at the middle. The manager must assure enough exchange and interchange to get the job done, yet avoid crossing two delicate lines: one, competing inappropriately (taking too much credit, refusing to help others, etc.) and two, trying to do it all alone (trying to be a "hero," as it is known in some organizations). People must act as if they were *not* in competition (a stance helped by a "contest against a clock" perception) even though in many ways, of course, they are.

Thus, "getting along" is among the most complex of the challenges to be managed by people in the middle. But this challenge, difficult enough when people are peers, becomes even more difficult for those promoted and suddenly a step above recent peers. Two things help in this connection. One is the rapid shift in attitudes associated with a change of role. Lieberman (1956) demonstrated this in a striking study of workers, some of whom were made union shop stewards, while others—equivalent at the outset—were promoted to foremen. Attitudes shifted markedly toward the union, for those who became stewards, and toward company management, for the new foremen. Moreover, when some of those promoted were subsequently demoted, their attitudes reverted to those held previously. In addition, other people readjust their attitudes toward an individual, depending on his or her role; the one promoted is readily seen as possessing characteristics that make him or her appropriate for the promotion.

The reason underlying all of this is, at least to some extent, simple. It is in everyone's interest to assume and believe that the organization, with its elaborate rational systems, is indeed "fair" and that decisions made are appropriate. This will be thought to be true, whether or not the reasons for a decision are apparent. If not obvious, they will either be assumed, invented, or regarded as a sign of the superior wisdom of those in charge. Organizations require, especially in the middle ranks at issue here, a general agreement that the system is fair. This belief, or myth, is important, and few will question it closely. Kermit Vandivier and his colleagues (chapter 9) are virtually unable to believe that Goodrich is being "dishonest" and violating perceived norms of fair play, even when evidence is overwhelming. And at every level, those involved rationalize the action so as to maintain their belief.

Thus, it may be said that organizational rationality is to a considerable degree in the service of a belief system, rather than in the service of "efficiency." The three managers suing their employers (chapter 7) are doing so only under extreme provocation and with the explicit belief that their treatment is *unfair*. It is in the middle particularly that this belief is important. At the bottom, it is irrelevant since no one feels either powerful or committed; people can even take comfort in the unfairness. At the top, the situation is much more particularistic, and decisions ordinarily *are* fair, because that is one of the chief criteria guiding their formulation. But the middle has a greater need to take things on faith.

JOBS IN THE MIDDLE

Many jobs in the middle are complex and mysterious, and their contribution to the overall effort is often unclear, even to other insiders. Thus, it is difficult for people to have a direct sense of significance in their work; rather, they must identify with the organization and their membership in it and take pride in belonging to an organization known and valued by others. Wheeler Stanley, for example (chapter 5), is personally rewarded when friends like a Ford. The converse is equally true, as we see in "Why Should My Conscience Bother Me?" (chapter 9) Kermit Vandivier and others at Goodrich are deeply shocked by the unethical and illegal behavior of their superiors, as much because of their image of the corporation as anything else. Over and over again, they seek out still more senior executives who will surely not allow these things to happen, and are ever more deeply disappointed each time. The final irony is that the same theme—the literal incredibility that a reputable and well-known corporation would countenance such actions—is used by the company's attorney to deny the charges before a Senate committee.

In a simple sense, there are three sorts of people in the middle—professionals, managers, and foremen or supervisors. By an equally simple standard, the professionals include those with expertise in a recognized body of knowledge, who help make it available to the organization. The managers link the authority at the top to those at the bottom by a direct chain-of-command hierarchy. The foremen and supervisors are the lowest link in that hierarchy, and are often differentiated, as here, because of their very delicate position between two worlds. Most managers' direct relationships tend to be with other managers or professionals; foremen/supervisors have most of their relationships with workers, the people at the bottom. Some companies differentiate between managers of managers, and managers of individual contributors, to make a similar point.

The point is important: a well-known article on the foreman as man-in-the-middle (Gardner and Whyte, 1945) pointed out some of the critical characteristics of such roles. From the present perspective, the special "middleness" of the foreman and supervisor derives from his or her need to represent and identify with "management" in "the organization," on the one hand, and on the other hand to gain the trust and respect of people for whom those images are either negative, meaningless, or laden with very different content. Managers, in general, deal both up and down with people whose identification and orientation is similar—in public if not in private—for their own role requires it. But the foreman or supervisor is in a very different position. Their role in management becomes still more difficult if their own route to that role was "up from the ranks," as used to be routinely the case. Where that is so, as with Wheeler Stanley, the problems of managing a group of former peers is especially complex. Here, unlike the cases described earlier in which someone is promoted out of a group of people *all* seeking and nominally expecting promotions, the former peers are likely to see the promotion as desertion and disloyalty, and to put pressure on the newly-promoted boss. As organizations have been increasingly using first-line supervisors' and foremen's jobs as an entry for management trainees, this latter problem is diluted, at the cost of hardening the barrier between labor (non-exempt) and management (exempt).

In general, however, people in the middle are becoming more universally professional. In large modern organizations, fewer and fewer people directly supervise actual production of the goods or services provided to customers or clients. More and more time, staff, and resources are devoted to the essential but ancillary functions, whose members tend to think of themselves as professionals, even where the label does not formally apply. For example, the salesmen and women in "the Gender Pioneers" (chapter 8) clearly think of themselves as "professionals" and speak of doing a "professional" job. Increasingly, as middle managers develop—and require—expertise to survive and prosper in the organization, they come to think of themselves as professionals, and often as representing a body of knowledge and expertise. And this is so despite the fact that what companies want in top managers is breadth and generalist skills (Stein, 1976). The traditional distinction between professionals and bureaucrats—between those with some allegiance to an essential body of standards and those with allegiance to the organization—is breaking down; recent studies have shown fewer sharp differences in behavior between the two groups (Hall, 1968).

What all people in the middle have in common is the sense of belonging, of being a part of a larger group; again, a sign that the middle *is* the organization, the holder of its traditions, the keeper of its faith. It is striking how many middle people build their life around the organization even without moving further; they generate their own sense of belonging. And organizations often encourage the feeling of being one big family, through benefit plans that take care of the person from birth to death, and through a variety of other events that create a sense of recreation and solidarity.

Thus, people in the middle are encouraged not to think about their relative powerlessness or status compared to the top, for they are made to feel safe and secure and as though they are sharing in the benefits of whatever the large organization is generating. In fact, most large organizations have managed to create a striking sense of "family" by such devices as frequent movement (lateral and vertical) among functions, roles, and geographical regions; emphasis on promotion from within; and a whole panoply of devices to keep people in touch (newsletters, national meetings, clubs for hobbyists, vacation opportunities and plans, etc.). And, of course, the frequent transfers from place to place tend to eliminate most friends but those in the organization. All in all, the loss, or possibility of loss, of a job "in the middle" is extremely threatening. It is a wonder that more people don't fight back, as did the three managers described in chapter 7.

DILEMMAS OF LIFE IN THE MIDDLE

Life in the middle, then, consists in making an accommodation to the diverse pulls and strains of the role. For some, this is relatively easy—merely a matter of settling into a comfortable groove, as with Alan Harrington's co-workers in "The Crystal Palace." (chapter 6) For others, such as the saleswomen in "The Gender Pioneers," (chapter 8) it is a continuing challenge and source of struggle as well as satisfaction. For all, the particular forms of accommodation represent some personal response to situations that constrain and limit the varieties of possible responses. If, as Kanter (1977) has shown, certain features of the organization's structure define and shape people's opportunities and power, their individual responses can still vary somewhat. The readings that follow (and others in the book) illustrate a variety of responses to circumstance. These may be seen in terms of a set of pulls, or tensions, surrounding life in the middle.

For example, Alan Harrington draws a vivid picture in

chapter 6 of what a "bland and creamy" safe environment his organization tries to create for its people in the middle. There is Muzak, the company dining room, and an atmosphere of politeness and decorum, as well as a luxurious set of surroundings. In fact, the routine itself becomes not deadening but soporific, not killing people off (as some jobs at the bottom do) but putting them to sleep. Conflict is smoothed over and avoided in what Harrington calls the "rabbit runs of nicety." The same characteristic is visible in "Why Should My Conscience Bother Me?" (chapter 9) Conflict is avoided and downplayed; routines are the final point of reference. What has been called "management by exception" (attending to the things that do *not* respond to routine) does not exist. Yet this "bland and creamy" life, by putting people to sleep, kills creativity, efficiency, and responsiveness. Harrington himself rebelled; so did Vandivier. And when an organization needs to change, as increasingly all do, no one is able to respond.

A related tension is that between following the rules or play-it-safe and personal autonomy or risk-taking. The middle is seen as relatively secure; a company, like a family, won't throw you out. (Some of this sense of security is misplaced; many middle managers do lose their jobs, though the *proportion* is certainly low.) Organizations, of course, see security and safety as a desirable way to assure loyalty—even pension and profit-sharing plans are often called "golden handcuffs" because their real benefits *require* continued loyalty (e.g., not leaving).

But the price for living in such a safe world (contrast this world with the risky ones—in different ways—at the top and bottom) is to have one's life bound by the rules as well as by the clock. It can even be argued that the rules are more restrictive in the middle than they are at the bottom, for the people at the bottom are treated more like machines, while people in the middle are still expected to be thinking persons who take responsibility for making decisions and acting on them. Thus the rules tend to govern only the work-related conduct of those at the bottom: they are free to think whatever they wish; they are not expected to develop loyalty and commitment to the organization; and no one much cares what they do with the rest of their life. But for those in the middle, the rules reach out to encompass their private lives, their appearance, and their attitudes and feelings. They must more often look the part. They must fit in and get along. But the clock, ironically enough, is just as demanding for Harrington's professional department in the crystal palace as it is for a factory worker.

These choices—safety or risk—are not often terribly clear. Safety slowly decreases as risk increases, and it is generally easy to avoid the hard decision because it is so convenient to stick to the safe path. People often "play it safe" in organizations not because they lack bravery or some other abstract quality but because the choices are rarely sharp. Organizational life admits of few black and white decisions; the middle is comprised of varying shades of gray. The decisions faced by Vandivier at B. F. Goodrich are therefore all the more striking because they expose the dilemma so sharply. Someone in high office—never identified, probably never known—decides to take an unethical path, in fact, to lie publicly and dramatically. Vandivier and his colleagues are expected, as good organization members, to follow the decision and to accept the thin rationalizations offered. They refuse, are placed under increasing pressue, and finally told in nearly this many words: "Go along or find other jobs." In most organizations, most of the time, people in the middle understand that that is the choice. But most organizations, most of the time, make it relatively easy to go along. Allegiance and loyalty are regarded as important, but, like power, they can only be drawn on up to a point. Much of life in the middle can be seen as a delicate interplay between individuals and organizations, maintaining enough loyalty to assure adherence to appropriately modest claims upon it.

Life in the middle also generates hostility and resentment. Older people tend to resent younger people who are on the move, as Wheeler Stanley pointed out in chapter 5, and people who never advance often resent anybody who's moving upwards. People still at the bottom may resent those in their ranks who get a chance to move up and are suddenly in a position superior to them. As noted earlier, people in the middle *especially* need the cooperation of those around them, including their subordinates, in order to do their own work, for they do not have total power; they have only a piece of the action. But the very resentments generated may work against them and make it difficult for them to gain this cooperation. The trick for a person in the middle is to be both firm and fair—to exercise authority but to be seen as justified in doing it.

Perhaps the most critical tension, just as at the top, comes from the problems of powerlessness. For those in the middle who feel most powerless, who feel that they are not in a position to get cooperation or that they do not have the authority they need are those who are most likely to handle the situation badly. Those low in power because their job is routinized, because their talents are considered irrelevant to the organization's design, but who are still held accountable for actions of others, often become rules minded because their control of the rules can represent one of their few areas of personal discretion. They are often measured on the basis of how well the rules made by those above are carried out by those below—a typical performance standard for supervisors. But also the organization's rules constitute the one arena in which they can exchange something for compliance; they can reward their favorites with a lighter application of the rules. But first, the rules must be experienced and honored. They can only be modified after demonstration that they can (and will) be enforced. So people in the middle are often put in, and put themselves in, the position of "watchdog" or "rule enforcer" (Kanter, 1977, 1978).

The greatest tension for individuals in the middle comes from seeing the alternatives—from knowing what they could do if they had fewer rules, more discretion, more control. Thus, the fact that Harrington's associate in chapter 6 could have a file in front of him but be prevented by the rules from passing it on to someone who wanted the information is more frustrating than not having access to the file in the first place. It is also more frustrating to have an answer that isn't used, to operate a plant but not control critical purse strings, as is the case of Mr. Hoffman ("The Managers," chapter 7), or to be responsible for disciplining employees for violating rules one may not fully believe in (a not infrequent organizational test). In one large company, during a discussion with production supervisors and managers about power-as-capacity-to-act, both groups knew what was meant immediately. "Sure I feel powerless," said one supervisor, "When there's a million dollars worth of inventory behind me on the line, and I can't get an essential part, and I can't get anyone to listen to me, and the rules say, go through channels, then I'm frustrated. I know what needs to be done to turn out a good product on time, and they won't let me do it."

Over time, for the middle, powerlessness coupled with accountability, with responsiblity for results dependent on the actions of others, provokes a cautious, low-risk, play-it-safe attitude. Those in the middle are often unwilling to jeopardize the privilege they have attained by rocking the boat. Getting everything right, and demanding that subordinates do the same, is the response of those who lack other ways to impress those above them or to secure their position; and in turn, they demand this kind of ritualistic conformity from subordinates, like a school teacher more concerned about the neatness of the paper than its ideas. Furthermore, such people often become controlling, coercive, and demanding in their relationships with those they supervise, and often supervise them too closely (Kanter, 1977). A Wheeler Stanley, who is on the way up, can afford to be generous with his subordinates, can afford to give them opportunities for growth and discipline them only when necessary. But for those who are stuck and feel relatively powerless, there is no such luxury.

Thus, styles of handling responsiblity that are often seen as pathologies of bureaucracy or of individuals can be attributed to the problems of middleness. Robert Merton (1961) has argued that bureaucrats adopt a domineering manner because whenever they use the authority of their office with clients or subordinates, they are acting as representatives of the power and prestige of the entire structure. Vicarious power, Merton seemed to say, power through identification with the strength of the organization, breeds bossiness. However, if we look more closely at the organizational structures he described, we can see that this aspect of the "bureaucratic personality" reflects a response to *powerlessness* rather than to power delegated or otherwise. The organization's concern with regulations reduces administrators' spheres of autonomy and limits their influence and decision-making power. The very provision of graded careers stressing seniority, in which incremental advances are relatively small and all must wait their turn, fosters dependency on the organization, which always holds back some rewards until the next advance. Strikingly, the chief organizational reward that is infinitely adjustable (*and* in principle, nearly as expandable) is also taboo and private—thus *invisible*. We refer, of course, to money.

Finally, in response to organizational insignificance, people in the middle often turn to their own small territory, their own piece of the system—their subordinates, their function, their expertise. They guard their domain jealously. They narrow their interests to focus exclusively on it. They try to insulate and protect it and to prevent anyone else from engaging in similar activities without their approval as "the experts" in that domain (Kanter, 1977). This syndrome has traditionally been found most often among professionals in organizations, and their conflicts with bureaucratic managers are well-known. But such behavior, such guarding of a narrow domain, only increases the sense of helplessness of people in the middle as they try to influence the organization. And as people develop expertise and territories more broadly, the same patterns can be seen in people-in-the-middle more generally.

THE SELECTIONS

Life in the middle, in short, is comfortable but not always easy. Its virtues and rewards are often bought at a high price, both for the people themselves and for organizations. The readings that follow illuminate different aspects of the middle, its dilemmas and its characteristics.

"Wheeler Stanley, Foreman" from Studs Terkel's celebrated book, *Working*, introduces one of the main themes of life in the middle, upward mobility. Here, Wheeler Stanley, starting his way up the hierarchy at the Ford Motor Co., talks about his job and its prospects. Stanley is most unusual; as we note in the introduction to "Life at the Bottom." Very few auto workers get promoted to foreman, perhaps one out of every several hundred. But his story illustrates some of the rewards and hopes held out to middle people.

"A Day at the Crystal Palace" is taken from Alan Harrington's account (disguised only as to names) of his experience as a professional writer at the headquarters of one of America's largest corporations, somewhere in Westchester County, just outside of New York City. Harrington wrote at a time (the late 1950s) when relatively few corporations chose to locate in the parklike splendor of the affluent suburbs. Since then, the Crystal Palace has been joined by dozens of others, all remarkably alike.

"The Managers" briefly describes six quite different people in six unique middle management positions. As the *Wall Street Journal* said in a prefatory note to the series from which these portraits were taken: "At the heart of American industry is the middle manager, the executive below the rank of vice president who carries out top management's instructions. Yet despite his vital function, he is a barely visible part of the industrial machine." The six managers include three who were fired and are suing their companies. One unusual case is that of a black woman manager; her experiences are also echoed in the next selection, dealing with those who are "different" from their peers.

Next, "The Gender Pioneers," comes from a report originally prepared for a major American corporation seeking to better understand some of the reports, comments, gossip, and problems arising from their decision to open the sales force to women. The data were derived from extensive interviews, group discussions, and meetings with the new women, their male peers, and a variety of managers. The report considers the problems the women faced as "outsiders" getting into the middle and trying to get along.

This section concludes with a most unusual selection, "Why Should My Conscience Bother Me?" by Kermit Vandivier. Vandivier was a young engineer at a division of the B. F. Goodrich Co., who became involved in a wholly illegal and unethical attempt by the company to fabricate information about a new product; information that was not only dead wrong, but put at risk an uncertain number of lives since the product in question was the brake for a new aircraft. Vandivier ultimately was unable to keep silent, and was fortunately prevailed on to write his own story. Blowing the whistle is dangerous; Vandivier is now a newspaper reporter. But his story clearly illustrates one dramatic pressure on people in the middle, which, under extreme circumstances, can turn into the story of the bureaucratic Eichmann who does great evil but sees it as "just doing my job."

5 / Wheeler Stanley, General Foreman

Studs Terkel

"I'M PROBABLY the youngest general foreman in the plant, yes, sir." He was invited to sit in the chair of the plant manager as Tom Brand went about his work. "I'm in the chassis line right now. There's 372 people working for us, hourly. And thirteen foremen. I'm the lead general foreman."

He grew up in this area, "not more than five minutes away. I watched the Ford plant grow from when I was a little boy." His father is a railroad man and he is the only son among four children. He is married and has two small children.

He has just turned thirty. He appears always to be "at attention." It is not accidental. "I always had one ambition. I wanted to go in the army and be a paratrooper. So I became a paratrooper. When I got out of the army, where I majored in communications, I applied at Illinois Bell. But nobody was hiring. So I came out here as an hourly man. Ten years ago. I was twenty."

I was a cushion builder. We made all the seats and trim. I could comprehend it real easy. I moved around considerably. I was a spot-welder. I went from cushion to trim to body shop, paint. I could look at a job and I could do it. My mind would just click. I could stand back, look at a job, and five minutes later I can go and do it. I enjoyed the work. I felt it was a man's job. You can do something with your hands. You can go home at night and feel you have accomplished something.

Did you find the assembly line boring?

No, uh-uh. Far from boring. There was a couple of us that we were hired together. We'd come up with different games—like

From *Working: People Talk About What They Do All Day and How They Feel About What They Do*, by Studs Terkel. Copyright © 1973, 1974 by Studs Terkel. Reprinted by permission of Pantheon Books, a Division of Random House, Inc. Pp. 181–87.

we'd take the number of the jeeps that went by. That guy loses, he buys coffee. I very rarely had any problems with the other guys. We had a lot of respect for each other. If you're a dead-head when you're an hourly man and you go on supervision, they don't have much use for you. But if they know the guy's aggressive and he tries to do a job, they tend to respect him.

I'm the kind of guy, if I was due for a raise I'm not gonna ask for it. If they don't feel I'm entitled to it, they're not gonna give it to me. If they think I'm entitled to it, they'll give it to me. If I don't deserve it, I'm not gonna get it. I don't question my boss, I don't question the company.

When I came here I wanted to be a utility man. He goes around and spot relieves everybody. I thought that was the greatest thing in the world. When the production manager asked me would I consider training for a foreman's job, boy! my sights left utility. I worked on all the assembly lines. I spent eighteen months on the lines, made foreman, and eighteen months later I made general foreman—March of '66.

A lot of the old-timers had more time in the plant than I had time in the world. Some of 'em had thirty, thirty-five years' service. I had to overcome their resentment and get their respect. I was taught one thing: to be firm but fair. Each man has got an assignment of work to do. If he has a problem, correct his problem. If he doesn't have a problem, correct him.

If an hourly man continued to let the work go, you have to take disciplinary action. You go progressively, depending on the situation. If it was me being a young guy and he resented it, I would overlook it and try to get him to think my way. If I couldn't, I had to go to the disciplinary route—which would be a reprimand, a warning.

If they respect you, they'll do anything for you. If they don't, they won't do nothin' for you. Be aggressive. You have to know each and every man and know how they react. I have to know each and every one of my foremen. I know how they react, all thirteen.

There's a few on the line you can associate with. I haven't as yet. When you get familiarity it causes—the more you get to know somebody, it's hard to distinguish between boss and friend. This isn't good for my profession. But I don't think we ever change much. Like I like to say, "We put our pants on the same way." We work together, we live together. But they always gotta realize you're the boss.

I want to get quality first, then everything else'll come. The line runs good, the production's good, you get your cost and you get your good workmanship. When they hire in, you gotta show 'em you're firm. We've got company rules. We've got about seventeen different rules here at Chicago Ford Assembly that we try to enforce from the beginning.

The case begins with a reprimand, a warning procedure. A lotta times they don't realize this is the first step to termination. If they've got thirty years' service, twenty years' service, they never realize it. There's always a first step to termination. If you catch a guy stealing, the first step *is* a termination. In the case of workmanship, it's a progressive period. A reprimand, docked time—three days, a week. Then a termination.

You mean discharge?

Discharge. This isn't always the end. You always try to correct it. It's not directly our responsibility to discharge. It's a labor relations responsibility. We initiate the discipline and support the case for a discharge.

Guys talk about the Green House . . .

I never call it a Green House. This is childish. It never seemed right to me: "I'll take you to the Green House." You wanted to tell a guy in a man's way, "If you don't do better, I'll take you to the office." Or "We'll go to labor relations to solve this thing." It sounds a lot more management. Not this: "I'm gonna take you to the Green House."

When you worked on the line, were you ever taken to the . . . office?

No. I didn't take no time off and I always did my job well, wore my glasses and everything. I don't think I've missed three days in the last five years. My wife likes to nag me, because if she gets sick I pick up my mother-in-law and bring her over. "You stay with my wife, she's not that bad. I'm going to work."

Dad never missed work. He worked hard. He used to work a lot of overtime. He'd work sixteen hours. They'd say, "He gets his wind on the second shift." He started off as a switchman. Now he's general yard master. He's been a company man all his life. I always admired him for it.

Do you feel your army training helped you?

Considerably. I learned respect. A lotta times you like to shoot your mouth off. You really don't know how to control your pride. Pride is a good attribute, but if you got too much of it . . . when it interferes with your good judgment and you don't know how to control it . . . In the army, you learn to shut up and do your job and eat a little crow now and then. It helps.

There's an old saying: The boss ain't always right but he's still the boss. He has things applied to him from top management, where they see the whole picture. A lot of times I don't agree with it. There's an instance now. We've been having problems with water leaks. It doesn't affect the chassis department, but it's so close we have to come up with the immediate fix. We have to suffer the penalty of two additional people. It reflects on your costs, which is one of my jobs. When the boss says pay 'em, we pay 'em. But I don't believe our department should be penalized because of a problem created in another department. There's a lot of pride between these departments. There's competition between the day shift and the night shift. Good, wholesome competition never hurt.

Prior to going on supervision, you think hourly. But when you become management, you have to look out for the company's best interests. You always have to present a management attitude. I view a management attitude as, number one, a neat-appearing-type foreman. You don't want to come in sloppy, dirty. You want to come in looking like a foreman. You always conduct yourself in a man's way.

I couldn't be a salesman. A salesman would be below me. I don't like to go and bother people or try to sell something to somebody that they don't really want, talk them into it. Not me. I like to come to work and do my job. Out here, it's a big job. There's a lot of responsibility. It's not like working in a soup factory, where all you do is make soup cans. If you get a can punched wrong, you put it on the side and don't worry about it. You can't do that with a five-thousand-dollar-car.

There's no difference between young and old workers. There's an old guy out here, he's a colored fella, he's on nights. He must be fifty-five years old, but he's been here only five years. He amazes me. He tells me, "I'll be here if I have to walk to work." Some young guys tell you the same thing. I don't feel age has any bearing on it. Colored or white, old or young, it's the caliber of the man himself.

In the old days, when they fought for the union, they might have needed the union then. But now the company is just as good to them as the union is. We had a baseball meeting a couple of nights ago and the guy's couldn't get over the way the company supported a banquet for them and the trophies and the jackets. And the way Tom Brand participated in the banquet himself.

A few years ago, it was hourly versus management—there was two sides of the world. Now it's more molded into one. It's not hourly and management; it's the company. Everybody is involved in the company. We've achieved many good things, as baseball tournaments, basketball leagues. We've had golf outings. Last year we started a softball league. The team they most wanted to beat was supervision—our team. It brought everybody so much closer together. It's one big family now. When we first started, this is '65, '66, it was the company against the union. It's not that way any more.

What's the next step for you?

Superintendent. I've been looking forward to it. I'd be department head of chassis. It's the largest department in the plant.

And after that?

Pre-delivery manager. And then production manager and then operation manager is the way it goes—chain of command. Last year our operation man went to Europe for four months. While he was gone I took the job as a training period.

And eventually?

Who knows? Superintendent, first. That's my next step. I've got a great feeling for Ford because it's been good to me. As far as I'm concerned, you couldn't ask for a better company. It's got great insurance benefits and everything else. I don't think it cost me two dollars to have my two children. My son, he's only six years old and I've taken him through the plant. I took him through one night and the electricians were working the body hoists. He pushed the button and he ran the hoist around and he couldn't get over that. He can now work a screw driver motor. I showed him that. He just enjoyed it. And that's all he talks about: "I'm going to work for Ford, too." And I say, "Oh, no you ain't." And my wife will shut me up and she'll say, "Why not?" Then I think to myself, "Why not? It's been good to me."

I like to see people on the street and when they say, "I got a new Ford," I ask how it is. You stop at a tavern, have a drink, or you're out for an evening, and they say, "I've got a new Ford," you like to be inquisitive. I like to find out if they like the product. It's a great feeling when you find someone says, "I like it, it rides good. It's quiet. Everything you said it would be."

Have you heard of Lordstown, where the Vega plant is?

I like to read the *Wall Street Journal*. I'd like to invest some in Wall Street. I'd like to learn more about the stock market. Financially, I can't do it yet—two small children . . . I read the entire Lordstown article they had in there. I think the union was unjustified. And I think management could have done a better job. A hundred cars an hour is quite excessive. But again, you're building a small car and it's easier to set a line up. But I understand there was some sabotage.

I think the president of the union is only twenty-nine years old. I imagine he's a real hardheaded type of individual. He's headstrong and he wants his way. If I was working with him, we'd probably be bumpin' heads quite a bit. I've been known to be hardheaded and hard-nosed and real stubborn if I have to be.

"I won a scholarship at Mendel High School, but I couldn't afford the books. At the time, my family was pretty hard up. So I went to Vocational High and it was the biggest mistake I ever made. I was used to a Catholic grammar school. I needed Catholic schooling to keep me in line 'cause I was a pretty hot-tempered type."

I'm the type of guy, sometimes you gotta chew me out to let me know you're still around. If you didn't, I might forget and relax. I don't like to relax. I can't afford it. I like to stay on my toes. I don't want to get stagnant, because if I do, I'm not doing anybody any good.

(He studies his watch. It has all the appurtenances: second, minute, hour, day, month, year . . .)

I refer to my watch all the time. I check different items. About every hour I tour my line. About six thirty, I'll tour labor relations to find out who is absent. At seven, I hit the end of the

line. I'll check paint, check my scratches and damage. Around
ten I'll start talking to all the foremen. I make sure they're all
awake, they're in the area of their responsibility. So we can
shut down the end of the line at two o'clock and everything's
clean. Friday night everybody'll get paid and they'll want to
get out of here as quickly as they can. I gotta keep 'em on the
line. I can't afford lettin' 'em get out early.

We can't have no holes, no nothing.

If a guy was hurt to the point where it would interfere with
production, then it stops. We had a fella some years ago, he was
trapped with body. The only way we could get him off was to
shut the line off. Reverse the belt, in order to get his fingers out.
We're gonna shut the line to see that he don't get hurt any
more. A slight laceration or something like that, that's an ev-
eryday occurrence. You have to handle 'em.

What's your feeling walking the floor?

Like when I take the superintendent's job, if he's going on
vacation for a week. They drive what they call an M-10 unit.
Their license plate is always a numeral 2, with a letter afterwards: like 2-A, 2-D—which reflects the manager's car.
When he's on vacation and I take his job, all his privileges become mine for a week. You're thirty years old and you're gonna
be a manager at forty. I couldn't ask for nothing better. When I
take the car home for a week, I'm proud of that license plate. It
says "Manufacturer" on it, and they know I work for Ford. It's a
good feeling.

*Tom Brand has returned. Wheeler Stanley rises from the chair in
soldier-like fashion. Brand is jovial. "In traveling around plants,
we're fortunate if we have two or three like him, that are real
comers. It isn't gonna be too long that these fellas are gonna take
our jobs. Always be kind to your sweeper, you never know when
you're going to be working for him." (Laughs.) Wheeler Stanley
smiles.*

6 / A Day at the Crystal Palace

Alan Harrington

9:00 A.M. The bus-commuters from the railroad station have arrived. Everybody holds the glass doors open for everybody else. We scatter through the great lobby and go down our various beige corridors to the interior and wings of the building. There are two bus-travelers in our department, George Browne and I. The others, like all but fifty or so of the employees at the palace, arrive in their own cars or in car pools.

Our good-mornings are jocular, and if somebody is late we laugh at him. There is a period of settling down. Austin Johnson, the tube-station attendant, grins at us as he arranges his projectiles to start the day. Soon they will be flying through the tube system to all corners of the building carrying pieces of paper, and torpedoes from other offices will arrive at our station with a thump, and a red light will flash on.

The girls are making up and chattering, and it is nice to look at them. Music by Muzak has started up and will give us its soft melodies for the next quarter-hour. Then it will go off for fifteen minutes, and on again, and continue in the fashion until we go home. Thus it is possible to space one's day by quarter-hours. It is said that this music increases office productivity by a sizable percentage, but I haven't noticed that it helps. Probably it quickens the output of those in more or less automatic jobs such as typing and adding-machine work, but I find that if I listen to it at all it puts me in a revery. It makes me feel as if I were in a cocktail lounge.

The girls are slow in getting down to work this Monday morning. I wonder why. It can't be that they are talking about skiing because that season passed several weeks ago. Then it must be golf, bowling, or some dance. They are all pretty and

From *Life in the Crystal Palace*, by Alan Harrington. Copyright © 1958, 1959 by Alan Harrington. Reprinted by permission of Alfred A. Knopf, Inc. Pp. 125–35, 137–43.

athletic, and have not been with the company long enough to take on the cheerfully resigned look. They have fun and remain irreverent, but must watch out lest they grow too contented with this harmless daily round.

I look out my picture window to watch the late-arriving car pools whirling up the long driveway. The stylish sedans and convertibles hold before my eyes like a snapshot of toy models, cleverly suggesting motion, placed outside the architect's model of our palace to give the "feel" of country office life. The cars will race around the building and find places in the chrome arc of prosperity that half-encircles our office. All our workers have cars, as everyone knows. And our employees also have a view unequaled by any offered to a group of employees since time began. Rolling hills go on to the horizon; they will burst into flower next week, and when autumn comes they will flare red and gold, and winter will put snow on them like frosting. Our landscaped grounds, too, will flower. We can smell honeysuckle; our lawns are so green that they hurt your eyes. Meadows extend to the hills and beyond like a perpetually green future.

It really is time for those girls to quiet down. Walt Comfort who is supposed to be the department's office manager clucks at them but dares not give an order. He will say something like: "Well, I didn't know we were having a three-day holiday." This has no effect. The only way to handle them is to shout: "Hey, quiet down!" in a friendly manner. Walt, a diffident and nice fellow, seldom exercises his full authority. In justice to him I should point out that discipline at the Palace is very lax indeed. People get away with all kinds of laziness and time-wasting without being reproved for it, let alone threatened. For some reason a great many of our executives have no courage when it comes to controlling the loud voices of office boys and inter-departmental loungers.

The chatter is suddenly broken off, and I hear a familiar squeak of shoes. (All our shoes squeak distinctively on the tile floors.) The head of our department, Mac Tyler, is coming down the hall. He stumps past with a gruff good-morning to every-one. The day begins in the public relations office.

I go to my typewriter. In the next office George Browne's machine is already going at top speed. The sound depresses me. George arrived at the Crystal Palace a year ago when he was pushing fifty. He began as a consultant, and has just received permanent status. He found safety here. I like this lively, youthful Teddy Bear of a man whose journalistic career took him all over the world. But then he felt the pressure of time and knocked on the door of the Palace, and now he is sub-editor of our harmless house organ. George says he will leave soon. I hope so. He who has covered invasions and surrenders must work under the aforementioned Walt Comfort who covered lodge meetings for a small-town paper. I must learn to mind my own business, and stop thinking of Justice.

As I start to work, the phone rings. The caller gives me a corrected production figure and I thank him. I will manage to work this into our public-health story. Music by Muzak has gone off and come on again. But it will be some time yet before the coffee cart reaches our area.

Meanwhile I have been unfair to Walt Comfort. He is a good and kind man who has managed small gifts with great skill. His talent is being nice. He is completely a company person, knows the rule book backwards and follows it absolutely. Any violation of the rules pains him, as though he *were* the company. He is, too, in a way. If corporations had an unknown soldier, Walt would be the one laid to rest under our cornerstone. He is unfailingly courteous and never mean to people unless they break a rule, and then only in a mild fashion. If he appropriates credit from his subordinates now and then, the thefts are minor. This petty larceny of credit is done merely to preserve his executive franchise; there is no greed involved. If everyone were like Walt Comfort the world would be a happier place, although there might not be too much going on. I think I have been unfair to him because our department head, Mac Tyler, whom Walt calls "the boss," has recently decreed that I must, among my other duties, help write his house organ. This is a terrible bore.

I am writing a story about the Elbridge family which has been represented in the company for ninety-eight years. Grandfather, father, and son have all been employed by us.

Looking out of the window I glimpse a small event that always makes me feel comfortable. The company limousine approaches the Crystal Palace, carrying the president to work. The black Cadillac rolls slowly to our front door. I can see the president's hand gripping the strap as they turn the corner. The black-liveried chauffeur leaps out and holds the door open. The president alights, followed by the chairman of the board. The president is a serene gentleman with white hair. The chairman has an alert but somber countenance. He makes me think of Scrooge. They stand for a moment surveying the palace façade with complete satisfaction. The president embraces the landscape with one arm, indicating the signs of spring. But the chairman has his eye on something else. He points to the roof. They examine some defect up there with great concern—a leaky gutter. A phone call will be made and action taken, I should imagine, within ninety seconds.

"If Rex Elbridge goes on to normal retirement—twenty-four years hence—the family will have served a total of 122 years. . . ."

This is a bad morning because the coffee cart will not arrive in our part of the building until ten-thirty. We have a half-hour to wait.

10:00 A.M. Coffee! Coffee! Where is that wagon? We all share this preoccupation. When our days extend in an almost unvarying routine I think that many of us develop a minor time-neurosis. We grow accustomed to our routine being partitioned or punctuated in a certain manner. If for some reason the coffee cart does not appear at a certain time, or lunch is delayed, or the Muzak is turned off, or the bus is late, we are disturbed. When routine is violated one's stomach joins in the protest. I find now that I have a perfect craving for coffee commencing at 9:30 A.M. I doesn't matter how many cups I may have had for breakfast; I must still have coffee at that time or I am slightly miserable. The same with lunch. If I cannot go down to the dining room at 12:00 noon I feel a bit dizzy.

Most of us at the Crystal Palace have the same craving for time to stop exactly when it is supposed to. The route of the coffee wagon changes every week, giving departments in different sections of the palace alternate "early" and "late" coffee breaks. This being our late week, I am irritable. Contributing to my mood are the dull chores I must perform in the service of the house organ.

Call this monthly newspaper the *Palace Voice*, since it is the voice of management. Nearly every big company has a paper of some kind, and it is certainly reasonable that such publications should exist. But why must they be so dull? The answer to that is easy: because they mustn't contain the smallest hint of con-

troversy or present any idea that is not pleasing and soothing—
"all the news that's print to fit." Every story in the *Voice* has to
be checked by higher authority to make sure that it is free of
roughage. In the end, therefore, the house organ is like the food
in the dining hall—smooth, bland, and creamy. . . .

Coffee! Now I feel better, and a good story has come in. One
of our people was in an airplane crash and survived without a
blemish. I will interview him in the afternoon. Having joshed
with my friends during the coffee break, I return to the *Voice* in
a positive frame of mind.

Eleven A.M. Just one more complaint about house-organ editors. After a while they develop corporate reflexes. So does everyone else at the Palace, of course, but it is a shame to see it
happen to newspapermen. In his *Inside Russia Today* (Harper &
Brothers, 1957) John Gunther tells us that Soviet journalists
never deviate from the party line because it is also their own
line. He points out that:

"The slant comes from within; the censorship is altogether self-imposed." . . .

Remarkably enough then, the editor of *Pravda* appears to be
freer than Walt Comfort and the other editors of the *Palace
Voice*. We toe the line too. Even so, we must clear everything
with department heads, and if the story is important, with a
director. If the editor of *Pravda* can be trusted, why can't we? I
can assure you that house-organ editors develop "spontaneous,
automatic and complete" acceptance of company policy. We
become excellent self-censors. If only given a chance, we could
censor ourselves as well as or better than any *Pravda* editor.
Well . . . occasionally we slip up, but not often.

For example, one story submitted to a director said that the
Voice complimented management on a certain move. This was
stricken out on the grounds that it implied that the paper had
the power *not* to compliment management. Sometimes an inexperienced contributor makes silly attempts to liven things up.
Once, writing an account of the annual jamboree I said that a
number of annuitants (pensioners) had come around to join in
the fun. Among them were John Smith, Bill Jones, Tom
Robinson, Old GrandDad, and Old Forester. A feeble joke
surely, but our situation breeds juvenile humor. Every author-

ity who saw that line cut it out. Actually, the more I look at the witticism I don't blame them too much. It was their unanimity that was depressing. Another time I wrote that a new span connecting the Palace grounds with the highway would be "our bridge to the outside world." Bam! Again all the blue pencils came down.

I think again without much conviction: "I've got to get out of here!" These rabbit runs of nicety are driving me crazy. I find myself like a schoolboy longing to commit a nuisance. My position is dignified (I ghostwrite speeches for the president to make before great national associations), and I am no longer a kid, but I have to put down impulses to clown and make a fool of myself. This, of course, is immature and, worse, ineffectual. It puts me in a class with that idiot who dropped an open bottle full of ketchup in the tube system, and the other, whoever he may be, who introduced a loose roll of scotch tape into the same wind tunnel.

Everyone asks sooner or later: "Who am I?" I sit at my typewriter and all at once realize that I'm playing the part of a sheer and uninteresting fool, an intellectual playboy. It is a moment of revelation that comes out of nowhere and passes. Nothing appears to change, not even one's expression. Music by Muzak is playing: "We Could Make Believe." But from this hour I know that I will be able to leave the Palace when I want to. Faces are gathered at my door, and my colleagues are grinning at me, which means that it is time for lunch.

Twelve noon. We eat in a gaily decorated dining room on the Terrace (lower ground) Floor, looking out on the side lawn. At one end of the room see our brick-walled Japanese moon gate; at the other, counters for those who wish to eat in a hurry. Most of us go to the assemblage of yellow and gray tables, sit down on bright red or blue chairs, and have a leisurely meal served by waitresses who expect no tips. (Tipping handled by the management.) We look at the menus and fill out our slips, and, still bathed by Muzak, relax.

When we first moved to the Palace a general memorandum (abetted by the *Voice*) encouraged headquarters personnel to mingle in the dining hall and get to know each other. The idea was that you should not necessarily eat with members of your own department, but sit with people doing other kinds of work. This suggestion has largely been ignored. We eat with about the same companions day after day. The result is to pile incestuousness on incestuousness, and our lunch conversations are for the most part, again, as bland and creamy as our food. I do not mean to say that *we* are duller than anybody else, but try lunching with the same group day after day. Conversation becomes a sort of filler, a means of avoiding silence.

Today we are involved in a familiar subject—traffic. . . .

The amount of time we can spend discussing traffic is fantastic. I think it is because the highway is almost the last place of adventure a suburbanite has left. They are able to talk about their journeys to and from work in the manner of knights, for the dangers are authentic, uncertainties always present, and individual skill is demanded of all.

Also like knights we talk about our chargers. "How is your old Buick holding up?" Dwight King is asked. Very well, in fact he wouldn't swap it for many of this year's new models. All, all honorable men! Next we go into driveways and lawns and mowing machines and clipping hedges. I am crushed with boredom, for a good reason. Living in the city as I do I don't own any property. Therefore, I can't contribute anything to conversations that deal with virtually nothing else but property of one kind or another. Of course, one is not supposed to discuss Socrates at lunch, but there must be something else. I bring up some plays and movies I have seen—but then my listeners are in the same fix. They practically never go to the movies. It comes down to this: most of the people at our table are good enough to talk with individually, but together at lunch we make the dullest lot you would ever want to avoid.

I notice that dozens of employees at neighboring tables are reading the same pamphlet. It is one of those handouts that are displayed in corporation reading racks. Craning my neck, I see that it is titled: "Are You a Knocker or a Booster?" After lunch I will read it myself.

I forgot to mention that in the beginning it was announced that the gentlemen of the board of directors would eat in the main dining room along with everybody else, although they would have a separate table. On important occasions, such as the need to entertain distinguished guests, they would repair to the Executive Dining Room. This arrangement lasted some thirty days. Now you dan't find a director in our eating place. I can understand why, after enjoying one meal in the Executive Dining Room where our department was allowed to entertain newsmen. We had shrimp cocktails and hunks of dripping-rare roast beef compared with the flat chicken à la king featured that day on the menu for lower employees. Rank has its privileges, to be sure, and the first place you can count on over-democracy breaking down is in the food department.

One P.M. In the quiet lounge, surrounded by employees playing cards, checkers, and chess, I will take a long lunch hour and read: "Are You a Knocker or a Booster?" At the far end of this room, shut off by curtains, is the TV annex. Behind me extends the company lending library filled with the latest good books, which I should be reading instead of this pamphlet.

But I am reading in order to make myself angry, and succeeding. As I suspected, "Are You a Knocker or a Booster?" is awful. I don't object so much to the booklet as I do to its distribution. There are a number of outfits that make money by keeping corporations in all parts of the country supplied with this pap. Whoever puts out the tracts must think that the American people are absolute morons. They are so written-down and over-simplified. There would be no reason to mention these booklets except that they are on display in hundreds of racks in corporate halls, and presumably should exert some influence on somebody. Yet it may be possible that they don't. Conceivably not one person has ever been influenced by the messages they carry, and management is being fooled by the pamphlet companies into thinking that their employees find them of more than passing interest. . . .

The pamphlets put out by this service also assume at all times that criticism of higher authority is unjustified and neurotic, and even unpatriotic. Thus: "The negative attitude—'it can't be done' or 'the boss is a square'—can be one of the biggest roadblocks to your progress. Worse still, it is contagious and can easily blight your home, your plant and even your community." The crude juxtaposition of these two negative attitudes is typical of the pamphlet's dishonesty. Most knockers complain about the boss either because he seems to them unfair or inefficient. Sometimes "it can't be done" precisely because the boss is a blockhead.

I have taken the test and done much better than I had hoped. The verdict: "You are not a KNOCKER but you veer in that direction. Correct the faults and carefully monitor your tongue. Make a recheck for progress in 30 days."

This has been a long lunch hour. I detect in myself a goldbricking attitude which I intend to monitor. The reason for goofing off in the army is that the soldier wants to avoid boring or meaningless tasks. This is also true in civilian and corporate life. I never goofed off until I was assigned to the house organ. I am in a dilemma. If I do a good job on the *Voice* I will be stuck with it. Somehow, with this attitude, I have wasted two hours at midday. It is now—

Two P.M. A strange and yet ordinary thing has happened. It tells so much about the Crystal Palace. To understand it you have to know something about the character of Phil Jester. I have spoken of many decent men at the Palace. Phil is more than that. This is a man of natural goodness. He does all the right things, not because he has been indoctrinated but because, it almost seems, he was born with a warm heart. We talk about someone's "disposition." Phil is disposed to kindness; he has become a fount of kindness. I have never met anyone with greater moral purity who manages nevertheless a high sense of humor. He is utterly responsive, too, to sadness and tragedy. A former Palace employee died in an oxygen tent without friends or relatives, not a good man, in some ways a bastard, and Phil was the one he called to sit with him through his last day.

With all this going for him, Phil remains a perfect corporation man. Big, heavy, genial, two hundred and twenty pounds, PTA executive, scout leader, officer in the reserves, he is a good father of two, fine husband, excellent drinking companion, splendid one-man audience for you and me, but also, a man who has, finally, not been able to specialize in anything. Instead he has been appointed Mac Tyler's odd-jobs executive in our department. He serves as an occasional shock-absorber (nothing serious) for the boss' bouts of crankiness. Tyler, who standing beside him is as a hydrant next to a tower, looks askance at big fellows and treats Phil with exasperation. But for better or for worse Phil's good heart seems to have neutralized his ego.

Last week he was visited in the office by a charming woman on an urgent research errand. She was working for a well-known writer who was preparing a book with an industrial background. Our files could supply important answers for her. But Mac Tyler, in a churlish mood that day, had instructed Phil not to give her any of this file material. There was no good reason for his admonition. Nothing she might discover would affect our company adversely. And it happened that Phil had found some of the information she was after.

Today, early this afternoon, it lay on his desk while she talked to him. Plainly her need for the material was urgent. She was warm and attractive, appealing in a mature way, a woman who had been all around the world and known famous people, but who was now up against an assignment that was proving too difficult. With all his manliness he longed to help her. But Mac Tyler had decreed otherwise. He wanted to rise above Tyler's edict, above the system, and respond as a man does to a woman in trouble. He could have killed a dragon for her, he could have (awed witnesses have testified) risen out of his mildness and cleaned up a barroom full of louts, he could have shielded her body with his in any moment of danger, but he *could not* lift his hand and push the file across the desk to her . . . because it was against the rules. He had to watch her go away and accept her thanks for being so good and helpful.

Phil has just come in to me and asked whether he has done the right thing. What can I say? Of course, for him it was the right thing. I want to say to him that I know he has courage. Even so, strong and honorable though he is, only a man with the corporation habit could respond according to the rule book in a situation that cried out for rules to be broken.

Three P.M. Once more the coffee wagon, the matched coins to see who buys, and a meeting called by Mac Tyler. This will be a conference on a company film to celebrate our organization. An outside script writer has been hired to prepare a scenario. I put off my interview with our air-crash survivor, and four of us troop into Mac Tyler's office. The writer waits there nervously. He is a pro with a reputation for turning out solid commercial dialogue, but in hiring him we overlooked one thing. Sick of the movies, he has retreated to the Florida Keys where he has half-built a house. He has returned to do our job only to make enough money in order to complete his project. Hence, his heart is somewhere else and his script outline is nowhere at all. His labored pages tell a familiar story: he doesn't have it anymore, at least so far as our project is concerned.

We trample around in his script for the rest of the day. Soon the writer is out of things altogether and the meeting falls into an old pattern. Jack Reese, the assistant manager of our department, and I versus Mac Tyler; the soft sell against the hard sell. We spend ten minutes trying to prevent Tyler from inserting a line: "Here employees enjoy their good, nourishing food." We maintain that the color closeups of the food indicate just how good and nourishing it is. The line stays in.

Four-forty P.M. Five minutes before quitting time the meeting ends. The bus to the railroad station has pulled up at the front door. There is a mass squeaking of shoes in the corridors. George Browne and I put on our topcoats. Goody-by, good-by, good night. On the way down the corridor I ask George what he has been doing. He has been with a photographer topping off a story on an accountant who has had his thirty-year button pinned on him. One of the directors comes down from the top floor to shake hands. The accountant grins and blinks. The flash bulbs go off. Another story, George says, has to do with the company's newest office boy who is looking forward to being the first Crystal Palace employee to retire in the year 2000. I don't know why this story depresses me.

We walk down the front steps toward the bus, and the wheel of the years seems all at once not to turn but to spin before my eyes. Looking about me, I don't have any consciousness of spring but of all the seasons coming upon us faster and faster, and overwhelming us in their quickening cycle. Yesterday the hillside was white with snow drifts, tomorrow it will be green, then parched, the day after for a few moments aflame with glorious red leaves, and then barren and November-hard.

Ten new college boys will be funneled into our hopper, a few pink-cheeked girls will take their places in the typing pool, and out another door will go ten old men and five old women. I may be projecting my own feelings onto them, but it seems to me that the ones stepping into the golden years of retirement have a stunned expression. They smile uncertainly and wave; they put on a brave face, but appear to be struck by the flat blade of time. I have noticed the same expression in milder form on employees who are having decades pinned on them in the form of buttons. It is a vaguely foolish, half-shrewd, half-goofy look, like that of a rube who has had a funny trick played on him at a carnival, and isn't quite sure whether he should enjoy it or not.

We who remain inside can't imagine this sensation. For most of us nothing much will have happened between winter and winter to make this year any different from the last one. At the Crystal Palace we are ignorant of time. We think that we will always have our year, and we are right. All the unnoticed years run together into one unchanging year. Only we age and change. It seems to me now that our group has always been getting into this bus. Oh, we are happy enough. It is just that whatever we do here, we have always done it before.

If all the world's a stage, so too the Crystal Palace may be viewed as a corporate theater in which all the actors are bit players. We have no star system here. Even directors and department managers who play relatively significant roles in our endless production never have the stage to themselves. In our show there are always dozens of people taking part in the smallest scene. No one but an insider can tell one actor from another. Yet we have no scene-stealing either. Far from lusting for prominence, our discreet thespians advance by *not* calling unseemly attention to themselves. They play not for the audience and its irrelevant applause but for Stage Management watching from the wing. . . .

7 / The Managers

Staff Reporters of *The Wall Street Journal*

> At the heart of American industry is the middle manager, the executive below the rank of vice president who carries out top management's instructions. Yet despite his vital function, he is a barely visible part of the industrial machine.

JOHN A. ARMBRUSTER, TRW, INC.
By Richard Martin

About this time every year John A. Armbruster faces the same problem. "It's that little box at the top of the 1040 federal tax form marked 'occupation.' I don't know what to put in it," he says.

Mr. Armbruster's employer is TRW Inc., and his title there is director of corporate planning. "But that isn't what I do," he says. "I always think about that little box quite awhile and then I put down 'engineer'—it isn't right either but it fits the space and people understand it."

People usually don't understand when he tells them what he really does for a living. As soon as he starts talking about "parametric growth curves" and TRW's "algebraic relationships with the environment," people's eyes glaze over. "I hope you can explain this job," he says. "I want to take the paper home for my wife and kids to read, because they don't understand what I do."

Mr. Armbruster is a prime example of the fastest growing segment of today's corporate America: the middle management "knowledge specialist." Typically steeped in a narrow field of expertise, these specialists have little or no political clout in the executive suite and command few subordinates. They neither set corporate policy, as does top management, nor produce a salable product, as do workers on the assembly line. Their job responsibilities often baffle co-workers down the hall, let alone family and friends.

But while their contributions to the corporate weal may be invisible to outsiders, and to many insiders, sometimes even themselves, knowledge specialists are having a marked impact on how big business operates. More and more these anonymous managers are handling problems of information management, psychology, politics, ecology, law, social policy and other areas that were unknown or ignored in the executive office as recently as a decade ago.

As the responsibilities of these specialists expand, amoeba-fashion, to engulf practically every aspect of running a huge corporation, their collective influence becomes apparent. Middle managers are making most of the day-to-day operating decisions and also are making nearly all of the specialized studies and recommendations on which top management is basing its long range decisions. As a result, "sometimes it appears that middle management is practically running the company," says Frederick A. Teague, a vice president at Booz Allen & Hamilton, the consulting firm. . . .

Yet although these often "faceless" middle-management specialists collectively have considerable influence within a company, as individuals they often face the frustration of little or no supervisory authority and working with little visibility in a position that isn't well understood. It isn't always easy for a knowledge specialist to feel appreciated or to see a bright future ahead of him in such a position. A specialist must constantly be building his own expertise. Yet to rise very far in management, says James E. Dunlap, TRW's vice president of human relations, "the specialist has to somehow or other get broader and become more of a generalist."

RANGING THE GLOBE

Nowhere is the impact of an emergent corporate staff of specialists in widely diverse areas of expertise more evident than at TRW, an innovative multinational concern with $3 billion of annual sales, ranging from auto parts and electronics systems to aerospace and industrial products. TRW's knowledge specialists range the globe, giving money to orchestras, colleges and hospitals, arguing with tax officials in Singapore, lobbying elected officials in California and creating computer programs to do such things as automatically audit purchases and sales between divisions. . . .

In the cramped little office where he daily pores over computer readouts, John Armbruster compares his work to the microwave oven his wife would like to buy. "I'm caught up here in providing something no one would miss if it weren't provided," he says.

Ruben F. Mettler, president and chief operating officer of TRW, calls Mr. Armbruster's contributions "very real and very large, but also diffuse and subtle." Over the past few years, he says, his work has had "a very positive effect on the bottom line," which rose 6 percent in 1974, 12 percent in 1975 and 28 percent in 1976, when net income was $133 million.

Mr. Armbruster is an intense, fussy man with dark, piercing eyes and nervous hands that are constantly drawing diagrams in the air. He worked summers in TRW's mail room while he was earning a degree in mechanical engineering at Case Western Reserve University. During six years in the Air Force he immersed himself in analytical research work and statistics. He earned a master's degree in industrial engineering and management at Oklahoma State University and later added an MBA degree in marketing and finance from Case Western. The advanced degrees, he believes, helped him "avoid being pigeonholed as a computer jock" early in his career at TRW.

That career began in 1965 as a reliability engineer in TRW's aircraft propulsion group. But that wasn't what he really wanted, so in 1967 he applied for a computer modeling job on the corporate staff and got it.

Computer modeling was then in its infancy as a forecasting tool for making long-range strategic decisions and for separating internal growth expectations from forecasts based on growth through acquisitions. A series of top-echelon memos and meetings had created the job. TRW's founder, Simon Ramo, in a 1966 memo first cited the need to start plotting mathematical growth curves that would project TRW's financial and operating results far into the future under difference economic conditions. By the time Mr. Armbruster had been appointed a year later, the scope of the job had broadened considerably, but it was still very fuzzy.

"I've been doing about the same kind of work since 1967, but I've been doing it in a lot of different offices, because they didn't quite know where to put me," he says. First it was the data processing department, then the controller's office, then with the vice president of finance. "That was the first real recognition of the nature of my work," says Mr. Armbruster. His next boss was the vice president, economist, another step up in status. In 1973 a new post was created, vice president, corporate planning and development, and Mr. Armbruster has been director in this office ever since.

Mr. Armbruster's salary is in the $40,000 to $50,000 range, and he participates in TRW's management incentive bonus program, which is based on annual profit gains. "I don't know where the topside is on this job," he says. "I think I could have a very fulfilling career right here."

Certainly, the moves he has made so far have been significant. "It isn't uncommon to find people like me stagnating in an accounting department somewhere," says Mr. Armbruster. "My product isn't something that can be pushed up through an organization. Top management has to understand it and want it enough to reach down and get it."

The main product Mr. Armbruster and his young MBA assistant, John Keogh, produce is TRW's "top-down forecast," a half-inch sheaf of typewritten pages, financial tables, charts and graphs that is delivered to Mr. Mettler three times a year. It forecasts key financial and operating data, including profits, working capital requirements and return on assets as far as five years ahead and separates TRW's sales into fifteen different business areas.

The object is to be able to understand how much of TRW's performance is really under the control of management and how much is subject to the vagaries of the economy," says Mr. Armbruster. "It gives top management an idea of what's possible under five or six different conditions. They can select the preferable future and see what actions to take to attempt to reach various goals, rather than just let the corporation meander off on its own."

For instance, "Rube (Mr. Mettler, the president) can look at the forecast and tell an operating guy: 'Forget those plans, that business is strictly at the mercy of the economy. Use your creative management time to concentrate on this business, where what you do can make a difference,'" says Mr. Armbruster. "We've found that management can exercise far more control over a company's fate than was thought possible before."

Over the past three years, the short-term quarter-to-quarter portion of the top-down forecast has come closer to forecasting actual operating profits than have the traditional "bottom-up" forecasts prepared quarterly by the operating divisions.

The forecast doesn't just spring out of the computer room 250 feet down the hall where Mr. Armbruster spends a big chunk of his day. Building the various computer models that make the forecast possible has been a painstaking research and development process. The forecast still is evolving, growing more detailed and refined all the time. "The data that are generated to meet federal requirements, the SEC, IRS, EPA or whoever, usually are not the most useful data for running a company, so we have to go out and develop most of our own," he says.

That takes lots of time on the phone, "digging out stuff like how many pumps they moved out the door last quarter," he says. Sometimes it requires personal visits to operating divisions' financial staffs "to make friends and convince them to pull the stuff I need out of their archives," says Mr. Armbruster. "The people down below are very sensitive about requests from the corporate staff for data that are going to require their time and effort to put together. It's always a question of how far can I go without stepping on the toes of the operating people."

The quality of the information is a constant worry. "We're trying to look at the future with pretty flaky data sometimes," he says. "I have a high tolerance for ambiguity, but sometimes it gets very frustrating to never be sure what's out there." He has built up his credibility carefully over the years, "and I guard it very jealously," he says. Still, bad information sometimes gets into a forecast because of aberrations caused by internal reorganizations, acquisitions and accounting changes over the years, and it can make things hot for an operating man who is meeting with top management. Recently a division vice president "phoned and really chewed my ear for a long while because I had bad data," says Mr. Armbruster.

Another worry is time. Mr. Armbruster, his assistant, Mr. Keogh, and TRW's econometrician, Van Bussmann, have spent about 80 percent of their time working together as a team lately in an effort to meet top management's increasing requests for more and faster information. "We're in danger of being loved to death," says Mr. Armbruster. "We just can't keep up with everything we want to do." Instead of going to lunch, he often sneaks off to the computer to run his own analyses.

Mr. Armbruster concedes that some of the time pressures he feels are self-imposed. "Sometimes if I didn't generate some particular report nobody would miss it because they don't even know it's coming," he says. "But I know it ought to be done and I feel like I've got to. My wife says I get compulsive when I have a project going. I enter into a one-track mind mode until I either solve the problem or fall over in complete frustration."

CHESTER A. HOFFMAN, ATLAS POWDER CO.
By June Kronholz

Atlas Powder Co. had a problem that was threatening to cost it business. Its salesmen were complaining that they needed a new, inexpensive dynamite product to sell to their strip-mine customers. The salesmen wanted to know what Atlas could do to prevent customers being lured away by competing products.

Atlas, a division of Dallas-based Tyler Corp., turned to Chester A. Hoffman, manager of its huge plant here in the Pocono Mountains of northeastern Pennsylvania. Mr. Hoffman designed a twenty-five-pound stick of dynamite that was stout enough for stripmining, cheap enough to be competitive and waterproof for use in wet holes where other explosives would get soggy.

Then, he set his plant to work: the engineers to adapting equipment to handle the new product; the power line to mixing the dynamite; the shell shop to turning out the casings, and the box factory to making shipping cartons. Within two weeks, the truckers of Mr. Hoffman's eighteen-van fleet were loading the new dynamite for delivery. Today, it is the Tamaqua plant's biggest volume item.

"That's one of the joys of the job," says Mr. Hoffman, a bespectacled 55-year-old manager whose mild manner belies the fact that he is a $50,000-a-year big gun at an explosives plant. "I have a hand in everything that goes on here," he says. Mr. Hoffman's responsibility for his plant is, in fact, a 24-hour assignment and of a complexity that top corporate executives rarely have to face.

Yet despite his wide-ranging responsibilities, his acknowledged expertise in his field and his 35-year career with the company, Mr. Hoffman, like most of the nation's plant managers, remains far down the corporate ladder. He has met Tyler's top officers only twice, has never visited the corporate offices and made his first and only trip to the Atlas division's home office in Dallas just last winter.

The plant manager is a pivotal figure in American industry and ranks among the most highly paid and valued of all middle managers. What's more, his responsibilities seem to be growing. . . .

But when it comes to making major corporate decisions, the plant manager usually has little say. . . .

Atlas's Mr. Hoffman says that he is content to "have enough input to affect the decisions concerning this plant." But making decisions, he says, is "the most challenging part of any job, and only the dullard doesn't want to be the top dog and make the top decisions."

Norman B. Keider, Atlas's president, rates Mr. Hoffman's chances of moving into upper management as "reasonable":

one chance in three of becoming an Atlas executive, one in five of becoming a top manager at another Tyler subsidiary and one chance in ten of moving into the corporate offices at Tyler.

As it is, it would seem that Mr. Hoffman's duties are considerable. They range from ordering the raw materials for dynamite, nitroglycerin, blasting caps and slurries (gelatinous ammonium nitrate-based explosives) to delivering the finished goods to customers in construction, mining and quarrying. He oversees the safety of 950 employes, the profitability of an operation that will report about $50 million in sales this year, the reliability of dangerous products and the general care and security of 500 buildings, a 2,700-acre wooded site and over a ton of stored explosives.

At times, his responsibilities even include the dramatic and the droll. When a forest fire threatened the plant, Mr. Hoffman manned the fire lines. When smoke began wafting from a dynamite magazine, he chopped open a rooftop vent to find the source. And when a herd of deer living on the grounds threatened the flower beds, he ordered protective fencing.

But while Atlas leaves all production policies up to Mr. Hoffman, it keeps the purse-string policies for itself. Thus Mr. Hoffman was powerless this winter to hire a badly needed draftsman until Atlas authorized creating a new salaried position, a process that took over two months.

Sometimes, though, Mr. Hoffman does find himself in a position to influence the company's course. He argued at a December 1975 meeting with Mr. Keider and fellow plant managers that a new explosive developed and patented by Atlas researchers was ready for commercial production at the Tamaqua plant. Atlas had been working on a product to combine the best characteristics of old-fashioned dynamite with the newer, safer slurries. But to put it into production would cost $550,000 for a new building and equipment.

"I asked Chet's advice and listened to what he had to say," recalls Mr. Keider. Before the meeting ended, Mr. Hoffman had approval for the project. . . .

More than just the explosives market has changed since Mr. Hoffman joined Atlas; so has the company's ownership. In 1971, Atlas Chemical Industries Inc., then an independent concern traded on the New York Stock Exchange, was acquired by ICI American Inc., a subsidiary of Imperial Chemical Industries

Ltd., the big British concern which is a major explosives maker.

"It was a traumatic period to go through," Mr. Hoffman recalls. ICI scrapped the Atlas name and ran it out of ICI America's corporate offices in Wilmington, Del. "Wilmington made the decisions and solved the problems," Mr. Hoffman recalls. It also did the engineering, job interviewing and special services that employees at the Tamaqua plant do now.

Such a centralized management style was irksome to Mr. Hoffman. "Literally every day there would be someone here from Wilmington," he says with displeasure. "You couldn't do anything until it cleared channels. That slowed development tremendously."

The association with ICI lasted two years. Then the Federal Trade Commission told ICI that it could keep the Atlas aerospace and chemical units, but had to divest itself of the explosives division. Tyler, which also has interests in transportation, engineering and pipe manufacture, bought it in 1973.

In taking control of the three explosives plants, Tyler resurrected the Atlas name, moved its headquarters west to be near seismographic and mining customers, and established a decentralized style of management. Mr. Hoffman keeps in daily telephone contact with his Dallas superiors, but the new owners "put a great emphasis on local decision-making," he says. "They dictate very little."

His contact with his own employees is more direct. He tours the plant daily, greeting people by name (an exception is identical twins; he says he still can't tell them apart) and asks about families, vacations, and health problems. He says he is pleased that the opening of the emulsion plant meant that this year, at least, Atlas didn't have to order its usual winter layoffs (much road building and strip mining is curtailed in the winter). Layoffs, says Mr. Hoffman, are "painful to watch."

Still, his reputation is as a tough manager, and full employment last winter will mean easier union negotiations this spring. Tamaqua workers have struck the plant twice since Mr. Hoffman became manager. They have called a work slowdown once and have taken their grievances, most of them medically related, to arbitration ten times in the past five years. John Tracy, president of the Oil, Chemical and Atomic Workers Union local, representing about 700 Tamaqua employes, calls Mr. Hoffman a "tough negotiator." The two men know each other well, and, says Mr. Tracy, "I know when I can squeeze the extra half pint out of him and he knows when we deserve it."

Mr. Hoffman's own management style is perhaps best illustrated by his attitude toward alcoholism on the job. Last year, on his own initiative, he began an alcohol and drug abuse counseling program for plant workers. He has been known to take midnight calls from inebriated workers asking for help. And he seldom fires anyone, regardless of the cause. "Think of the hardship that would cause the family," he says. But in the past he has had to force employees with alcohol problems to take early retirement and reduced benefits. "I'm sympathetic, but I can't keep people like that on the job," he says.

Not surprisingly, Mr. Hoffman is a leading citizen in tiny Tamaqua, an old coal town where Atlas is the major employer. Evenings, when he's not at his hobby, making grandfather clocks, he works on civic affairs: He chairs a school board committee; he headed the Salvation Army advisory board the year it built a community center; he helped found the local United Fund; and he is an elder in the local Presbyterian church, a member of the choir, and vice president of the county manufacturers association.

His wife, Esther, sits on the board of the county meals-on-wheels program for the elderly, and together they hosted eight foreign exchange students while their own three children, now married, were in school.

"In a company town like this, nobody in management is 100 percent liked, even if he's the nicest guy in the world," says union official Mr. Tracy. "But people have respect for Mr. Hoffman, which he deserves."

CHALLIS M. LOWE, CONTINENTAL BANK
By Joann S. Lublin

"Your secretary came outside to inspect the no-parking signs we put up at the drive-in teller," the police lieutenant told Martin Hartmann, an assistant branch manager for Continental Bank.

"Hey, that was no secretary," objected Mr. Hartmann. "That was my boss."

His boss is Challis M. Lowe, a thirty-one-year-old black woman who earns more than $25,000 a year running the bank's first branch office, which opened last September in a sky-scraper lobby at the north end of Chicago's financial district. Well aware that Mrs. Lowe is in charge, her staff of twenty-six bankers, tellers and clerks have dubbed the branch "Challis's palace." But outsiders, unaccustomed to dealing with a woman executive, sometimes mistake her for a secretary. . . .

The pressures and frustrations of being a woman middle manager are clearly apparent in Challis Lowe's career. But there also is satisfaction, and her experience suggests that some aspects of corporate life may get easier as the ranks of female executives swell.

At first glance, Challis Lowe doesn't appear to fit the part she plays: an ambitious, hard-driving executive who is determined to reach a high management position. She is a thin, seemingly shy person who speaks in a soft voice. Her carefully tailored suits and large, thick glasses give her the appearance of a schoolteacher.

In fact, her early ambition was to be a high school math teacher, and she substituted in an elementary school after the birth of her first daughter. Daphne, in 1966. But after her second daughter was born two years later, she acted against her husband John's wishes and decided to seek a fulltime business career. She wasn't looking for fulfillment or power, she says, so much as "peace of mind from getting out of the house during the day."

She did counseling for an employment agency for two years, and it was there that she heard about opportunities for women in banking. So in 1971 she became a customer representative for Continental Illinois National Bank & Trust Co.'s personal banking division, which services individual customers, rather than business and commercial accounts.

After a few years spent opening accounts and counseling, Mrs. Lowe began to wonder if she would ever go higher in the bank. She was dubious because there was only one female officer in her section of personal banking. And when she asked her supervisor about a promotion, he suggested that she transfer to another area of the bank.

She ignored his suggestion and, instead, took a personnel department test, which indicated she had management talents.

As a result, her work was watched more closely, and in mid-1974, at the age of twenty-eight, Mrs. Lowe was made assistant sales manager and, later that year, an officer. Early in 1975 she became sales manager.

Mrs. Lowe was Continental Bank's first black woman officer. Now the bank employs about 100 women executives—up from only 30 in 1973—three of whom are black. Altogether, the bank has 1,123 individuals in management.

As sales manager, Mrs. Lowe was in charge of half of the bank's family banking center, which handles all types of customer services. The promotion put her in charge of 30 bankers, most of whom were men. Uncomfortable about the situation, a few of the male veterans complained to her boss. One older woman took early retirement rather than take orders from the new manager. To this day, Mrs. Lowe says she doesn't know whether they resented her because she was black, female, or under thirty—or all three.

Sometimes, customers also were skeptical of her authority, refusing to talk to her and insisting that they be allowed "to see an officer." One elderly man was finally persuaded to confer with her, and was so pleased with the results that he told her, "You can be my secretary any time." Mrs. Lowe coolly replied, "I don't think you can afford me."

When Continental Bank decided to launch its first branch four blocks from the main office, Mrs. Lowe was tapped to manage the branch. At the time, Illinois law prohibited branch banking except for an additional office offering personal and limited commercial banking-services within 1,500 feet of a bank's headquarters. (The law was amended last summer to allow another branch within two miles.)

She took over her new job in February 1976, months before the lobby office opened, to direct the construction, design and equipping of the facility. In the process, Mrs. Lowe learned some lessons about being a woman middle manager. For the first time she had to deal with men in other bank departments, few of whom knew her or had worked with a female executive before. This explains why, she says, "they tended to put my priorities on the back burner. I found I had to prove myself with many of them."

One bank official stalled on her request for some signs, because, she thinks, he resented taking orders from a woman. Undaunted, she called the official's boss and made arrangements directly with him.

Getting what she wants for her branch also requires Mrs. Lowe to work closely with the three men and one woman who are her fellow executives in personal banking. All of these executives have profit responsibilities and all compete for staff and budget allocations from their boss, vice president Lawrence A. Eldridge.

Two or three times every day, Mrs. Lowe leaves her thickly carpeted, glassed-in office on the branch's mezzanine level for meetings or a working lunch at the main office with the other managers. At these meetings she sometimes finds herself fighting to protect her turf. One recent, and still unresolved, dispute concerned dinner plates that the bank gives away as premiums. She argued with her colleagues that she shouldn't have to absorb the marketing expenses when customers with accounts at the main bank pick up free plates at her branch.

But the competition among the personal banking executives is more often friendly and low-keyed, and Mrs. Lowe deliberately tries to encourage bonhomie. Whether it's a marketing strategy conference or an occasional drink after work, Mrs. Lowe prepares diligently, keeping posted on the latest sports scores, even though she hates sports. It's vital for a woman "to work at becoming part of a company's informal social network," she observes.

Her quick adaptation to office politics and her smooth operation of the new office (its deposit volume is running four months ahead of schedule) are winning her praise. Staff morale is high, customers are pleased, "and we're getting a good business there," says John H. Perkins, Continental Bank's president. "It's got to be because she's running the place well." . . .

Despite her guilt feelings [about leaving her two preteen daughters], Challis Lowe wouldn't think of giving up her management job because, she says, it gives her a deep sense of accomplishment. Her "personal drive," she says, wasn't being "fulfilled" by staying at home.

Her drive is fueled by ambition. With a note of determination in her voice, she declares that her sights "aren't limited to becoming a second vice president." Her race and sex may help more than hinder her further advancement at Continental Bank, which is currently the target of a sex discrimination suit by Women Employed, an organization of Chicago working women.

But conflicting loyalties between work and home make Mrs. Lowe unsure that she would like to be president of Continental Bank. The road to the top is filled with more and more commitment to the job and less and less time with your family," she says, her voice growing softer and less steady. Laughing nervously, she adds, "If I spent any more hours away from home, I might not have a family."

THREE WHO AREN'T MAKING IT

By Terry P. Brown

MARVIN E. WALDEN. In only five years at GM, Marvin E. Walden was promoted to senior mathematician at the company's technical center, receiving several merit pay increases and extensive training at company expense. He felt, however, that his chances of entering management would be better at a company with "less technical depth" in personnel and facilities. "I was young and ambitious, so I sent out resumes to Ford and Chrysler," he says. In mid-1969, he joined Chrysler for a "substantial pay increase."

Within a few months, Mr. Walden became head of a thirty-two-man department assigned to computerize the process of turning clay models of car designs into precisely measured body components. For nearly a year and a half, he ran the department and developed facilities which, he claims, now save Chrysler about $1 million annually. During that time, Mr. Walden says he received a "favorable" oral performance review from the head of Chrysler's technical computer center. He says this was the only performance appraisal he has had in eight years with the company.

With a managerial position that paid about $24,000 a year, Mr. Walden's career seemed "on track." In addition, he was completing his doctorate in mathematics at Detroit's Wayne State University, where he had graduated Phi Beta Kappa with a physics degree and earned a master's degree in math.

His job prospects changed dramatically, however, when his boss was promoted and, according to Mr. Walden, a "personality clash" developed with the new man. In May 1971, Mr. Walden's department was disbanded without warning, and he was demoted to a supervisor without any cut in pay. Chrysler says the move was necessary to eliminate duplication of work with another department; Mr. Walden thinks he was "set up" as part of an inter-departmental political struggle.

"At first, I was angry and wanted to quit," says forty-one-year-old Mr. Walden, "but after sending out hundreds of resumes, I quickly learned I'd have to take a substantial cut in pay." He decided to stay on at Chrysler, hoping that he might eventually be promoted back to his former level. Instead, Mr. Walden says he has been given a series of "make-work, letter-writing assignments, leading nowhere."

In 1975, Mr. Walden was laid off, along with about 20,000 other Chrysler salaried workers, due to the recession. When he returned he found that several younger men had been promoted to positions he thought himself qualified to fill. So Mr. Walden sued his employer, seeking reinstatement to his former management position and $500,000 in damages. "My demotion was without cause, but if they had treated me like a gentleman, I would have saluted and waited for a promotion back to a manager's level," he says. "But there was no internal due process, no mediation procedure."

As part of his suit, Mr. Walden is demanding to see Chrysler's list of " exceptional" employes. Chrysler admits that it centrally compiles such lists to assist it in selecting candidates for internal openings, but the company denies that it uses the list in a discriminatory manner. "One's name on such a list doesn't guarantee advancement," company lawyers say. "There are many, many employees whose names haven't been on such a list who have been advanced much further than most of the employes so listed." Chrysler has been ordered by Wayne County Circuit Court to produce certain details of the list for inspection.

"Usually in Chrysler," contends Mr. Walden, "you get on the list, and you get promoted if you know a director (a management level one step below vice president). It's a 100 percent sponsor- or godfather-type system and has nothing to do with any kind of scientific management system."

"What results," he feels, "is that many people are underutilized; yet they continue to pay us high salaries, wasting millions." He says his total economic package, including such benefits as medical insurance, is about $35,000 a year. He lives in a comfortable brick ranch house in the affluent Detroit suburb of Bloomfield Hills, has two cars, and sends his three children to private schools. "I've lost a lot of sleep over this," he says. "I started grinding my teeth so much I had to buy a teeth protector." He adds: "It won't be possible for me to take less money and change my life style now."

RICHARD E. MATHEWS. "If they thought they were clearing out some deadwood, they picked the wrong man," declares Richard E. Mathews, who has worked for Ford for nearly thirty-eight years. "No one ever told me I didn't do a good job, and I certainly never felt I was ready to retire." But Mr. Mathews asserts that in rough times Ford "makes the mistake of assuming that young is good, older is bad, or now is our chance to weed out the older employees." Mr. Mathews never thought he would be one of those "eased out the door."

In 1939 at the age of nineteen, Mr. Mathews joined Ford as an assembly-line worker. He left in 1942 to fly B29s during World War II, rising to the rank of captain. He returned to Ford in 1947, and was assigned to testing Ford's German-made trucks. Except for three years on the assembly line, Mr. Mathews's entire career has been in testing and developing products for Ford's foreign affiliates and export markets.

Despite the lack of a college degree, Mr. Mathews rose to the post of supervisor, with as many as twenty-two engineers and technicians under him. After eight years, he was asked to take a lateral transfer to become supervisor of another department's Latin American section. "I thought the move was made to train younger supervisors and to expand my overall experience," says Mr. Mathews. Two years later, in 1974, however, the department was eliminated, and Mr. Mathews, then 53 years old, was demoted and transferred back to his old department as an engineer.

An indignant Mr. Mathews fired off a letter to chairman Henry Ford II. But the only response was a call from the personnel department saying his complaint wasn't "valid." Mr. Mathews sued, asking for reinstatement to his former position. Ford argues that Mr. Mathews was demoted without any cut in pay at a time when "thousands of employees were being released outright" due to the recession. Mr. Mathews claims that in his department there was a net gain in personnel of about 15 percent during the recession.

Although his salary wasn't cut (last year, he earned about $45,000, including $10,000 of overtime), he says he "lost prestige, a private office, a secretary and any right to a bonus, which probably would have amounted to about $4,500 last year." He declares: "I didn't have any illusions that I could go much higher than one more notch, but the demotion put me further back in the pack for any future advancement."

Sitting in the living room of his Dearborn Heights, Mich., home, not far from Ford's world headquarters, Mr. Mathews says: "I don't disagree with the idea of bringing fresh blood into an organization, but you have to try to hit a happy medium between the young world-beaters and your loyal, experienced people. A lot of the stars burn themselves out at an early age."

EDWARD B. MAZZOTTA. In 1953, Edward B. Mazzotta joined Ford as a project engineer designing vehicle components. Eight years later, he left to work for two smaller Detroit-area engineering firms, but rejoined Ford in 1971. Within fifteen months, he was promoted two pay grades to resident engineer of the Dearborn engine plant, a $30,000-a-year management job.

"In any corporation, nine times out of ten, you need an angel to watch over you if you're going to get ahead," says the fifty-six-year-old Mr. Mazzotta. "I had an angel, but when a new regime came in to head up the resident engineering staff, my angel got his wings clipped and was forced into early retirement."

What resulted, in Mr. Mazzotta's view, was a "humiliating, systematic step-by-step discrediting" by his new supervisors. Within about three months, Mr. Mazzotta received two poor performance reviews. "These were unwarranted and based on a lack of facts," he claims. "When the reviews were presented to me, I was told to read them and then sign them, but I had no opportunity to discuss them." In March 1974, Mr. Mazzotta, then fifty-three, was demoted two pay grades without a cut in pay and transferred to another department. Now, he says, he's "a paper shuffler, doing nothing that any high school graduate couldn't do," at a salary of about $35,000 a year.

"Some people will tolerate a lot of abuse before they do

anything: they'll sit there and take the money. But the desire to feel useful and constructive was too great for me," he says. Mr. Mazzotta says he tried to appeal his case through Ford's personnel department, asking for a promotional transfer, but "it was like going to a priest for confession. Once you've been demoted, it's unlikely you'll ever shake the stigma and be promoted again."

In a lawsuit filed last year in Wayne County Circuit Court, seeking reinstatement and $500,000 in damages, Mr. Mazzotta charges that younger men "with far less experience" have been promoted within the department, while several older men "in my age range" have been either demoted or forced into early retirement. Ford says that Mr. Mazzotta's lack of promotion is a function of "few position openings" and of his performance "in relation to others seeking the positions."

The demotion and the decision to sue Ford haven't been easy on Mr. Mazzotta. Eight months after his demotion, he required medical treatment for a duodenal ulcer. At his request, he was interviewed for this story in his hospital room after suffering a heart attack while on the job. Mr. Mazzotta blames his health problems on the way he was treated at Ford.

"You can't eliminate politics from a corporation, but you can try to minimize it," he reasons. "In my case, the performance review was used as a weapon, and I had no way to refute or rebut what was happening to me.

"I don't agree with the idea that a man slows down as he gets older," he says. "If a man is slow at fifty-five, he was slow at thirty-five, and the company has an obligation to tell him of his limited potential then—and not wait twenty years to shelve him or sweep him out the door."

8 / The Gender Pioneers: Women in an Industrial Sales Force

Rosabeth Moss Kanter and Barry A. Stein

WOMEN are the latest addition to many companies' sales forces, in fields once covered exclusively by men, the *New York Times* financial pages reported on January 5, 1975. The areas range from pharmaceuticals to brass products, computers to industrial chemicals. In August 1974, *Chemical Week* reported on the progress of large chemical companies in upgrading women employees.

A large number of businesses have opened increased opportunities to women in sales—and have attracted a group of highly-motivated women who see sales as a challenge en route to management.

As with any new phenomenon, the presence of women in the sales force can create a number of questions and uncertainties: Do women encounter any special difficulties as "travelling salesmen?" How do men in the company react to these new opportunities for women? How do the traditional relationships between men and women affect this new career for women? What helps women succeed in a sales position?

This report is an attempt to help answer some of these questions by drawing on experiences in one company as of spring, 1975.

The women currently in the sales force are typically very excited about what an industrial sales position offers them. They are ambitious, energetic, committed to their work and to seeing themselves as professionals. Several of them have always been intrigued by a career in sales: "I love selling: encountering

Adapted from "Women at [Company X]: The Sales Force," a handbook prepared for use at a leading American corporation, which granted permission for publication on the condition that the company remain anonymous.

different people, the lack of structure, haggling over prices." "I enjoy the customers. I like setting my own schedule and running my own small business within a large company." One said she felt fortunate to work for a company that cared about its people and was continually trying to improve.

The challenge and the opportunities also appeal to these women: "I have an opportunity to do some technical teaching as well as selling. There's variety." "I like the opportunity to move and learn. I'm impressed by the broad field. I can go all over the place. I also wanted a challenge, and I feel I will be given a chance if I ask and my background is appropriate." For several women, sales is also a route to bigger challenges, including top management positions.

SUCCESS STRATEGIES

The women who are succeeding in sales are generally aware of the problems they might face as women in the business world. But many of them have also developed their own sucess strategies and coping mechanisms. Some of these began much earlier in life, when they first became used to operating in a "man's world." Particularly the women with technical backgrounds were accustomed to being in a minority studying science in school. One woman was the only girl in her neighborhood and had an older brother, enabling her to learn to deal with boys as equals from an early age and making it easier to go into a "man's field". Another attended a nearly all-male college and had reached positions of leadership among men in past jobs, before taking her present position. Some women had been working for the company in other capacities before joining the sales force and similarly were experienced in dealing with mostly men in the business environment, even through they were in typical "women's jobs." Many of the successful sales women also recalled being free of many traditional restraints on women and women's career aspirations. "I always did what I wanted despite my parents' restrictions," one women recalled, and this theme of "doing what I want" rang through other women's stories.

Thus, many of the successful women in sales bring with them

a history of self-assertion and experience with the minority status of career women. They rely heavily on technical knowledge, competence, and expertise to create their successes in a field in which several of them still see: "the decks stacked against women's success. Take your average woman—she is going to fail if things don't change in business." Yet these women don't want to just "get by"; they want to do an outstanding job. Competence, and particularly knowledge of the company and the product, is by far the most important factor in the effectiveness of women as well as men. There is no substitute for competence. But women also include a series of specific coping mechanisms that help them deal with the special situations they encounter as females.

"Guts and a good sense of humor" are the capacities one woman stresses. "It's important to help men to adjust. Around chairs and doors, men may not know how to handle themselves. I try to make a light joke out of it." "I develop my ability to see the funny side of situations, and I wait for men to get over their problems." Tolerance is another important ability. "Some people will always make snide remarks about a woman. You have to learn to let them roll off your back . . . You also have to learn to be patient the 300th time a man makes the same joke in your presence, like 'You're better looking than the *last* salesman.' When I get frustrated I try to remember what the situation is like for the other person."

Many of the women are very concerned about their treatment and willing to stand up for themselves when they feel unfairly treated or discriminated against. But they also have learned to put their energies into those areas where they will pay off and not to fight impossible battles just to make a point. For example, a customer who had previously been called on by a black man told the new woman assigned to his account, "I get all of your company's minority salesmen." The woman involved considered whether she was engendering more ill will than necessary, and whether the energy it would take to "convert" this man to accept her was worth the trouble. In another kind of situation, a woman reported that she does not go out of her way to prove she can behave "just like a man" in every circumstance. For example, she does not try to get in on the raunchy story-telling that can be part of male culture, feeling it would fall flat.

The women also feel they have to speak up for themselves.

One tends not to let comments about what a woman can or cannot do go by without stopping them and engaging the man involved in a dialogue. She has thus helped many men see that the presence of a woman does not necessarily mean a change in the activities a group will engage in, such as sports or fishing. Another stresses the importance of letting people know what she hopes and wants rather than leaving them to guess or to make decisions for her. "If I don't say what I want, people guess ten different futures for me. I make a point of seeing my manager, I don't let anyone speak *for* me. Everything that has been decided for me has been what I've wanted. Men have a difficult time anticipating *for* a woman—you have to tell them."

WHY WOMEN DON'T ALWAYS MAKE IT

Despite their own successes and ability to cope, a few of the women stressed the extra energy that it took to deal with many of the situations they faced because they were women. "It's not that I can't make it okay," one said. "It's just that there are so many more things I have to deal with than a man does." Another asked, "Will a woman always have to be twice as good just to stay at her present level? That's an additional burden." One woman put it bluntly and directly: "Let's face it. Men are biased against women and our success. They're lined up with a whole set of traditional attitudes and weapons to keep us from getting ahead."

The women had clear ideas about the specific factors involved for those women who did not succeed in the sales force and have since left. They were not necessarily laying the blame at everyone else's feet but the woman's, but they were trying to identify those circumstances that can make it more likely that a woman won't make it. Lack of "indoctrination" and feedback were considered to have influenced one woman's chances to perform adequately and effectively: hired too quickly, assigned too quickly, not properly indoctrinated, and not given feedback on what to do to improve. In this case the woman herself had felt she had *sought* feedback and was given the impression that she was doing fine, so that she was doubly surprised when she learned about the negative evaluations made of her.

In another case, of a woman who eventually left the company, her failure was attributed to over-protection by management, that she was never really pushed to perform all of the work that would be expected of a man, that she was treated too easily and thus never experienced pressure to measure up. In other instances, the sales women felt that the company was not selective enough in hiring nor sensitive enough to the needs for support of a new female trainee. A story was told about a new hire who had brought someone with her on a visit to the Director of Sales and on every visit thereafter. "I talked to the manager about her interviews, and he said the interviewers had been impressed with her. She had won them over as a *girl* that they could feel comfortable with, but they didn't look beyond that into selling . . . Then she was assigned to an office. There was no way for her to get to know the neighborhood or get integrated, alone among three male trainees. She left after a few months." Another person asked about this incident: Would a man have been hired who brought someone along on an interview? She also asked: How well was the woman chosen and prepared?

Lack of a support system for women, lack of adequate integration into a world of mostly men, lack of female role models, and lack of feedback, then, were among the circumstances making it harder for a woman in sales. The successful women indicated that those who had left the sales force had to bear their share of the responsibility for the problems, either through ignorance or inappropriate behavior, but they also felt that many of the situations could have been eased or avoided.

The first women in sales face a situation that probably has as much to do with being *rare* as being *female*. The first women are a curiosity; they stand out. They may be the subject of conversation, questioning, and perhaps even more careful scrutiny than would be given to a man. Reported a manager, "Every woman hired gets screened through a 100-mesh screen, men through a ten mesh. Then the women get watched a lot more. I hear the names of female trainees coming up in conversation, yet I don't hear the men wondering about Sam Jones' placement." In one case, a woman was told by her manager that she was watched more closely than men, that her dress and appearance were important, and that her performance could affect the prospects for other women in the company. When women are rare, it is true that they may be judged as a category—that what one woman does may be seen to reflect both positively and negatively on all women. There simply are not enough women to permit recognition of the range of differences *among* women, and the first women naturally bear the brunt of the questions, "How will women do? How will women handle the work?"

One woman was told about the big business deal her female predecessor "blew" and warned to be careful about mistakes. Another recalled that when she first came to the company, she heard "how great a few of the other women in sales were, I was told, 'you are expected to be like this.' This was my first indication that you are going to be watched forever and compared to the others—you have to meet their standards. It was like working in a fishbowl."

There are both advantages and disadvantages to the visibility of the women in sales. Women are easily noticed and can more easily make an impression to get the attention of higher management: "One of the advantages that I think women have is we don't have to go out of our way to be noticed. I've been at sales meetings where all the trainees were running up to the managers—Hi, Mr. So and So. Really trying to make that impression, wearing a strawberry tie, whatever, something that they could be remembered by. Whereas there were three of us (women) in a group of fifty, and all we had to do was walk in, and everyone recognized us. I was introduced to people when I was just passing by: 'Well, this is our woman sales trainee . . .' "
A man also felt that women presently have an attention-getting edge: "You know you're going to be listened to. When a woman speaks in a meeting I think people are going to listen—if for no other reason just to hear what this woman has to say. The first time she calls on a customer, especially if it's the first time he's seen a woman, she's definitely going to have the attention of that specific customer because it's a totally new experience."

In addition to the attention that novelty brings, a woman's minority status may also give her some freedom to deviate from norms men feel they must obey. The woman is already different; in some situations she can afford to be a non-conformist. "In a technical training course there was an unspoken understanding that people were to be bored and slightly negative. Yet a woman could get away with being enthusiastic—and in the process learn a lot more."

There are also *disadvantages* to the high visibility of the first women. "If it seems good to be noticed, wait until you make your first major mistake." "It's a burden for the manager who gets asked about a woman and has to answer behind-the-back stuff about her. It doesn't reach the woman unless he tells her. The manager gets it and has to deal with it." "I don't have as much freedom of behavior as men do; I can't be as independent. I carry the burden of all womankind." What is often the most visible to men is not the woman's competence but her appearance and sexual attributes. "Sure they notice me! But they are looking at my body, not listening to what I say." "Some of the attention is nice, but some of is demeaning to a professional. When a man gets a job, they don't tell him he's better looking than the man who was here before—but they say this to me."

A young salesman confirmed the fact that what is often most visible about women is their physical rather than intellectual sides: "Some of our competition, like ourselves, have women salespeople in the field. It's interesting that when you go in to see a purchasing agent what he has to say about the woman sales person. It is always what kind of body she has or how good looking she is or 'Boy, are you in trouble on this account now.' They don't tell you how good looking your competitors are if they're males. But I've never heard about a woman's technical competence or what kind of a sales person she was—only what her body was like."

Some women like getting compliments on their appearance and feel flattered when men notice their dress or looks. But those who object, say they object because this might be the *only* attention a woman gets or that it may block out the business matters the woman is trying to accomplish. Some women can use this kind of attention to their advantage but others, particularly young-looking women, feel that their female appearance means they have to work twice as hard to prove their competence, since men may have little experience with professional women. "There are times when I would rather say to a man, 'Hey, listen, you can have our looks and look like a female and have the advantage of walking in the room and being noticed.' But the noticeability also has attached to it that surprise on the part of men that you can talk and talk intelligently. Recognition works against you as much as it does for you. So I envy men because as soon as they walk in and sit down, you automatically assume they know what they're talking about. I never get that automatically."

The keys to changing the disadvantages of visibility to advantages are competence, knowledge and professionalism. Women must clearly demonstrate their competence, and when they have the attention of managers or customers, they must know what they are talking about. Company knowledge and product knowledge are essential. "Men are going to test women the first time around," said one woman. "I get asked a lot of nonessential questions just to find out how much I know. That's where I use my technical background." "My success is based on confidence and knowledge," said another. "There are customers who would rather deal with me than with a man because they know I have the answers."

Women in the high-visibility situation of the women in the sales force also cannot afford to engage in any less than professional behavior. "The company's a rumor factory. You must be careful how you conduct yourself and what you say to whom. I saw how one woman in the office was discussed endlessly, and I decided it would be better to keep my personal life and personal affairs separate. This woman also feels that it is better for a woman not to go out drinking after work with men from the office, but others do not necessarily agree. Said one: "This is a decision each woman has to make for herself for each set of circumstances, and I am confident that there are women, including myself, who drink after work with men from the office with no repercussions!"

LONE WOMEN IN GROUPS OF MEN

Women's minority status in the sales force means that they are likely to be the only woman (or one of two or three) in otherwise all-male groups—at meetings, on business calls, and in training programs. Being the only woman in a group of men can have a variety of consequences that might range from discomfort to outright exclusion and isolation. At minimum, there can be a slight social awkwardness which can be handled by good communication between the woman and her male peers. "I was the only woman in a group, and I was sensitive to

whether the guys wanted me included in their dinner plans. I
didn't want to be a tagalong or impose, and I was hesitant to in-
trude. I discussed it with some of the guys. One said he didn't
ask me to join them for dinner because it felt like dating, that
he'd rather I took the initiative. So I did, and the rest was much
better for me."

The culture that sometimes develops in male groups, involving drinking, off-color stories, and sexual innuendoes, can be a
source of awkwardness and discomfort for the only woman,
even one who can easily become "one of the boys." Said one of
a trainees group, "I felt like one of the guys for a while. Then I
got tired of it. They had crude mouths and were very immature. I began to dread the next week because I was tired of their
company. Finally, when we were all out drinking, I admitted to
myself, this is not me; I don't want to play their game." "I was
at a dinner where the men were telling dirty jokes. It was fun
for a while, then it got to me. I moved and tried to have a real
conversation with a guy at the other end of the table. It started
out as a comrade thing, but it loses its flavor, especially if you're
the only woman." "I didn't want them to stop on my account,
but I wish I had had an alternative conversation."

On occasion this "male culture" may be heightened in the
presence of a woman—as a form of male solidarity, as a way of
testing the woman, as a way of ensuring that the woman's presence won't threaten the things men have learned about what it
means to be a man in sales. (This partly depends on the matu-
rity and professionalism of the men themselves.) Women may
find sexual innuendoes or displays of locker room humor offen-
sive when they think that it is being put on for their benefit.
One woman was a team leader at a workshop when her team
decided to use an off-color slogan. "When they said it, they
looked at me for my reaction. Then they jumped on me for
not liking it. But I thought it didn't belong in a professional
atmosphere.

Though occasionally tempted to retaliate, many women
have learned that it is better not to compete with this culture.
Said one:"If a woman told the same joke the men tell, it
wouldn't go over too well. A clean joke would be like a wet
blanket. So I don't tell jokes." "Some people will always make
snide remarks. You have to learn to let them roll off your back.
You don't want to give them the satisfaction of a reaction."

Perhaps the heightening of male culture in a woman's presence comes out of uncertainty. Some men express concern that
they cannot "be themselves" in the presence of women, particularly female peers, and particularly around the issue of language. Several women said they had picked up the message
that men feel constrained to censor their language when
women are around, eliminate dirty words, refrain from swear-
ing, and tell no off-color stories. One male purchasing agent
was unhappy about dealing with a female customer service
representative and expressed this to the salesman, who told the
woman. She confronted the man and learned that he felt: "I
can't say what I want to a woman . . . I can't swear." (She told
him to go ahead, and now they have a good relationship.) In
another case, "the customer was short and nasty at first. I began
joking with him a little, and he loosened up. At one time he
started to say 'goddamn' and stopped, so I repeated the 'goddamn.' He cracked up . . . Humor can be a good coping device."
(A female peer added "when they say they can't swear around a
woman it's a crutch.")

But women have similar issues. Having been told that they
are "gentle and soft-spoken" (as one woman present was told),
they in turn may feel inhibited in expressing themselves
strongly or using foul language around men.

The women who reported such experiences said that they
were more common inside the company, rarely happening
with customers. "Customers seem to know what words they can
use." "Customers are gentlemanly. It's the snide remarks in the
office that are the problem. The men always ask if you run into
any problems on the road—assuming you will." With customers, as with male peers, it's a matter of establishing a relationship in which both parties feel comfortable with their
modes of expression.

The more serious things that can happen to women in their
minority status in groups of men include stereotyping and exclusion. Occasionally women can be isolated and made to feel
like outsiders so that they neither have the chance to demonstrate their competence or benefit from the group's activity.
Such outright exclusion was *not* reported by the sales women,
but several women did recall occasions on which they were not
taken seriously, were the target of male jokes, about which they
learned only indirectly, or, in one case, were given less impor-

tant and less educational work to do as a trainee than the men were.

The first women and the rare women in a male field also have to contend with their unexpectedness; the fact that women are not expected to be doing what they are doing. One consequence is "mistaken identity." Women in sales and even customer service may be taken for something else, for what a "typical" woman would be doing in such a situation. This is not a serious problem or one that cannot be easily solved, but it represents a nuisance, an annoyance, a reminder of second-class citizenship, and a source of extra energy to correct. In the office or answering the phone, for example, a woman may be taken for a secretary. "Many times when my supervisor is out I fill in for him if any special problems come up. And everytime someone'll come and say, please take a call for X. I'll go out and they'll say—ok, are you his secretary? As soon as I give my hand, it is automatically assumed I'm his secretary. And another question they always ask—are you Miss or Mrs.? Why that makes a difference, I don't know. They constantly say—are you Miss or Mrs. And I'll say Ms. and they'd say, ok, Miss, ok."

One professional woman solved this on the telephone by answering the phone by her last name, something no secretary does. Another sales woman has decided not to treat other women in the way she's been treated when *she* makes calls. "I call and somebody will answer and I'll give my name and say, this is the question I have and I just relate the question and usually they'll say, well I'm not the right person to answer it, or something like that. That way, you don't have to ask the question: Are you his secretary? Are you his assistant?"

Sometimes the mistaken identity issue can arouse enough anger in the women involved that she mis-handles the situation. One woman was part of a trainee group with three men. The manager called all four in to the office to tell them who would sit in for whom as summer replacements. The men were assigned to sit in for sales reps, she for a secretary—even though a rep's job was open. She became so angry that she walked away, leaving the phones ringing and going over to sales anyway, probably hurting herself in the process. Another woman commented: "This problem's typical and the trainee's reaction is explainable. It points out the need for women to participate in training to gain skills in how to handle such frustrations so that we can maintain our own integrity and pursue our goals.

Other confusions of identity can happen while travelling in or out of the office. The woman out with a man may be assumed to be a wife or a lover rather than a professional colleague. When a woman goes out of town on sales calls with a man: "On the road there are insinuations all the time—at motels, especially if we ask for rooms close to each other, the desk clerk hands the key to the man and winks, giving me an adjoining room." "When we first walk in, customers assume I'm the wife." "Even if I make the reservations and I'm paying the bill, restaurants assume he's in charge and that he's my husband or date." Most of these situations, again, are more a source of annoyance and embarrassment than a detriment to effective business performance.

But one mistaken identity issue that may arise does have business consequences: the assumption that when a man and woman are together, he is in charge and she is the secretary-wife-assistant-subordinate. One experienced sales woman says that when she goes on a call with a man she is used to the customer talking to the man rather than to her; this does not necessarily change the nature of her relationship to that account, but the fact that men are used to talking to other men as though they are in charge does change the tempo of the call.

Sexual overtures stemming from the assumption that a woman travelling or seen alone is sexually available—some from almost total strangers—are easy to handle by, as one woman put it, "freezing them out." (While this kind of mistaken identity can be relatively simply corrected, the annoyance may not be worth the energy to some women. One woman has wondered aloud whether some competent women may be scared away from sales because they don't want to have to deal with these kinds of situations.) All but one of the women interviewed had never been approached sexually by a customer. Customers may have tried to flirt a little or pick up the check for lunch, despite the woman's expense account, but male peers within the company (in training programs and at work)—not customers—seemed the only ones likely to "sexualize" the atmosphere and make encounters "date"-like rather than business-like.

Women handle instances of mistaken identity by forthright self-assertion. If women are clear about their own identity and their own purposes in a situation, they can easily communicate this to others. ("When I'm on business I try to keep my business purposes firmly in mind and communicate these in every possible way." "I let people know who I am by my manner and bearing.") If, on the other hand, a woman is unsure of herself or confused about her role and motives, then it is harder to make the necessary corrections. One woman reported that another one complained about how men with whom she had business dealings continually treated her in sexual rather than business terms. But according to the woman observing her, her own signals were mixed and unclear, and she never quite declared herself off limits.

The counterpart of incorrect assumptions about a woman's identity and role is the surprise that may occur when women are found in "male" roles or realms. It is common for saleswomen who use their initials to be taken for a man. Sally J. Smith gets mail addressed to Mr. and Mrs. S. J. Smith; an insurance agent assumes Sally Smith is Mr. Smith; Sally Smith's name on the American Express mailing list reads "Mr." The first woman to enter men's domains may create all kinds of surprises. "The guys in the office used to say, I've never seen anyone get so excited about [technical products], let alone a *girl*." When a woman was given a managerial job, some of her subordinates said, "Now there'll be no more fishing trips." She said, "Why not?" and proceeded to surprise them with her interest in fishing.

A man reported both his surprise and new awareness when he had to deal with a woman in a new way: "I remember when I was younger, if ever I called up, especially if I was calling for something regarding a mechanical part or replace a part for a car, or something like that. There's a woman on the phone, invariably my immediate reaction is, oh, I'm gonna have to explain everything, of course women don't know anything about technical stuff or things like that. And just last week I guess it kind of hit home. I had to call some company. I guess it was about a dunning letter about not paying a bill, and I had to call and straighten it out, and it was signed C. Blish. So I asked for Mr. Blish and ended up speaking to *Miss* Blish. And I remember my reaction when it ended up being Miss Blish. We started talking and she said she was the Credit Manager. My immediate reaction was to think negatively. But as I talked to her, I found out she really knew what she was talking about. That started to turn my head around. I wonder how we can translate that enlightenment to other people."

One salesman told about the surprise he caused a customer by bringing a woman along on a call—but the story had an even more surprising ending. "I remember making a joint call with Joan when I was on the road and she was a trainee. I went in and introduced her to a customer. And he just laughed for about ten minutes. I don't know if it was funny, or he was amused. He just laughed." "Had you told him that you were bringing her in?" someone else asked. "No, I just said I was bringing in a sales trainee. He couldn't believe it; he said, What will they do next. . . . But it ended up that the person who ran the company, his chief engineer, was a *woman*. Joan spent about forty minutes with her, and they hit it off famously. That probably did me a lot of good on the account."

There is a moral to these stories. It may be surprising at first to see women doing things formerly reserved for men, but it can be even more surprising to discover that the woman who was mistaken for a secretary or a wife or an easy pick-up in a hotel can turn out to be the chief engineer. The *second* time a woman is discovered in unexpected circumstances is not so surprising. And the third time her presence and behavior may even be taken for granted.

MAKING PERSONAL RELATIONS IN A BUSINESS CONTEXT

The fact is, people in business do not always relate to each other in strictly business terms. There is often the question of friendships, of social life, and of how much of one's personal life becomes connected to the job and the office. This may be a particular issue in sales, since part of what salesmen do is to entertain customers and to be available for socializing outside of the routine office setting. For women, a number of issues arise about managing these more personal relations—with customers as well as fellow workers—so as to remain professional at all times.

Several of the women made it clear that a woman absolutely needs to avoid even the appearance of compromising situations. The company gossip network guarantees that everyone will know about it if a woman gets involved with someone in the company or at a training program. "Two people in the office were dating, and everyone else knew everything that happened." "There was an office party, and one of the women brought a date at the request of the men, who said they'd feel more comfortable if she did. So she brought a man, and he was talked about all next week." The solution for a single woman, according to one successful sales woman, is to "have a booming social life outside the company. After I saw how another woman was discussed endlessly. I decided it was better, it was protection, to keep my personal life separate."

One of the problems for women is that many men seem available for "nonprofessional" relationships, and women need to be careful not to get involved. Said one: "When I first went into the business world I was depressed about men, like the creeps in the elevator who try to pick you up and have wives at home, kids. It was a shock. The men have lots of opportunities, and wives sometimes choose not to see that their men have them. There are opportunities for women too, because there's always a guy who is willing."

Training programs represent a time when personal management is important. Women, particularly the only woman, get a lot of attention from the men who are now away from home. How to have a social life at programs was an issue for several women. "The group develops fast, and if you begin to join in, there is pressure to continue. The togetherness is okay for guys, but not for a woman. It's difficult because you do want to be part of the group, don't want to be ostracized. But you can't be overwhelmed by the attention and must keep it in perspective. And above all, you must be careful of what you do, because openness stops when you leave."

Several women, especially single ones, were concerned to maintain good relations with wives, of both customers and men from the office. One reports that when she first came to the office, the men were uncertain about how their wives would react to her presence: "The men didn't know how to act around me in their wives' presences because they didn't know me that well. They were acting differently all of a sudden with their wives around. But that changed after a while, and I know the wives pretty well now." An experienced sales woman makes it a point to seek the wives out at parties, and she also tries to include the customer's wife, along with a date for herself, if she takes a male customer out for dinner. Another one takes customers out on a boat in nice weather, with her husband and their wives included.

Relations with wives seem to work out very smoothly for the sales women interviewed—even in those few cases where the husband's behavior might have created a problem. In several situations, men going out on the road with women might make or receive "jokes" such as, "We're going to share a room," or, "Good luck: his wife is the jealous type." In one case a man made a fuss to his wife about how he was playing golf with a trainee that turned out to be a woman. She later met the wife and they established a good relationship, but she also felt angry at and a little used by the man. One message here is that men's *fantasies* about a woman could cause problems for her even if her behavior is absolutely businesslike and absolutely above reproach. In this case, men need to change.

Each woman sets her own standards and draws her own limits. One refuses to go out drinking after work with men from the office, while another one enjoys doing it in a group. One prefers to see customers over lunch rather than dinner: "You don't have to fight anyone to pick up the tab for lunch, but dinner is different—dressier, more date-like." One effective saleswoman has another rule: she refuses to get cornered into listening to men's personal troubles, especially of the my-wife-doesn't-understand-me variety. "Men talking about their personal lives represent trouble. For example, a salesman in family difficulties wanted to take me out to dinner just to talk . . . I turned him down." She also stressed the importance of saying something to men *before* they make advances. "Men have a tendency to take women out and test them about their sexual availability, just as a matter of course. So I head them off before that happens, sometimes making a joke—like, 'I'll pay for dessert, because I'm not it.'"

For the most part, when women are clear about the messages they send, know themselves what kinds of things are "off limits," and are not bringing their own social needs into the office, then they have very few problems. This is one area where the burden of good conduct falls on the woman, even though men's approaches and men's fantasies may create the difficult situations. Professional women learn to manage these more personal situations, but they also indicate a wish that men would change *their* attitudes and behavior.

WOMAN TO WOMAN:
SALES WOMEN AND SECRETARIES

There has occasionally been uncertainty in the business world about how women behave as bosses and managers and how secretaries would feel about working for a woman rather than a man. For the saleswoman, working with secretaries has turned out to be one of the least problematic aspects of their jobs—once they have learned about good management. The amount of personal, woman-to-woman contact between saleswomen and secretaries varies. Some women never see secretaries socially, while others make a point to do it occasionally. Personal contacts can interfere with a business relationship, but only if the saleswoman involved lets them. Said one, "I saw my secretary socially. Once in a while I had a problem when I wanted to get something done. I had to push her because there was too much work for the number of secretaries in the office. But the advantages of our relationship outweighed the disadvantages; areas of correspondence opened up."

A saleswoman indicated the learning she acquired about how to use a secretary's talents and energies: "I had been taught to defer, to do it myself rather than ask. One day I wanted a letter typed, and the secretary couldn't do it because she was going to the bank for another salesman. I decided that was the end. Now I use her, and that frees up a lot of my time . . . It is harder for a woman to get good work from a secretary when the woman is self-effacing and acts like the low man on the totem pole. I've learned that when I'm demanding I get equal time."

Some secretaries are concerned at first about working with women, either in sales or customer service. But the women interviewed indicated that this concern tended to go away. Eventually, in some cases, a hidden advantage of working for a professional woman opened up; the professional was a role model for the secretary and could help develop her talents and aspirations. Several women reported helping their secretaries to see their own potential.

FIGHTING STEREOTYPES

There are still a number of stereotypes and traditional attitudes that women in sales must fight and that affect the prospects for the success of exempt women in the company in general. Several people, both women and men, have remarked
that women must overcome a vague and persisting feeling that
women simply cannot do certain jobs. Said a staff member,
"There are many cases where sales trainees, young people, resent women doing the same job they are doing. Time and time
again, I am asked by sales trainees, How do you feel about
women being in sales? And in my typical way I say, 'What's
behind the question.' What it usually is is that they resent the
women doing the same thing that they are because women
should be nurses or secretaries or school teachers. The implication is, they shouldn't be doing what I'm doing because then
they're as good as I am. It exists."

Even in customer service, which employs a much greater
number of women than sales, a similar feeling lingers: "The
same kind of feeling: 'Hey, *she* can't do the job,' persists. I don't
think it's nearly as strong as it was two years ago, three years
ago, but it's still there."

The persistence of negative attitudes can mean that men will
look for excuses not to use women in certain capacities. But
even well-meaning men sometimes base their assumptions and
decisions around women on stereotypes rather than accurate,
up-to-date information. The issue about which women had
most complaints in this regard was what men said about
women and marriage.

The issue of marriage is often used to exclude women from
desirable positions and from challenging opportunities such as
travel. The excuse is contradictory, in the experience of the
women interviewed; sometimes the message is that being single
is an advantage, sometimes that it's a disadvantage. Single
women are told that they cannot be given important jobs because they're likely to get married and leave (even 40 year old
single women have been told this). One manager said that he
would wait about five years before promoting a competent
woman to see if she "falls into marriage." On the other hand,
married women cannot be given important jobs because of

their family responsibilities—their children, if they are working mothers; their unborn children and the danger that they'll
leave with pregnancy, if currently childless. One manager
present indicated that he has never even considered asking a
married woman to do anything that involved travel, even if
this was in the interests of her career development.

Married women also face the prevalent feeling that "married
women are absent more;" yet one woman, married with children, had taken off only one day in 11 years. The stories the
women told are revealing. One asked her manager for a promotion; he replied, "You're probably going to get pregnant!" So
she pointed out to him that he told her that eight years ago, and
she hadn't. She wondered how long she had to work to prove
she was serious about her career. A divorced woman similarly
discussed promotion with her manager and was asked, "How
long do you want the job? Do you think you'll get married
again?"

One important conclusion to be drawn from the experiences
of [the industrial sales] women is that what they want most of
all is the opportunity to demonstrate their talents. They want
to do not just a good job, but an outstanding one. The things
that get in their way are: inappropriate selection and orientation to the company; insufficient feedback from managers;
some stereotyped feedback held by men; the visibility of and
not always-welcomed attention paid to the "first" women; and
some difficulties of being nearly the only woman in a group of
men. There are also a number of heartening success stories: of
outstanding women developing their own strategies for business success and coping with a world of men.

If women face a set of new experiences as they enter positions
formerly held only by men, the same can be said for men in the
company as they deal with the women coming in. Women need
to listen to men as much as men need to listen to women, in
order to maximize their own effectiveness.

A GAMUT OF MEN'S REACTIONS

The presence of women and heightened awareness of the
women's issue can create a great deal of uncertainty and awkwardness for men that might make them want to avoid women.

As relations between the sexes change and women appear in men's territories, even routine encounters become problematic: opening doors, pulling out chairs, shaking hands. Some men have little problem with these routines, but others express concerns: "I have a problem in day-to-day dealings with women—it's a personal hang-up. Just that when I'm introduced to a woman, I never extend my hand. I wait for her to move to shake hands. Should I, I guess I'm saying? I guess I should; why not?" One man said that his awkwardness comes from confusing messages. He learned how to treat women from relating to his wife, who wants the traditional treatment. Now he finds that those old courtesies make the women at work angry. When he meets a new woman, he finds it hard to figure out whether to behave the old way or not, and he doesn't want to offend her by being wrong. "I wish women would help us out more," he said, "by saying what they want."

Language becomes a sensitive issue. A manager reflected: "There's a problem of vocabulary in dealing with women who are now sensitive to what they are being called. And do you call them females? They don't like that in some cases. Johnson and Johnson, which has a great number of female employees, has actually stated a principle: in all communications, in all vocal interchanges, you use the word female. You don't talk about women, you don't talk about girls, they are females . . . In conversations I'll hear men switch back two or three times in terms of what they call them."

Because of such new awarenesses in the relations between men and women, because once taken for granted behavior can no longer be automatically invoked, men sometimes feel on edge around women in new situations, particularly if they want to make a good impression. Said one man: "That need to make an impression, plus the fact that the interaction can be like a mating dance, maybe that's a pressure that comes when you have women in a group. You have to choose your words very carefully, smile, grin, be agreeable."

Concerns that women might be ready to attack men for "chauvinist" treatment can also lead to feelings of resentment on the part of men. Even liberal men admit resenting the discomfort women sometimes cause, the special attention given to women's complaints. Said one: "I have a vision of a manager in New York with a cigar saying, 'Oh, there they go bitching again about this because they're women again. Don't bother me with that garbage.' And that's pretty much what I myself was thinking."

Anger and negativity on the part of women is likely to arouse defensiveness as well as resentment from men. Men often report feeling unfairly stereotyped and unfairly accused of mistreating women—and sometimes not as individuals, but as part of a generic category. One man reported, "At times I feel myself defending either men, in general, from being stereotyped, or me in particular from being stereotyped as a male with certain ideas." This kind of concern can make it difficult for men to listen to women's complaints about their situation, for instead of empathizing fully with the woman, they may be putting themselves in the situation of the other men, wondering how they have acted or reacted in a similar role. This can be one explanation for an impatience some men exhibit around the women's issue, out of their identification with the "men" or "the system" being accused.

Sometimes, too, men can feel attacked by women just by having the issues raised at all. Suddenly the power is in the hands of women—to evaluate men by some new and occasionally hidden standards. Men may perceive women talking about the issue with the righteous security of the traditional victim, the one who is "done to" and who has the right to accuse without accepting any of the responsibility. But men see themselves being labelled as the bad guys—and resent it. One man offered a vivid and revealing image of how it felt to be part of a men's group talking while women listened: "I was sitting there in that circle, and the image came to mind that it was like being in a wagon train. There we were with our wagons together and here were these spear throwers or arrow shooters. I was really conscious of what was going on behind my back. I thought I was almost talking too much. I felt that strong arrows could be shot."

Men can feel that it's easy for women to talk about the issue because they see themselves as being in the right, but men find it hard to get into the issue if it appears to be equivalent to admitting guilt. Said one: "Women do talk in specifics, and men in generalities about this issue. It's okay for women to talk about themselves and their relations and interfaces with men and how they're treated and mistreated. But I find what I'm asked to do is bare my soul and admit, yes, I do act like that, or I've said that, and then I don't even get a sympathetic response. I find it very difficult to do. I *do* get defensive."

If men can resent being labelled and attacked, they can also resent it when women don't accept any of the responsibility for their situation. Men have sometimes seen women as deliberately playing into the very roles women complain about. One man said: "I think there are two sides to every issue. I think women are totally justified in being angry if they're thought of as sex objects and those kinds of things. But there is another side to it that could really tick a man off, and that is I think women use their sexuality to their advantage very often." The message from men to women is: You can't have it both ways.

Some men perceive women as having power now in the business as well as interpersonal realm, as being singled out for special treatment and gaining an unfair advantage. Men do not automatically resent this (or admit to resenting it) if they are confident in their own abilities and if the women in question are qualified and competent. A young salesman talked about not having concerns about competing with women but letting the attention they're getting spur him on to greater effort: "I'm not worried yet. I feel I've got a couple of years on them—but they're getting closer. You look at the situation and you say, now [an executive] has to bring women up, so they will go zooming by. And, you tell yourself: boy, you're not going to let them. So maybe it's an incentive. You're going to work just as hard, if not harder, than they are. And if they do beat you to it because they're more qualified, then they're a better person. And if they do—fine. They deserve it."

But there still lingers the question about whether women are getting ahead because of their competence or because of their sex and affirmative action pressure. Said one man "When a woman gets a promotion, my guess is that most men would tend to react: it isn't because she's better qualified than me, it's because the company wants to have women in certain positions regardless of whether that was the reason or not. I think I would react that way." Said another: "My personal feeling is, if they're qualified, okay. If they're using their sex as a political weapon to get ahead, I don't like it. Maybe I'm envious, that that's the game. I don't choose to play. They choose to play politics and get ahead. And maybe that's envy because I don't want to play the game . . . But yeah, I do think I resent it. I resent it when a guy does it too."

Undeniably competition is one of the underlying concerns men have as women enter former men's territories. The uncertainty about how to behave around women or how women will respond to them is only part of a larger uncertainty about what will happen to men as workers, company members, husbands, and men, as the women's movement marches forward. The issue, as one man put it, is not door openings or language or whether women have the technical competence to do men's work, but: "Business! We're going to be competing for the same standards increasingly. We're going to be out there selling to the same kinds of customers and therefore measurable along the same dimensions. Now suppose I get out-competed by one woman, more women, lots of women—that really is an issue in terms of my whole self-image, my masculinity, my definition of what's important about me, what it means to be a man in this society. I think it's different for different people, and I don't want to overstate it, but people have to be scared about it. A lot of the fright is simply from unknown issues. We don't know, we can't talk about it, we all assume that all kinds of things are going to happen, but since we can never show it, I build it up inside myself, and I can't admit to you, another man, that I'm scared—what do you care? How can I say that to somebody? So there's a whole set of patterns that make it very difficult to deal with the problem . . . These ripples of fear go right through the company. That's why the rumors go around so fast about the women: There's another one in Dallas . . ."

IT'S POSSIBLE TO CHANGE ATTITUDES

Attitude change can sometimes occur surprisingly fast. Some men retain traditional attitudes toward women simply because they have never experienced anything different. The first time a woman is encountered in a new way can be awkward and surprising, but once the surprise is over, new sets of expectations are put into motion. Three men talked about three different situations in which their awareness was enlarged.

Seeing women as a promotable resource: (After watching a

film made by IBM in which a competent woman was ignored for a promotion because it never occurred to her manager and she had never expressed an interest.) "I had a situation in which I fired a black man in the job and pressure was on to replace him with another minority. My vision focused on black as a minority. But now I see that there was my resource potential right in the office—an experienced woman—and she and I never talked about it. I never thought about her as interested in doing the job, never really gave it a thought. This has been a real awakening for me. Not just from the film, but when I did hear afterward when I left the office that she had accepted the job, I said, wow, what did I miss. My vision was very narrow. But now I see that when looking at the total human resources you have within an organization, there are a lot more people available if you just open your mind."

A woman taking charge: "I stopped by a program to visit with a sales woman calling on one of my account's purchasing locations. We went out to a bar after the program. We were sitting there, having a few drinks, talking about the customer, and it was about 6:30 or 7. I thought, gee, here we've been talking about an hour, certainly I planned to ask her if she would like to have dinner. And before I had a chance—which would be a new thing that I had planned to do—she said, 'I really enjoyed this; I would like you to be my guest for dinner tonight. I thought, *'You're* going to take me out to dinner. This is a whole new experience for me.' . . . This was an unusual and very rewarding experience for me to have a young, attractive woman take an old guy like me out for dinner. We talked business. Then it came time for the check. And obviously I reached for it. She grabbed the check ahead of me. We were having this big confrontation in the restaurant, but this was very flattering to me, and I certainly enjoyed it. I can imagine now that if this woman were calling on me on business—I'm the customer—and she takes me out to lunch and picks up the check, I would think that relationship would be very interesting and rewarding. I must say that this was a new and novel experience for me."

Stereotypes of women: "When I was younger, my mother programmed me to think of women as being gentle, quiet, nice. You don't play football with women because they might get hurt—that kind of thing. And I guess the first representative that I found who was not that way was my wife. She's very strong and outspoken. I have to admit that the first time I met her, I got that kind of interaction, and I was shocked. I was shocked because everything that I had been told was suddenly maybe not right. You know: here's something different, here was a person who did not fit into the criteria which had been described for me all the way along. Now I find it very refreshing. But I can still remember that day when I think she told me to go—in my hat—her exact words. I blubbered, 'You're not supposed to . . . You're a woman . . . You don't say that.' It was quite a shocking experience which I'm glad happened. And it changed my idea of what a woman was."

A FEW CONCLUSIONS

Some problems are not "women's" problems at all. Some of the issues discussed in this Handbook are certainly encountered by women but should not be labelled "women's" problems; they are, rather, the problems of the *young*, the *inexperienced*, the *new-hire* in general. In fact, many men have reported that they have or face a number of the same problems as women report; a section of the report discusses these reactions in greater detail. To provide solutions to some of these problems for women can thus be beneficial to men, too—it is recognized that many issues arise because of *situation*, because of organizational circumstance, and not because of sex. Women per se do *not* necessarily have special needs in organizations; although the traditional roles open to women and their relative rarity in sales positions *might* create a special set of circumstances for the first women to break out of traditional roles. Perhaps this report will be useful for managers of all new-hires—men as well as women.

Women are not all alike. In talking about the *consequences* of unfair stereotyping of women in the past, we do not want to be creating a *new* set of stereotypes about the problems of women in fields formerly open only to men. There are great differences as well as similarities among women—in attitudes, feelings, and behavior, and in the problems (if any) they have encountered in sales. This report can be read as a set of "probabilities"—things that *might* happen because they have happened to at least some of the women in sales. But it is not a picture of all women under all circumstances. Awareness and support for women's success also means acknowledging the uniqueness of each woman as a distinctive person in a distinctive situation.

It is harder at first. Many of the problem situations described here are the problems of new-ness: the *first* few women in sales, the *first* time a woman does something, the *first* time a man encounters a woman in a new way, the *first* few minutes of a new relationship, the *first* entrance of a woman into a group. Some of the kinds of things women face get easier or even disappear with time. As relationships are built, as men get used to women, as customers look beyond a woman's appearance at her competence, then a woman's sex becomes less and less relevant to her business performance and the responses she gets may be indistinguishable from those given to a man. Over time, people become capable of seeing each other as individuals rather than as members of categories like "woman" or "youth." When women talk about the problems they have faced, they almost invariably report that *time* helps solve them. There is a period of adjustment for women, even a trial period in which a woman has to work harder to gain acceptance, but once that period is over, her problems may disappear. So, more experienced women, or women with longer-standing relationships with peers, managers and customers, are much less likely to encounter the problems that are faced by newer women or faced briefly each time a woman enters a new situation with new people who do not yet know her.

Parts of the country are different. Regional variations should also be kept in mind. The South, for example, is more traditional in its attitudes toward women, and women may find it more difficult to operate in non-traditional ways. New York and other major metropolitan areas are less traditional, and women in these regions are unlikely to have some of the problems we have identified, such as restaurants not wanting to provide separate expense records or hotels assuming a woman must be somebody's wife.

Male-female communication is sometimes cross-cultural communication. Finally, it is important to remember that just because men and women come together under so many circumstances in our society and appear to be speaking English, they do not necessarily understand each other. To some extent,

women and men constitute different cultures with different
languages and cannot always automatically understand the experience of the other sex. More of the male-female difficulties
we discovered in preparing this report came from misunder-
standings than from ill will. Sometimes a woman thought that
what a man said was petty and couldn't understand why it was
so important to him; and men sometimes had difficulty understanding what women were complaining about. Women, too,
can easily be unaware of the problem other women face and
unable to empathize. So it is important to try to understand
where the other person—or another sex or same sex—is coming
from, to try to put yourself in his or her shoes, just as we would
for somebody coming from a strange or different culture.

9 / "Why Should My Conscience Bother Me?"

Kermit Vandivier

THE B. F. GOODRICH CO. is what business magazines like to
speak of as "a major American corporation." It has operations
in a dozen states and as many foreign countries, and of these
far-flung facilities, the Goodrich plant at Troy, Ohio, is not the
most imposing. It is a small, one-story building, employing only
about six hundred people. Nevertheless, it is one of the three
largest manufacturers of aircraft wheels and brakes, a leader in
a most profitable industry. . . .

Contracts for aircraft wheels and brakes often run into millions of dollars, and ordinarily a contract with a total value of
less than $70,000, though welcome, would not create any spe-
cial stir of joy in the hearts of Goodrich sales personnel. But
purchase order P-23718, issued on June 18, 1967, by the LTV

Aerospace Corporation, and ordering 202 brake assemblies for a new Air Force plane at a total price of $69,417, was received by Goodrich with considerable glee. And there was a good reason. Some ten years previously, Goodrich had built a brake for LTV that was, to say the least, considerably less than a rousing success. The brake had not lived up to Goodrich's promises, and after experiencing considerable difficulty, LTV had written off Goodrich as a source of brakes. Since that time, Goodrich salesmen had been unable to sell so much as a shot of brake fluid to LTV. So in 1967, when LTV requested bids on wheels and brakes for the new A7D light attack aircraft it proposed to build for the Air Force, Goodrich submitted a bid that was absurdly low, so low that LTV could not, in all prudence, turn it down.

Goodrich had, in industry parlance, "bought into the business." Not only did the company not expect to make a profit on the deal; it was prepared, if necessary, to lose money. For aircraft brakes are not something that can be ordered off the shelf. They are designed for a particular aircraft, and once an aircraft manufacturer buys a brake, he is forced to purchase all replacement parts from the brake manufacturer. The $70,000 that Goodrich would get for making the brake would be a drop in the bucket when compared with the cost of the linings and other parts the Air Force would have to buy from Goodrich during the lifetime of the aircraft. Furthermore, the company which manufactures brakes for one particular model of an aircraft quite naturally has the inside track to supply other brakes when the planes are updated and improved.

Thus, that first contract, regardless of the money involved, is very important, and Goodrich, when it learned that it had been awarded the A7D contract, was determined that while it may have slammed the door on its own foot ten years before, this time, the second time around, things would be different. The word was soon circulated throughout the plant: "We can't bungle it this time. We've got to give them a good brake, regardless of the cost."

There was another factor which had undoubtedly influenced LTV. All aircraft brakes made today are of the disk type, and the bid submitted by Goodrich called for a relatively small brake, one containing four disks and weighing only 106 pounds. The weight of any aircraft part is extremely important. The lighter a part is, the heavier the plane's payload can be. The four-rotor, 106-pound brake promised by Goodrich was about as light as could be expected, and this undoubtedly had helped move LTV to award the contract to Goodrich.

The brake was designed by one of Goodrich's most capable engineers, John Warren. A tall, lanky blond and a graduate of Purdue, Warren had come from the Chrysler Corporation seven years before and had become adept at aircraft brake design. The happy-go-lucky manner he usually maintained belied a temper which exploded whenever anyone ventured to offer any criticism of his work, no matter how small. On these occasions, Warren would turn red in the face, often throwing or slamming something and then stalking from the scene. As his coworkers learned the consequences of criticizing him, they did so less and less readily, and when he submitted his preliminary design for the A7D brake, it was accepted without question.

Warren was named project engineer for the A7D, and he, in turn, assigned the task of producing the final production design to a newcomer to the Goodrich engineering stable, Searle Lawson. Just turned twenty-six, Lawson had been out of the Northrup Institute of Technology only one year when he came to Goodrich in January 1967. . . .

Procedures for new brakes were highly standardized. After preliminary testing and after the brake was judged ready for production, one whole brake assembly would undergo a series of grueling, simulated braking stops and other severe trials called qualification tests. These tests are required by the military, which gives very detailed specifications on how they are to be conducted, the criteria for failure, and so on. They are performed in the Goodrich plant's test laboratory, where huge machines called dynamometers can simulate the weight and speed of almost any aircraft. After the brakes pass the laboratory tests, they are approved for production, but before the brakes are accepted for use in military service, they must undergo further extensive flight tests.

Searle Lawson was well aware that much work had to be done before the A7D brake could go into production, and he knew that LTV had set the last two weeks in June, 1968, as the starting dates for flight tests. So he decided to begin testing immediately. . . . The main purpose of these preliminary tests was to learn what temperatures would develop within the brake during the simulated stops and to evaluate the lining materials tentatively selected for use.

During a normal aircraft landing the temperatures inside the brake may reach 1000 degrees, and occasionally a bit higher. During Lawson's first simulated landings, the temperature of his prototype brake reached 1500 degrees. The brake glowed a bright cherry-red and threw off incandescent particles of metal and lining material as the temperature reached its peak. After a few such stops, the brake was dismantled and the linings were found to be almost completely disintegrated. Lawson chalked this first failure up to chance and, ordering new lining materials, tried again.

The second attempt was a repeat of the first. The brake became extremely hot, causing the lining materials to crumble into dust.

After the third such failure, Lawson, inexperienced though he was, knew that the fault lay not in defective parts or unsuitable lining material but in the basic design of the brake itself. Ignoring Warren's original computations, Lawson made his own, and it didn't take him long to discover where the trouble lay—the brake was too small. There simply was not enough surface area on the disks to stop the aircraft without generating the excessive heat that caused the linings to fail.

The answer to the problem was obvious but far from simple—the four-disk brake would have to be scrapped, and a new design, using five disks, would have to be developed. The implications were not lost on Lawson. Such a step would require the junking of all the four-disk-brake subassemblies, many of which had now begun to arrive from the various suppliers. It would also mean several weeks of preliminary design and testing and many more weeks of waiting while the suppliers made and delivered the new subassemblies.

Yet, several weeks had already gone by since LTV's order had arrived, and the date for delivery of the first production brakes for flight testing was only a few months away.

Although project engineer John Warren had more or less turned the A7D over to Lawson, he knew of the difficulties Lawson had been experiencing. He had assured the young engineer that the problem revolved around getting the right kind of lining material. Once that was found, he said, the difficulties would end.

Despite the evidence of the abortive tests and Lawson's careful computations, Warren rejected the suggestion that the four-disk brake was too light for the job. Warren knew that his superior had already told LTV, in rather glowing terms, that the preliminary tests on the A7D brake were very successful. Indeed, Warren's superiors weren't aware at this time of the troubles on the brake. It would have been difficult for Warren to admit not only that he had made a serious error in his calculations and original design but that his mistakes had been caught by a green kid, barely out of college.

Warren's reaction to a five-disk brake was not unexpected by Lawson, and, seeing that the four-disk brake was not to be abandoned so easily, he took his calculations and dismal test results one step up the corporate ladder.

At Goodrich, the man who supervises the engineers working on projects slated for production is called, predictably, the projects manager. The job was held by a short, chubby and bald man named Robert Sink. . . . Some fifteen years before, Sink had begun working at Goodrich as a lowly draftsman. Slowly, he worked his way up. Despite his geniality, Sink was neither respected nor liked by the majority of the engineers, and his appointment as their supervisor did not improve their feelings about him. They thought he had only gone to high school. It quite naturally rankled those who had gone through years of college and acquired impressive specialities such as thermodynamics and astronautics to be commanded by a man whom they considered their intellectual inferior. But, though Sink had no college training, he had something even more useful: a fine working knowledge of company politics.

Puffing upon a Meerschaum pipe, Sink listened gravely as young Lawson confided his fears about the four-disk brake. Then he examined Lawson's calculations and the results of the abortive tests. Despite the fact that he was not a qualified engineer, in the strictest sense of the word, it must certainly have been obvious to Sink that Lawson's calculations were correct and that a four-disk brake would never have worked on the A7D.

But other things of equal importance were also obvious. First, to concede that Lawson's calculations were correct would also mean conceding that Warren's calculations were incorrect. As projects manager, he not only was responsible for Warren's activities, but, in admitting that Warren had erred, he would have to admit that he had erred in trusting Warren's judgment. It also meant that, as projects manager, it would be he who would have to explain the whole messy situation to the

Goodrich hierarchy, not only at Troy but possibly on the corporate level at Goodrich's Akron offices. And, having taken Warren's judgment of the four-disk brake at face value (he was forced to do this since, not being an engineer, he was unable to exercise any engineering judgment of his own), he had assured LTV, not once but several times, that about all there was left to do on the brake was pack it in a crate and ship it out the back door.

There's really no problem at all, he told Lawson. After all, Warren was an experienced engineer, and if he said the brake would work, it would work. Just keep on testing and probably, maybe even on the very next try, it'll work out just fine. . . .

The first qualification attempts went exactly as the tests on the prototype had. Terrific heat developed within the brakes and, after a few, short, simulated stops, the linings crumbled. A new type of lining material was ordered and once again an attempt to qualify the brake was made. Again, failure.

Experts were called in from lining manufacturers, and new lining "mixes" were tried, always with the same result. Failure.

It was now the last week in March 1968, and flight tests were scheduled to begin in seventy days. Twelve separate attempts had been made to formally qualify the brake, and all had failed. It was no longer possible for anyone to ignore the glaring truth that the brake was a dismal failure and that nothing short of a major design change could ever make it work.

In the engineering department, panic set in. . . .

On April 4, the thirteenth attempt at qualification was begun. This time no attempt was made to conduct the tests by the methods and techniques spelled out in the military specifications. Regardless of how it had to be done, the brake was to be "nursed" through the required fifty simulated stops. . . .

By various methods, all clearly contrary to the techniques established by the military specifications, the brake was coaxed through the fifty stops. But even using these methods, the brake could not meet all the requirements. On one stop the wheel rolled for a distance of 16,000 feet, nearly three miles, before the brake could bring it to a stop. The normal distance required for such a stop was around 3500 feet.

On April 11, the day the thirteenth test was completed, I became personally involved in the A7D situation.

I had worked in the Goodrich test laboratory for five years, starting first as an instrumentation engineer, then later becoming a data analyst and technical writer. As part of my duties, I analyzed the reams and reams of instrumentation data that came from the many testing machines in the laboratory, then transcribed it to a more usable form for the engineering department. And when a new-type brake had successfully completed the required qualification tests, I would issue a formal qualification report.

Qualification reports were an accumulation of all the data and test logs compiled by the test technicians during the qualification tests, and were documentary proof that a brake had met all the requirements established by the military specifications and was therefore presumed safe for flight testing. Before actual flight tests were conducted on a brake, qualification reports had to be delivered to the customer and to various government officials.

On April 11, I was looking over the data from the latest A7D test, and I noticed that many irregularities in testing methods had been noted on the test logs.

Technically, of course, there was nothing wrong with conducting tests in any manner desired, so long as the test was for research purposes only. But qualification test methods are clearly delineated by the military, and I knew that this test had been a formal qualification attempt. One particular notation on the test logs caught my eye. For some of the stops, the instrument which recorded the brake pressure had been deliberately miscalibrated so that, while the brake pressure used during the stops was recorded as 1000 psi (the maximum pressure that would be available on the A7D aircraft), the pressure had actually been 1100 psi!

I showed the test logs to the test lab supervisor, Ralph Gretzinger, who said he had learned from the technician who had miscalibrated the instrument that he had been asked to do so by Lawson. Lawson, said Gretzinger, readily admitted asking for the miscalibration, saying he had been told to do so by Sink.

I asked Gretzinger why anyone would want to miscalibrate the data-recording instruments.

"Why? I'll tell you why," he snorted. "That brake is a failure. It's way too small for the job, and they're not ever going to get it to work. They're getting desperate, and instead of scrapping the damned thing and starting over, they figure they can horse around down here in the lab and qualify it that way." . . .

"If you want to find out what's going on," said Gretzinger, "ask Lawson, he'll tell you."

Curious, I did ask Lawson the next time he came into the lab. He seemed eager to discuss the A7D and gave me the history of his months of frustrating efforts to get Warren and Sink to change the brake design. "I just can't believe this is really happening," said Lawson, shaking his head slowly. "This isn't engineering, at least not what I thought it would be. Back in school, I thought that when you were an engineer, you tried to do your best, no matter what it cost. But this is something else."

He sat across the desk from me, his chin propped in his hand. "Just wait," he warned. "You'll get a chance to see what I'm talking about. You're going to get in the act, too, because I've already had the word that we're going to make one more attempt to qualify the brake, and that's it. Win or lose, we're going to issue a qualification report!"

I reminded him that a qualification report could only be issued after a brake had successfully met all military requirements, and therefore, unless the next qualification attempt was a success, no report would be issued.

"You'll find out," retorted Lawson. "I was already told that regardless of what the brake does on test, it's going to be qualified." He said he had been told in those exact words at a conference with Sink and Russell Van Horn.

This was the first indication that Sink had brought his boss, Van Horn, into the mess. Although Van Horn, as manager of the design engineering section, was responsible for the entire department, he was not necessarily familiar with all phases of every project, and it was not uncommon for those under him to exercise the what-he-doesn't-know-won't-hurt-him philosophy. . . .

If Van Horn had said, "regardless what the brake does on test, it's going to be qualified," then it could only mean that, if necessary, a false qualification report would be issued! I discussed this possibility with Gretzinger, and he assured me that under no circumstances would such a report ever be issued.

"If they want a qualification report, we'll write them one, but we'll tell it just like it is," he declared emphatically. "No false data or false reports are going to come out of this lab."

On May 2, 1968, the fourteenth and final attempt to qualify the brake was begun. Although the same improper methods used to nurse the brake through the previous tests were employed, it soon became obvious that this too would end in failure.

When the tests were about half completed, Lawson asked if I would start preparing the various engineering curves and graphic displays which were normally incorporated in a qualification report. "It looks as though you'll be writing a qualification report shortly," he said.

I flatly refused to have anything to do with the matter and immediately told Gretzinger what I had been asked to do. He was furious and repeated his previous declaration that under no circumstances would any false data or other matter be issued from the lab.

"I'm going to get this settled right now, once and for all," he declared. "I'm going to see Line [Russell Line, manager of the Goodrich Technical Services Section, of which the test lab was a part] and find out just how far this thing is going to go!" He stormed out of the room.

In about an hour, he returned and called me to his desk. He sat silently for a few moments, then muttered, half to himself, "I wonder what the hell they'd do if I just quit?" . . .

"You know," he went on uncertainly, looking down at his desk, "I've been an engineer for a long time, and I've always believed that ethics and integrity were every bit as important as theorems and formulas, and never once has anything happened to change my beliefs. Now this . . . Hell, I've got two sons I've got to put through school and I just . . ." His voice trailed off.

He sat for a few more minutes, then, looking over the top of his glasses, said hoarsely, "Well, it looks like we're licked. The way it stands now, we're to go ahead and prepare the data and other things for the graphic presentation in the report, and when we're finished, someone upstairs will actually write the report.

"After all," he continued, "we're just drawing some curves, and what happens to them after they leave here, well, we're not responsible for that."

He was trying to persuade himself that as long as we were concerned with only one part of the puzzle and didn't see the completed picture, we really weren't doing anything wrong. He didn't believe what he was saying, and he knew I didn't believe it either. It was an embarrassing and shameful moment for both of us.

I wasn't at all satisfied with the situation and decided that I too would discuss the matter with Russell Line, the senior executive in our section. ... He listened sympathetically while I explained how I felt about the A7D situation, and when I had finished, he asked me what I wanted him to do about it. I said that as employees of the Goodrich Company we had a responsibility to protect the company and its reputation if at all possible. I said I was certain that officers on the corporate level would never knowingly allow such tactics as had been employed on the A7D.

"I agree with you," he remarked, "but I still want to know what you want me to do about it."

I suggested that in all probability the chief engineer at the Troy plant, H. C. "Bud" Sunderman, was unaware of the A7D problem and that he, Line, should tell him what was going on.

Line laughed, good-humoredly. "Sure, I could, but I'm not going to. Bud probably already knows about this thing anyway, and if he doesn't, I'm sure not going to be the one to tell him."

"But why?"

"Because it's none of my business, and it's none of yours. I learned a long time ago not to worry about things over which I had no control. I have no control over this."

I wasn't satisfied with this answer, and I asked him if his conscience wouldn't bother him if, say, during flight tests on the brake, something should happen resulting in death or injury to the test pilot.

"Look," he said, becoming somewhat exasperated, "I just told you I have no control over this thing. Why should my conscience bother me?"

His voice took on a quiet, soothing tone as he continued. "You're just getting all upset over this thing for nothing. I just do as I'm told, and I'd advise you to do the same."

He had made his decision, and now I had to make mine. . . .

Before coming to Goodrich in 1963, I had held a variety of jobs, each a little more pleasant, a little more rewarding than the last. At forty-two, with seven children, I had decided that the Goodrich Company would probably be my "home" for the rest of my working life. The job paid well, it was pleasant and challenging, and the future looked reasonably bright. My wife and I had bought a home and we were ready to settle down into a comfortable, middle-age, middle-class rut. If I refused to take part in the A7D fraud, I would have to either resign or be fired. The report would be written by someone anyway, but I would have the satisfaction of knowing I had had no part in the matter. But bills aren't paid with personal satisfaction, nor house payments with ethical principles. I made my decision. The next morning, I telephoned Lawson and told him I was ready to begin on the qualification report.

In a few minutes, he was at my desk, ready to begin. Before we started, I asked him, "Do you realize what we are going to do?"

"Yeah," he replied bitterly, "we're going to screw LTV. And speaking of screwing," he continued, "I know now how a whore feels, because that's exactly what I've become, an engineering whore. I've sold myself. It's all I can do to look at myself in the mirror when I shave. I make me sick."

I was surprised at his vehemence. It was obvious that he too had done his share of soul-searching and didn't like what he had found. Somehow, though, the air seemed clearer after his outburst, and we began working on the report.

I had written dozens of qualification reports, and I knew what a "good" one looked like. Resorting to the actual test data only on occasion, Lawson and I proceeded to prepare page after page of elaborate, detailed engineering curves, charts, and test logs, which purported to show what had happened during the formal qualification tests. . . .

Occasionally, we would find that some test either hadn't been performed at all or had been conducted improperly. On those occasions, we "conducted" the test—successfully, of course—on paper.

For nearly a month we worked on the graphic presentation that would be a part of the report. Meanwhile, the fourteenth and final qualification attempt had been completed, and the brake, not unexpectedly, had failed again. . . .

I saw Lawson's boss, John Warren, at least twice during that month and needled him about what we were doing. He didn't take the jibes too kindly but managed to laugh the situation off as "one of those things." One day I remarked that what we were doing amounted to fraud, and he pulled out an engineering handbook and turned to a section on laws as they related to the engineering profession.

He read the definition of fraud aloud, then said, "Well, technically I don't think what we're doing can be called fraud. I'll admit it's not right, but it's just one of those things. We're just kinda caught in the middle. About all I can tell you is, Do like I'm doing. Make copies of everything and put them in your SYA file."

"What's an 'SYA' file?" I asked.

"That's a 'save your ass' file." He laughed.

Although I hadn't known it was called that, I had been keeping an SYA file since the beginning of the A7D fiasco. I had made a copy of every scrap of paper connected even remotely with the A7D and had even had copies of 16mm movies that had been made during some of the simulated stops. Lawson, too, had an SYA file, and we both maintained them for one reason: Should the true state of events on the A7D ever be questioned, we wanted to have access to a complete set of factual data. We were afraid that should the question ever come up, the test data might accidentally be "lost."

We finished our work on the graphic portion of the report around the first of June. Altogether, we had prepared nearly two hundred pages of data, containing dozens of deliberate falsifications and misrepresentations. I delivered the data to Gretzinger, who said he had been instructed to deliver it personally to the chief engineer, Bud Sunderman, who in turn would assign someone in the engineering department to complete the written portion of the report. He gathered the bundle of data and left the office. Within minutes, he was back with the data, his face white with anger.

"That damned Sink's beat me to it," he said furiously. "He's already talked to Bud about this, and now Sunderman says no one in the engineering department has time to write the report. He wants us to do it, and I told him we couldn't."

The words had barely left his mouth when Russell Line burst in the door. "What the hell's all the fuss about this damned report?" he demanded loudly.

Patiently, Gretzinger explained. "There's no fuss. Sunderman just told me that we'd have to write the report down here, and I said we couldn't. Russ," he went on, "I've told you before that we weren't going to write the report. I made my position clear on that a long time ago."

Line shut him up with a wave of his hand and, turning to me, bellowed, "I'm getting sick and tired of hearing about this damned report. Now, write the goddam thing and shut up about it!" He slammed out of the office.

Gretzinger and I just sat for a few seconds looking at each other. Then he spoke.

"Well, I guess he's made it pretty clear, hasn't he? We can either write the thing or quit. You know, what we should have done was quit a long time ago. Now, it's too late." . . .

Still, Line's order came as something of a shock. All the time Lawson and I were working on the report, I felt, deep down, that somewhere, somehow, something would come along and the whole thing would blow over. But Russell Line had crushed that hope. The report was actually going to be issued. Intelligent, law-abiding officials of B. F. Goodrich, one of the oldest and most respected of American corporations, were actually going to deliver to a customer a product that was known to be defective and dangerous and which could very possibly cause death or serious injury. . . .

On June 5, 1968, the report was officially published and copies were delivered in person to the Air Force and LTV. Within a week, flight tests were begun at Edwards Air Force Base in California. Searle Lawson was sent to California as Goodrich's representative. Within approximately two weeks, he returned because some rather unusual incidents during the tests had caused them to be canceled.

His face was grim as he related stories of several near crashes during landings—caused by brake troubles. . . .

That evening I left work early and went to see my attorney. After I told him the story, he advised that, while I was probably not actually guilty of fraud, I was certainly part of a conspiracy to defraud. He advised me to go to the Federal Bureau of Investigation and offered to arrange an appointment. The following week he took me to the Dayton office of the FBI, and after I had been warned that I would not be immune from prosecution, I disclosed the A7D matter to one of the agents. The agent told me to say nothing about the episode to anyone and to report any further incident to him. He said he would forward the story to his superiors in Washington.

A few days later, Lawson returned from [a] conference [with LTV] in Dallas and said that the Air Force, which had previously approved the qualification report, had suddenly rescinded that approval and was demanding to see some of the raw test data taken during the tests. I gathered that the FBI had passed the word.

Omitting any reference to the FBI, I told Lawson I had been to an attorney and that we were probably guilty of conspiracy.

"Can you get me an appointment with your attorney?" he asked. Within a week, he had been to the FBI and told them of his part in the mess. He too was advised to say nothing but to keep on the job reporting any new development.

Naturally, with the rescinding of Air Force approval and the demand to see raw test data, Goodrich officials were in a panic. . . .

[A series of conferences with Lawson, Sink, Warren, and myself] were held during August and September, and the summer was punctuated with frequent treks between Dallas and Troy, and demands by the Air Force to see the raw test data. Tempers were short and matters seemed to grow worse.

Finally, early in October 1968, Lawson submitted his resignation, to take effect on October 25. On October 18, I submitted my own resignation, to take effect on November 1. In my resignation, addressed to Russell Line, I cited the A7D report and stated: "As you are aware, this report contained numerous deliberate and willful misrepresentations which, according to legal counsel, constitute fraud and expose both myself and others to criminal charges of conspiracy to defraud . . . The events of the past seven months have created an atmosphere of deceit and distrust in which it is impossible to work . . ."

On October 25, I received a sharp summons to the office of Bud Sunderman, [who] was responsible for the entire engineering division. . . . He motioned me to a chair. "I have your resignation here," he snapped, "and I must say you have made some rather shocking, I might even say irresponsible, charges. This is very serious."

Before I could reply, he was demanding an explanation. "I want to know exactly what the fraud is in connection with the A7D and how you can dare accuse this company of such a thing!"

I started to tell some of the things that had happened during the testing, but he shut me off saying, "There's nothing wrong with anything we've done here. You aren't aware of all the things that have been going on behind the scenes. If you had known the true situation, you would never have made these charges." He said that in view of my apparent "disloyalty" he had decided to accept my resignation "right now," and said it would be better for all concerned if I left the plant immediately. As I got up to leave he asked me if I intended to "carry this thing further."

I answered simply, "Yes," to which he replied, "Suit yourself." Within twenty minutes, I had cleaned out my desk and left. Forty-eight hours later, the B. F. Goodrich Company recalled the qualification report and the four-disk brake, announcing that it would replace the brake with a new, improved, five-disk brake at no cost to LTV.

Ten months later, on August 13, 1969, I was the chief government witness at a hearing conducted before Senator William Proxmire's Economy in Government Subcommittee of the Congress's Joint Economic Committee. I related the A7D story to the committee, and my testimony was supported by Searle Lawson, who followed me to the witness stand. Air Force officers also testified, as well as a four-man team from the General Accounting Office, which had conducted an investigation of the A7D brake at the request of Senator Proxmire. Both Air Force and GAO investigators declared that the brake was dangerous and had not been tested properly.

Testifying for Goodrich was R. G. Jeter, vice-president and general counsel of the company, from the Akron headquarters. Representing the Troy plant was Robert Sink. These two denied any wrongdoing on the part of the Goodrich Company, despite expert testimony to the contrary by Air Force and GAO officials. Sink was quick to deny any connection with the writing of the report or of directing any falsifications, claiming to be on the West Coast at the time. John Warren was the man who supervised its writing, said Sink. . . .

Jeter pooh-poohed the suggestion that anything improper occurred, saying: "We have thirty-odd engineers at this plant . . . and I say to you that it is incredible that these men would stand idly by and see reports changed or falsified. . . . I mean you just do not have to do that working for anybody. . . . Just nobody does that."

The four-hour hearing adjourned with no real conclusion reached by the committee. But, the following day the Department of Defense made sweeping changes in its inspection, testing and reporting procedures. A spokesman for the DOD said the changes were a result of the Goodrich episode.

The A7D is now in service, sporting a Goodrich-made five-disk brake, a brake that works very well, I'm told. Business at the Goodrich plant is good. Lawson is now an engineer for LTV and has been assigned to the A7D project. And I am now a newspaper reporter.

At this writing, those remaining at Goodrich are still secure in the same positions, all except Russell Line and Robert Sink. Line has been rewarded with a promotion to production superintendent, a large step upward on the corporate ladder. As for Sink, he moved up into Line's old job.

SECTION THREE

Making a Life at the Bottom

WHAT CONSTITUTES the "bottom" of an organization? It consists of those who stand lowest in the organization's hierarchy of command. The people at the bottom are often also rewarded the least, valued the least, and considered the most expendable and replaceable—in a sense, not fully members of the organization at all. One large company recently moved its headquarters from midtown New York City to a suburban town about seventy miles away. It paid to move all of the office personnel except the secretaries and some clerical workers, a clear sign that these were the most tenuous members of the organization, at least in its own view.

On the company's side, it could be argued that this was a mere matter of costs and benefits; that the cost of moving these people would exceed the cost of replacing and retraining them locally. This is probably true, though it is certainly less sharply so than the company thinks, because such people in fact always know more than is assumed by top management. So long as calculations are made on the basis of the work people are *supposed* to do, as against what they *actually* do, not to mention what they *could* do, the result will favor replacement. However, the key point is that the calculations are not made for individuals at all, but for categories. Secretaries and clerical personnel, with a few exceptions, are simply assumed to fall under different standards of appropriateness than the managers. Because of this and related behavior, we are entitled to see "the bottom" as a category fairly sharply bounded from "the middle."

But the real sign of being at the bottom is the degree to which a person is controlled. Tasks are defined elsewhere, other people are giving orders, and those at the bottom do not, in turn, have the right to define tasks themselves and develop commands. What distinguishes the quality of tasks at the bottom is not merely their distance from the top of the organization, but also the extent of minute specialization and the number of areas that are considered under the organization's control—in short, how little discretion, how little autonomy, how little freedom, how little influence remains. The worker, in short, is treated as though he were a child—or worse, a machine. The ultimate in lack of control is exemplified in those situations in which the worker is forced to conform to the rhythm of the machine, as on an assembly line, and is, simultaneously, forced by the rules to deny any responsiveness to the rhythm of his or her own body. For example, going to the bathroom is something workers at the Fair Plan Insurance Company were expected to do on their own time, as described by Barbara Garson in chapter 12. Similarly, on the assembly line at Lordstown, workers take bathroom breaks when scheduled. There's a clear absence of creature comforts for people at the bottom—no food or coffee, except at specified times, no chairs for sales people.

Boredom, repetition and monotony—classic features of jobs at the bottom—are themselves a product of an attempt to reduce the control of the worker over his or her work. By subdividing tasks into minute parts that can be performed repetitively by workers with relatively little skill, commitment to the organization, or knowledge of overall purposes, the organization makes workers expendable and interchangeable. Indeed, the extent to which workers at the bottom are considered easily replaceable is also indicated by the extremely short training periods that workers undergo for certain jobs—in Donald Roy's case (chapter 10), a few demonstrations of how to operate a machine; in Louisa Howe's case (chapter 13), less than a half-hour's worth of instruction.

The traditional economic argument, presented full-blown by Adam Smith in 1776, is that a minute division of labor enormously increases productivity and lowers costs, and is thus an arguable benefit. This is one principle behind "scientific management," developed by Frederic Taylor at the turn of the century. There is some evidence that Smith rather overstated the case, but even if he did not, the classical economists who followed were quick to recognize an additional benefit, namely replaceability. Workers became, almost at once, an indistinguishable swarm—the proletariat, as Marx called them. Companies have taken two routes in following up this important potential advantage to owners of many replaceable workers. One has been to maximize the potential interchangeability by setting up production systems that are built around the temporary employment of large numbers of such workers, who serve as an admirably effective buffer. When orders rise, hire more; when orders fall, lay them off. And since by definition, little or no skill or training is required, extra costs for this scheme, as compared to full-time employees, are nil. The second route has been to use machines instead of well-trained and highly skilled workers who may represent a costly investment.

But of course, by breaking down tasks into their monotonous components so as to cope with the problem of potential turnover, organizations create their own turnover problem, in response to the very monotony of the tasks. Among the many causes of the heavily publicized Lordstown, Ohio, Vega plant strike in 1972 (chapter 11) was the layoff of a large proportion of workers, thus increasing the amount of work and the pace of work for those remaining. The union was some help and protection in that situation, and the workers could strike against management. But in other situations, such as the department store, described by Louisa Howe in chapter 13, the union was little help and offered little protection. Part-time workers were hired, and many of them would leave before they developed many rights or benefits. Similarly, people at the bottom tend to be seen as part of a vast mass—for example, the 350 new people hired by Howe's store for the Christmas rush. Since power often comes out of a sense of uniqueness and non-replaceability, it is very hard for people at the bottom to gain much power. When David Mechanic (1962) wrote about power through expertise for lower participants, he assumed that they have a monopoly on knowledge that is not held elsewhere. But the minute division of labor is a way of "de-skilling" workers, confining their work to such small tasks that they can be easily replaced.

Pay is not the only indication that a job exists at the organizational bottom, for some jobs at the bottom *may* pay extremely well, while those at middle levels and in middle kinds of positions may come with less material and more symbolic reward, or less immediate and more long-term payoff. Many of the auto workers at Lordstown, indeed, commented that the pay was good (chapter 11). What concerned them was the poor quality of the work. In general, of course, pay and organizational rank go together, but under some circumstances, promotions may mean a pay cut. The most common instance is probably the transition from non-exempt skilled labor, paid at hourly rates and often including overtime, to first-line supervisor, an exempt salaried position. In some companies, the drop in real income associated with this step is enough to be a serious consideration for candidates.

Lack of power in positions at the bottom tends to be coupled with lack of opportunity—with minimal, if any, chance to grow and develop. This is especially true for the jobs with least acquired skill attached. There are, of course, some "good" jobs at the bottom for crafts workers and skilled laborers who are highly paid and who, because they exercise clear individual skills, work with a relatively high degree of autonomy and control. And a few jobs at the bottom are considered "entry positions," vehicles for people to enter the organization, with a clear expectation that they will soon move on. But for the most part, people at the bottom—in our use of "bottom"—cannot hope for much mobility. The sales clerks Louisa Howe met in the department store could aspire only to become assistant managers or managers. The best jobs were reserved for men (though most of the clerks were women), and even there, pay and control were very limited. Auto workers, such as those at Lordstown, are a classic case of blocked opportunity, as Eli Chinoy (1955) found in his studies in the 1950s. Several thousand workers competed, if that's the word, for fewer than twelve openings a year for foreman. It is also striking in the accounts presented here how many workers at the bottom remain in the same position doing practically the same thing for their entire work lives—for example, the grandmother at the Reader's Digest who had been there in essentially the same job for twenty-five years; the older workers on Donald Roy's crew. Because no future at higher levels of the organization is envisioned for many workers at the bottom, no attention has to be given to their training and development. Thus, blocked mobility or limited opportunity reinforces lack of power.

DIFFERENCES IN BOTTOM POSITIONS AND THEIR HUMAN EFFECTS

Organizational bottoms come in several different forms. One classic distinction is between blue collar and white collar jobs; between office work which takes place in cleaner more pleasant surroundings and machine work, which tends to take place in more physically demanding and dirtier circumstances. White collar workers long enjoyed the illusion of superior status, of being closer to the top of the organization, and thus supposedly more motivated by symbolic rewards—signs of their prestige, status, and closer connection to power—than by money. (White collar jobs often pay less than "dirtier" factory jobs.) The women at the Reader's Digest, for example, were thought to be motivated by monthly visits from the founders of the magazine, who would tell them how important their work is. This is supposed to substitute for pay and other fringe benefits which many blue collar workers have won through unionization. But it is clear that many distinctions between white and blue collar work are breaking down. The new Vega factory at Lordstown was a clean, modern, well-lit facility. On the other hand, many office workers are becoming little more than machine operators. Thus, other distinctions seem to be more important.

We can contrast machine-paced and individually-paced work. We can also contrast work which requires very little skill, discretion and expertise, and work which includes a great deal. Another important difference is between work where one has very little personal connection with the final product and work where one's identity is bound up with the product, one represents the product to the public—as in the case of sales clerks, who can take some pride in ownership over their small territory and become personally involved in what they are selling to other people. Louisa Howe pleased a customer, and thus, to her surprise, felt pleased.

There is, finally, a distinction between work which is essentially done alone and that which is dependent on the acts of others and therefore, both requires more cooperation and reduces autonomy, and also makes possible cooperation that enhances the freedom of each member. The assembly line is most restricting because the pace of the line forces the worker's pace; yet here, because there is a group involved, it was also possible for a group of workers at Lordstown to figure out a way to beat the system, to earn a half-hour's rest for each of its members by doubling up and speeding up the work for the other half-hour. In independent machine work, the worker lacks a sense of contribution to a totality and the sort of involvement that joint work on a task can create, but the worker at least controls his or her own pace and thus, can make a game out of the work in order to provide some mental stimulation, as Donald Roy did in "Banana Time," in chapter 10.

Based on such distinctions, Robert Blauner (1964) uncovered four dimensions of alienation at work: powerlessness, meaninglessness, isolation, and self-estrangement. Assembly lines classically had the most alienated workers on these dimensions, while technically skilled work, even in a factory setting at a chemical refinery, tended to have the least alienated workers. However, the correspondence was not exact, for alienation is also a result of people's expectations. Thus, textile workers in the South, who had very limited expectations of what work could and would provide, showed limited alienation in Blauner's measures.

And it is also clear that people may develop a strong feeling of commitment and involvement despite any objective sense in which their work is boring, meaningless, or demeaning. People want to invest in work and can make surprising investments in organizations that offer them very little in return. We see this throughout the selections: Margie in books and records in Howe's department store came in early to get her area in order; many older men in the automobile factories never considered the kind of militancy the young workers were developing; the older men in Roy's factory remained loyal to the company.

PERSONAL INVESTMENTS: CREATING LIFE AT THE BOTTOM

The problem at the bottom, then, is *making* a life—that is, creating something human and humanly involving in a situation which may try to suppress the human. Given half a chance, people will create their own sources of stimulation. They will become playful about work, inventing games amidst the drudgery. They will create relationships and involvements that create a bit of drama and excitement out of otherwise drab routines. They will take pride in what might seem like absurdly small aspects of their work. They will invent their own standards and measure themselves against them. They will take such basic and simple matters as going to the bathroom, getting a drink of water, or eating a meal, and make those the high points of their day, the places, in fact, where their humanness comes through despite the attempts of the organization to suppress it. "Banana time"—and its accompaniments in peach time, coke time, pick-up time, fish time, etc.—is the most striking example of the development of involving rituals that create something at least interesting, if not positively meaningful, about work.

Many workers do have warm feelings about their companies, feeling they have been good to them. Said one woman about to retire from a factory making telephones, the company

has been like a big family. I've been in one department for thirty years and I've had loads of people working with me, and they're spread through the whole plant by this time. So no matter where you go, you always see somebody you know and everybody says hi and how are you? Some of them now, when I see them out in the parking lot going home from the first shift and they haven't seen me for a long time, they say hi Helen, and they give me a big hug and kiss like a lost friend, it's nice. I feel at home here. They treat you like a human being here. It may not look like they do, they're a big outfit and it may look like they are not partial to your problems, but they are. I think so. And I know I'm not the only one. I really like this company, and a girl and myself we always talk about it. She says, "Helen, I feel the same way you do about this company, it's been our bread and butter for thirty years." These kids today, they haven't worked in places like we have before, and they've been treated decent and they don't know anything different. But we do. I worked in the mills when I was a teenager and they didn't treat you with any respect. I hated it. [Balzer, 1976:225–226]

It used to be said by professionals that informal work groups were set up in opposition to the routines and goals of the organization. Then it was said by others that such groups were positive forces that enabled workers to produce more and to be more satisfied with their jobs. Both positions are probably exaggerated. In chapter 10, Roy speculates that the men of "Banana Time" were fairly inefficient and might have cost the company something in quantity, though perhaps not in quality. Yet, it is not clear that they could have done the job at all, day in and day out for twelve hours a day, if they had not been able to create for themselves some variation, some ritual, some aspects of life that they controlled. Similarly, Barbara Garson indicates in chapter 12 that the women in the college payroll office may have been rather inefficient by the standards of modern organizations, but she also pointed to the fact that they are, indeed, getting the job done, they are willing to admit and therefore correct mistakes, and they are not characterized by the degree of sabotage and subterfuge she found in other offices. And what is the cost of sabotage?

The workers at Lordstown who invented the doubling up system insist that their work under the new system is in fact of a higher quality than when they each had to work all of the time at a slower pace. The question of humanism versus efficiency has never been satisfactorily resolved. Reviews of the literature on productivity and job satisfaction (Srivastva, 1975; Katzell and Yankelovich, 1975) show equivocal results—that there is no direct or clear-cut relationship nor lack of it between the extent to which workers feel satisfied and happy with their jobs and the extent to which they are able to be productive. *But perhaps the question should be asked differently.* Perhaps what is important is not the development of strong worker-support groups that create meaning and involvement at work and do not function so much to boost productivity in the short run, but to make it possible for people to *survive their work* in the long run, to remain human and therefore, in fact, to have the energy to continue to come to work year after year—and to contribute to their families and society.

It is ironic that the major source of reward for work at the bottom, besides pay, seems to be friendship, something the organization does not provide and in many cases works hard to suppress, for it is considered inimicable to organizational discipline (Schrank, 1978). At the Fair Plan Insurance Company, in chapter 12, we see a supervisor trying to curtail eating and talking at desks. We see how hard it is to ask someone a simple personal question. At the Reader's Digest, we see friends separated, and lunch times varied to make it impossible for friends from different parts of the organization to get together. The good office at the college was one which offered a rich social life, freedom to come and go and attend to personal needs, small conveniences such as a refrigerator so that working women could shop at lunch, a boss who allowed flexibility as long as the work got done, and an organization of tasks that enabled people to use their judgment, to exercise their mental capacities.

We saw in life at the top that work spills over to encompass much of personal life, that personal life gets implicated in one's performance of one's role. At the bottom, work often swamps personal life, too, but in a negative sense—by making personal life subordinate to work disciplines and work rhythms. Work experiences may also shape the quality of private life. Several researchers, for example, found that blue collar workers whose work was limited in control, participation, and self-direction were less democratic in their politics and less creative in their leisure (Torbert and Rodgers, 1973). Similarly, fathers in low-autonomy jobs were more hostile as parents (McKinley, 1964). As Barbara Garson puts it: "Private lives get crimped into little cubby holes imposed by office routine." Mothers in offices can't take time off to stay home with sick children for fear of losing their jobs and can't take personal calls at the office because that interferes with office discipline; men at Lordstown don't come home until late at night—and then take three or four hours to unwind or to turn their brains on again after being numbed by routine all day long.

There is clearly reflected here a variation in the degree to which organizations make it possible to make a life at the bottom work. And we must consider what kind of a life. Is "any" life a real life? "Banana time" is creative and interesting, but it is also sad, childish, frenetic, and depressing. That's a life?

THE BOTTOM'S SOURCES OF POWER

One lesson is that when people are treated as irresponsible, they behave irresponsibly. "If they give me a robot's job to do, I'm going to do it like a robot." This has at least two sources. On the one hand, people are being prevented from investing themselves, from feeling involved in the whole task, from feeling that their work has purpose and meaning and that they are making a clear and defined contribution. (Contrast the women in a college business office who are very clear about what their contribution is to the whole and who have measurable milestones for achievement.) On the other hand, being irresponsible is one of the few sources of power that lower participants have in an organization. At least they can exercise control by keeping quiet, slowing down, or not contributing when they could. Some forms of sabotage also serve to protect the worker against what appears to him or her to be arbitrary forms of discipline, exercised at the whim of the supervisor to whom they cost little, but which have major repercussions for the worker him or herself. The worker who has no right to say "You're throwing work at me too fast, and it is humanly impossible to do it" resorts to subterfuge: hiding the mail, letting mistakes go through. The person who doesn't care about the organization because the organization doesn't care about him may merely resort to passive minimization: doing only the minimum to put in the time to get done the least amount possible. The worker who wants to exercise power may stubbornly use the rules or the routine to insist that a demand of a higher participant in the organization cannot be met.

Or a kind of negative power may be exercised through sabotage—deliberately doing things to a car that will cause problems for the organization down the line. The worker is not exercising power of a positive sort, but he or she is clearly making the assertion that she cannot be completely controlled, that she cannot be reduced to a mere machine mechanically following orders. It is possible to overoptimistically portray the possibilities for power inherent in lower positions in organizations (Mechanic, 1962). But it is clear that complete surveillance is never possible—despite the best attempts of supervisors at the insurance company office or of foremen at the automobile factory—nor is it desirable, for the organization needs the cooperation of even its lowest members, and especially of its lowest members when they control the handling of details that higher officials cannot be bothered with. Thus, those at the bottom are given, at best, bargaining tools, and at least, the power to subvert.

More positive power is often exercised through unions. The 1972 Lordstown strike was a particularly significant public event and one that has been interpreted from a variety of different frameworks. The articles in chapter 11 tend to view it primarily in terms of new worker attitudes that a "new breed of worker" has developed—one who is young and cannot be bought with money alone but is interested in the quality of the work he does. This was put negatively by United Auto Workers Vice President Ken Bannon in *Newsweek* (March 4, 1972): "The young don't accept the idea anymore that hard work is a virtue and a duty." His solution: pay them more and cut work time. There are indications that Bannon's solution would be fine with at least some of the workers, as in this exchange: "How come you're working four days a week?" a reporter asked a worker who tended to disappear on the fifth day routinely. The reply: "Because I can't make enough in three" (*Newsweek*, February 7, 1972).

Some commentators feel that the extent to which the Lordstown strike reflects new workers attitudes was unduly exaggerated. In this view, the age of the workers and the rhetoric of meaningful work was irrelevant; the strike reflected classic union issues—a response to speedups on the line as a result of worker layoffs. The pace of work and not its quality was what was at issue.

But for the most part, the interviews with Lordstown workers reflected here do indicate new attitudes on the part of those at the bottom. The "work ethic'" of earlier generations that kept men chained to industrial discipline regardless of the machine-like quality of the work may have instead been a "mobility ethic," which held that hard work was a necessary ingredient to improving oneself and one's family and to insuring an education for one's children so that they would not have to do the same kind of work. However, one's children may have found themselves, despite their increased education, on the assembly line at Lordstown. For these workers, the mobility ethic no longer made much sense. Their education had led them to expect something better (Kanter 1978b). Their pay was high enough that they could be affluent already, so pay itself was not enough. But their hopes for the future were certainly not tied to the automobile plant. Like many workers in blocked opportunity situations, in jobs that are stuck and lead nowhere, many of the Lordstown workers dreamed of escape, just as the automobile worker in Detroit interviewed earlier by Chinoy (1955) did: to leave the factory, to establish their own small business where they would at least have some control and sense of purpose—like the 27-year-old auto worker in chapter 11 who ran a real estate business on the side.

Whatever was going on at Lordstown, it certainly aroused strong feelings. The strike vote had the heaviest turnout in the history of UAW Local 1112, and 97 percent of those voting supported the strike (*New York Times*, February 3, 1972). Some of the lessons of Lordstown did not go unheard by General Motors and other auto companies, nor was Lordstown the only factory that was full of aggrieved workers. But the auto industry's solutions missed a great deal of the problem. They attributed the problem to poor communications between workers and management and set about to work on that, with Ford giving sensitivity training to foremen so that they could better relate to younger workers, and another General Motors plant instituting worker-management "rap" sessions on absenteeism and improving assembly processes. In a few other cases there were attempts to "enlarge" jobs, giving workers more than one task to perform so that they could have some variation in the assembly line routine.

TOWARD A BETTER LIFE AT THE BOTTOM

But all of these missed the point: control. Workers did not necessarily want more to do—quite the opposite, that was often seen as another form of speed-up—but rather workers wanted to have more power over the tasks they were performing. It was not participation that was at issue, but power—putting the locus of control, as far as possible, back in the hands of the individuals and work groups actually performing the tasks. The control theme emerges in a large number of studies or current attitudes toward work in America. In fact, people's sense of power and control—really efficacy—are the best general predictors of alienation, and are closely linked to job satisfaction, mental health, political attitudes, and family relations (Kanter, 1978b). It has also been argued, by Melvin Seeman (1975), a leading student of alienation, that control aspirations seem implicated in such major industrial disputes as the strikes at Lordstown and at Luton in France.

This raises a critical question. To what extent is it possible to modify organizations so that life at the bottom includes more control for workers? The answer is that although it is difficult to show uniform and unequivocal results, there is a large body of data on a wide variety of work alternatives that demonstrate the feasibility of increasing personal control, power, and autonomy without decreasing production efficiency. Often, indeed, productivity increases. General Motors has itself been pioneering in such quality-of-work-life alternatives, with much of the credit for initiation belonging to its organizational research department and Delmar ("Dutch") Landen, a GM psychologist (Psychology Today, 1978).

Even in the automobile companies, then, whose size and traditional reliance on assembly lines would seem to offer one of the most difficult challenges to the attempt to redesign work, it is possible to develop better systems. Volvo, under the leadership of its president, Perr Gyllenhammer, has pioneered in the development and construction of entire factories built around assembly by more-or-less independent, self-managed work teams (Gyllenhammar, 1975). Though initial costs seem higher, there is evidence that final costs will approximate those of more conventional plants. More critical, however, is the change in less public or less widely reported data, or in longer-term effects. For example, sabotage is virtually nil, and quality is high, in contrast to American lines, where sabotage beats out quality. And turnover and absenteeism are very reduced at Volvo, again, in contrast to the American experience. If all costs of dehumanized work are included, including the loss of individual health, self-respect, and sense of competence (as reflected in the Lordstown pieces), these alternatives would clearly be superior, even on economic grounds. General Motors measures many of these human issues in its monitoring of its quality-of-work-life programs.

A number of scholars have investigated the conditions that make jobs satisfying to the people in them, and they tend to come down to a few variables especially relevant to people at the bottom: variety, autonomy, feedback, and task identity, and a sense of how parts fit into the whole (Hackman, 1977). To these we should add mobility (Kanter, 1977). That is, one solution to the problem of jobs at the bottom is to get them better connected to jobs further up the organizational ladder. This is one way that Japan solves its problem of undesirable work. No one ends up doing it for very long. The minute people are seen as promotable, as movable into other and better jobs, as needing opportunity to develop their skills, they have to be treated differently, less as dispensable resources incapable of making their own decisions and more as thinking, feeling human beings.

Job design will be a key issue for the next decade, we predict. The challenge will be to enhance opportunity and power for workers at all levels in the face of a growing labor force and a more nearly static economy. This will call for more *variety* of opportunities: more upward mobility, suitably distributed, but also greater access to challenge, growth, control, and participation even in jobs at the bottom.

Ultimately, the question that needs to be faced is this: do organizations need to have a clear-cut bottom? Of course, all organizations have some people who are newer, who are paid less, who do the less desirable tasks. But there is still the question of whether it is possible to create autonomous purposeful work with some measure of control given to workers and with allowance made for their human dignity, as opposed to minutely subdivided work in which even workers' bodily functions are controlled by the organization. One way, in principle, is by rotation mechanisms. Even though the job appears the same, its occupant could rotate (as is true in some organizations now). The second way is to redefine jobs so that none unequivocally contain all such work. Rather, jobs could contain elements of both: a fraction of "dirty work" and another component with more meaningful, competence-embracing aspects.

That these possibilities would be valuable even to the organization is demonstrated by the articles here, which clearly show that people would rather invest themselves in work than not and will find ways to do so on their own if the organization does not provide the tools for doing it. They also demonstrate that workers are often exercising their intelligence and are entirely capable of developing quite innovative solutions to the problems facing them at work (Cohen, 1976). Yet, most organizations have no way to take account of this intelligence and expertise. This is a tremendous cost. The Lordstown solution, doubling-up on the line, is a remarkably innovative example that shows the potential for much greater productivity. Note also in chapter 12 the story of Mrs. Kline in the college business office who knew how to handle payroll problems such as workers returning from leave in the middle of the month in such a way as to minimize paperwork problems and financial complications later. There are in fact many other examples in the literature that make a similar point (Stein, 1974; Hollander, 1965).

We have seen numerous examples of unrecognized worker talent in our consulting practice—and the infusion of energy a company gets when it decides to tap that talent. In one project at a large computer company, first-line supervisors and shop floor workers formed teams to investigate organizational problems and consider the redesign of assembly line jobs. An early step was to formulate proposals that team representatives took to higher management—about ten levels higher. The management people were impressed and astounded, commenting that these workers were helping the company by taking over functions of the personnel department for the first time. Ironically, the workers were not flattered by this response, because they felt management was *too* surprised. "Didn't they think we could think?" one said. "Didn't they think we know what's going on and what needs to be done?"

We can only speculate about the result of organizations that are so designed as to tap the latent talents of their workers, and especially those at the bottom. Why shouldn't organizations *help* their workers "make a life"?

THE SELECTIONS

If all people at the bottom have to cope with the threat of insignificance and lack of control, still some find it easier to fashion a more fully human life at the bottom than others, depending on organizational circumstances. The circumstances depicted in the articles that follow cover a wide range: individual machine operators, assembly line workers, paper processors, clothing sales clerks. They work in factories, insurance companies, universities, department stores, and publishing companies. They are women and men, young (in Lordstown) and old (in "Banana Time"), union and non-union. These group memberships and cultural expectations intersect with job conditions to give people the material for making their own kind of life at the bottom.

Donald Roy went to work in a machine shop as a graduate student and soon learned how much he needed to invent games to break the dull monotony of the job. While he was young and could escape, the older workers were there for the long term, and thus, Roy discovered, they developed more elaborate games as a group ("Banana Time" and other rituals). There is something both admirable and pathetic about the culture of that work group, given their limited resources and minimal freedom.

If "Banana Time" reflects older workers resigned to their fate and doing what they can with it, the cluster of articles on the Lordstown, Ohio, Vega plant perhaps represents the "new breed" of younger workers. Automobile factories have long been considered by social scientists as an extreme version of alienated labor, and thus, the strike at Lordstown in 1972 was taken as a sign that younger workers would no longer stand for meaningless, robot-like assembly line work. *Time*'s report provides the factual background; B. J. Widick's article from the *Nation*, also written at the time of the strike, is one commentator's view. Barbara Garson interviewed and lived with some of the younger Lordstown workers. And Bennett Kremen from the *New York Times* spoke to them a year later and was struck by the talent and inventiveness of the assembly workers, who, when left to their own devices, could develop better systems for running the line.

Next, we move from the factory to the office, but we also see that some offices are very much like factories. In "Women's Work," Barbara Garson describes some good and bad offices, based on her own experiences as an employee as well as long conversations with other workers. "Women's Work" and her Lordstown observations are both part of her book on the ordinary worker, *All the Livelong Day*.

"Retail Sales" is a first-hand account from *Pink Collar Workers* by Louisa Kapp Howe. Howe, a writer, took a job in a large New York department store at Christmas, but found that she became too fond of her sister employees to keep up the pretense very long. This excerpt describes her first day on the job, her reactions to it, and how the store regarded and treated its clerks.

Is life possible at the bottom? Certainly. And most workers

are far from discontent. But perhaps only in "good offices" like the one Garson describes, can those at the bottom gain much power.

10 / "Banana Time": Job Satisfaction and Informal Interaction

Donald F. Roy

MY ACCOUNT of how one group of machine operators kept from "going nuts" in a situation of monotonous work activity attempts to lay bare the tissues of interaction which made up the content of their adjustment, the talking, fun, and fooling which provided solution to the elemental problem of "psychological survival." . . .

My fellow operatives and I spent our long days of simple repetitive work in relative isolation from other employees of the factory. Our line of machines was sealed off from other work areas of the plant by the four walls of the clicking room. The one door of this room was usually closed. Even when it was kept open, during periods of hot weather, the consequences were not social; it opened on an uninhabited storage room of the shipping department. Not even the sounds of work activity going on elsewhere in the factory carried to this isolated work place. There were occasional contacts with "outside" employees, usually on matters connected with the work; but, with the exception of the daily calls of one fellow who came to pick up finished materials for the next step in processing, such visits were sporadic and infrequent.

Moreover, face-to-face contact with members of the managerial hierarchy were few and far between. No one bearing the title of foreman ever came around. The only company official

Reproduced by permission of the Society for Applied Anthropology from *Human Organization* 18:158–168, 1959.

who showed himself more than once during the two-month observation period was the plant superintendent. Evidently overloaded with supervisory duties and production problems which kept him busy elsewhere, he managed to pay his respects every week or two. His visits were in the nature of short, businesslike, but friendly exchanges. Otherwise he confined his observable communications with the group to occasional utilization of a public address system. During the two-month period, the company president and the chief chemist paid one friendly call apiece. One man, who may or may not have been of managerial status, was seen on various occasions lurking about in a manner which excited suspicion. Although no observable consequences accrued from the peculiar visitations of this silent fellow, it was assumed that he was some sort of efficiency expert, and he was referred to as "The Snooper."

As far as our work group was concerned, this was truly a situation of laissez-faire management. There was no interference from staff experts, no hounding by time-study engineers or personnel men hot on the scent of efficiency or good human relations. Nor were there any signs of industrial democracy in the form of safety, recreational, or production committees. There was an international union, and there was a highly publicized union-management cooperation program; but actual interactional processes of cooperation were carried on somewhere beyond my range of observation and without participation of members of my work group. Furthermore, these union-management get-togethers had no determinable connection with the problem of "toughing out" a twelve-hour day of monotonous work.

Our work group was thus not only abandoned to its own sources for creating job satisfaction, but left without that basic reservoir of ill-will toward management which can sometimes be counted on to stimulate the development of interesting activities to occupy hand and brain. Lacking was the challenge of intergroup conflict, that perennial source of creative experience to fill the otherwise empty hours of meaningless work routine.

The clicking machines were housed in a room approximately thirty by twenty-four feet. They were four in number, set in a row, and so arranged along one wall that the busy operator could, merely by raising his head from his work, freshen his reveries with a glance through one of three large barred windows. To the rear of one of the end machines sat a long cutting table; here the operators cut up rolls of plastic materials into small sheets manageable for further processing at the clickers. Behind the machine at the opposite end of the line sat another table which was intermittently the work station of a female employee who performed sundry scissors operations of a more intricate nature on raincoat parts. Boxed in on all sides by shelves and stocks of materials, this latter locus of work appeared a cell within a cell. . . .

Introduction to the new job, with its relatively simple machine skills and work routines, was accomplished with what proved to be, in my experience, an all-time minimum of job training. The clicking machine assigned to me was situated at one end of the row. Here the superintendent and one of the operators gave a few brief demonstrations, accompanied by bits of advice which included a warning to keep hands clear of the descending hammer. After a short practice period, at the end of which the superintendent expressed satisfaction with progress and potentialities, I was left to develop my learning curve with no other supervision than that afforded by members of the work group. Further advice and assistance did come, from time to time, from my fellow operatives, sometimes upon request, sometimes unsolicited.

THE WORK GROUP

Absorbed at first in three related goals of improving my clicking skill, increasing my rate of output, and keeping my left hand unclicked, I paid little attention to my fellow operatives save to observe that they were friendly, middle-aged, foreign-born, full of advice, and very talkative. Their names, according to the way they addressed each other, were George, Ike, and Sammy. George, a stocky fellow in his late fifties, operated the machine at the opposite end of the line; he, I later discovered, had emigrated in early youth from a country in Southeastern Europe. Ike, stationed at George's left, was tall, slender, in his early fifties, and Jewish; he had come from Eastern Europe in his youth. Sammy, number three man in the line, and my neighbor, was heavy set, in his late fifties, and Jewish; he had escaped from a country in Eastern Europe just before Hitler's legions had moved in. All three men had been downwardly mobile as to occupation in recent years. George and Sammy had been proprietors of small businesses; the former had been "wiped out" when his uninsured establishment burned down; the latter had been entrepreneuring on a small scale before he left all behind him to flee the Germans. According to his account, Ike had left a highly skilled trade which he had practiced for years in Chicago.

I discovered also that the clicker line represented a ranking system in descending order from George to myself. George not only had top seniority for the group, but functioned as a sort of leadman. His superior status was marked in the fact that he received five cents more per hour than the other clickermen, put in the longest workday, made daily contact, outside the workroom, with the superintendent on work matters which concerned the entire line, and communicated to the rest of us the directives which he received. The narrow margin of superordination was seen in the fact that directives were always relayed in the superintendent's name; they were on the order of, "You'd better let that go now, and get on the green. Joe says they're running low on the fifth floor," or, "Joe says he wants two boxes of the 3-die today." The narrow margin was also seen in the fact that the superintendent would communicate directly with his operatives over the public address system; and, on occasion, Ike or Sammy would leave the workroom to confer with him for decisions or advice in regard to work orders.

Ike was next to George in seniority, then Sammy. I was, of course, low man on the totem pole. Other indices to status differentiation lay in informal interaction, to be described later.

With one exception, job status tended to be matched by length of workday. George worked a thirteen-hour day, from 7 A.M. to 8:30 P.M. Ike worked eleven hours, from 7 A.M. to 6:30 P.M.; occasionally he worked until 7 or 7:30 for an eleven and a half- or a twelve-hour day. Sammy put in a nine-hour day, from 8 A.M. to 5:30 P.M. My twelve hours spanned from 8 A.M to 8:30 P.M. We had a half hour for lunch, from 12 to 12:30.

The female who worked at the secluded table behind George's machine put in a regular plant-wide eight-hour shift from 8 to 4:30. Two women held this job during the period of my employment; Mable was succeeded by Baby. Both were Negroes, and in their late twenties.

A fifth clicker operator, an Arabian *emigré* called Boo, worked a night shift by himself. He usually arrived about 7 P.M. to take over Ike's machine.

THE WORK

It was evident to me, before my first workday drew to a weary close, that my clicking career was going to be a grim process of fighting the clock, the particular timepiece in this situation being an old-fashioned alarm clock which ticked away on a shelf near George's machine. I had struggled through many dreary rounds with the minutes and hours during the various phases of my industrial experience, but never had I been confronted with such a dismal combination of working conditions as the extra-long workday, the infinitesimal cerebral excitation, and the extreme limitation of physical movement. The contrast with a recent stint in the California oil fields was striking. This was no eight-hour day of racing hither and yon over desert and foothills with a rollicking crew of "roustabouts" on a variety of repair missions at oil wells, pipe lines, and storage tanks. Here there were no afternoon dallyings to search the sands for horned toads, tarantulas, and rattlesnakes, or to climb old wooden derricks for raven's nests, with an eye out, of course, for the telltale streak of dust in the distance which gave ample warning of the approach of the boss. This was standing all day in one spot beside three old codgers in a dingy room looking out through barred windows at the bare walls of a brick warehouse, leg movements largely restricted to the shifting of body weight from one foot to the other, hand and arm movements confined, for the most part, to a simple repetitive sequence of place the die, ——— punch the clicker, ——— place the die, ——— punch the clicker, and intellectual activity reduced to computing the hours to quitting time. It is true that from time to time a fresh stack of sheets would have to be substituted for the clicked-out old one; but the stack would have been prepared by someone else, and the exchange would be only a minute or two in the making. Now and then a box of finished work would have to be moved back out of the way, and an empty box brought up; but the moving back and the bringing up involved only a step or two. And there was the half hour for lunch, and occasional trips to the lavatory or the drinking fountain to break up the day into digestible parts. But after each momentary respite, hammer and die were moving again: click, ——— move die, ——— click, ——— move die. . . .

The next day was the same: the monotony of the work, the tired legs and sore feet and thoughts of quitting.

THE GAME OF WORK

In discussing the factory operative's struggle to "cling to the remnants of joy in work," Henri de Man makes the general observations that "it is psychologically impossible to deprive any kind of work of all its positive emotional elements," that the worker will find *some* meaning in any activity assigned to him, a "certain scope for initiative which can satisfy after a fashion the instinct for play and the creative impulse," that "even in the Taylor system there is found luxury of self-determination." De Man cites the case of one worker who wrapped 13,000 incandescent bulbs a day; she found her outlet for creative impulse, her self-determination, her meaning in work by varying her wrapping movements a little from time to time.

So did I search for *some* meaning in my continuous mincing of plastic sheets into small ovals, fingers, and trapezoids. The richness of possibility for creative expression previously discovered in my experience with the "Taylor system" did not reveal itself here. There was no piecework, so no piecework game. There was no conflict with management, so no war game. But, like the light bulb wrapper, I did find a "certain scope for initiative," and out of this slight freedom to vary activity, I developed a game of work, [which] might be described as a continuous sequence of short-range production goals with achievement rewards in the form of activity change. . . .

But a hasty conclusion that I was having lots of fun playing my clicking game should be avoided. These games were not as interesting in the experiencing as they might seem to be from the telling. Emotional tone of the activity was low, and intellectual currents weak. Such rewards as scraping the block or "getting to do the blue ones" were not very exciting, and the stretches of repetitive movement involved in achieving them were long enough to permit lapses into obsessive reverie. Henri de Man speaks of "clinging to the remnants of joy in work," and this situation represented just that. How tenacious the clinging was, how long I could have "stuck it out" with my remnants, was never determined. Before the first week was out this adjustment to the work situation was complicated by other developments. The game of work continued, but in a different context. Its influence became decidedly subordinated to, if not completely overshadowed by, another source of job satisfaction.

INFORMAL SOCIAL ACTIVITY OF THE WORK GROUP: TIMES AND THEMES

The change came about when I began to take serious note of the social activity going on around me; my attentiveness to this activity came with growing involvement in it. What I heard at first, before I started to listen, was a stream of disconnected bits of communication which did not make much sense. Foreign accents were strong and referents were not joined to coherent contexts of meaning. It was just "jabbering." What I saw at first, before I began to observe, was occasional flurries of horseplay so simple and unvarying in pattern and so childish in quality that they made no strong bid for attention. For example, Ike would regularly switch off the power at Sammy's machine whenever Sammy made a trip to the lavatory or the drinking fountain. Correlatively, Sammy invariably fell victim to the plot by making an attempt to operate his clicking hammer after returning to the shop. And, as the simple pattern went, this blind stumbling into the trap was always followed by indignation and reproach from Sammy, smirking satisfaction from Ike, and mild paternal scolding from George. My interest in this procedure was at first confined to wondering when Ike would weary of his tedious joke or when Sammy would learn to check his power switch before trying the hammer.

But, as I began to pay closer attention, as I began to develop familiarity with the communication system, the disconnected became connected, the nonsense made sense, the obscure became clear, and the silly actually funny. . . .

This emerging awareness of structure and meaning included recognition that the long day's grind was broken by interruptions of a kind other than the formally instituted or idiosyncratically developed disjunctions in work routine previously described. These additional interruptions appeared in daily repetition in an ordered series of informal interactions. They were, in part, but only in part and in very rough comparison, similar to those common fractures of the production process known as the coffee break, the coke break, and the cigarette break. Their distinction lay in frequency of occurrence and in brevity. As phases of the daily series, they occurred almost hourly, and so short were they in duration that they disrupted work activity only slightly. Their significance lay not so much in their function as rest pauses, although it cannot be denied that physical refreshment was involved. Nor did their chief importance lie in the accentuation of progress points in the passage of time, although they could perform that function far more strikingly than the hour hand on the dull face of George's alarm clock. If the daily series of interruptions be likened to a clock, then the comparison might best be made with a special kind of cuckoo clock, one with a cuckoo which can provide variation in its announcements and can create such an interest in them that the intervening minutes become filled with intellectual content. The major significance of the interactional interruptions lay in such a carryover of interest. The physical interplay which momentarily halted work activity would initiate verbal exchanges and thought processes to occupy group members until the next interruption. The group interactions thus not only marked off the time; they gave it content and hurried it along.

Most of the breaks in the daily series were designated as "times" in the parlance of the clicker operators, and they featured the consumption of food or drink of one sort or another. There was coffee time, peach time, banana time, fish time, coke time, and, of course, lunch time. Other interruptions, which formed part of the series but were not verbally recognized as times, were window time, pickup time, and the staggered quitting times of Sammy and Ike. These latter unnamed times did not involve the partaking of refreshments.

My attention was first drawn to this times business during my first week of employment when I was encouraged to join in the sharing of two peaches. It was Sammy who provided the peaches; he drew them from his lunch box after making the announcement, "Peach time!" On this first occasion I refused the proffered fruit, but thereafter regularly consumed my half peach. Sammy continued to provide the peaches and to make the "Peach time!" announcement, although there were days when Ike would remind him that it was peach time, urging him to hurry up with the mid-morning snack. Ike invariably complained about the quality of the fruit, and his complaints fed the fires of continued banter between peach donor and critical recipient. I did find the fruit a bit on the scrubby side but felt, before I achieved insight into the function of peach time, that Ike was showing poor manners by looking a gift horse in the mouth. I wondered why Sammy continued to share his peaches with such an ingrate.

Banana time followed peach time by approximately an hour. Sammy again provided the refreshments, namely, one banana. There was, however, no four-way sharing of Sammy's banana. Ike would gulp it down by himself after surreptitiously extracting it from Sammy's lunch box, kept on a shelf behind Sammy's work station. Each morning, after making the snatch, Ike would call out, "Banana time!" and proceed to down his prize while Sammy made futile protests and denunciations. George would join in with mild remonstrances, sometimes scolding Sammy for making so much fuss. The banana was one which Sammy brought for his own consumption at lunch time; he never did get to eat his banana, but kept bringing one for his lunch. At first this daily theft startled and amazed me. Then I grew to look forward to the daily seizure and the verbal interaction which followed.

Window time came next. It followed banana time as a regular consequence of Ike's castigation by the indignant Sammy. After "taking" repeated references to himself as a person badly lacking in morality and character, Ike would "finally" retaliate by opening the window which faced Sammy's machine, to let the "cold air" blow in on Sammy. The slandering which would, in its echolalic repetition, wear down Ike's patience and forbearance usually took the form of the invidious comparison: "George is a good daddy! Ike is a bad man! A very bad man!" Opening the window would take a little time to accomplish and would involve a great deal of verbal interplay between Ike and Sammy, both before and after the event. Ike would threaten, make feints toward the window, then finally open it. Sammy would protest, argue, and make claims that the air blowing in on him would give him a cold; he would eventually have to leave his machine to close the window. . . .

Following window time came lunch time, a formally designated half-hour for the midday repast and rest break. At this time, informal interaction would feature exchanges between Ike and George. The former would start eating his lunch a few minutes before noon, and the latter, in his role as straw boss, would censure him for malobservance of the rules. Ike's off-beat luncheon usually involved a previous tampering with George's alarm clock. Ike would set the clock ahead a few minutes in order to maintain his eating schedule without detection, and George would discover these small daylight saving changes. . . .

Pickup time, fish time, and coke time came in the afternoon. I name it pickup time to represent the official visit of the man who made daily calls to cart away boxes of clicked materials. The arrival of the pickup man, a Negro, was always a noisy one, like the arrival of a daily passenger train in an isolated small town. Interaction attained a quick peak of intensity to crowd into a few minutes all communications, necessary and otherwise. Exchanges invariably included loud depreciations by the pickup man of the amount of work accomplished in the clicking department during the preceding twenty-four hours. Such scoffing would be on the order of "Is that all you've got done? What do the boys do all day?" These devaluations would be countered with allusions to the "soft job" enjoyed by the pickup man. During the course of the exchanges news items would be dropped, some of serious import, such as reports of accomplished or impending layoffs in the various plants of the company, or of gains or losses in orders for company products. Most of the news items, however, involved bits of information on plant employees told in a light vein. Information relayed by the clicker operators was usually told about each other, mainly in the form of summaries of the most recent kidding sequences. Some of this material was repetitive, carried over from day to day. Sammy would be the butt of most of this newscasting, although he would make occasional counter-reports on Ike and George. . . .

About mid-afternoon came fish time. George and Ike would

stop work for a few minutes to consume some sort of pickled fish which Ike provided. Neither Sammy nor I partook of this nourishment, nor were we invited. For this omission I was grateful; the fish, brought in a newspaper and with head and tail intact, produced a reverse effect on my appetite. . . .

Coke time came late in the afternoon, and was an occasion for total participation. The four of us took turns in buying the drinks and in making the trip for them to a fourth floor vending machine. . . .

Themes

To put flesh, so to speak, on this interactional frame of "times," my work group had developed various "themes" of verbal interplay which had become standardized in their repetition. These topics of conversation ranged in quality from an extreme of nonsensical chatter to another extreme of serious discourse. Unlike the times, these themes flowed one into the other in no particular sequence of predictability. Serious conversation could suddenly melt into horseplay, and vice versa. In the middle of a serious discussion on the high cost of living, Ike might drop a weight behind the easily startled Sammy, or hit him over the head with a dusty paper sack. Interaction would immediately drop to a low comedy exchange of slaps, threats, guffaws, and disapprobations which would invariably include a ten-minute echolalia of "Ike is a bad man, a bad man! George is a good daddy, a very fine man!" Or, on the other hand, a stream of such invidious comparisons as followed a surreptitious switching-off of Sammy's machine by the playful Ike might merge suddenly into a discussion of the pros and cons of saving for one's funeral. "Kidding themes" were usually started by George or Ike, and Sammy was usually the butt of the joke. . . .

The "poom poom" theme was one that caused no sting. It would come up several times a day to be enjoyed as unbarbed fun by the three older clicker operators. Ike was usually the one to raise the question, "How many times you go poom poom last night?" The person questioned usually replied with claims of being "too old for poom poom." If this theme did develop a goat, it was I. When it was pointed out that I was a younger man, this provided further grist for the poom poom mill. I soon grew weary of this poom poom business, so dear to the hearts of the three old satyrs, and, knowing where the conversation would inevitably lead, winced whenever Ike brought up the subject. . . .

Another kidding theme which developed out of serious discussion could be labelled "helping Danelly find a cheaper apartment." It became known to the group that Danelly had a pending housing problem, that he would need new quarters for his family when the permanent resident of his temporary summer dwelling returned from a vacation. This information engendered at first a great deal of sympathetic concern and, of course, advice on apartment hunting. Development into a kidding theme was immediately related to previous exchanges between Ike and George on the quality of their respective dwelling areas. Ike lived in "Lawndale," and George dwelt in the "Woodlawn" area. The new pattern featured the reading aloud of bogus "apartment for rent" ads in newspapers which were brought into the shop. Studying his paper at lunchtime, George would call out, "Here's an apartment for you, Danelly! Five rooms, stove heat, $20 a month, Lawndale Avenue!" Later, Ike would read from his paper, "Here's one! Six rooms, stove heat, dirt floor. $18.50 a month! At 55th and Woodlawn." Bantering would then go on in regard to the quality of housing or population in the two areas. The search for an apartment for Dannelly was not successful.

Serious themes included the relating of major misfortunes suffered in the past by group members. George referred again and again to the loss, by fire, of his business establishment. Ike's chief complaints centered around a chronically ill wife who had undergone various operations and periods of hospital care. Ike spoke with discouragement of the expenses attendant upon hiring a housekeeper for himself and his children; he referred with disappointment and disgust to a teen-age son, an inept lad who "couldn't even fix his own lunch. He couldn't even make himself a sandwich!" Sammy's reminiscences centered on the loss of a flourishing business when he had to flee Europe ahead of Nazi invasion.

But all serious topics were not tales of woe. One favorite serious theme which was optimistic in tone could be called either "Danelly's future" or "getting Danelly a better job." It was known that I had been attending "college," the magic door to opportunity, although my specific course of study remained somewhat obscure. Suggestions poured forth on good lines of work to get into, and these suggestions were backed with accounts of friends, and friends of friends, who had made good via the academic route. My answer to the expected question, "Why are you working here?" always stressed the "lots of overtime" feature, and this explanation seemed to suffice for short-range goals. . . .

The "professor theme" was the cream of verbal interaction. It involved George's connection with higher learning. His daughter had married the son of a professor who instructed in one of the local colleges. This professor theme was not in the strictest sense a conversation piece; when the subject came up, George did all the talking. The two Jewish operatives remained silent as they listened with deep respect, if not actual awe, to George's accounts of the Big Wedding which, including the wedding pictures, entailed an expense of $1,000. It was monologue, but there was listening, there was communication, the sacred communication of a temple, when George told of going for Sunday afternoon walks on the Midway with the professor, or of joining the professor for a Sunday dinner. Whenever he spoke of the professor, his daughter, the wedding, or even of the new son-in-law, who remained for the most part in the background, a sort of incidental like the wedding cake, George was complete master of the interaction. His manner, in speaking to the rank-and-file of clicker operators, was indeed that of master deigning to notice his underlings. I came to the conclusion that it was the professor connection, not the strawboss-ship or the extra nickel an hour, which provided the fount of George's superior status in the group. . . .

So initial discouragement with the meagerness of social interaction I now recognized as due to lack of observation. The interaction was there, in constant flow. It captured attention and held interest to make the long day pass. The twelve hours of "click, —— move die, —— click, —— move die" became as easy to endure as eight hours of varied activity in the oil fields or eight hours of playing the piecework game in a machine shop. The "beast of boredom" was gentled to the harmlessness of a kitten. . . .

In regard to possible practical application to problems of industrial management, these observations seem to support the generally accepted notion that one key source of job satisfaction lies in the informal interaction shared by members of a work group. In the clicking-room situation the spontaneous development of a patterned combination of horseplay, serious conversation, and frequent sharing of food and drink reduced the monotony of simple, repetitive operations to the point where a regular schedule of long work days became livable. This kind of group interplay may be termed "consumatory" in the sense indicated by Dewey, when he makes a basic distinction between "instrumental" and "consumatory" communication. The enjoyment of communication "for its own sake" as "mere sociabilities," as "free, aimless social intercourse," brings job satisfaction, at least job endurance, to work situations largely bereft of creative experience.

In regard to another managerial concern, employee productivity, any appraisal of the influence of group interaction upon clicking-room output could be no more than roughly impressionistic. I obtained no evidence to warrant a claim that banana time, or any of its accompaniments in consumatory interaction, boosted production. To the contrary, my diary recordings express an occasional perplexity in the form of "How does this company manage to stay in business?" However, I did not obtain sufficient evidence to indicate that, under the prevailing conditions of laissez-faire management, the output of our group would have been more impressive if the playful cavorting of three middle-aged gentlemen about the barred windows had never been. As far as achievement of managerial goals is concerned, the most that could be suggested is that leavening the deadly boredom of individualized work routines with a concurrent flow of group festivities had a negative effect on turnover. I left the group, with sad reluctance, under the pressure of strong urgings to accept a research fellowship which would involve no factory toil. My fellow clickers stayed with their machines to carry on their labors in the spirit of banana time.

11 / The Lordstown Auto Workers

SABOTAGE AT LORDSTOWN?
Editors of *Time*

General Motors' Lordstown, Ohio, plant is a hub of superlatives. Its assembly line is the most highly automated one in the industry; it has 26 bellows-like armed robots that can bend around corners and that make some 520 welds in each car. The line is also the fastest in the U.S., capable of producing 100 cars an hour. The labor force—long-haired, pigtailed and bell-bottomed—is the youngest of any G.M. plant, with an average age of 24 to 25. Now Lordstown, the only U.S. plant that turns out subcompact Vegas, has the industry's worst labor problem, and so far it has cost G.M. about $40 million in lost production.

Hardly anybody calls it sabotage—yet. But last October somebody deliberately set fire to an assembly-line control box shed, causing the line to shut down. Autos regularly roll off the line with slit upholstery, scratched paint, dented bodies, bent gear-shift levers, cut ignition wires, and loose or missing bolts. In some cars, the trunk key is broken off right in the lock, thereby jamming it. The plant's repair lot has space for 2,000 autos, but often becomes too crowded to accept more. When that happens, as it did last week, the assembly line is stopped and workers are sent home payless.

SPEEDUP

Trouble began in mid-1971, about a year after the automated line was put into operation. Partly because the bugs had been worked out of the line and partly because the assembly plant consolidated with an adjacent Fisher Body plant, there were layoffs in what G.M. now will only say was an "8,000-plus" work force. The United Auto Workers claims that 750 or more were laid off; management contends the total was only half that. Those still on the job complained that they were being forced to speed up, do extra jobs and generally work too hard. The grievances got little response from G.M., but as they grew, so did the number of damaged cars. In mid-January, U.A.W. Local 1112 at Lordstown leaked a story to the press that G.M. was shipping defective Vegas to its dealers, a charge that G.M. vehemently denies. Cracks Gary Bryner, the mustachioed, hip-talking, 29-year-old president of Local 1112: "We warned them that we were going to get our story out if they wouldn't work with us."

Led by its angry young, the local has threatened to take a strike vote this week unless G.M. makes concessions. Money is not the issue; the workers earn about $4.50 an hour, plus $2.50 in fringes. What the union wants is a redefinition of the work rules that will result in some rehiring and elimination of extra chores, which workers claim rush them as the autos move by at an average of one every 36 seconds. G.M. added some of these chores partly in the hope of alleviating the mindnumbing boredom of endlessly doing just one task.

After interviewing both sides at Lordstown, TIME's Detroit Bureau Chief Edwin Reingold reports: "There has been much talk of 'job enrichment,' assigning a worker more tasks in order to give him a sense of fulfillment. But some union leaders charge that 'enriching' a worker's job by making him do two jobs each 30 times an hour instead of one job 60 times an hour is a 'con.' At Lordstown the workers want more time to do their single, simple job—and that is certainly the opposite of what many outsiders think they want. Many workers complain that they do not want to work as hard as they are being asked to do. It may well be that what were considered ordinary norms in the past are no longer acceptable."

THE MEN WON'T TOE THE VEGA LINE
By B. J. Widick

The world's fastest assembly line was shut down on March 3 [1972] in what General Motors declared was a dispute over work standards. The United Auto Workers (UAW) said the walkout, involving more than 7,700 workers, was caused by speedups. By confining or reducing the issues in conflict to the problem of speed, and not considering the nature of the job, whatever the speed, both sides have made a mistake that will add to the difficulties of settlement.

The site of the dispute is Lordstown, Ohio, part of the Cleveland-Warren industrial complex. The plant is GM's new, highly automated Vega assembly operation. This plant and the Vega were to be GM's answers to small imports. The factory has been designed to turn out 100 vehicles an hour. The Vega is put together from 578 different body parts; the average car, by contrast, has 996. This reduction, plus the latest automated equipment, seems to make the compact a sure manufacturing success.

As further assurance, GM carefully screened its work applicants, seeking and obtaining mainly young (average age less than 25), white workers with a better than average education (more years of high school). Less than 500 of the plant employees are women and only 100 are black. The pay scale is about $36 a day, not counting fringe benefits. Relief time is about twenty-three minutes twice a day. Only a year ago, GM wrote its Vega employees a letter thanking them for a job well done.

What factors changed this relationship? The passage of time alone turned the excitement of new jobs into the humdrum of assembly line drudgery. Furthermore, GM never achieved its goal of 100 cars per hour off the assembly line, which meant that the work pace never met the arbitrary standards set by GM's time-study engineers. Last October, therefore, GM placed the Vega plant under the control of its General Motors Assembly Division (GMAD), which soon began eliminating or changing jobs and increasing workloads.

B. J. Widick, "The Men Won't Toe the Vega Line," *The Nation*, Vol. 214 (March 27, 1972), copyright 1972, The Nation Associates. Pp. 403–4.

Leonard Woodcock, president of the UAW, remarked recently that GMAD is "probably the roughest, toughest division in GM. They admit they jerked 300 workers out of the system; our people say 700. The men are fighting back. That's all." For management, the issue soon became one of prestige as well as work output. GMAD's reputation was at stake, and that is one factor in the inability of the two parties to negotiate the grievances peacefully and satisfactorily. Before GMAD took over, there had been 300 grievances; under the new management there were more than 5,000 with hundreds of discipline cases to boot.

GMAD's operational techniques are standard in the auto industry. Works standards engineers determine the number of seconds required for an operation and foremen are given the manpower to perform at that rate. Failure to meet the standard results in disciplinary action against the employee: being sent home, given days off, ultimately discharge. As men resist in one form or another, usually by not meeting the workload, the cars go down the line incomplete. When repairs have piled up to a predetermined point, management sends the entire work force home. The key to understanding this performance conflict is that the assembly line determines the pace of the men, not the other way around. Hence workers feel manacled to the line.

In the management theory, when "send homes" have occurred a number of times, the men not working directly on the line and thus unaffected by the works standards dispute will begin to put pressure on the assembly workers. "We need the pay; write a grievance. Let's not lose all our power in small fights." This attitude, plus disciplinary measures, is expected to break the resistance to the new works standards, which have been "scientifically" calculated and must therefore be "right." Frequently this process fails, and management faces and accepts a strike, which usually ends in compromise. Then management begins the whole process over again. (That is a thumbnail history of all auto assembly plants.)

When C. E. Wilson, GM president, introduced in 1949 the concept of an "annual improvement factor wage increase," the company wasn't kidding when it said it knew that the workers would increase productivity annually. GM's works standards department was and is strictly professional and totally impersonal when it comes to viewing the human factor.

At the Lordstown plant, management entirely miscalculated the reaction of its carefully selected young to the time-study coercion. The resistance was direct, hostile and brutal. Pressure for a strike was immediate, and the hatred of GMAD universal. Among the management's jokes, as many workers saw it, was the attempt to solve employee attitudes by sensitivity training! In response, young workers irritated management by singing *Solidarity Forever* in the cafeteria during mealtime. The college-trained management personnel, who have never worked on an assembly line, are a special focus of disrespect among the young and new breed of workers.

Their attitudes and views are symbolized by the kind of union leader they elected in 1970 to be their spokesman. Local 1112 president is Gary Bryner, aged 29, who doesn't fit the ordinary image of a local union leader. Like so many of his followers, he uses the language of contemporary youth. "Let's rap," he says. "Right-on," he agrees. Bryner ends phone conversations with the slogan, "Peace." His desk has a peace symbol in prominent display, next to his favorite book, *Revolutionary Quotations of Great Americans*. Neither he nor his members stand in awe of GM, or anybody else.

Since striking over works standards disputes is a right retained by the UAW during the life of a contract, the local union leadership and membership overwhelmingly and eagerly voted to exercise that right, and the battle has been joined, with costs for both sides soon to mount. The UAW was organized primarily to resist speedups and decisions made unilaterally by the auto barons. The oldtimers did their part, made many sacrifices to build the union as an organization of worker protection against the huge companies. But try as they might, they could never solve the problem that work on an assembly line was a rotten way to make a living. Only peripheral improvement, like more adequate relief time, relieved the strain. Walter Reuther used to characterize the assembly plant a "golden-plated sweat shop." Now the young workers are taking the work issues a step further. They are irreverent of all decision makers; they simply don't see working GM's way all their lives, no matter what the pay. Even Henry Ford recently remarked that the auto industry had never solved the problem of boredom on the assembly line. That is the issue projecting itself once again in the negotiations at Lordstown. The young workers give every indication that they won't put up with what were considered hard but "normal" work conditions. Assembly lines going at the rate of sixty-five an hour add a factor of fatigue by their very pace. How high it must be on a line designed to run at 100 jobs an hour hasn't been calculated; nor can it be, since no one yet has worked under those conditions.

The prospect of spending a lifetime that way is a basic ingredient of dissatisfaction in the Vega factory. As a consultant to GM recently told *Iron Age* magazine, "Constant, repetitive work is being resisted by workers, and when you put in tough management to make a car every forty seconds, instead of fifty-five, the whole thing falls apart. You can't take a young man, average age 22, and subject him to the dreadful, dismal future of a production line."

That's the real challenge in the Lordstown strike, and the negotiators can't answer it if they confine the argument exclusively to the pace of work, rather than the kind of work. Both count in the minds of the young workers, and that is why the current strike has such unusual importance. A new element is being introduced into the old argument of man versus machine. Who runs whom for what purpose? And at what human cost? The young workers are asking good questions, which will come increasingly to the fore in the decade of the 1970s.

LUDDITES IN LORDSTOWN

By Barbara Garson

Is it true," an auto worker asked wistfully, "that you get to do fifteen different jobs on a Cadillac?" "I heard," said another, "that with Volvos you follow one car all the way down the line."

Such are the yearnings of young auto workers at the Vega plant in Lordstown, Ohio. Their average age is twenty-four, and they work on the fastest auto assembly line in the world. Their jobs are so subdivided that few workers can feel they are making a car.

The assembly line carries 101 cars past each worker every

hour. Most GM lines run under sixty. At 101 cars an hour, a worker has thirty-six seconds to perform his assigned snaps, knocks, twists, or squirts on each car. The line was running at this speed in October when a new management group, General Motors Assembly Division (GMAD or Gee-Mad), took over the plant. Within four months they fired 500 to 800 [out of 7000 assembly line] workers. Their jobs were divided among the remaining workers, adding a few more snaps, knocks, twists, or squirts to each man's task. The job had been boring and unbearable before. When it remained boring and became a bit more unbearable there was a 97 percent vote to strike. More amazing—85 percent went down to the union hall to vote. . . .

Hanging around the parking lot between shifts, I learned immediately that to these young workers, "It's not the money."

"It pays good," said one, "but it's driving me crazy."

"I don't want more money," said another. "None of us do."

"I do," said his friend. "So I can quit quicker."

"It's the job," everyone said. But they found it hard to describe the job itself.

"My father worked in auto for thirty-five years," said a clean-cut lad, "and he never talked about the job. What's there to say? A car comes, I weld it. A car comes, I weld it. A car comes, I weld it. One hundred and one times an hour."

I asked a young wife, "What does your husband tell you about his work?"

"He doesn't say what he does. Only if something happened like, 'My hair caught on fire,' or, 'Something fell in my face.' "

"There's a lot of variety in the paint shop," said a dapper twenty-two-year-old up from West Virginia. "You clip on the color hose, bleed out the old color, and squirt. Clip, bleed, squirt, think; clip, bleed, squirt, yawn; clip, bleed, squirt, scratch your nose. Only now the Gee-Mads have taken away the time to scratch your nose."

A long-hair reminisced; "Before the Go-Mads, when I had a good job like door handles, I could get a couple of cars ahead and have a whole minute to relax."

I asked about diversions. "What do you do to keep from going crazy?"

"Well, certain jobs like the pit you can light up a cigarette without them seeing."

"I go to the wastepaper basket. I wait a certain number of cars, then find a piece of paper to throw away."

"I have fantasies. You know what I keep imagining? I see a car coming down. It's red. So I know it's gonna have a black seat, black dash, black interiors. But I keep thinking what if somebody up there sends down the wrong color interiors—like orange, and me putting in yellow cushions, bright yellow!"

"There's always water fights, paint fights, or laugh, talk, tell jokes. Anything so you don't feel like a machine."

But everyone had the same hope: "You're always waiting for the line to break down." . . .

I took the guided tour of the plant. It's new, it's clean, it's well lit without windows, and it's noisy. Hanging car bodies move past at the speed of a Coney Island ride slowing down. Most men work alongside the line but some stand in a man-sized pit craning their necks to work on the undersides of the cars.

I stopped to shout at a worker drinking coffee, *"Is there any quiet place to take a break?"* He shouted back, *"Can't hear you, ma'am. Too noisy to chat on a break."* . . .

That evening I visited Duane [and a] couple of [his] high-school friends, Stan and Eddie. . . . Duane had invited them over to tell me what it's like working at the plant.

"I'll tell you what it's like," said Duane. "It's like the Army. They even use the same words like *direct order.* Supposedly you have a contract so there's some things they just can't make you do. Except, if the foreman gives you a direct order, you do it, or you're out."

"Out?" I asked.

"Yeah, fired—or else they give you a DLO."

"DLO?"

"Disciplinary layoff. Which means you're out without pay for however long they say. Like maybe it'll be a three-day DLO or a week DLO."

Eddie explained it further: "Like this foreman comes up to me and says, 'Pick up that piece of paper.' Only he says it a little nastier, with a few references to my race, creed, and length of hair. So I says, 'That's not my job.' He says, 'I'm giving you a direct order to pick up that piece of paper.' Finally he takes me up to the office. My committeeman comes over and tells me I could of lost my job because you can't refuse a direct order. You do it, and then you put in a grievance—ha!"

"Calling your committeeman," says Duane. "That's just like the Army too. If your CO [commanding officer] is harassing you, you can file a complaint with the IG [Inspector General].

Only thing is you gotta go up to your CO and say, 'Sir, request permission to see the Inspector General to tell him my commanding officer is a shit.' Same thing here. Before you can get your committeeman, you got to tell the foreman exactly what your grievance is in detail. So meantime he's working out ways to tell the story different."

Here Stan took out an actual DLO form from his wallet. "Last week someone up the line put a stink bomb in a car. I do rear cushions, and the foreman says, 'You get in that car.' We said, 'If you can put your head in that car we'll do the job.' So the foreman says, 'I'm giving you a direct order.' So I hold my breath and do it. My job is every other car so I let the next one pass. He gets on me, and I say, 'It ain't my car. Please, I done your dirty work and the other one wasn't mine.' But he keeps at me, and I wind up with a week off. Now, I got a hot committeeman who really stuck up for me. So you know what? They sent *him* home too. Gave the committeeman a DLO!"

"See, just like the Army," Duane repeats. "No, it's worse 'cause you're welded to the line. You just about need a pass to piss."

"That ain't no joke," says Eddie. "You raise your little hand if you want to go wee-wee. Then wait maybe half an hour till they find a relief man. And they write it down every time too. 'Cause you're supposed to do it on your own time, not theirs. Try it too often, and you'll get a week off."

"I'd rather work in a gas station," said Stan wistfully. "That way you pump gas, then you patch a tire, then you go the bathroom. You do what needs doing."

"Why don't you work in a gas station?" I asked.

"You know what they pay in a gas station? I got a kid. Besides, I couldn't even get a job in a gas station. Before I got in here I was so hard up I wound up selling vacuum cleaners— $297 door to door. In a month I earned exactly $10 selling one vacuum cleaner to a laid-off steel worker for which I'll never forgive myself." . . .

Later in the week I stay at an auto-workers' commune. . . . Throughout the evening, six to twelve people drifted through the old house waiting for Indian Nut (out working night shift at Lordstown) and his wife Jane (out baby-sitting).

Jane returned at midnight to prepare dinner for her husband. By 2:00 A.M. she complained: "They can keep them two, three, four hours over." Overtime is mandatory for auto workers, but it's not as popular at Lordstown as it is among older workers at other plants.

At two-thirty the Nut burst in, wild-haired, wild-eyed, and sweet-smiled. He had a mildly maniacal look because his glasses were speckled with welding spatter.

"New foreman, a real Gee-mad-man. Sent a guy home for farting in a car. And another one home for yodeling."

"Yodeling?" I asked.

"Yeah, you know." (And he yodeled.)

(It's common in auto plants for men to break the monotony with noise, like the banging of tin cans in jail. Someone will drop something, his partner will yell "Whaa," and then "Whaa" gets transmitted all along the line.)

"I bet there's no shop rule against farting," the Nut conjectured. "You know those porkers have been getting their 101 off the line again, and not that many of them need repairs. It's the hillbillies. Those cats have no stamina. The union calls them to a meeting, says, 'Now don't you sabotage, but don't you run. Don't do more than you can do.' And everybody cheers. But in a few days it's back to where it was. Hillbillies working so fast they ain't got time to scratch their balls. Meantime these porkers is making money even faster than they're making cars."

I ask who he means by the hillbillies. "Hillbillies is the general Ohio term for assholes, except if you happen to be a hillbilly. Then you say Polack. Fact is everybody is a hillbilly out here except me and two other guys. And they must work day shift 'cause I never see them.

"Sabotage?" says the Nut. "Just a way of letting off steam. You can't keep up with the car so you scratch it on the way past. I once saw a hillbilly drop an ignition key down the gas tank. Last week I watched a guy light a glove and lock it in the trunk. We all waited to see how far down the line they'd discover it. . . . If you miss a car, they call that sabotage. They expect the sixty-second minute. Even a machine has to sneeze. Look how they call us in weekends, hold us extra, send us home early, give us layoffs. You'd think we were machines the way they turn us on and off."

I apologized for getting Indian Nut so steamed up and keeping him awake late. "No," sighed Jane. "It always takes a couple of hours to calm him down. We never get to bed before four." . . .

As I proceeded with my unscientific survey, I found that I

couldn't predict a man's militancy from his hair length, age, or general freakiness. . . .

A nineteen-year-old told me bitterly: "A black guy worked next to me putting sealer into the cracks. He used to get cut all the time on sharp edges of metal. One day his finger really got stuck and he was bleeding all over the car. So I stopped the line [There's a button every so many feet.] Sure they rushed him to the hospital, but boy did they get down on me for stopping the line. That line runs no matter what the cost."

The mildest man I met was driving a Vega. He was a long-haired, or at least shaggy-haired, twenty-one-year-old. He thought the Vega was a "pretty little thing." When I asked about his job he said, "It's a very important job. After all, everybody's got to have a car." Yes, he had voted for the strike. "Myself, I'd rather work, but if they're gonna keep laying people off, might as well strike now and get it over with." . . .

At the Pink Elephant Bar I met a man who'd voted against the strike, one of the rare 3 percent. He was an older man who'd worked in other auto plants. "I seen it before. The international [union] is just giving them enough rope to hang themselves. They don't ever take on speed-up or safety. And they don't ever help with any strike *they* didn't call. . . .

"Like I was saying, they see a kicky young local so they go along. They authorize the strike. . . .

"So they let 'em go ahead. But they don't give 'em no help. They don't give 'em no funds. They don't even let the other locals come out with you. When it comes to humanizing working contitions you might as well be back before there was any unions.

"So the strike drags on, it's lost, or they 'settle' in Detroit. Everybody says, 'There, it didn't pay.' And the next time around the leadership gets unelected." . . .

The underlying assumption in an auto plant is that no worker wants to work. The plant is arranged so that employees can be controlled, checked, and supervised at every point. The efficiency of an assembly line is not only in its speed but in the fact that the workers are easily replaced. This allows the employer to cope with high turnover. But it's a vicious cycle. The job is so unpleasantly subdivided that men are constantly quitting and absenteeism is common. Even an accident is a welcome diversion. Because of the high turnover, management further simplifies the job, and more men quit. But the company has learned to cope with high turnover. So they don't have to worry if men quit or go crazy before they're forty.

The UAW is not a particularly undemocratic union. Still, it is as hard for the majority of its members to influence their international as it is for the majority of Americans to end the war in Vietnam. The desire to reduce alienation is hard to express as a union demand, and it's hard to get union leaders to insist upon this demand. Harder still will be the actual struggle to take more control over production away from corporate management. It is a fight that questions the right to private ownership of the means of production.

LORDSTOWN—SEARCHING FOR
A BETTER WAY OF WORK

By Bennett Kremen

Lordstown, Ohio—*In some places, the lightning always seems to strike. Surely one is Lordstown, Ohio, where General Motors builds the Chevrolet Vega. . . .*

After a week of nights in barrooms in nearby Warren and Youngstown, and hours at the factory gate and after slipping into the plant on the second shift the other night, early hints of more lightning in Lordstown flashed again.

.   .   .

For during those eight hours along the line, a rush of curses directed at the plant's managers hissed from the mouths of both assemblers and their elected committeemen as I pressed questions incessantly, determined to grasp finally what lay at the nerve and marrow of this plant. Repeatedly I was informed that more than 5,000 grievances have piled up within the last six months and that hundreds more are sure to come.

And before leaving the roar of the plant with its incessant assembly line binding like a halter, forcing hours of tedious movements from thousands in its service who stand in fixed stations for blocks, I could conclude only that Lordstown's reputation as an extraordinary site in the industrial environment was not in the least larger than it warranted, but indeed, smaller. For what I'd been told there, I'd never heard before.

Eleven committeemen and standard assemblers, convinced of the need to spell out the smoldering tensions, agreed to meet me in the union hall and explain everything. Their ages range from early twenties to early thirties—an age group whose numbers will dominate the American work force within six years.

QUESTION: Why don't you introduce yourselves, fellows?

ANSWER: Al Alli, committeeman, trim department.

I'm Bill Bowers, committeeman for final line and cushion.

George Brayner, material department, committeeman.

Jim Baird, assembler, final line.

Carol Crawford, assembler, cushion.

Joe Alfona, absentee replacement operator.

Dave McGarvey, final 3, rank and file.

Gary Brainard, final assembler.

Dennis McGee, committeeman, first shift.

Dennis Lawrence, committeeman, body shop.

Robert Dickerson, committeeman.

Q: When I came into this place in the strike in '72 I was amazed at the level of anger that I heard. And now I'm hearing it again. What's the yelling about?

ALLI: The working conditions. General Motors' attitude's no damn good!

Q: In what way?

ALLI: They break their agreements. You settle a grievance, then they turn right on you and break the agreement. It just tees us off!

Q: I talked to some people recently who say the whole thing about the alienation of the younger working men is an invention of the journalists—that they made it up. Does that sound like it has any reason to it? You must represent about 3,000 men, just sitting at this table.

LAWRENCE: There's no rationale at all. The press, the news media may have coined certain phrases that are attached to the workers of today. But as far as the dissension, it's there; it's live.

Q: Is it growing or getting less?

LAWRENCE: It's growing. It's going to continue to grow until corporations realize that it's not a bunch of kids they're playing with. These guys out there—I don't give a damn if they're 18 or 50—they're serious, they're disgusted, they're fed up with it. And goddamn it, it's going to change, it's got to change, because if it doesn't, they just won't build the goddamned cars.

Q: Is there a distinct difference between the way you people are seeing things, or feeling, or what's going on in the plant and the way your fathers saw it?

BRAINARD: Our fathers range between 50 and 60 years old, and most of them are established people. They almost have to bend to the corporation. This being a young plant, and most of the people out there being of a younger set, we don't have to take the garbage they're giving us now.

MCGEE: I think we're different. Our parents were motivated to a lesser degree than we were. Maybe they didn't have the education we had. Maybe they were immigrant families that wanted to prove themselves, that their nationality was real good. They're hard workers.

But we, the younger workers, have been through high school and have had advanced subjects compared to our parents. Most of us have had monetary gains, but we know that isn't all there is. We're not narrow-minded people. We know we're down here in the plant, and we know we've got to have a good time about doing it.

Q: So it's not money that is bothering you. And Alli says working conditions are the main issue. Is that right?

MCGEE: Yeah. Absolutely.

Q: O.K., what is it about the working conditions that's creating the intensity of your anger? I've heard it for eight nights all over the place.

ALFONA: Well, like all men when they used to work, they had a specific job to do. They told them to shovel 100 tons of coal within X amount of time, and that's what they did. And they left them alone.

But like now they tell you, "Put in 10 screws," and you do it. Then a couple of weeks later they say, "Put in 15" and next they say, "Well, we don't need you no more, give it to the next man."

From day to day, you don't know what your job's going to be. They always either add to your job or take a man off. I mean management's word is no good. They guarantee you—they write to the union—that this is the settlement on the job, this is the way it's going to run—103 cars an hour, and we're the only ones in the world could do that pace. Know what I mean?

They agree that so many men are going to do so many things, period! Fine, the union will buy that because they negotiated it. Two weeks later management comes down and says, "Hey, listen, let's add something else to that guy." They don't even tell the union. And management says, if you don't do it, they'll throw you out, which they do. No problem. Zap! away you go. . . .

Q: O.K., let's get to it now—to those 5,000 grievances. After my research and getting the history of this plant back to the beginning, what has really come to a head is an issue we've never heard of before, which even your international is either unaware of or denies exists—and that's "doubling up."

Relay teams rather than doubling up may describe this better. On your own, without the aid of the company or the union, you're doing the same amount of work on the line, but in teams relieving each other, half an hour on, half an hour off. By doubling your

speed, this method produces an equal amount of quality and productivity, but gives each person more time off the line. And this has
never been done before. Am I on the track?

LAWRENCE: That's it basically.

Q: How did it start?

MCGEE: Well, our local union has a normal work pace out there. In
other words, we don't want a guy killing himself speeding eight
hours a day. I believe an individual should do his task and have a
recovery time in which he can turn around and look at the car coming up next, take a breather and go on. Okay? A normal pace—not
hustling, normal.

Now what happens is that the guys who have their operations
side by side, they're relating together.

In other words, they all worked in the same area. They started
saying, "Go ahead, take off." It started like an 'E' break—you asked
for emergency bathroom call. The utility man might be tied up.

I'd say, "Go ahead, man, I think I can handle it." I'd run to the
front of the car and I'd stick in the ring we used to have, and I'd run
to the back then. I mean, I'm not running, really running, but I'm
moving. I put the gas in, I go up to the front of the car again . . . go
back again. I'm getting it done, and I'm not having any recovery
time. I'm going right back again.

Well, the guys started doing this on a larger scale.

Q: How far back did it start, Al?

ALLI: I'd say three years, four years ago.

Q: All right. Why do people at the international say that there's no
such thing as doubling up?

LAWRENCE: God damn it—they're just not that concerned.

DICKERSON: Yeah, they'd just as soon ignore it.

Q: Why?

LAWRENCE: They don't want to take it on. They have certain set attitudes. See, you're talking there again to older people, your executive board are older people, every one of them. They don't have any
young people.

Q: All right, here's another argument from the company. They say
that if you double up the quality is going to go down.

DICKERSON: They're wrong.

SEVERAL: No way.

Q: You have any evidence they're wrong?

ALLI: Damn right. We had better quality when they doubled up.

Q: How do you know?

ALFONA: The audit tickets.

Q: What are audit tickets?

ALFONA: They come down there with the corporation and they check X
amount of jobs, like maybe 10 out of 100. And they check the
tickets, the repair tickets which were inspected. And they see how
much repair was done to this car before it hit the end of the line.

DICKERSON: It's an inspection ticket.

ALFONA: Right, it's a rating. Like if so many repairs were on this ticket within the 10 jobs per 100 it was a good audit. But if more repairs were on it, that means that the quality was bad in certain areas. And they could detect which areas.

Q: So you're saying that during the doubling up the quality, in terms of audit tickets, does not go down or does go down?

ALFONA: It goes up. I can prove it to you, because I work the line, see. And we used to double up in tail lights. It's a four-man operation— you do every other car, two people do every other car.

Q: A half-hour on, a half-hour off?

ALFONA: Right. I got thrown out of the plant for a week over this issue.

Q: Are the 5,000 grievances related to a lot of this?

ALFONA: Absolutely. Two people would be working the job. The other two people would usually stay right there if something should happen—if the gun broke down, or if I missed a screw, I'd call my partner, who was sitting down. "Hey, catch that before it goes down to the repair station." He'd jump up, put the screw in for me. No repair. I got the next car behind me.

I'm working, working, working. If something else should happen, if I fell in the hole and missed a job, I call my sidekick again. He catches it, repairs it. It's never marked on the ticket. You get 100 percent, perfect. Because we don't want no problems, you know what I mean? We're doing a good job. And I defy you to find some-body who's doubling up disciplined for bad work!

LAWRENCE: The only reason we started doubling up was to break the boredom on the damned line.

DICKERSON: I think there's a better word than relay team—anti-dehumanization team.

MCGEE: I think something else should be noted about the doubling up. We had a lot of press releases concerning assembly-line work being dehumanizing. It's the hardest mental type work in the world. Poli-ticans have gotten on the bandwagon and started committees, they've come to the plant and rapped with people about it.

But the ones that found a way finally to beat it were the same dudes, so-called dodos they wrote about in Playboy. Well, these do-dos devised the system, the working man himself, the assembler himself devised this system.

Playboy called us long-haired hippies, spaced-out, or whatever words they used. They're a bunch of idiots; it makes no difference how long a guy's hair is. Most of the long-haired dudes in there, they're not dummies any of them. Nor are the short-hairs. It makes no difference.

Q: Would you say that that system was a redesign of assembly line methods?

MCGEE: Definitely. There's no question about it.

Q: This is an astounding thing if it's true. It's an absolutely amazing thing. If you, by doing it your own way produce the same quality and the same amount through your doubling, then you have rede-signed the assembly line. Does that make sense?

MCGARVEY: You have to double up and break the boredom to get an immediate feed-back from your job, because the only gratification you get is a paycheck once a week, and that's too long to go without any kind of gratification from the job.

q: Well, management's argument is this: If you stay on the line and do a full hour's pace—a day's work for a day's pay—meaning you stand there and take the standard breaks as worked out in your negotiations, you should be able to do more work. You should be able to produce more at the end of the day.

But you were telling me the other night that in the eight-hour day, if you did it that way, the boredom would begin to affect the quality before the day was over. That, with the doubling up, you break the boredom, and when you get back to it, you work harder.

LAWRENCE: What their [management's] reasoning is against doubling up—and the only answer that I can get out of them is basic quality. But where is your quality? Where do you show me that your quality went down?

Then they come and say, "Well, it's our plant." But this idea of doubling up where you put a man on for eight hours and—after he learns that job, gets set in his ways, he no longer pays any attention to what he's doing because it's automatic—bang, bang, bang.

He's dreaming about something he's going to do tomorrow, something he did last night, whatever.

q: So the quality suffers?

LAWRENCE: The quality goes down. That's my experience. He don't care any more. But at the point where you're doubling up, you've got the responsibility for two jobs. You've got to keep your mind working at all times. Because if that car when it comes off the end of the line, if it isn't right, it goes back to the repair yard.

q: Do you have evidence that during doubling up fewer cars go to the yard?

BROWER: The quality index board reflected that.

q: Would that be related to resentment at working in the traditional manner or to the fact that the boredom came into it?

GENERAL: Oh, boredom.

q: So why would the company have anything against doubling up?

MCGEE: This is what I just realized. Honest to God, I believe right now that they're so goddamned scared of doubling up because every job that people doubled up on the final line, they took that man away, they took him away, every single man.

q: But despite all the hassle with their clamping down and the 5000 grievances in the last six months, you manage to double up.

SEVERAL: Oh, yes.

MCGARVEY: Even if they say don't double up, what you do—it's not as good as doubling up the way we normally do it—but we'll hang on the car and we'll stand there while the other guy does it. And the minute somebody comes round, we'll just put our hand in the car. We'll just play the game with them.

And they get tired of harrassing us because they keep checking like bird dogs. And every time they look we're over there. Yeah, we're doing the job—but we're not really. Just to play the game.

ALFONA: You know, there were instances out there where foremen on the floor actually paid guys to double up. They paid them.

Q: Why?

MCGEE: Because they want the area to run smooth. That's why.

ALFONA: They turned their backs on it. You're not allowed to double up. In other words the foreman says, "I'm going to go over to the next line for a couple of hours." Normally the guys know what they mean, and they'll do a good job for that foreman.

Then when this foreman turns to the general foreman, he tells the general foreman, "Well, my area is running perfect." Sure, because his guys are doubling up. If he had four guys working in this one spot at the normal pace eight hours, without doubling up, he's going to get less good work out of them. Even if the guys don't want to sabotage.

Q: You mean the foreman knows that?

GENERAL: Right.

ALFONA: He says, "To hell with it. I'm going to walk over to the other line and get a Coca-Cola," because he wants the productivity and the quality.

Q: Do a lot of foremen do this?

GENERAL: Quite a few.

And now I suddenly realize that without the tacit approval of foremen on the line, efforts to double up would halt, or lead to even more explosive conflict than exists. I wonder also if the foremen might silently agree that part of the answer to the humanization of the assembly line lies in this simple antidote of doubling up: Perhaps it's not a waste of manpower.

Although G.M. seems convinced otherwise, even the company, like the U.A.W. International, will not admit for the record what the Dennis McGees and Dave McGarveys are evolving on the line.

Joseph Godfrey, general manager of General Motors' assembly division has said, "Yes, workers in our plants are less willing to give maximum effort than they used to be. . . . There is a lot of unrest in the world and we feel it on the assembly lines—war, youth rebellion, drugs, race, inflation, moral degeneration. Marriage isn't what it used to be. We feel it. Their minds are on other things."

Yet the question remains, does doubling up lead to an equal, or even better, degree of quality because it lessens boredom? And does doubling up, thus, lead to less absenteeism, as some of the men have been telling me?

*Could it diminish the mounting alienation of labor? Most
serious, can the young, imaginative, work force coming up so rapidly bear a blue-collar lifestyle other than the one they're developing at Lordstown?*

Q: So there's a philosophy behind doubling up?

GENERAL: Definitely.

MCGEE: Sure, if you're on the damned line here and you've found a
way to double up and you've found a way for me to shuck and
jive—all day long, have a good time, help each other and get out
the work. I don't have to take these pain pills no more. My ulcer's
gone. Now what are you going to tell a dude? "You ain't going to do
it?" My nerves was bad. I'm not kidding you.

Q: Has it—and your doubling up—come from laziness or inventiveness?

DICKERSON: Inventiveness. One way to explain the thing is that any-
time there's a human need, there's always an invention, or a way to
get around it.

MCGARVEY: I'd say inventiveness definitely. I was explaining to my father what the line was like. He said, "Well, why don't you push a
broom?" He doesn't understand that pushing a broom is a priority
job out there.

LAWRENCE: Yeah—it gets you off that line.

Q: When they eliminate the doubling up, are there more drugs? More
alcohol?

MCGEE: Drugs aren't necessarily connected with it. I'm saying some
people on that line run out of things to think about, man. And when
you get through singing that song, and telling every joke, what is
there? You know, that's all there is to it.

ALFONA: And really there's no such thing as an eight-hour day. There's
10, 12, six days a week. You have no social life. The only social life
you have is in that plant, and if you're stuck on that line all that
time—nothing!

But if you can get that break where you can go down and rap to
your buddy or make a phone call to some chick, it's different.

Q: You know, you read all these articles about humanizing the work
place, and boredom. And I was beginning to think it was an invention of journalists myself. Now, according to what you're telling
me, you've gone way beyond that. It's what they're trying to do at
Volvo—redesign the line. Chrysler claims it's doing this in one of its
experimental plants. And here you are doing it almost unconsciously in a highly productive plant.

ALFONA: I'd explain it to the people on the outside very simply, about
Lordstown and the doubling up situation. They should think about
themselves at work not at Lordstown but some other place—either
in an office or in a steel mill. If they say, "Gee, I'd like to go and get
a drink of water," and they go. Now I might be on the line, and my
break doesn't come for four hours. What am I going to do?

I'd also tell people on the outside, "Listen, if you had a job paying $4 an hour, you and your buddy, and you're each going to carry a package"—I bring it down to very easy words so the average man can understand—"You're going to get paid $4 an hour to each carry a package up the steps and down."

"Well, isn't it a little easier for you to break your back and carry two packages up and down for half an hour and your buddy resting, and then let him take over and you rest your back. If you want to go get your drink of water or go call your chick, you got the simple freedom to go, see?"

And then they understand it a little bit more. I mean, they said, "Hey, yeah, that makes life a little easier." That's all we want.

12 / Women's Work: Some Lousy Offices to Work in, and One Good One

Barbara Garson

I WORKED for a while at the Fair Plan Insurance Company, where hundreds of women sat typing up and breaking down sextuplicate insurance forms. My job was in endorsements: *First, third, and fourth copies staple together/Place the pink sheet in back of the yellow/If the endorsement shows a new mortgagee/Stamp the fifth copy "certificate needed. . . ."*

Other sections, like coding, checks, filing, and endorsement typing, did similar subdivided parts of the paperwork. The women in the other sections sat at steel desks like mine, each working separately on a stack of forms or cards. Every section had a supervisor who counted and checked the work. She recorded the number of pieces we completed, and the number of errors we made, on our individual production sheets. These production sheets were the basis for our periodic merit raises.

Aside from counting and checking, the supervisor also tried to curtail talking and eating at the desks.

Across the room from endorsements—the room was an entire floor in a Manhattan skyscraper—sat a black woman named Marlene. I stared at her often because she wore the largest earrings I had ever seen. I used those gigantic gold hoops to refocus my eyes when the forms got blurry. (*First, third, and fourth copies staple together/Place the pink sheet in back of the yellow/If the endorsement shows a new mortgagee. . . .*)

I had never spoken to Marlene because the sections had staggered breaks and ours never coincided. One day when I came back from coffee, the women in the section next to me were questioning each other.

"Who was that ran out crying?"

"I don't know. She's in coding I think."

"They called her to the phone. That's what Mary told me."

"I thought you weren't allowed to receive any personal phone calls."

"It must have been an emergency."

"Something about her kid Mary said."

It turned out that Marlene's two-year-old son had pneumonia. She had been going to the hospital every day before and after work.

The morning after the phone call she was back at her desk on time, earrings gleaming, working steadily.

The way our jobs were arranged at Fair Plan, none of us really worked with each other. Occasionally someone may have borrowed a stapler off Marlene's desk, and someone else may have brought back errors for her to do over. But our work certainly didn't facilitate personal contact. As a matter of fact it required a contrivance for me to ask her how her son was. Since a clerk can't just saunter across the room, I went to the bathroom when I saw Marlene's section go for their break. At the sink I asked her how her son was and she said, "Junior's doing just fine." When I got back, my supervisor reminded me that I should attend to my personal needs on my own time.

Even if we had been allowed to talk, the job would not have encouraged closeness. Though all of our desks were as close together as they could be, we worked far apart from each other; each woman stapling, stamping, sorting, or figuring over her own pile. None of us would sense Marlene's distraction in the course of our work. And there was no subtlety about the job that would make her production a little "off." As long as she could manage to stamp and staple, she could fulfill her function for Fair Plan. The bosses didn't have to notice her distress until she actually cracked up. And then they could replace her in one day with someone who would pick up her speed in less than a week. The job was deliberately designed that way.

At the Reader's Digest plant near Pleasantville, New York, about 2,000 women work in the business sections handling complaints, processing subscriptions, flipping through special promotions to separate the "Yesses—I would like to subscribe" from the "Nos—but please enter me in your contest." This work, called fulfillment, is arranged very much like the jobs at Fair Plan. There's the same extreme division of labor, the same close supervision with the same production sheets and merit raises. At the Digest the raises are based not only upon quantity and quality of production, but also on cooperativeness, dependability, flexibility, and attendance. In periodic conferences with the supervisor, each clerk may see her number and letter grades in each category.

Fair Plan is a low-paying firm in the middle of Manhattan. It has a very high turnover. Reader's Digest, on the other hand, is the main employer in a suburban region. The Digest has its own bus system, which brings women to work from the surrounding towns and countryside. Like Fair Plan, the Digest pays low wages. Most of the women who work in the business sections bring home under $100 a week. But unlike Fair Plan, the Digest has bonuses, outings, insurance, and other benefits. More than half the women at the Digest have worked there for over ten years. There are twenty and twenty-five year workers in just about every department.

A gray-haired grandmother, still working as a clerk at Reader's Digest, recalled the days when her daughter was in elementary school.

"The worst thing of all was when she was sick and I had to leave her home. Actually I worked well on those days. I guess I was so nervous that my fingers went fast. Somehow you feel like if you work faster the day will go faster. Anyway I remember my supervisor always used to compliment me on those days."

I asked if she ever thought of telling her supervisor about a child's illness. "Oh, goodness no! And my husband and I had a policy if anything ever happened at home he wouldn't call me at work. They don't like you to get personal phone calls. I couldn't do anything about it in the office anyway."

The women at Fair Plan agreed that Marlene would have been foolish to tell her supervisor about her problem. In fact some were saying at lunch that it was too bad the hospital had called. "Now they'll know she's got a sick kid and what do they want with someone who'll be out all the time?" "You wait, the next time they're slow I bet she's the first one they let go."

They may have been right. When I applied for my job at Fair Plan no one bothered to check my phony record of previous employment. But the personnel officer and the department manager both questioned me closely about child-care arrangements. Was I certain, they wanted to know, that I could get to work if my child was sick?

WORK AT THE COLLEGE

I know a lady named Mrs. Klein who works in the payroll office of a fair-sized community college. She said she wouldn't mind being interviewed and suggested that I come to her office at lunch hour.

I walked through the business wing of the main building past Accounting, Purchasing, Bursar, Personnel . . . until I came to a funny little corner. There I found Payroll, a small office with four desks shared by five middle-aged women. The phone was ringing when I got there. A four-year-old picked it up and squeaked, "Hello, payroll office." She listened carefully and called, "Grandma, it's for you!"

Grandma was assistant accountant Sylvia Klein. On the other end Edna Gillers, administrative assistant in biological sciences, was calling to get several social security numbers. "Sure I could get it through personnel," Edna explained, "but it's such a pleasure to go through your new secretary. Sylvia, she is precious! Absolutely precious! I told my grandson Carl— that's my oldest one's youngest one—I have the perfect girl for him to meet. . . ."

Edna took down the social security numbers and wound up

the phone call. "Listen, Sylvia, about twenty minutes after two send your little secretary over. I'll have the time sheets for the lab assistants ready. OK? Thanks."

Now that it was noon the payroll women were getting ready to leave for lunch.

"Sylvia," said Pearl Arronstein, getting her purse out of the drawer. "I'm going over to the gym. I'll take your granddaughter if you want."

"You're going folk dancing?" asked Mimi Dworkin, a lady who kept herself in very good shape with yoga and yogurt and transcendental meditation.

"Why not?" answered the shapeless Pearl. "They didn't have any sign 'no old ladies allowed.' " Then turning back to Sylvia, "What do you say? Should I take the little one? She'll love it."

The little one answered for herself. "Can I take my shoes off in the gym, Grandma?"

"Oh that would be a godsend, Pearl. This young lady is here to interview me, and. . . ."

"I'll just be five minutes, Jessie," Pearl explained to the child. "I want to get these things xeroxed now before it gets crowded. If I can just get the 138's out to central payroll this afternoon I'll be all right for the rest of the week."

"Fine," said Sylvia. "We'll be over in the business office. I told Lillian I'd cover for her."

Mrs. Klein led me down the hall. "Lillian is the business manager's secretary," she explained. "Her grandson was bar-mitzvahed last week—wait till you see her, you'll never believe she could have a grandchild that age—so she's giving a coffee hour for the girls. I told her I'd cover her phones while she's setting up."

At the business office Lillian was waiting with her two grown daughters, each carrying three shopping bags full of strudels, halvah, nuts, fruits, and coffee cakes. She quickly gave Mrs. Klein some instructions and left to set up the coffee hour in the conference room. Sylvia Klein sat down at Lillian's desk in front of the business manager's closed door. Mr. Johnson was a timid enough, or wise enough, executive to stay strictly inside his office as long as the work was getting done. Nevertheless, the women generally lowered their voices when they passed his door.

While her granddaughter was out folk dancing, while Lillian

was setting up the bar-mitzvah spread, while Mimi Dworkin was practicing yoga in the next office, Sylvia Klein explained her job to me.

"There's three different categories, three different payroll banks we handle. Full-time faculty get paid monthly, full-time non-academics like clerks and janitors get paid bi-weekly, and all the hourlies get paid every week. I handle the full-time faculty.

"Prior to September I get all the information I need on P.D.F. forms from the Dean of Faculty. I take the information from these personnel data forms and make individual history cards. Then I code them, that is I figure each faculty member's annual salary, and I place them on a budget line that reserves a certain amount of money for them with the city. You see I pay them each month out of the money in their 'bank.' If I don't set aside enough at the beginning of the year I'll have a hard time paying them by the end.

"By the fifteenth of the month I have to project each individual's pay (there's 400 to 500 in my bank) on an A-221 and send them to central payroll. They send back payroll sheets and I have to be sure everything adds up. They use computers so sometimes they make ridiculous errors. Like one man was hired at $5,350 a year but they had him down as $53,500. His first check was equal to his whole annual salary. You should have seen the taxes he had to pay! Most of the time the mistakes aren't so obvious. It takes a lot of going over.

"When it's all right, or at least the computer errors are all accounted for, I make out a final payroll which my boss signs. I get it out to central payroll and they send me the checks. First I alphabetize them. A few, maybe fifteen, get delivered personally to the V.I.P.'s. Others I mail out. Whoever leaves me addressed envelopes I'll mail their checks to them. It's no trouble to us. The rest of the people come to the payroll window to pick up their checks.

"Very often you can't get the errors on the payroll sheets corrected by payday. If someone's check is really messed up I try to get them a month's advance from the special college fund. It's as if I'm borrowing it for them. I pay them 70 percent of their gross salaries as a rough estimate of their pay after taxes."

I asked Mrs. Klein if there were any other things like advances that she had to arrange on her own.

At that point a woman crossed the room with a load of groceries. She put them into a refrigerator in the corner of the office.

"The refrigerator," Mrs. Klein explained, "is big enough so you can shop at lunch hour. You'd be surprised what a difference that makes when you work full-time.

"Now what were you asking? Oh yes, things I have to look out for for myself. Well, for one thing I don't get new data each month except on new hires. I have to figure from their payroll history cards if someone is scheduled for a raise or a leave. If someone is due back from a leave I call up and find out if they're really gonna be here. Or sometimes someone will call me and say "I'm back.' Now I may not be able to get official confirmation of that till after the fifteenth but I try to get them on an A-221 before the fifteenth because I'd rather not let it go and then have to pay them for two months. First of all most people can't wait a month and a half for their pay when they're just back from leave. But secondly, as I may have mentioned, that computer isn't any too bright. If someone gets paid for two months they make deductions as though his salary was twice as high. And till you can straighten it out is two reams of forms and half a dozen phone calls. So I take a chance and use my judgment. If they weren't supposed to be paid I'd be in trouble. But I know most of the faculty here and if I don't know them I know who to call to say 'look, is so-and-so here or not?' "

Then Mrs. Klein summed up some of her other duties. "Aside from the monthly payroll, there are quarterly budget modifications. Then we have the state labor report. I handle that for all three banks because the women doing the weeklies and biweeklies have plenty to do without that. There's withholding. We distribute the W-2's. When someone requests to have union dues taken out or some deductions added, I send an E-138 to central payroll. Then during the year there's United Fund, bonds, all kinds of deductions.

"Sometimes one of the women from another office will help at the window on payday. The pressure really piles up certain times of the month. If you plan a vacation you've got to plan it away from the deadlines. Same thing for the flu or a funeral. A person can't drop dead around the fifteenth or the thirtieth."

"It sounds like a very heavy job," I said. "Is your granddaughter much help?"

"Well," she smiled, "she's a very good little secretary. I really should put her on the payroll. But she's only going to be here today and tomorrow. It's a Jewish holiday and we managed to get her into a Yeshiva nursery school until my daughter gets settled."

Mrs. Klein filled me in on her daughter's situation.

"She's been divorced two years—not even divorced. Her husband just left to go have a 'life style.'

"So Beth finally decided to move back to New York. She found a job pretty quickly—she's a very talented girl. So she's been working three weeks in a publishing house, spending her lunch hours and after work looking for an apartment and a nursery school in the city. Of course she couldn't take Jessie to work on the holidays. It's not that kind of place. So who's gonna take care of the child? The grandmother of course."

"Doesn't your boss mind?"

She shrugged at the business manager's closed door. "As long as we get the work done. But you know the Yeshiva doesn't start till nine and it's been almost a month I've been coming in a little late. And I can't stay late because I have to pick the baby up. So I told my boss, 'Listen, there's nothing I can do. I'll stay and work through lunch if you want.' He doesn't care as long as the payroll gets out.

"But it's not fair to the other women. On the fifteenth those A-221's have to get out. People have to be paid. If you have to stay late you stay late. But you don't leave a four-year-old standing on the sidewalk either. So the other women have had to pitch in. Well we always help each other if there's a problem. Like when Pearl's son had the accident or when Rose's daughter was getting married. But this has been a month already.

"Anyway my daughter has a job now and I think she may have found an apartment yesterday. One bedroom for $225, but what can you do? Now she just has to find a nursery school. You know," said Mrs. Klein with a very real sigh, "what she really needs to find is a husband."

"If you know where to find one," said Mimi Dworkin, relaxing from her exercises, "you tell me for my Marcia." And she went back into modified lotus. . . .

MAIL READING

The ladies in the college business offices are not afraid to point out their own errors. No one would juggle figures or hide papers in order to cover for themselves. After all, everyone has a common goal: to get the payroll out.

At Reader's Digest and Fair Plan, close supervision, production sheets, and merit raises are supposed to replace the goal as a way of keeping the women working. Certainly everyone works quietly and diligently at the Digest. But sometimes their anxious energies go into covering for themselves, regardless of the actual output.

Mail reading is one of the larger and more diversified departments at the Digest. It handles items that require individual responses. Of course, with hundreds of thousands of letters a week, the possible responses have been categorized and simplified as much as possible. There is a standard form for someone who received a bill after he'd already mailed a check. A change of address has to be "V coded." That is, the letter has to be read and certain items need to be underlined. The material has to be put into a standard form for the keypunch operators with, for instance, the "reet" deleted from "street." A deceased has to have his name removed from the subscription lists. There are about twenty different operations that the women learn to handle. The new clerks are taught the simplest and most common items. Gradually, as a woman's repertoire increases, other items are deposited in her basket.

Just as the clerks are graded and rewarded for their output, so are the supervisors. The goal, of course, is to turn out the most work at the least cost to the company. At the beginning of each period the supervisors estimate the number of woman-hours they will need to handle the up-and-coming work. It's good to have a low estimate, but it's better to be a little high than dead wrong.

Ruth Anne Yuba had always been a somewhat nervous and severe supervisor, but in one period the pressure and tensions were noticeably increased.

"I was in mail reading three years," said a relative newcomer to the Digest, "and it was never very cozy. You know the place;

you've seen it . . . the long tables with the wooden cubbies with the slots in front of you. They were always patrolling around to stop any talking. Even if we talked between baskets—sometimes we had to wait for work, you weren't allowed to just get up and get some more, that wasn't the system—even if you talked between baskets she'd yell and separate you. If she thought two women were getting to be friends she'd always separate them. There was never a nice word from her. If you had a question about a new form all they'd say was 'That was explained to you.'

"But then it seemed to be getting even worse. And I knew what it was. She had underestimated the help she was going to need and I guess she was afraid to tell them. She couldn't keep up with the work and finally she started hiding back mail. I knew it because she hid boxes of it near my desk.

"The women that knew it were very disturbed. I mean there are women who've been here fifteen, twenty years in mail reading. And they were proud of the fact that every letter to the Digest gets answered. It's the propaganda. The Wallaces come around thanking you personally for the fact that millions of pieces of mail get answered all within a week. And here was the supervisor hiding mail underneath the desks.

"I think some of the women sent a secret letter. I'm not sure about that but I know the office must have been tipped off because a big boss came in and went right to the boxes of hidden mail.

"Even though she made my life miserable, I really felt sorry for Ruth Anne Yuba. Because you know what? I was doing the same thing she was.

"At the time I was handling complaints from Christmas gift donors and a few things like that. But sometimes I'd come up with something I wasn't sure how to handle. So I'd take those things and put them on the bottom of my basket. Then when someone nearby went to the bathroom I'd slip it into her basket. So wasn't I doing the same thing as the supervisor—hiding the mail?"

At Fair Plan I heard about another form of "evasion" that was inspired by the production sheets. A young woman named Ellen told me this story.

"The other day I was proofreading an endorsement and I noticed some guy had insured his store for $165,000 against vandalism and $5,000 against fire. Now that's bound to be a mistake. They probably got it backwards.

"I was just about to show it to Gloria [the supervisor] when I figured, 'Wait a minute! I'm not supposed to read these forms. I'm just supposed to check one column against another. And they do check. So it couldn't be counted as my error.'

"Then I thought about this poor guy when his store burns down and they tell him he's only covered for $5,000. But I figured, the hell with it. It'll get straightened out one way or another."

I must have looked disapproving.

"Listen," she apologized slightly, "for all I know he took out the insurance just to burn down the store himself." Then, growing angry, "God damn it. They don't explain this stuff to me. I'm not supposed to understand it. I'm just supposed to check one column against the other.

"If they're gonna give me a robot's job to do, I'm gonna do it like a robot! Anyway it just lowers my production record to get up and point out someone else's error."

At the college, the point was to get the payroll out. To get it out correctly and on time.

At Fair Plan the extreme division of labor and the close supervision sparked Ellen's resentful refusal to use any initiative. Almost gleefully she lets large mistakes go past because she's only hired to do one small operation.

At the Digest, the supervisors, the report cards, the unstated quotas created a generalized fear. It caused a clerk to stash away work in another woman's basket, and frightened a supervisor into hiding whole boxes of mail.

Yet any industrial engineer could tell you that it's the payroll office that is inefficiently organized. For one thing, women with the title of assistant bookkeeper are spending hours each week alphabetizing and copying figures. It's absurd to pay skilled people to do unskilled work. The job could be broken down so that it would require one assistant bookkeeper and four clerks.

Second, the payroll office is obviously inefficient in that the women spend time chatting, eating, and cooing to and about children during work hours. More exasperating than the length of their breaks is the fact that they seem to take them when and where they want. This is something no efficient firm can tolerate. And it looks as if the college is finally going to do something about it.

"Well, they've been talking about it for two years," said Pearl. "But it looks like they're finally coming, girls. The time clocks."

"Oy," said Tillie Grossberg. "How can you give anyone a birthday luncheon? You can't go out to a restaurant and get back door-to-door in one hour."

"It won't make any difference here," said Mimi Dworkin. "The business sections put in a full day. But over in the academic offices—none of those deans come in till twelve, so naturally their secretaries don't come in till ten-thirty."

"In the end they'll get less out of us," said Mrs. Klein. And she explained to me. "As it is now you're not supposed to work overtime without preauthorization. If you know you're gonna need a whole Saturday to do something you put in a request. But if you just need another ten minutes to finish up, you stay and finish up. And if it turns into a half hour so it's a half hour. But you tell me who is going to clock out at five o'clock and then work an extra ten minutes? I tell you, wherever they have time clocks, they clock out and run."

Will the ladies at the college be tamed by the time clocks? They may be slowed down at first. But eventually they'll learn how to clock in and out for each other or continue luncheons at their desks.

. . .

The amazing thing about these women is not just the energy with which they get out the payroll, but the energy of personality by which they have expanded the office routine to encompass their own rich and purposeful lives.

At the Digest and Fair Plan the opposite happens. Private lives tend to get crimped into the little cubby holes imposed by the office routine.

Formally, Reader's Digest promotes social life. They have basketball, softball, and golf teams. They organize outings to baseball games. If a department is planning a party, the company will reserve a table in the cafeteria. They will even allow someone to come in early and decorate it. Happily for Digest efficiency, a party in the company cafeteria, with the supervisor present, rarely runs much over the 35-minute lunch "hour."

Though the Digest encourages social groups, it also reserves the right to break them up in accordance with the needs of production.

I interviewed a very nervous girl named Catherine who came to Reader's Digest because her roommate worked there. One day, without notice, she was transferred to a very remote wing of the building (remote at least from her friends). At first she tried to continue meeting the girls for lunch. But in her new department, lunch hours were often switched at the last moment. When this happened there was no way for Catherine to get word to her friends. She was extremely anxious and insecure about keeping them waiting outside the cafeteria for 10 minutes of their 35-minute lunch hour. Eventually she just gave up making any arrangements at all.

Aside from transferring and loaning women to other departments, the Digest upsets people's plans by requiring overtime. Several clerks said that they were afraid to turn down extra hours. While overtime is not mandatory, "flexibility" is one of the traits the supervisors rate. And so, to be flexible with the company, they have to be inflexible with their lives.

"I needed the job too bad to refuse overtime," said a widow. "I was supposed to get out at four, but lots of times they'd ask you to work till five and they wrote you down if you didn't. I had to pull my boy out of cub scouts one year because I couldn't do my part in the carpool."

An elderly woman told me, "When I first came here I used to cry, actually cry, because of all the things I couldn't do anymore. I was a young girl then. I wanted to take sewing classes and I wanted to go out dancing. But you never know when you can make Saturday classes, and doing the same thing over and over all day you get too tired to go dancing. By now it doesn't bother me anymore. They give you sick days, they give you holidays, they give you time off for funerals, and at this stage of my life that's all that comes up anyway."

DECENT WORK

It makes an enormous difference in your life whether you work at a place like the Digest or a place like the college. For some women it almost makes the difference between having a life or not. If Marlene worked in the payroll office she could have spent unharried hours in the hospital with her two-year-old. The other women would have pitched in with her work and they probably would have visited the hospital also. To the little boy, it might have made the difference between growing up scared and growing up secure.

You never see a want ad that describes these special working conditions. Occasionally the ads will mention fellow workers as an attraction like "meet interesting people," "assist young execs." But the want ads never say "work with together women."

It is their "togetherness" that enables the ladies at the college to humanize their job. How these particular women in their particular setting have pulled it off so well is hard to analyze. Among the factors may be: the size of the offices, the job security, the defined and useful nature of the work, the inferiority complex of the boss, the ethnic and individual traits of the women. . . .

There is nothing like the élan of the payroll office. Part of the reason may be the size and the physical layout of the place. But I think the most important factor is the job itself. The monthly, biweekly, and weekly results are invigorating. Where clerks process endless forms or have discouraging tasks like interviewing unemployables about nonexistent employment, there's usually lethargy. They may spend twice as much office time on breaks, luncheons, and working the *New York Times* crossword puzzle, but they don't feel good. Yet it's wonderful to go to the Van Gogh exhibition during working hours with an old friend's daughter, when you've just gotten those hourlies out of the way.

At the Digest and at Fair Plan there's no way to experience the satisfaction of autonomous and purposeful work. The job is minutely subdivided and so is any possible sense of accomplishment. At these offices you put your mind and your emotions into limbo for seven hours a day while you process papers. That makes it hard to get the gears going again even after quitting time.

Some blessed combination of personal and sociological traits, plus the logistics of the office and the significance of the job, has enabled the payroll women to "get it together." They share a notion of what's important in the world: work, education, families and friends, Bar-Mitzvahs, and above all, children.

The women themselves have arranged their office time to encompass the important things in life. Included among those things is getting out the payroll.

13 / Retail Sales Worker

Louise Kapp Howe

FIFTY women and men are standing in line in the basement of one of Manhattan's most popular discount department stores. Filling out forms, fidgeting, waiting for their turn. Yesterday and today there were help-wanted ads for Christmas jobs here and at other stores in the *Times* and *Daily News. Earn extra cash. . . . Be in the center of things for Christmas. . . . Come meet the nicest people. . . . Apply now.*

The line moves slowly, or feels that way at least. "Two hours now I've been waiting," says a tiny woman with delicate features in a high soprano voice. "You'd think they'd have the courtesy to provide us some chairs."

"Why should they?" a basso profundo behind her rejoins. "You don't get to sit when you're on the job." And then, flirtatiously; "Maybe you can't take it."

The soprano, half an octave lower now: "Buzz off, honey."

In front of the line, a door marked PERSONNEL. Every three or so minutes it flashes open, an applicant departs (did she or he get it?) and the next is ushered in. Meantime, for those still waiting there is an arithmetic test to complete in addition to the ritual (name-address-age-education-experience-references) application form. A two page test. Add up a column of figures, then another a little longer. Subtract the following. Now multiply and divide. What's 7 percent of $5,794.89?

Nervous or simply restless, many on the line go over and over and over their answers. Including me. I am here to learn first-hand, if I can, what it is like to work at a large store such as this, and although I ostensibly mastered simple arithmetic a thousand years ago, now for some reason I find myself hesitating too, checking and rechecking as the line inches up. Perhaps I'm really concerned about all the blank spaces I left in the application form under "experience." In any case, I'm working on $5,794.89 for the third time when a young man comes out of the office and nods, "You next."

Inside, a thin blonde woman sits behind a desk overflowing with applications and arithmetic tests. She indicates a chair by her side. Glances quickly at me, my filled out papers (too rapidly to evaluate the answers *or* the blank spaces), looks up and asks what I'd prefer, sales or cashiering.

"Sales."

"Any special department?"

"Yes, coats. Or suits. Dresses. Something like that."

Then she gets to the questions about my previous selling experience (I have none, I admit, as the application shows; I would like to find out what it's like). She consults a chart on her desk. Makes a large check in one of the boxes. "I think coats and suits will be okay."

'And the pay?" I asked, relieved that it was all this easy.

"Two fifteen an hour."

Which is even lower than the low wages I had supposed. No wonder it was so easy. "Any commission above that?"

"No, two dollars and fifteen cents straight for the Christmas help. Of course you also get ten percent off on most of our merchandise."

She smiles a take it or leave it smile. I ask her when I can begin. She says in two weeks, and that being that I leave the office to be immediately replaced by the next person on the still growing line of applicants hoping for the opportunity to earn $86 a week before taxes, about $70 after, in one of the most expensive cities in the world. Did someone say people don't want to work anymore? . . .

BIRTH OF A SALESWOMAN

Standing in line again, two weeks later, fifty or more of us as before.

"Do you know what department you're going to?" the woman on my right asks. She is a short plump woman with fluffy red hair. Late fifties, or so.

"Coats and suits," I say.

"Oh, then you'll be with Peggy," she says, tapping the back of the large black woman standing in front of her. "I'm Lillian," she continues. "Dresses."

Then my new co-worker, Peggy, turns around and introduces herself, too. Seems she and Lillian met earlier in the lunchroom where we all had to go first to pick up our "Kit for Employees." (Contents of kit: One large blue and white badge reading TRAINEE, one employee discount card, one locker room key, one brochure about the store, one plastic see-through case for I don't know what.) Unlike me, Peggy and Lillian are both old hands at department store selling, but Peggy turns out to be the one with the particular information we are all avid for now: she worked in *this* store once before, only six months ago in fact.

So how is it? we both ask, what's it like?

"Well, you know, like everywhere else it all depends on which department you're in," Peggy answers, keeping her voice low. "Naturally it's how your manager and the other people you work with treat you, and that's different all over the store."

"Which manager is—" Lillian starts to ask but she is interrupted by a voice from the front of the line: "PLEASE FOLLOW ME UP THE STAIRS INTO THE MAIN FLOOR AND THEN UP THE ESCALATOR TO THE TOP OF THE STORE WHERE THE TRAINING ROOM IS."

The voice is that of the blonde woman from Personnel and we follow her now. Out of the dim basement into the bright main floor, a typical department store main floor—*cosmetics, blouses, jewelry, perfume, scarves, gloves.* Up the escalator passing the second floor—*books and records, small appliances, men's wear;* the third floor—*robes and lingerie, women's and junior sportswear;* the fourth—*coats and suits* (Peggy's and my new home) and *dresses* (where Lillian will be) and *shoes;* and then the fifth—*toys, infants' and children's wear, nursery furniture, sporting goods;* and the sixth—*vacuum cleaners, major appliances, fishing equipment, silverware and dishes;* and the seventh—*luggage, stereo sets and television, tools, furniture, carpeting, hardware;* and finally up a flight of stairs into the attic, the main stock area for the store. At the end of a long corridor full of cartons of all sizes is the training room, a tiny room with a blackboard, a desk, wooden chairs lined up in rows.

The woman from personnel is sitting behind the desk when we arrive waiting for us to be seated too. Peggy, Lillian and I find three chairs together.

The woman rises, a thick looseleaf manual in her hand. Tells us her name (Andrea), her title (assistant to the manager of personnel) and apologizes for the long wait we had downstairs.

"But it's a crazy day as you can all see. We have over 150 people starting today alone, 350 in all for the Christmas season. So it's quite hectic to say the least. But what I have to say now shouldn't take that long."

Sits down again, placing the manual on the desk in front of her. Flips slowly through the pages, stopping at certain places to inform us of company regulations. About:

Time: "Naturally it's important not to forget to punch in or out. If you want to get paid, that is. The company gives you a ten-minute leeway for lateness in the morning, anything above that you're docked. The usual system. Since it's the Christmas rush, you'll all be working some nights and most Saturdays. Your manager will let you know by the preceding Thursday what your schedule the next week will be."

Breaks: "You get a half hour each day, usually divided fifteen in the morning and afternoon, but some take it all at once."

Lunch: "You get an hour each day, although by state law the company doesn't have to give you more than 45 minutes when you work an eight-hour day. Only thing we require is you don't take lunch between twelve and two, since that's the busiest time of our day."

Dress: "Women are allowed to wear pants if they're selling, so long as it's not dungarees or anything that doesn't look proper. We don't ask you to wear only dark colors or only dresses like some stores. Try to look decent, is all we ask."

Shoplifting: "It happens all the time, you wouldn't believe how often. If you catch someone, you get an award, fifteen or twenty dollars. But don't ever try to apprehend a shoplifter yourself. The secret is: Be alert. If you see someone suspicious, call the security officer on the phone in your department right away, describe the suspect and let the officer take it from there. You'll get the award if the person is caught. And another thing. I know this sounds like a terrible thing to say. I know it sounds insulting. But I have to. *Don't shoplift yourself.* That may seem like a crazy idea to you, why should a person who comes to work want to do that, but you'd be surprised how many try. And that's very dumb of them. There are security cops and one-way mirrors all over. And if you're caught we don't only fire you, we prosecute. So if you're going to steal something, go to a bank and take a million, not a little item here. Another thing. If you catch a fellow employee in your department stealing, you'll get an award of twenty-five dollars or more if you report it."

Lockers: "You must check your coats and other street clothes in your locker before punching in. Women must check their handbags, too. Take your wallet out and anything else you'll be needing during the day and put it in that plastic case we gave you in the employee kit." (So that's what the see-through case is for: to make sure we're not stealing anything.)

With that, Andrea closes the manual. "Unless you have any questions, that's all for now. Those of you who will be cashiers keep your seats, you'll be getting special training this week. The rest of you line up and proceed downstairs back into the basement where someone from your department will come to pick you up."

COATS

Back in the basement Peggy and I stand together, waiting to start work. Very soon our names are called and we're introduced to a middle-aged woman named Alice, who has come to escort us to coats and suits. Short gray hair, stern expression.

On the escalator, Alice gives us a bit of advice. "It a nice department, coats, but one thing, you really have to *worrrrkk.*"

"Oh, is that what we're here for—to work?" I joke to break the tension.

Bad joke, bad start.

Alice stares straight ahead, silently, as the escalator carries us up.

Peggy fills in the gap. "Are you the department manager, Alice?"

"No."

"Assistant manager?"

"No, Peggy, but I have quite a bit of authority here, as you'll both be seeing."

Peggy mentions she only asked because she's hoping there'll be a permanent spot for her after Christmas, does Alice think that's possible?

"Well maybe, it's very hard to tell." Continued ice cubes and silence the rest of the way up.

Arrive safely at coats. Meet Ed, our manager, early forties, curly brown hair, Bugs Bunny smile. Seems surprised to be getting two full-timers, only expected one. Also seems preoccupied (it's the noon rush hour by now) but amiable enough in a distracted sort of way.

"Well, I guess I should show you girls around." (Yes, sisters, I know he should call us women, but this is *not* the time to argue.) Peggy and I follow him to the middle of the department, a huge department really, taking up at least half the entire fourth floor. . . .

Out of the stock room and over to the cashier booth—a kind of circular cage near the front of the department. Peggy and I are introduced to two cashiers standing inside the booth, both about nineteen or twenty. One works full-time, the other 12 to 4. We also meet two other saleswomen in the department, again one full- and one part-time and they are in their late fifties. So we come in many categories here, I'm learning. Sales and cashiers. Full-time and part-time. Permanent and Christmas.

Ed shows us how to write out a layaway form, which looks simple enough, and our training period is pronounced over. Took, figuring generously, about eleven minutes.

"Now why don't you go and help the customers?" Ed says. Can he be serious? I think. There are about a dozen customers roaming around, all of whom must know the department better than I. Peggy goes to one side of the floor and I to the other.

I approach a woman in a black and white checked coat. "May I help you?"

"No, thank you."

On to the next. "May I help you?"

"Just looking."

A woman in green. "May I help you find something?"

"Not right now, thanks."

A woman of ample proportions. "May I help you?"

"Yes, miss, do you have any cashmere coats in black, size eighteen?"

Look vacantly around the room. Racks and racks and racks and racks of mysterious garments. "Black cashmere? Well, let's see. Over there are our fur-trimmed coats I believe and . . ."

"Not fur-trimmed. Cashmere. Plain black cashmere."

"Right, but next to the fur-trimmed I think are the plain coats. Shall we walk over?"

We do. The coats I saw turn out to be midi lengths, but next to *them* are the real untrimmed regular lengths. Relieved at finding them, I start to look through the rack.

"You don't call those cashmere, do you, miss? Cardboard would be more like it."

"Something the matter over here?" says a voice behind me. It is Alice, our escalator escort.

I turn to her. "Black cashmere. Size eighteen."

"Cashmere? Are you kidding? Someone told you we had black cashmere? Here? Sorry for wasting your time, madam," she says and stalks away.

Next: "May I help you?"

"No, just looking."

"May I help you?" A stunning black woman in a brown wool suit.

"Yes, I'm looking for a plain camel colored coat, size six or eight."

Scan the floor again, then remember. In front, near the cashier's booth. Walk decisively over. Finger through the racks, find three for her to try on. The last looks wonderful, and at $48 is a good buy. She takes it, looking immensely pleased. I'm a bit surprised to find I'm feeling pleased myself.

LUNCH

At 3:30 Ed says go to lunch. He's apologetic; usually we are to eat earlier, but today, because of all the training (sic) and confusion we're behind schedule. After punching out, I wander outside the store, find a coffee shop across the street. As I enter a woman waves to me from the counter. It is Lillian, the red-headed woman in dresses I met earlier, sitting with another woman also on her first day. I take the stool next to them, order a hamburger and coffee.

Lillian wants to know how I like it so far and I tell her, I don't know, it seems okay, but it's probably too soon to tell.

"How about the people?" she goes on, very curious. "The manager and the people in your department, they're nice? You like them?"

I tell her I don't like them or not like them yet. "I've hardly said a word to any of them really, except for Peggy, the woman you introduced me to, and except for the woman who came to pick us up—we sort of brushed each other the wrong way on the escalator."

"Oh, that's too bad," Lillian says, but she's obviously bubbling over with her own news. Good news. "In my department they're very friendly. All the women—there are four I've met so far, seem very sweet. Including my manager. She's a woman about my age. She's very sweet and friendly, too."

"So it looks good for you?' says the woman sitting on the other side of Lillian. She is an attractive blonde, heavily made up, with an accent hard to figure out. Her name is Marlene. Robes and lingerie.

"And you?" Lillian asks Marlene.

"Me, not so bad, I don't know yet. They keep me busy so far taking nightgowns out of boxes and putting labels on them. That's all I do so far."

"You want to work here after Christmas?" Lillian asks.

"Yes. If it works out. I go crazy at home all alone since my boy went away to college. What about you?"

Lillian nods. "I'm hoping they'll let me stay." She looks questioningly at me.

"No, I'm just here for Christmas," I say, feeling uneasy about not telling her more about myself yet.

Lillian looks at me closely. "I bet you'd rather work in an office, wouldn't you? I know I would. But at my age they almost never hire you. They want younger girls." She takes a sip of her coffee. "Or if they do give you a chance, the few places that do, they make you take a typing test, and that I could never never pass. I don't know why, I can type fine, really. But if there's a test my fingers start to freeze."

"Why do you think office work is so much better than selling?" I ask.

"Well, for one thing, the hours. You don't have to work nights or Saturdays. And the pay is better usually, and the conditions in general, and the way people act toward you."

"And you can *sit*," Marlene says and we all laugh and groan for a minute about our feet. Then Marlene goes on: "But really I don't want to sit all day. I think I like selling better—if they would let me sell. Not just put labels on nightgowns.". . .

EMPLOYEE QUARTERS

If you work in this store you must enter and leave through the Employee Entrance on a side street next to the trucking zone. You will push open a heavy green door and then walk down a flight of stairs (dousing your cigarette, because you can't smoke inside except in prescribed areas) until you reach the basement, which also serves as a general stock area. Cartons and cartons of merchandise all around. A uniformed guard will check to see that you have your employee badge, and then you may proceed to the locker room—there's one for each sex. Luck in the morning, if you happen to be fighting the time clock, is having no one blocking your way in the tiny locker room aisles, so you can get your coat and handbag tucked away fast. Luck is also not having to share your locker with more than one other person. During the Christmas rush some had as many as five. Finally, if you happen to own a navy blue jacket, as I do, luck is never having to share your locker with a white angora sweater, as I do.

Leaving the locker room, you walk down a long narrow corridor. Announcements on the wall of new union stewards, of salespeople who have won awards for catching shoplifters, of scholarships being given to children of employees, of a special employee discount day coming up during which you can get twenty percent off instead of the usual ten. In the middle of the corridor you will find, on one side, the time clock; on the other the employee lunchroom. Lunchroom, not cafeteria. A small square room with six or seven rectangular tables and matching benches, plus a half dozen coin machines for coffee, cigarettes, potato chips, soda, cookies. On the wall more announcements; one reminding you of that scholarship program for children, another of the $25 award you can get for reporting a dishonest fellow worker.

In addition to coming here to eat the sandwiches that you, like most employees, will probably bring from home, it is here in the lunchroom that you will usually take your breaks. It is here that you will begin to meet people from other departments. And to hear the latest rumors making the rounds.

Such as (during the first week I was there):

They've overhired for Christmas.

Business is slow and everyone's worried.

They're going to be laying off like crazy.

A nurse is coming and all the Christmas help is going to have to take urine tests. (This was already a regular practice among the permanent employees, to spot drug users.)

The last two rumors prove not to be true. . . .

PERSONNEL

Today is payday, and her little office is jammed. People asking questions about deductions, about the amount of their checks in general. I could come back another day, I say to Andrea, but, no, she says, sit down, it won't be long.

My first question, when the office finally clears out, has to do with the ages of the women who work there. I mention the pattern I've noticed; young women in their late teens and early twenties mainly working part-time as cashiers or in sales; and then the women in their forties or older, working full-time for many years in the same spot. Andrea agrees that that is the general pattern, not only here but at other department stores as well. "Does that mean there is a trend toward recruiting mainly part-time now?" Andrea says yes. Aside from the special situation at Christmas they have reached the point where there are now more part-timers than full-timers. "We are developing four shifts," she says: nine thirty to two thirty; eleven to three; three to seven; and five to nine. "The early shifts are mainly young mothers with school kids. The three to seven are high school and college students coming after school. And the five to nine are mostly students again and people who moonlight. We still hire full-time, when someone good comes along, but we're doing very little recruiting of women there."

"Is that because the company saves money on part-timers?"

"Yes, that's certainly one of the factors. You can cover yourself during your rush hours and have less people around when it's quieter. Also there can be some savings on fringe benefits a company has to pay. If you work here a month you have to join the union, and that means, if you're full-time you're immediately eligible for health insurance. But if you're part-time you have to wait six months, by which time many of our part-timers are gone. Also we only have to provide health insurance if you're not covered elsewhere, and almost all of our part-timers are covered by someone else in their family."

I ask about the wage scale, and she says, "This is the way it works. If you get a job with us you make $2.15 an hour for the first month. Then after thirty days, if your manager gives you a good evaluation, and if there's an opening in your department and you want to stay, you get raised ten cents an hour and you have to join the union. Then after six months, if everything's still okay, you get another ten cents an hour."

I shake my head, wonder how people in New York can manage on this.

Andrea agrees. "I certainly couldn't live on it, even with my husband's wages." Then she quickly becomes her company's spokesperson again: "But of course the kind of work they do is nothing they should be paid much for. There's no responsibility, the jobs are not difficult or challenging. What's the big deal in folding a pair of pajamas and putting them away in a drawer?" I think of Marlene going crazy folding those pajamas and start to say perhaps people should get paid more precisely to the degree they're not *allowed* to do the more challenging work, but now there is a young black man, about twenty, standing by Andrea's desk, waiting to be noticed.

"Yes, John," Andrea says. He is a Christmas full-time, toys.

"I'm wondering when I can join the union," he says. "I want to stay for good if I can."

"Well, we'll have to wait until January 15 to see what our needs are going to be, John, and also to see what your manager says about your work. So until then, why don't you just keep doing what you're doing?"

The subject closed, he leaves the room and I remark that even at these absurdly low wages they obviously have no problem getting workers and that that is perhaps the chief difficulty.

"Oh, yes, well you saw what happened when we put in the

Christmas help-wanted ads, the place was flooded for days. Many were happy to get anything we could give them; they didn't even ask about the salary, some of them."

I mention that there seemed to be a great deal more black women on the line that first day I came to apply—perhaps 80 percent were black—than those with me—about 40 percent—when I returned to start work. And most of the black women were hired as cashiers.

"Oh, yes," Andrea agrees readily. "That's one of the first things I notice when people come to apply. We have a kind of quota system here, all stores do."

Since there is a massive equal employment opportunity sign outside her office door. I'm rather surprised she is admitting this so easily.

"How does the quota system work?"

"Well, the rule of thumb in most places is that your sales help should be as much like your clientele as possible. In other words if this were the suburbs and your help was all black and your customers all white, well most of them might just walk out. So there, our help is mostly white. Here, our customers are more mixed so our help can be pretty mixed too. But I try to see that it's equally divided; you know, that there aren't all blacks in one department or floor, that it's pretty much spread out through the store."

"And what about the male-female differences?" I ask. "The fact that the men are in the big commission departments, and not the women."

"We're trying to equalize that, too." she says. "But certain departments—the heavy stock departments, for example, like major appliances, are mostly requested by men, and certain jobs, like cashiers, tend to be female. Even though I try to spread things out. See, men don't ask for cashier jobs, and I try to put people in places they want to be. And women almost always ask for soft goods, for sportswear or dresses nine out of ten times, so I don't have too much chance to do what I'd like, do I?"

"And managers?" I ask.

"Probably about sixty percent men, forty percent women. But remember we're a young company, we're still changing, and the tendency now is to push women into the better jobs. But even here there are problems. We recruit from outside for these kinds of jobs, because our managers usually have to have college degrees and most of our sales help don't have that much education."

Meaning Terry or Peggy or Lillian or Marlene could never be managers.

I think about Ed. "How much does a department manager make?"

"Oh, maybe, at the beginning about $175 or $180 a week, after a while say $200 a week."

So even the King of Coats is barely topping $10,000 a year.

"I'm just amazed by these salaries."

"It's true," Andrea says. "Retail salaries are notoriously low, even in management jobs. Only on the top, where they make $125,000 a year or more, does it seem to pay anything."

"And one final thing," I ask. "Why isn't it possible to have chairs for the workers? Particularly for the cashiers. But also for the sales help. Couldn't there be chairs so the employees would be able to rest their feet when business is slow?"

"I can't answer that," Andrea says. "I don't know why. I guess it's just always been that way."

PART II

LIFE TIMES

SECTION FOUR

Growing Pains

THE PIONEERS in an organization usually feel wonderful. In on the ground floor, they can watch the system being constructed, decide how the territory should be divided up, and choose the character of each area. For these risk takers, the promise of eventual rewards and the community of those who share the struggle of beginnings drives them to their finest efforts. "Growing" the organization is one of their tasks, and, in a sense, the organization is their product in addition to whatever goods or services the organization itself produces. But if growth is both inevitable and a state to be desired, it also creates its own tensions and dilemmas for those who live in the organization—its "growing pains."

No organization comes into being full-blown or resembles at the start its final form, just as the child is not merely a miniature adult. Every organization must live through a series of developmental stages, each with its own characteristic flavor. Even spin-offs of larger organizations must often repeat the sequence. Indeed, it is impossible to short-circuit the growth phase, because:

—Not everything can be predicted in advance; some decisions can only be made as circumstances arise.

—An organization rests not only on formal procedures that can be planned before action begins, but also on relationships and people's individual knowledge of how to act; and these take time to develop.

—It is more realistic to develop in stages, with decisions made and units added gradually over time. Each development is impossible until earlier ones have been completed, since each represents a building block for those that follow.

Growth can mean two things: maturation or an increase in size. Although each kind of growth generates slightly different issues for the people living in the organization, there are also similarities. Even maturing organizations that do not increase in overall size still face turnover, and must change by adding new people, because of environmental shifts, or by adding new units or new procedures.

We live in a society that stresses growth in size as a measure of success. It is easier to feel a sense of progress by seeking change that simultaneously involves growth rather than by holding a course. One consequence is that most measures of progress in the organizational sense, and most of the kinds of organizational change generally regarded as positive, are those associated with such growth. So the impetus for growth in size or profits in modern American organizations is a cultural given, whether or not it is an automatic organizational or human imperative. Indeed, a number of contemporary social critics have pointed out that growth-in-size—economic growth—may be anti-human in some fundamental sense, and that it has little to do with maturation or evolution to a higher developmental stage.

These are difficult issues, philosophically as well as empirically. For our purposes—to look at the human experiences of organizations that are changing and getting larger—we will not try to address them, other than to say that getting bigger does not necessarily mean getting better. This is true even in economic terms (Stein, 1974). But getting bigger does create a variety of human and managerial dilemmas.

The issues of adding people who have not lived through earlier phases of the organization is as clear for maturing organizations as for those that grow in size, even though, of course, the problems are multiplied for the latter. What is it about earlier periods of an organization's history that can create problems as that same organization begins to succeed and grows in size?

LIFE AT THE BEGINNING: DELIGHTS AND DILEMMAS

When organizations are smaller and newer, they are often less secure with respect to their environments, but more able to create the internal conditions that make it possible for them to grow. Paradoxically, once they start growing, those internal conditions are lost.

When the organization is small or just developing, it is harder for people to get trapped in limited routines. The routines are not there yet, and, anyway, anything that is new tends to be more interesting. People get a chance to do more because they are often needed to perform multiple functions and to invent new procedures. Work is more easily shared; there is less division between so-called creative work and scut work.

Information also tends to be shared more easily, there is access to managers and top leaders of an easy and natural sort, and in general, there tends to be less bureaucracy. Accountability is also easier; there is less slippage between a decision to do something and actually doing it, and people have an enhanced sense of responsibility, because they know how much rests on them. Since everyone is learning, there is often less reliance on formal training programs and more emphasis on stretching to meet the challenge of new jobs. The paths upward are clear—the chance to move into greater responsibility (though it may be limited)—and people get to know more about what goes on at higher levels of the system, if we can even talk about "levels" in such circumstances.

Offices and other facilities tend to be smaller and more accessible to one another, with people flowing in and out rather freely. There is often a cluttered and just-moved-in and not-quite-organized look, in part because new people and materials may be arriving periodically, in part because there are too many other areas for investment to put money into fancy facilities right away, in part because there is too much else to do to get the physical plant in shape, and in part because so much is changing rapidly anyway. (Contrast this picture with the ossified offices Rosabeth Kanter described in chapter 1, "How the Top Is Different.") At Andrews Winery, as Barry Stein tells us (chapter 15), Bill Andrews, the company president, did not even have an office to call his own for the first few years, until an elegant permanent facility was built.

There are different bases for commitment earlier in an organization's life than later. In the early stages, the atmosphere is more familial, there is more mutual identification, people invest themselves in a shared struggle, and there is more opportunity and power (key dimensions in Kanter's, 1977, theory of organizational behavior).

Initially, for example, when uncertainty is great and procedures are minimal, people must rely on trust of one another as a basis for operating in the organization. Later, jobs are routinized and the reliance on personal trust is that much lower. Because people are much more likely to come into contact, they are also likely to get to know one another better. And, because the early years of building and struggling together are so demanding, the organization is also likely to absorb more of people's time and energy and even to draw in and implicate their families, so that the line between work and non-work life is blurred, and, as at Andrews Winery, there is likely to be a great deal of organizational social activity outside of work. All of these constitute "commitment mechanisms" found in successful communities that rely on commitment even more than businesses do (Kanter, 1972). And the concept of commitment is appropriate, since people are often willing to work for less pay in new and developing organizations because of the other rewards they obtain—present sense of community as well as investment in the future. So there is an element of sacrifice, too. This was true at Andrews Winery.

Opportunity is also great in the early years. Expansion means that new positions will constantly be opening up, and most organizations have some preference for filling them from inside. But growing organizations will not be able to wait until their own employees are "ready," for growth is likely to plunge people into jobs that they must stretch to meet and that give them a sense of continual challenge. The situation is also likely to be empowering, in Kanter's sense, for jobs are not yet routinized and the potential for extraordinary or creative action is there. Visibility too is great, so that people can become known for their contributions. And nearly every activity is likely to be relevant (a third criterion for power), since they all represent contingencies that must somehow be handled and problems that must be solved.

For all the excitement and joy of the start-up phase, there are also a number of tensions that can emerge—beyond the extra hard work that people often have to put in. Leadership may be *too* personal, and people may feel dependent on a parent for favors rather than feeling entitled to them when they are earned as a matter of course in an impersonal and just system. Roles and tasks may be *too* ambiguous. People may find themselves getting in each other's way as they all jump in to do things that are no one's clear responsibility. Or, since no one is clearly responsible, no one may think of doing the task. And, easy access and communication potential may mean that since people all assume that everyone else knows, all fail to share the information. These are among the critical issues facing new, small organizations; we see them in the first year of the Andrews Winery in chapter 15. Resolving them—establishing responsibilities and procedures—often brings an organization into its next stage of life.

GETTING BIGGER: ITS HUMAN MEANING

In the very beginning, even the most business-like organizations with the most pragmatic goals may have a communal flavor, intentionally or not. Some of this is an issue of sheer size, as well as a reflection of the quality of start-up phases. But as organizations grow, it is difficult to share the same amount of information as easily and across as many boundaries. There is more reliance on formal procedures and training programs. Jobs become solidified and tightly bounded, and while opportunities for promotion increase, the paths become more obscure. Layers are inserted between the boss and the staff, as at Andrews Winery. Newcomers, who don't have old ties and friendships and who missed out on the legendary events of the past, are at a special disadvantage. And oldtimers may feel they are missing something—the spirit of pulling together, a voice in policy, the chance to create, a special and close relationship to the boss, ritualistic celebrations of first-time accomplishments—and resent its absence, though the organization may, objectively, still be a happy place to work.

There can be a particular split between newcomers and old hands that reflects the fact that these groups experience two entirely different organizations. In one high-growth company that developed just after World War II, the oldtimers were part of a close-knit community with not only shared memories but also a shared culture of language, events, symbols, and rituals that constitutes part of what tied them to the organization. They often sacrificed to be part of a risky new venture, and they were now ready to reap the rewards. But for newcomers, a decade or so later, the organization was instead "just a job" because it now resembled any one of thousands of established entities. They heard about the old days and the special culture, but they never experienced them themselves, so they do not see their importance, and they wonder why everyone else seems to make such a fuss about their having to know about those times, since they have nothing to do with job performance.

For their part, the old hands recalled how they got to be where they were in the company: by inventing a job, by seeing something that needed doing and doing it, by attracting the attention of one of the bosses, by pushing themselves into a job before they had much training. They could not understand why, in such an open world in which all is possible, the newcomers (who instead experience a place of large size, a bit awesome and impersonal, where the creation process is long over) failed to share their optimism and complained that no one was helping them and that there were too few advancement prospects.

The oldtimers said, in effect, "Anyone who wants to and shows the stuff can move as fast as he or she wishes around here," concluding that there must be something wrong with "the kinds of people we hire today." The newcomers said, "This is a formidable and somewhat closed system; where's the room for me?" Ironically, the *individualistic* ethic of the old generation was nurtured in a communal atmosphere; they took community for granted (meaning automatic access, support, shared experience, and help) and so came to believe in individual talent. They had the right organizational conditions and supports to encourage the development and use of their talent and failed to see that new people—who may be just as intrinsically talented—lacked these important enabling conditions. In this particular company, the old hands constituted practically all of the top decision- and policy-makers, so they continued to make policy based on their own experience, without fully appreciating the new organizational realities. Is this a serious problem? It can be, if new systems and procedures, cultures and relationships, appropriate to a later growth stage, do not replace the vacuum left by the inevitable disappearance of the earlier conditions, and if leaders do not acknowledge the changes.

OTHER TENSIONS OF GROWTH

There are a number of pessimistic views in classical social theory about what growth brings to organizations. Robert Michels felt that even organizations with democratic intents could not remain in that state very long, and he framed the "iron law of oligarchy" to describe the tendency for control to increasingly centralize and fall into fewer hands (Michels, 1949). For Max Weber, it was bureaucracy that was inevitable—a similar outcome (in its lack of control by the average employee or member) but with a slightly different process. Even organizations that begin out of attraction to a charismatic leader and to the promise that such a founder represents, eventually must routinize to stay alive. Eventually the functions of the charismatic founder, Weber theorized, must be divided and taken over by at least two kinds of leaders: an administrator and a visionary. (This is not unlike the issues of leadership succession discussed in "Life at the Top.")

As organizations grow in size, they also tend eventually to differentiate, and thus to create diverging interests and perspectives. They become too large for a few people to manage themselves via personal control, and so delegation of responsibilities must take place. But this creates a major source of dilemmas, which some social scientists have framed in terms of "sub-optimization"—the tendency for the goals of each subgroup or smaller unit to become more important to them than the goals and objectives of the overall organization. To guard against sub-optimization, some managers try to retain as much personal control as possible, even when size makes this no longer feasible, as with Bill Andrews of the Andrews Winery. He finally had to give up and substitute more formal integrating devices—such as more specific responsibilities for other managers—for the pleasure of poking his nose into every function of the winery.

George Downing drew a number of lessons about the human responses to organizational growth from examining the history of General Electric, a company he knew from inside, a company that underwent a major structural change in the 1950s:

—As new technology is created or absorbed, it leads to more complexity resulting, in turn, in physical growth and spatial expansion. The corporation will initially accomodate these changes within its existing structure by building additional layers of the hierarchy. But as the hierarchical growth increases, coordination between work functions becomes more complex and more difficult, and executives find it harder to do their work as the work centers become farther away organizationally and spatially.

—Those parts of the organization with the strong culture—traditionally oriented beliefs and commonly shared "meanings," symbols, rituals, and legends—find it harder to accomodate the new technology. So those parts that survive from earlier eras and have had time and circumstances to nourish their own strong sense of what it means to be a member of the organization, will be the most resistant to change.

—But drastic and "rational" imposed organization structure changes will put pressure on members of the organization to adjust their social relations and modes of behavior. Thus, change from the top, that immediately puts in place a new status system, a new system of expectations and rewards, and new performance measures, will often result in the most rapid change and ready adaptation.

—Changes in formal organization structure do not occur in isolation; they also result in changes in "old" ways of doing things and in the symbolic meaning of various ritualistic and ceremonial processes.*

—If changes in formal structure do not accompany the addition of new technology, then, as the converse of the above propositions, the resistance to change in behavior and relationships will be greater. And this resistance to change will itself increase, the stronger the shared culture is as a basis for membership and participation in the organization. With stronger traditions and symbol systems, with stronger investments of meaning in the organization, there will be heightened anxiety and conflict within the organization when its members perceive imminent imposed structural change. And if it is eventually imposed, those areas with strong traditions and cultures will show the greatest lag in ultimate adjustment and the longest period of anxiety, frustration, and conflict.

—If, in the process of social change, time-honored symbol systems are threatened, altered, or destroyed, new symbol systems must emerge to keep pace with the social system change, and behavioral adaptation to the change will vary directly with the speed of evolution and strength of such new symbols. (Downing, 1967:238–40)

Thus, life in organizations is not merely a matter of rational calculus. Even in corporate giants such as General Electric,

---

* Yet, we might add, there is a lag, in that the old cultural myths persist long past the time where they directly reflect the reality that organization members are currently living. As in the example of the successful company that has been doubling in size every few years, managers who remember the early days still persist in believing that all it takes to get ahead is "doing the right thing," because someone higher up is sure to notice.

people need some things to invest and believe in, and some symbols to weave them together in their cooperative effort. As old ones disappear, new ones must be created if people are going to work well together.

INTEGRATION OF NEW PEOPLE

How do organizations grow? They grow by adding parts, and that almost inevitably means adding *people*, as individuals or as members of ongoing groups. So the next issue of growth is how to do this so that the new elements are smoothly absorbed. In fact, if the problem of adding new parts or new people is not adequately handled, the organization may eventually find itself in trouble. One observer wrote about the crisis of growth in Olin Mathieson, a once-great chemical company that declined in the 1950s. According to Richard Austin Smith:

In great corporations, particularly those whose size is more the result of acquiring other firms than of self-development, failure to take a firm hand inevitably brings on crisis. The trouble with this great chemical company in September of 1958 was rooted in the fact that for years Olin Mathieson had piled one inharmonious acquisition upon another, building up debt, eroding profits, scattering its strength, and paralyzing management. [Smith, 1966:18]

One way the structural and human problems of growth in size can be avoided is merely to add comparable units that operate on a relatively autonomous basis. Franchise organizations, a special breed, grow by duplicating units over and over again, a process that requires minimum accommodation on the part of the overall organization. Thus, the American company that has grown to annual sales of a billion dollars fastest, at least in modern times, is McDonald's, a franchise firm. But the problem of integrating new members, so that the overall culture and coherence as well as effectiveness of the organization is preserved, is still a problem for companies like McDonald's. It has partly solved this problem by creating "Hamburger University," a national training ground for new batches of managerial talent. Hamburger University, in Elk Grove, Illinois, not only trains managers in procedures that keep McDonald's uniform across the country, but it also indoctrinates them in a company culture to which it is hoped they will become committed. McDonald's is not the only fast food chain to have its own elaborate training facility (Quincy, Massachusetts, is the home of Dunkin Donuts University) but Hamburger University is perhaps the most elaborate and the fanciest. Though extreme and moderately amusing in many of their activities, the training programs offered at Hamburger University are not very different from the way many companies attempt to solve one of their "growing pains" by bringing new members up to speed quickly.

Hamburger University is dedicated to laying the foundations of success by passing on the founder's idea: to put the hamburger on the assembly line, the way Henry Ford did it with the Model T (Haden-Guest, 1973). The course lasts nine days, with audio-visual aids, closed circuit television systems, and units on such matters as the shake machine, carbonation principles, and how people steal in stores. There are pep talks about ideal management and attempts to build pride in the company. "Wearables," such as ties and jackets with the McDonald golden arches on the pocket, are also geared toward promoting an ideal image and identification with the company. Tests are given on the subjects of the courses, with scores totalled: hamburgers, fries and fryers, store maintenance, ice machine, teenagers, shortening, and apple pie. Then there are snappy graduation ceremonies with cocktails, diplomas and the "Archie Award" to the top person in the class, consisting of a McDonald's-shaped base on which rests a symbolic burger.

Anthony Haden-Guest, who visited Hamburger University, watched the rehearsal of a McDonald's musical spectacular to be produced in front of 2,000 McDonald's conventioneers in Hawaii, complete with song and dance routines, and actors playing such characters as the hamburger, the french fry, and the milkshake, One song was the "customers' song," with lines like "Everytime I look you sell a billion more. I never cease to wonder how they multiply . . . I hope and trust you realize to put those billions in the air. It's guys like me that got you there, never mind the 8 billion, just the one in my hand." "This is big business nowadays," Haden-Guest observed. "General Motors spends a million dollars a year on theatrical industrials, and more money is invested in live theatrical entertainment by industry than by all the Broadway backers put together" (Haden-Guest, 1973:209).

Lavish productions and training programs are used especially for salesmen, often to build company identification as
well as to inspire people not to rest on past successes. It is interesting to note how training programs and sales conferences
function to "artificially" build in the kinds of commitment
mechanisms that are a more "natural" part of a newer, smaller
organization: relationships of trust, ceremonies and rituals,
uniforms and identifying symbols, ideologies and traditions,
chances for communal sharing.

Finally, if attention to the integration of new units is important, then it is also possible to see how growth in itself demands
more growth, at least in the development of new functions.
Adding new people might also necessitate the development of
new mechanisms for integration and socialization, such as
training units and orientation programs. Those people who are
part of the early days learn the ropes together, in part because
they are inventing the ropes as they go along, but for later additions, there are not only ropes to be mastered but also increased
problems of coordination to solve. Thus, another way organizations change as they grow—and in this society it is almost an organizational imperative—is that they add functions. They
bring under their own control activities that they might have
relied on the environment to provide, or not considered very
self-consciously at all, just as American industrial organizations
in the early years of this century first used independent contrac-
tors for their sales and warehousing needs, then gradually
brought these and other functions inside. This is a way of coming to control more and more areas of uncertainty, making
manageable and predictable what would otherwise rest on
some outside figures' whims.

THEORIES OF ORGANIZATIONAL GROWTH AND DEVELOPMENT

As organizations age, they exhibit a wide variety of behaviors. Most simply, some die, others live. But while they live,
their structures, internal characters, behaviors, and sizes (measured variously) often exhibit continuing and idiosyncratic
changes. Theorists and researchers have sought the laws governing these aging processes, or at the very least, some observa-

ble regularities. The ones most commonly explored by far are those concerned with changes in size as measured by employment or membership. Indeed, the phrase "growth and development" tends to carry this sort of restricted meaning. For example, William Starbuck, in a major review (1965), defines growth as "change in an organization's employment size" and development as "change in an organization's age." But as William Torbert (1975) points out, "changes in size and age do not necessarily generate changes in quality."

Indeed, it is essential to differentiate changes in size (growth), which in itself *forces* changes in structure, from changes in the internal character of the organization and the way it operates. Torbert's use of the word "quality," as in "qualitatively different," expresses the difference neatly. Although it is difficult to prove rigorously that the changes due to growth are not synonomous with the changes due to qualitative development, the two are plainly of different conceptual character, and their results are also different.

In some ways, one of the most striking features of small organizations is that they often tend to replicate large ones, or at least to set themselves apart by explicitly contrasting themselves to large organizations, rather than by developing uniquely applicable arrangements of their own. For example, the General Electric Company (chapter 14) changed its structure in a major way to accommodate changes in both size and technical/market environment. All of the resultant changes involved formal structures composed of large groups within the company (total employment was then in the neighborhood of 200,000 people). Contrast that with the growth of Andrews Winery (chapter 15), from its entrepreneurial inception to an employment of fifty or so at a point approaching stability. Andrews operated with a structure not possible for GE, an entrepreneurial one characterized by wholly informal processes, but the structure was "selected" by rejecting such models as GE used, rather than by taking deliberate advantage of Andrews' size and character. It is fair to say that Andrews could get away with its structure.

Yet on another level, these two organizations of vastly different size underwent similar changes. Both decentralized to accommodate growth in the sense that legitimate decision-making capacity was more broadly distributed after the change than before. This is one of the things that will always occur from time to time over the continued growth of any hierarchical organization. This and related structural effects explain some of the regularity observed in organizations as they grow. Whatever else happens, and regardless of the particular form that the growth takes, a pre-existing structure can only be expanded so far before it becomes unacceptably inappropriate. At the limit, if nothing else occurs first, organizations become too centralized. As many have shown, size and structure are closely linked, in nature as well as in social organizations (Stinchcombe, 1965; Blau and Schoenherr, 1971; and Heydebrand, 1973). But the specific form that linkage takes varies, depending among other things on many factors bearing on the organization's relationship with its environment. Paul Lawrence and Jay Lorsch (1967) have made this the basis of an important theory of organizational behavior, contingent on the extent to which organizations need to continually accommodate a changing environment.

However, it is more interesting here to note that none of these effects of growth are accidents; they are the result of specific decisions and actions by people or groups within organizations. From the standpoint of life in organizations, these structural adjustments reflect the impact of some perceived need or awareness on members. Alfred Chandler (1962) specifically used the concept of organizational strategy to account for the deliberate shifts in structure visible in many large organizations, arguing, in effect, that to continue growing in size, organizations were forced to develop new strategies, necessarily with important structural consequences. The General Electric case in chapter 14 illustrates this point: form followed function.

Minimally, designing forms appropriate to functions requires an important awareness on the part of organizational leaders: how to make plainly deliberate modifications aimed at particular objectives. The very concept of "strategy" is a self-conscious one. Yet how common is deliberate strategy? Organizations also change, probably more often if the truth be known, in response to internal pressures that are less obviously related to thoughtful design lessons. After the fact, of course, organizations and leaders seek to take greater credit for decisions that turn out in retrospect to be useful, in the process rewriting the history through which they lived. Bill Andrews was "fortunate" enough to run across people accidentally who could help him in the development of Andrews Winery—but he would argue that he knew how to take advantage of these opportunities and to create in the organization the conditions for success. And surely one formulation is as true as the other. There are no more simple causes in organizations than in individuals; most behavior reflects complex interdependencies and events.

A number of people have attempted to analyze the growth processes of organizations in terms of these internal pressures—essentially put as crises—that force managers to act. Their basic features may be illustrated by reference to three specific frameworks. First, Lawrence Steinmetz, a business professor, specifically addressed issues of "small business," but insisted that there is no possibility of staying small; grow or die is the message.

Anyone who commits himself to managing a small business must recognize one irrefutable fact: the minute he commits himself, he is on the treadmill of forced growth ... Furthermore, there is no escape from this escalator unless he is willing to accept the demise of his small business. [1969:36]

Thus, Steinmetz denied the possibility of stability at modest size, despite the obvious fact that the economy is heavily populated with firms that survive and maintain reasonable prosperity without marked change in size. Indeed, many of these are handed down from generation to generation. In effect, Steinmetz confused development with growth, failing to recognize that even if there are crises, their resolution does not require further growth. In fact, it is that prescription that creates the problems, for if growth resolves crises only at the cost of another crisis, there is no end. This, indeed, is the message of Steinmetz as well as other theorists.

What are the crises? There are three: (1) the transition from direct supervision to supervised supervision (the first that Andrews Winery managed); (2) the transition from supervised supervision to indirect control (the one Andrews Winery is managing next); and (3) the transition from indirect control to divisional organization (the stage of General Electric when Downing began his article). It is plain from Steinmetz' labels that these are crises that arise because of size and size alone, and the nature of the solutions are bureaucratic and hierarchical.

What is perhaps most striking is that it is flatly impossible to demonstrate that mere success in transitions of this sort will in itself cause great growth, still less turn a small business into a large one. The factors responsible for *that* transition go far beyond managerial crises. Most large organizations arose out of complex circumstances, technological, historical, and institutional, in addition to managerial, and exceed our capacity for deliberate creation, except by sheer bulk of expenditure.

Larry Greiner proposed a related framework to explain organizational growth in systems of all sizes. However, Greiner recognized explicitly that "A management that is aware of the problems ahead could well decide *not* to grow" and indeed, that because "the informal practices of a small company . . . [are] inherent in the organization's limited size . . . [growth] may do [managers] out of . . . a way of life they enjoy." (1972:46) For Bill Andrews and many of those around him, this is a very real issue. Nevertheless, Greiner agreed with Steinmetz in seeing crises of growth as discreet problems for management to resolve. His five phases of growth, each terminated by a "leadership crisis," are: (1) creativity (small, informal, entrepreneurial); (2) direction (more or less equivalent to "supervised supervision"); (3) delegation (indirect control); (4) coordination (a formal balance between centralized and decentralized activities); and (5) collaboration (based on teams and informal structures with sophisticated and interpersonally skillful members in a highly supportive context). Greiner explicitly tied this sequence to growth, indicating only that the time to reach these various stages will differ. Nevertheless, the critical fact is that such shifts are driven by changes in size—by the conventional measure of success.

Finally, George Strauss focused on particular problems at the stage of growth he calls adolescence. He makes the most explicit statement that development (maturing) requires growth in size:

there's a considerable uniformity in the stresses and strains undergone by corporations as they pass from youth (50 to 200 employees or fewer) to adolescence (200 to 1000 employees) . . . however . . . organizational adolescence is not inevitable—some organizations can and do reject the growing-up process, by choosing to stay small. [1975:3]

Thus, an organization cannot "grow up" without "growing." And somehow, to choose not to grow, is also to give up. Yet, if growth brings continued problems and crises, it is not clear what end is served.

Fortunately, there is one theorist who has sharply differentiated growth and development, and who has produced a genuine theory of development not at all necessarily related to size. William Torbert squarely confronts the conventional wisdom:

A significant problem in developing a theory of qualitatively distinct stages of organization development is that the particular organizational form called bureaucracy is . . . virtually synonymous with the term organization itself. The theory to be articulated here will, by contrast, place bureaucracy as a middle stage of organization development. [1975:2]

Torbert's theory involves nine stages, of which the last remains purely conceptual and uncharted. The fifth is well-developed bureaucracy. The first six stages and their key characteristics are as follows:

   1.   Parentage and conception: the genesis of the organization. The individuals who participate in initial conversations are not to be thought of as the "parents" of an organization. Instead, other organized structures, whether these be public occasions, ideologies or institutions, parent new organizations. (And not necessarily just two, for ideas are not monogamous.)
   2.   Investments:
      a.   Organizers make a definite commitment to the enterprise;
      b.   parent institutions make financial, structural, and spiritual commitments;
      c.   early relationship building takes place among potential first leaders and members; and
      d.   leadership style is negotiated.
   3.   Determinations:
      a.   Specific goals, clients, staff, and members are determined;
      b.   recognizable territory is delineated;
      c.   first common tasks and time commitments are worked out; and
      d.   psychological contracts of various parties are defined implicitly or explicitly.
   4.   Experiments: Alternative legal, governing, administrative, physical, production, communication, planning, scheduling and/or interpersonal structures and processes are developed and tried out.
   5.   Predefined productivity (e.g., bureaucracy):
      a.   Focus on doing the predefined task;
      b.   viability of the product becomes the overriding criterion of success;
      c.   standards and structures are taken for granted;
      d.   there is a focus on quantitative results based on defined standards; and

    e. reality is conceived as dichotomous and competitive (e.g., success/failure, education/therapy, in-group/out-group, leader/follower, legitimate/illegitimate, work/play, reason/emotional).

This ends the list of those stages that most organizations reach. However, Torbert goes on to suggest other developmental stages, which are more open, more humane, more just, and (Torbert says) more effective:

  6. Openly chosen structure:
    a. Shared reflection about the larger purposes of the organization;
    b. development of norms of disclosure, support and confrontation;
    c. evaluation of effects of one's own behavior on others in the organization, and formative research on the effects of the organization on its environment;
    d. non-conventional solutions to conflicts;
    e. deliberately chosen structure unique in the experience of the participants or among similar organizations, with commitment over time;
    f. primary emphasis on horizontal rather than vertical role differentiation.

One striking implication of this theory is that it may be possible for an organization to become prematurely fixed in any given stage of development, though it may still grow in other senses. From this perspective, bureaucracy is perhaps a temporary, culturally and historically specific phase of organizational development which is able to grow (in size) without further development. The question for the future—a future that increasingly bodes to differ sharply from the past—is whether that form, driven by size-related measures of success, is as appropriate as other alternatives. Torbert's path offers a glimpse of some potential alternatives.

WHERE IS ORGANIZATIONAL CONTINUITY?

As we look at the growth process, it is clear that increasing size brings with it a number of other changes: new people with a different set of experiences; new internal structural arrangements, including differentiated functions; and new areas of activity, both to integrate the new people and to take over functions from the environment.

In what sense, then, can an organization be said to be the "same one?" There are several possible answers:

• *Legal definition.* Legally, an organization is the same if its legal persona (corporate identity or unincorporated identification for tax or registration purposes) is maintained. Corporations in particular, having essentially unlimited life, may appear to be the same by simple virtue of this institutional feature, though everything else may change.

• *Structure.* An organization could be said to be the same to the extent that its formal structure is maintained. Though this is at first glance a doubtful proposition, it is exactly this sort of argument that underlies the very common attempt to categorize organizations in terms of their formal structure, and to see as similar those organizations that have certain structural elements in common. But of course, as we have seen, structure is itself constantly changing. One company keeps its organization chart on movable magnets attached to a board, so it can move them around monthly as the system changes.

• *Functions.* Organizations could be said to be the same if they occupy functionally identical positions in the socioeconomic environment and keep on doing the same things. That is, an organization might be treated as a black box, seen to be the same as long as its inputs and outputs continue unchanged—as long as General Motors continues to turn out cars and the State Department to conduct diplomacy.

• *Culture.* One could also say that an organization stays the same if it is characterized by the same culture—the same behavior patterns, beliefs, and modes of expression. This is a particularly tricky argument since the concept of culture is itself complex and pervasive. To some extent, it is always changing and it would therefore be necessary to single out key components or aspects, by which the culture would be appraised.

• *People.* Obviously, an organization could be said to stay the same if it is composed of the same people. Equally obviously, it is the criterion least likely to be met for organizations other than very small ones, or for any organization over a moderate time span. Indeed, what is most striking is precisely the fact that people turn over, yet organizations are still seen as the same.

But from the standpoint of the people in an organization, there is perhaps one relatively unequivocal answer:

• *Identity.* An organization is the same to the extent that over the period in question, members of the organization continue to identify with its past, and see themselves as a collectivity extending through time.

If and as people feel themselves to be an outgrowth of an earlier organization, and if the culture and symbolic system exhibit at least adequate continuity to reinforce that in the conscious sense, then the present organization is the same as that in the past. George Downing clearly shows in chapter 14 how, in G.E., the Elfun Society and associated rituals served this purpose for years. The implication of this particular definition is that organizational continuity exists to an important degree because people choose to believe that it is so, and invest energy in maintaining that view, even though in every other respect the organization may in fact be very different. To accomplish this requires some accommodation by the people themselves; a sort of organizational collusion in the interest of reducing temporal uncertainty and ambiguity, to pretend that because they remember a shared past and look forward to a shared future, they *are* in the same organization.

THE SELECTIONS

This section looks at growth issues in a large and a small company. George Downing, author of "The Changing Structure of a Large Corporation," was an executive at General Electric who later returned to school and became a professor of marketing. His perspective is valuable because he had access to his own experiences and inside information, combined with the objectivity of the scholar and analyst. This article is excerpted from a much longer description of the changes at G.E., offering organization charts as well as personal reflections.

In "The Company Family," Barry Stein presents snapshots of a small but highly successful company at two times in its early history and points out the human problems it had to solve at each stage. The Andrews Winery (not its real name) was the product of Bill Andrews' founding genius, and he had to find a way to make into a stable business what began as a kind of quasi-family with Bill as the father. Along the way, there were a number of other issues to resolve.

Both the G.E. and Andrews Winery stories are successes. Both organizations faced normal "growing pains" but managed to move on to new forms and new kinds of life with little more than the average predictable tensions. Some of this can be attributed to their leaderships, who were willing to admit, and thus face squarely, the problems of growth.

14 / The Changing Structure of a Great Corporation

George D. Downing

THE GENERAL ELECTRIC COMPANY is one of many very large-scale organizations that have been changing their internal structures to meet the demands of a rapidly changing society and technology. Many corporations have changed their management structure from a vertical hierarchy in which decisions were made at the top to several hierarchies, each involved with one product or group of products. In effect, portions of the organization and technological systems have been reassembled and decision making moved down in the organizational structure. The product departments in the new hierarchy are smaller profit-making business organizations but are still integral parts of the company. . . . This change is in part a reaction to the vast number and variety of activities, products, and people that have to be managed and to the changing competitive demands of a rapidly changing society. If decisions were to remain with top management alone, there would be misunderstanding, confusion, and slow and inefficient timing in relation to the demands of the competitive markets. . . .

Charles E. Wilson was elected president and chief executive officer [in 1940]. Wilson had long been an outstanding advocate

Reprinted by permission from Yale University Press, from *The Emergent American Society: Large-Scale Organizations*, vol. 1, by W. Lloyd Warner et al. Copyright © 1967 by Yale University. Pp. 158, 175–78, 181–82, 197, 217–21, 224–28, 230–33, 235–37.

of organization-structure change and probably would have engineered change had it not been for the war effort. . . .

But during this period Wilson, [an] advocate of organization change, prepared for change. In 1946 he charged Ralph Cordiner, first as an assistant to the president and later as executive vice president, to formalize plans for vast reorganization. This was not a sudden executive move. During World War II officers of the company were predicting a future for the company of "almost explosive growth which caused its managers to question whether it might not be necessary to evolve new techniques of organizing and managing the company." . . .

It was stated repeatedly and publicly by company officers that a company with such growth characteristics and operating on such a scale required a different managerial approach than the company of the 1920s and 1930s.

Decentralization in General Electric was much beyond, and much deeper than, merely a reshuffling and reorganizing of facilities and organizational components, for underlying was a philosophy of the managerial process radically different from the one that had existed prior to decentralization. . . .

Although it is true that there was a physical decentralization or rearranging of organizational units into smaller, more manageable pieces, and although decentralization was undertaken with respect to products, markets, geographical locations, and functional types of work, the real key to General Electric's concept lay in the decentralization of responsibility and authority for making business decisions.

The former vertical, functional hierarchies of engineering, manufacturing, and sales were dissolved, and the organization was reformed into a three-part structure, distinguishing between the product departments (operating components), the services (company-wide staff), and the executive office. . . .

The management structure of the company [before and] after decentralization is shown schematically in Figure 1. Whereas under the former centralized structure the line of communication between an operating executive and individual workers was long and tenuous with a great multiplicity of management layers and the horizontal linkages between the long vertical functions were accomplished only by committees that possessed no decision-making authority, *after decentral-*

Figure 1. Centralized and Decentralized Formal Organization Structures

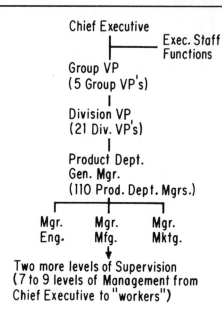

Chief Executive
— Exec. Staff Functions
Group VP
(5 Group VP's)
Division VP
(21 Div. VP's)
Product Dept.
Gen. Mgr.
(110 Prod. Dept. Mgrs.)

Mgr. Eng.   Mgr. Mfg.   Mgr. Mktg.

Two more levels of Supervision
(7 to 9 levels of Management from
Chief Executive to "workers")

170 plants

"Decentralized" structure. Delegation of decision-making authority, but with "accountability" and increasing degree of quantitatitive measurement

Affiliated companies absorbed as operating divisions or departments.

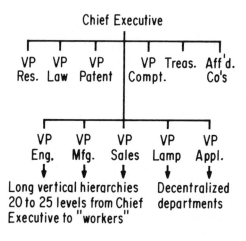

Chief Executive

VP Res.   VP Law   VP Patent   VP Compt.   Treas.   Aff'd. Co's

VP Eng.   VP Mfg.   VP Sales   VP Lamp   VP Appl.

Long vertical hierarchies 20 to 25 levels from Chief Executive to "workers"

Decentralized departments

25-54 plants

Highly centralized structure. Lamp and appliance separately organized, but centralized within themselves.

Long vertical hierarchies of engineers, manufacturing, sales throughout rest of company.

Acquired companies retained their names and identities, and were "independent."

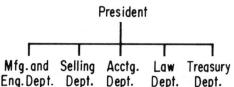

President

Mfg. and Eng. Dept.   Selling Dept.   Acctg. Dept.   Law Dept.   Treasury Dept.

3-10 plants

Original structure.
Simple line and staff, highly centralized structure.

Figure 1 has been adapted by the authors from "The Changing Structure of a Great American Corporation" by George D. Downing in W. Lloyd Warner et al., eds., The Emergent American Society: Large-Scale Organizations, vol. 1 (New Haven: Yale University Press, 1967).

ization the line of communication from chief executive to individual workers was greatly shortened to only seven levels. In a few cases there was one additional level. Further, the functional work was horizontally linked or coordinated, with firm decision-making authority at the product operating level. Thus, each of the product departments became a semiautonomous business with a simple line and staff structure but housed "under the same roof"—highly reminiscent of the total company in its early days. . . .

The General Electric Company's organizational change from a centralized functional management structure to a decentralized structure. . . . was one of change in formal management organizational structure. But within this formal structure, what processes were there for enabling the individual, or groups of individuals, or systems of individuals to learn what the company meant, to come to understand what the individual work functions meant, to learn the do's and don'ts of managerial behavior, to learn how they were to be rewarded? All this, of course, was learned as it is in any social system, through the complex web of structure, norms of behavior, and social relationships, or in terms of a shared value system, shared sentiments, and shared corporate goals congruent with, and interacting with, personal goals. . . . Two activities in the company deserve special attention because of their influence on the conception of managerial positions and their strong reinforcement of the traditionally based symbol system.

The company owned an island in Lake Ontario near the headwaters of the St. Lawrence River. It had been equipped as a summer meeting place and, beginning about the mid-1920s, was used each summer for the purpose of assembling managers above a certain level.

The facilities on the island were relatively simple. Tents on board flooring spread in a semicircle around a large parade ground on a central campus. Each tent housed two men, and there were facilities for approximately two hundred.

The island quickly became a most evocative symbol. Merely to be invited to attend an island meeting was equated with success. The meetings were conducted with great ceremony and ritual. Top executives of the company were always in attendance; ties and coats were forbidden, and everyone was on a first-name basis. When arriving attendees disembarked at the docks, they were met by a small band playing music composed for the island and a reception line of company executives; a holiday spirit prevailed. After sunset on the first night of each camp meeting a ceremony was held underneath a large elm tree, known throughout the management ranks simply as "The Elm"; the executives spoke to the newcomers to the island (always known as the "rookies"), speaking of the greatness of the company and charging the "rookie" managers with the responsibility of carrying on the great traditions of the company. All this was done with colored lights, background music, and always culminated with the appearance of an Indian in full battle regalia, who paddled a canoe to the shore of the island, disembarked, and made a sentiment-charged speech.

The island meetings lasted three days with business sessions in the morning and recreation in the afternoon. Normally there were short business meetings after dinner with guest speakers from outside the company, such as noted industrialists and university presidents. Usually there was one camp session during each summer known as "Camp General," which was attended by the top management of all functions. But most island meetings were held by work function and were oriented to the parochial vertical hierarchies.

To this day management in the company speak of the island with great sentiment. A vice-president of the company stated:

> The island was simply great. It provided tremendous appeal to management people. I think it was a mistake on the company's part to abandon it. The management meetings being held now are not substitutes for the old island. At the Island there was a feeling of esprit de corps. It gave management people an emotional feeling, a feeling of G.E.'s image and a feeling of G.E.'s greatness. Management's meetings today are held on some specific problem such as the profit situation, etc. The island, on the other hand, had its meetings focused on the traditions of the company themselves.

During an island meeting in 1929 the chief executive of the company proposed forming a group of management personnel destined to have great impact on managerial thinking for the next twenty years. The overt reason for the formation of this group or society was to provide a means for managers above a certain level to make investments on a personal basis through a trust fund to be administered at essentially no cost by company officials. The group was therefore called the Elfun Society, a contraction of the term "Electrical Fund." But this society quickly became something more than that, for the chief executive encouraged the development of this management group into a powerful informal management policy-making body and at one time called the Elfun Society "my informal board of directors." Perhaps a thousand managers throughout the company held the rank and stature for eligibility to the society. Local chapters were established at all plant cities and throughout the sales regions. The local chapters met monthly to discuss management problems within the company generally and developed projects for studies of management policy to be forwarded to the chief executive.

Powerful symbolic meaning built up around the Elfun Society. To be an Elfun meant status, recognition, and a feeling of participation in management policy making. Elfun did something more; it began to integrate management thinking across the functional vertical hierarchical barriers. The local monthly meetings of each chapter were attended by managers of all functions. The sales people usually had their cocktails with other sales people, of course, and there was a definite tendency for managers of like jobs to hang together. Nevertheless, the extracurricular projects of various Elfun chapters were carried on by study committees composed of managers from various functions.

With changing executive and managerial philosophy after decentralization, changes in organization structure, objectives, and role expectations and need for training throughout all age groups became acute. This was particularly true for the positions of operating general managers for product departments since those positions called for executive management blending of all aspects of business—technical, production, marketing, financial, etc. Except for a small handful of executives at the very top echelon of the former centralized functional organization, there were almost no men in the company with training and experience in more than a single function. At the outset of decentralization this was a most critical problem.

Recognizing the deficiency of broadly trained executive personnel, in 1949 the company initiated a program dubbed the "Crown Prince" by many because it involved the selection of functional managers generally in the age group thirty-five to forty who had demonstrated potential for general management. Each of these men was completely relieved of work assignments and given special assignments as assistants to top level managers in another function for a period of six months to one year. A sales manager in apparatus sales may have been appointed assistant to the comptroller for a period of six months and may then have been assigned as assistant to a top level engineering manager. It was hoped that within a year, or two at the most, such outstanding men would receive broad practical experience in many functions that would qualify them to assume in the future the exacting executive roles of general managers of product departments. This program was short-lived for several reasons. It was expensive because of the temporary waste of highly competent management manpower; the experience of the first few individuals demonstrated that the program did not provide adequate developmental training. The program was discontinued in 1950.

Meetings at the island in 1950, 1951, and 1952 served in a sense as managerial training media. They were not formal training programs, but they served a descriptive, analytical, and explanatory purpose. The meaning of, and reasons for, decentralization were thoroughly and analytically presented to approximately 3,000 managers who, through these meetings, began to perceive the company's new managerial philosophy.

After the Island Camp sessions in the first three years of the decentralization program were completed, the island was no longer used as a meeting place. It was finally dismantled and sold in 1956. Hence, a great old tradition in the company disappeared.

At the outset of decentralization the chief executive rejected the activities of the Elfun Society. Elfun activities attempting solutions of company problems and making recommendations to formal management were stopped. Elfun itself was not disbanded and continued to hold monthly meetings. But it was no longer "part of top management." Its meaning had changed.

In 1955 the company invested over $2 million in its well known Advanced Management Institute. An estate overlooking the Hudson River about five miles north of New York City was purchased; a number of facilities were added, including excellent living quarters and a classroom building. Removed from an urban atmosphere, the Advanced Management Institute had the environment of a college campus.

The Advanced Management Course began in 1956 as a "crash" program to train top level business managers. There were thirteen-week programs, and attending managers were temporarily relieved of all operating responsibilities and lived at the Institute. The program was aimed primarily at . . . managers from the level of chief executive down through the functional managers reporting to the product department general managers. By March, 1961, the Advanced Management Course . . . graduates included 80 percent of all the product department general managers, all but one division manager, and all five group executives. Directors of the program state that the objective was simply to improve the quality of managerial performance in present positions. . . .

Reactions to the Advanced Management Course, its objectives, and its methods varied from enthusiastic acceptance to outright disdain. Possibly the most recurrent criticism was that the Advanced Management Course preached the doctrine of decentralization and the principles of management as dogma.

Regardless of criticism, however, many managers in the company did in fact approach the work of their positions using the so-called "managerial principles" emphasized during the early days of decentralization at the Advanced Management Course. Further, it developed a common language among division, department, and functional sectional managers throughout the company. . . .

Over time . . . the General Electric Company used the mechanics of decentralization to adapt its formal structure as the product departments were formed. . . . For market reasons the apparatus sales division [a traditional unit] had to be retained as the field selling arm of the apparatus type product departments, and it remained, in a sense, an island in a sea of organizational change. As the social system changes were activated and accelerated by executive action in much of the company, in the apparatus sales division the meanings of the company and the meanings of jobs remained traditionally based and strongly reinforced by symbolic meanings of rituals, practices, and procedures. Change was instituted deliberately in the product department subsystem but not within the apparatus sales subsystem; the apparatus sales subsystem resisted change, but change occurred nonetheless. . . .

The apparatus sales division enjoyed high prestige both in

and out of the company. Individual apparatus sales managers and sales engineers were generally regarded with esteem, which was reflected in levels of compensation and such kudos as invitations to island meetings and the Elfun Society, which, although nominally restricted to management, were extended to a relatively large number of outstanding nonmanagerial and professional individuals in apparatus sales.

The individual sales engineer was regarded as an "executive type" in customer circles, where he had access to customer executive levels and, in a significant number of cases, became intimately acquainted socially with top management.

From the very start of the company the field sales organization was independently structured; in a sense, it had to be because of the continually growing complexity of engineered products and engineered systems applications with which it dealt. Even in the days of decentralization after World War II the main qualities of the complex industrial selling organization seemed to defy objective analysis through such techniques as operations research or the application of measurements.

This independence within the company was seen in a number of ways. Prior to decentralization, when product sales groups in the general office were part of the apparatus sales organization, it was normally the product sales manager who "ran the show" in unifying engineering and manufacturing efforts and integrating them with sales efforts. Within the sales organization itself the regional sales operations were quite independent and at least until the middle 1950s did "run their shows" quite independently. Apparatus sales management regarded individual sales engineers as executive businessmen and overtly recognized the sales engineer as the "manager" of his business and of his territory.

Thus, for many years a high value had been placed on individuality throughout this organization, and a considerable amount of freedom of operation and freedom to make decisions had been developed by all individuals. All this contributed to making a very proud organization, a social as well as organizational system with high esprit de corps, a very close "family" feeling, and intense loyalty to the company and to apparatus sales.

All this was reinforced by the nonrational aura of the selection and training of the members for this social subsystem. In selecting its trainees from the company pool of recently employed college graduates, apparatus sales management had a definite image of "the typical" apparatus sales person. In the initial sales training programs the lore of the division was internalized by the young trainee. Later, even after two to three years of general office training, he was required to "compete" for his ultimate job in regional sales. Regional managers or a manager of the regional staff periodically visited the various sales training locations at major plant cities and interviewed prospective candidates for regional jobs; sales trainees in turn had a choice of several regions and attempted to "sell" themselves to these regions. When a trainee accepted an offer to come to a region, he was "tagged" for that region until the conclusion of his training program. Great store was set on being "tagged."

In the region he often spent as much as two years as a sort of apprentice—answering telephone inquiries, handling quotation work for sales engineers—before being assigned to industrial customers as a full-fledged sales engineer.

Another significant tradition was the mobility pattern. Promotion came almost entirely from within; high-level management jobs at apparatus sales headquarters were filled with apparatus sales people; even within regions promotion was largely from within the region. The result was very little change in the social system relative to the function itself and in the perceptions by individuals of the meaning of apparatus sales as a social system. Technologies changed and technical knowledge increased, but the structure, management ideology, methods, the life itself were very much the same in apparatus sales from one generation to the next.

When decentralization brought drastic changes in the product department operations of the company, the function of apparatus sales remained essentially the same.

But by the middle 1950s the top executive management in apparatus sales foresaw change being forced on them. Vis-a-vis the new ebullient product department system, with no traditional past but with a high degree of emerging, rational structure and a new organization, new managerial ideology, and new techniques of business operations, apparatus sales found its external environment (within the company) rapidly and radically changing. There were two independent but interdependent and interacting social systems: one traditionally oriented with a rich history, proud of the past, and in one sense living in the past but sensing the future moving in and the other born of dynamic change and accorded a high level of status and authority by the chief executive. The stage was set for ideological conflict. . . .

[This] can be seen in the following statements; the first is from a high-level executive of the apparatus sales division who in 1962 (then recently retired) commented:

The product departments were insisting on change. Yet they would not hold long enough for an adequate test period. The real way to examine the efficiency of an operation is to develop a theory, set up a model, apply the theory and test it. But the product department would not wait for the test. There were many things during those difficult days that I tried to do to eliminate criticisms of the product departments, but long before what we did could be proven right or wrong, the product departments were insisting on still further change. When Mr. Blank was apparatus sales division general manager, he took too long to make changes and was defensive, and tried to hold apparatus sales exactly as it was. I recognized that we had to make some changes and I attempted to do so. But I learned that it wasn't change that the product departments wanted, it was power and authority over us. The product department management and other executive management of the company were seeking change for the sake of change. Change itself became almost a fetish. It appeared to me that if an organization were in place and doing a good job, but had not made some kind of change during the last couple of years, eyebrows were raised, and it was assumed that the organization was less than completely competent. Change itself seemed to become an objective in the late 1950s.

Contrast this with comments about the apparatus sales division of the mid-1950s made in 1962 by a group executive vice-president of the company:

The "old" apparatus sales division was an organization which had been so rooted in its own past that it never changed. This organization never replaced the manager except when incumbents became sixty-five years old and were required to retire. This simply doesn't make sense. There were management people in the "old" apparatus sales division who simply could not understand or accept the changes in the present—could not realize that the whole nature of our business was changing—could not adjust themselves to it. Yet, this organization tried to keep itself fixed organizationally, and tried to keep its managerial individuals in their jobs indefinitely. Here is a case where I agree that change for the sake of change was probably a good thing.

The product department managers faced a serious personal dilemma stemming from the organizational dilemma previously discussed. In general, they were given great autonomy in decision making and in return were held highly accountable for results. They were not however given control over one critically important function: field sales.

Product department managements adopted several techniques to erode the authority of the apparatus sales department. The control of sales quotas and of the expense budgets of the sales department was taken over. The product managers threatened to appoint their own distribution agencies and underlined their threat by instituting formal studies of the organization required for such a move. That forced apparatus sales to institute their own organization studies, which then exposed them to criticism of their salary and level structures. The product managers showed personal favoritism toward sales personnel they thought shared their views. Often these sales personnel were specialists in a product line and were only loosely allied with the apparatus sales organization. As the culmination of the bid for supremacy the product departments formed an effective coalition and were able to exercise a veto in the selection of apparatus sales management personnel. . . .

Under the concept of decentralization each product department general manager theoretically had the freedom to choose his channels of distribution in the organization of his marketing effort. Although the apparatus sales division had been kept intact as a pooled selling organization, each product department general manager knew that if he wished, he could in fact withdraw from this arrangement and establish his own field selling organization. Ample evidence exists that most of them would have preferred to do this in order to secure complete control over their entire marketing and selling operations. Only the forces of the market prevented this.

Moves on the part of the product department management—some merely threats and others actual formal studies for an independent sales force—became apparent first to top management and then to all members of apparatus sales, causing resentment and, finally, fear and anxiety.

The formal studies by several product departments, and in some cases entire divisions, for setting up their own sales organizations had another effect: apparatus sales began studies of its own organization. One rather extensive study by an outside consulting firm showed that the current apparatus sales organization was highly desired by customers. A number of product department management people unofficially indicated that they felt this report was "rigged."

Other internal studies resulted in several previously described organizational changes. Each change was announced by apparatus sales executive management as "in tune with the times," adjusting the structure to fit the changing internal and external company environments. These self-studies were the beginning of a series of defensive maneuvers on the part of apparatus sales against the increasingly rational product department operations. None of these changes deterred the product departments in their continuing and increasing criticisms.

As product departments were organized during the decentralization period and as the respective managerial positions were established, each position was assigned an appropriate "level number." . . . Most product department general managers, for example, ranged from level 18 to 22, and their marketing managers were in levels 16 to 18. The level structure achieved by apparatus sales was relatively higher than this. Many regional managers, for example, were assigned levels and received compensation as high as some of the general managers of the smaller product departments. Similarly, one managerial step below regional manager, the district sales manager had levels equal to, and in some cases greater than, many of the marketing managers of product departments. This was a bone of contention. Perhaps even more serious was the fact that whereas all jobs, managerial and professional, in the product departments had specific level numbers beyond which the incumbents could not rise unless promoted to another job, the levels assigned to apparatus sales engineers and application engineers were flexible. A sales engineer could retain the same job and yet be progressively increased up to level 14; . . . professional men in apparatus sales were at a higher level (and had more opportunity to increase this level) than in a product department.

Of course, apparatus sales division management stoutly maintained that to the "executive type" sales engineers jobs could not be specifically pegged; that changing conditions in the marketplace, such as increased competition, changing customer practices, increasing complexity of technology, changed the characteristics of the selling job from year to year, and that by increased creative application and engineering ability a sales engineer in a specific job did have a potential to enlarge that job. Nevertheless, the power of the product departments prevailed, and by about 1959 or 1960 the apparatus sales division was required by executive management to restructure all its levels and completely change its managerial concept of levels. Each job in each of the regions was specifically pegged, that is, assigned value to the company and specific, unchanging level.

Perhaps more subtle behavior in securing greater control over apparatus sales came from some product department management's calculated favoritism (or conversely, lack of favoritism) for certain apparatus sales management and personnel. Such behavior was especially engaged in by those product departments most vociferous in overt and formal criticisms of apparatus sales. To understand this maneuver one must realize that much of the industrial capital type of business involved very large dollar volume orders; large steam turbines had a selling price of from $6 million to $12 million, and large power transformers sold for $50,000 to $500,000. Further, during this period . . .—1955–60—prices were extremely competitive. On such large orders prices were usually negotiated; that is, a "normal" price was quoted to a customer, but very often the product department, with its complete control of pricing, extended to the sales engineer a certain leeway to try to secure the business. There were often other special concessions that product departments sometimes made to customers, through apparatus sales, in order to secure business.

But these price negotiations with their "leeway" and other concessions were not allowed "across the board," which would have been tantamount to a general overall lowering of the price structure in the entiré industry. Hence, certain jobs were selected that the product department, for one reason or another, wanted very much to have; but they were often chosen on the basis of personal friendship or favoritism to selected apparatus sales management or professional personnel. The product department could use pricing to make certain apparatus sales personnel who they felt were "on the team" "look good" and others "look bad." This is a severe indictment, but there is validating evidence in numerous statements by informants in the company. When asked about organization conflict between product departments and apparatus sales, very specifically with reference to the seeking of power by product department management, a marketing manager of a large product department replied:

> Yes, there was a lot of conflict, in fact it was probably a lot worse than you might suspect. The product department management at that time, and I won't name any names, was certainly out to 'get' apparatus sales. Further, there were certain individuals in apparatus sales who were on the black list and they were particularly shot at. Further, our own departmental sales managers were told in no uncertain terms to approach apparatus sales with a chip on their shoulders. They were specifically told to be arrogant. I know I heard a lot of complaints from some of my friends in apparatus sales about the arrogancy of management—but you really mustn't blame the sales managers of our product departments—this was an edict from top management. It was part of an overall strategy to alienate apparatus sales, to pin it up against the wall, and finally to completely dissolve our division relationships with it.

Some of the tactics described above were initiated by separate product department management people, particularly by the product department marketing managers; but then they began to "get together" and coordinate their critical activities—according to informants—particularly exercising veto power.

Until the period 1955–58 apparatus sales held virtually complete authority for the selection of managerial and other key positions within its own structure. In appointing a new district manager the regional manager would select his candidate and ask approval from his own headquarters, which was almost always granted.

The power and high status of the product department marketing management system, however, began to erode this apparatus sales authority beginning about the middle 1950s. Aware of increasing criticism of apparatus sales by product department general management, apparatus sales executive management became acutely sensitive to personal relationships between its own management group at headquarters and in the field and the product department general managers and their marketing managers. Whether apparatus sales executive management was forced to begin submitting recommendations for managerial appointments within its own hierarchy to the product department management or whether it was done simply as a defensive measure is obscure; much evidence, however, indicates that beginning about the middle 1950s apparatus sales top management began to abdicate its authority on managerial appointments. Whenever a new regional manager, or even district managers and certain key sales engineers, was [to be] named, a list of candidates was submitted to relevant product department management for comments. For some time, even as late as 1959, apparatus sales executive management denied that the product departments had any direct influence on the selection of personnel within the apparatus sales organization and said they were merely being asked for advice. However, one high level apparatus sales executive flatly told this author:

The reason that Mr. Blank did not get the position of ———— was that three important products departments blackballed him.

And here is a comment from a product department general manager.

I think probably our dissatisfaction with apparatus sales started before we had any degree of say-so about apparatus sales personnel. But when apparatus sales finally did contemplate some degree of management specialization, we did have the opportunity to indicate our feelings about candidates for district sales manager positions. We would receive from apparatus sales headquarters a list of men being considered for sales positions in which we had interest, and we gave our comments on each.

When asked if this meant that he had the right to veto these candidates and a right to make additional suggestions for other candidates, this same product department general manager replied:

The answer is yes to both questions, although in some cases it was done somewhat informally. But, yes, I would say we had a degree of power of selection of people in apparatus sales.

Another marketing manager of a product department stated:

Well, I would say that if apparatus sales wanted to appoint a new regional manager or district manager, the product departments of our division would have a chance to look over a list of suggested names for this position as submitted to us by apparatus sales headquarters. If there was an apparatus sales individual on this list whom the product department general manager or his marketing manager did not like or did not feel was a "member of the team," that guy was dead.

Ample evidence from informants indicates considerable anxiety among apparatus sales personnel; some management embarked upon "programs" of improving personal relationships with various product departments management people; some, with faith in the traditional past, resolutely resisted what they called "politicking" with product department management; others adopted an anxious do-nothing attitude.

Ultimately, . . . the proud, traditionally oriented apparatus sales division was reorganized drastically and fragmented into a number of more highly specialized work functions more directly in structural alignment with product department groupings. . . .

15 / The Company Family: The Early Years of the Andrews Winery

Barry A. Stein

THE FOUNDING

The Andrews Winery was the result of Bill Andrews' dream, and a series of coincidences. Previously employed by a large market research corporation, Andrews had always been interested in wines. Because of that, he eventually decided to retire early, move to upstate New York and start a vineyard of his own. At the same time, several investors who foresaw major growth in American wine consumption, but who had little direct experience in that business, decided to explore their entry into that market and retained Andrews' firm to carry out the study. Though he was leaving, the firm asked him to do it because of his interest. After several months of work, Andrews concluded that there was a potential market for a particular class of wines, produced and marketed to fit a carefully devel-

Prepared especially for this book.

oped strategy. After Andrews made his report, the group of investors promptly asked him to implement the strategy, as president of the Andrews Winery.

Andrews, though bright and experienced as a planner and marketer, had never managed anything bigger than a project team. Moreover, his ideas on wine were based on his own amateur wine-making and an intellectual appreciation of the processes involved. His vision of the future firm was therefore exciting and innovative—the qualities that had appealed to the investors—but short on operating details. Andrews was sure these could be worked out as things went along.

Andrews' vision was of a company producing fine wines, of the sort not routinely produced in New York State, and of an organization not as bound by bureaucratic procedures as his old firm, and the many larger organizations he had served as a consultant. To Andrews, most bureaucracy was not only wasted energy, but a block to the real potential for people to contribute. "No wonder companies are so inefficient," Andrews would say, "with all these formal requirements and controls, it's a wonder anyone gets anything done at all." And he knew, from conversations with many other people over the years, that most of them shared his views. His company would be different.

THE EARLY YEARS

At the outset, Andrews worked alone, with a secretary, in an office in his home. But by the end of the second year, the winery had purchased land for vineyards, and rented office space nearby. There were three staff members; all were the result of coincidence, just as was the winery itself.

One of them, John Carver, was an itinerant musician passing through on his way to Ohio, and trying to find work to tide him over for a while. Though he had no experience in either the wine industry or agriculture, and wasn't particularly interested in a full time job, Andrews hired him as a care-taker, handyman and helper at his house, adjacent to one of the new vineyards. Since Carver had no place to live, Andrews let him fix up a barn on the property; he concentrated on learning something about agriculture, setting out, under Andrews' direction, the new vines that were being planted. The second staff member, Louisa Wilkins, came to Andrews' attention as the friend of another wine maker in the area. She, too, had no experience with either wine or business, but she did have a college degree, was smart and was interested. She became Andrews' secretary and assistant and soon, virtually indispensable. The third early staff member, Alice Derabian, was a neighbor of the Andrews. When Bill discovered that she was a junior accountant for a large firm nearby, she was promptly hired to set up the financial and accounting systems for the Winery, areas in which Bill himself felt relatively ill at ease. These four, and a part-time stenographer/switchboard operator constituted the initial staff in the new offices.

During this period, and over the next year or so, it was easy enough for Andrews to act on his dislike for bureaucratic procedures. There was no need to organize tightly. With lots to do and a close-knit group united by a common enthusiasm for Bill Andrews personally, things worked and worked well. People had plentiful opportunities to learn, and almost unlimited flexibility as to the tasks to be done. It was very much a happy family. As John Carver said, "Lots of things about this company are because of Bill, his personality and his drive. That's the way it's grown. He didn't go out and get some guy with twenty years experience, who probably wouldn't have made the mistakes I did. To me, it's a very personal operation. Working here is one way of expressing my affection."

By the time another year had passed, the winery staff had grown to about a dozen people, not counting a substantial part-time group of field workers, planting, pruning and taking care of the vines in the new land purchased earlier. In general, the new employees of Andrews had also been found by accident. In one case, a young man with some architectural training stopped into the office because local friends thought there might be a job at the winery, because the president had peculiar habits—peculiar at least for the area—such as a willingness to hire hippies and others without a conventional background. Sure enough, Skip promptly became involved in helping make use of a rented winery so that Andrews could produce its first product. Most other people arrived by a similar route, as it became clear that the winery was a place interested in people for themselves, and providing an unusually open atmosphere.

There were two exceptions to the "drop-in" hiring. One was a young man named Sam Harriman, hired to do the winery's marketing. Harriman had actually been on the marketing staff of a wine company and therefore came with specific credentials in his field. The other exception, an older man named Phil North, had been teaching agricultural management at the local community college in the valley where Andrews is located. Whereas Sam had been found by a fairly conventional search, Phil was suggested by two of his ex-students, who had earlier been added to the vineyard staff as the vineyard development and planting program expanded.

By this time, the firm was complex, though small. With only a dozen or so full-time employees, the winery was in several different businesses. It was managing vineyards and planting grapes on about 700 acres of land. It was crushing and making wine from purchased grapes, and bottling the product, a substantial manufacturing operation. Finally, it was in the business of marketing and distributing the wines both locally and in more distant areas. As if that were not enough, there was also a considerable amount of planning and preliminary work denoted to the task of designing and building the company's own facility. Although it was possible for Bill Andrews personally to attend to all of these in the early days, it became steadily less so as time went on. One of the major tensions that developed at the winery was due to Bill's continuing attempt to be involved in everything himself, and to do it without any "bureaucracy" (e.g., procedures).

Some of the staff summed the situation up in the following words:

Skip: "The pioneering is over, so maybe the interest is over. . . . The good part was that everyone was close, no structure needed—whoever knew how to do something would lead the team. There were no permanent bosses, no permanent slaves. Now things are getting more routine, more normal. If it gets too normal, I'd easily leave. . . . Bill is one of the magic people, but I see him less now. His previous experience was in the abstract level; he's not so knowledgeable about field issues, like how slippery mud gets. So planning is poor here."

Alice: "This company's getting very big, very fast. In the beginning it was lots of fun, everything was like a party. Now people say, 'oh, another party' and feel required to go . . . I feel underpaid. I didn't at first, I thought there wasn't enough money and everyone was underpaid, now I see a new guy getting 50 percent more than me . . . I feel passed over, Bill is going to hire experts from outside."

Louisa: "Many people are worrying about how things are going, but are concerned about saying because it seems like a personal attack on Bill. . . . I told him when I came that I wanted to grow, not do clerical work very long or frustrations would build up. So we'd talk about it, not much would happen, and I'd get frustrated again . . . I'm the mother of this company, just like Bill is the father. I'm the balance to his imagination. . . . He's got a finger in every pie, and doesn't want to compartmentalize people, so they become interchangeable parts. . . . If he doesn't like something, everything gets paralyzed."

THE STATE OF THE WINERY: I

At about this time, Bill had a visitor, an old friend and colleague who had also left the old firm, but to start an organizational consulting practice. Although the visit was strictly personal, it seemed to Bill another one of those lucky coincidences. Following some conversation with Bill and others, the visitor had agreed to carry out a small program for the winery, to gather some information about the state of affairs, and then to use it so that Bill and his staff could consider options for dealing with the issues that emerged.

Over the next few months, the consultants visited several times, extensively interviewed most of the staff, participated in a number of informal activities, and read most of what was available. This was the situation:

—The winery provided many ways for people to invest themselves. It permitted people to invest more of themselves than they could in a conventional business because there were more opportunities to pitch in, change jobs, and become active in a variety of areas. People are not restricted to narrow or limited territories.

—The winery provided a special sense of community for many people, who saw the company as a place where people worked together on shared tasks and in shared rituals.

—People felt committed because their work was meaningful

and their effort contributed to something worthwhile. The winery was making a product of high quality, providing consumers with something special. The care and concern manifested for people in the winery also provided a sense of meaning and specialness—that this was a place set apart. Finally, Bill's attractiveness as a person was important to many people.

—Essentially everyone was strongly motivated by these feelings about Bill. People spoke of him positively in such terms as these: great guy, good boss, high energy, creative, makes me feel included, considerate, very friendly, generates loyalty, gives everyone a chance, and cares about people. People spoke of having joined the winery or of having decided to stay because of Bill and his ideas, drive, and warmth.

—But from great goals, high expectations, and perceived promises, disappointment and disenchantment were natural outcomes. Other comments about Bill included: manipulates people, standards are hidden, doesn't give recognition, flares up easily, doesn't share decisions, too busy, not straight, and paralyzes other people's initiative.

—As the winery grew, it had become simply impossible for Bill to work as before. The company had changed. It started with Bill as lone entrepreneur. It became a sort of proprietorship, with Bill exercising all the key roles and functions personally, while working with a few others to form a relatively close-knit ("family") group. Thereafter, it shifted toward an organization with differentiated functions and roles, several geographically and technically distinct units, and a more complex structure.

—Though Bill was caught in the same pressures as others, he perceived them very differently by virtue of his position and experience (1) Bill offered bonuses that he saw as *extra* gifts and benefits (deserving of gratitude), whereas others saw them as having been *earned* and as potentially capriciously withheld by Bill (thus generating anger). (2) Bill saw people increasingly concerned with their private goals and less with the winery and its goals (and felt let down), whereas others saw the winery becoming more of a private preserve for Bill, with others increasingly acting as "mere" employees (and therefore *also* feeling let down).

—People liked the flexibility and openness of the winery: the opportunity to create their own position and the chance to move from job to job. Some people, however, would have preferred more clarity about their roles and functions, a better sense of what was expected of them, more clarity about the basis on which people were rewarded (either in pay, job changes, responsibilities, or bonuses), and any "hidden" standards.

—Equity of rewards was similarly concerning: some people found them quite unfair. There did seem to be two systems of rewards: people who came early in the company's history were paid on a more personal basis, while people who came as "experts" were more often paid according to "market value."

—The lack of clear limits to demands, definition of responsibilities, or standards for reward inevitably made Bill very central and powerful, regardless of intent. He was the only one who could decide if someone was doing "enough," if someone had overstepped or underreached the boundaries of his responsibility, and if someone was meeting the organization's standards. Because of this, people felt paralyzed and consequently unable to exercise their best judgment.

—Members of the organization had made certain assumptions, and even perceived themselves to have definite agreements, about their future jobs and rewards, and their timing. As these expectations failed to be met or as people perceived inconsistencies, anger and mistrust developed. Employees were also very conscious of the fact that upon completion of the firm's own winery, and its major entry into the marketplace, the firm's needs and its operation were likely to change substantially. Since these potential changes had not been discussed in detail, existing concerns were exacerbated.

In addition to these specifics, the winery was described in strikingly "family-like" images by many of the staff. At the time, they said, it seemed to be much more of a community than a conventional business; it was considered a place where people cared for one another. The word "family" was often used in referring to the company, and several people remarked that it was "more than just a job." The social connections appeared strong. One person said: "Everyone I know is somehow connected with the winery." The words "father" and "mother" were used by people to describe themselves or others, with Bill most often described as a father or as treating people paternalistically. The company had also been seen by some as a kind of home where unattached people came and found care and a job.

The "family" image was therefore a mixed blessing. On the

positive side, it was one source of the great commitment and attachment that many people had to the company and that motivated them to do more than just their job. However, the "family" culture was also a source of difficulties. One person
commented, "Sometimes I wish it were more like a conventional business." Family-like and businesslike behavior and activities were sometimes in tension. For example:

—Some people entered the company primarily as "members of the
family" and not as workers hired for specific jobs.
—Despite Bill's statements to the contrary, there was a prevalent feeling that people would be retained by the company and taken care
of (within reasonable limits), even if this would not be good for "the
business."
—There was some confusion between Bill as father and as president of
Andrews Winery. People sometimes talked about doing things for
Bill when they were for the company. And sometimes Bill took personally things that were meant as comments about the company as
a whole.
—The "family" image created problems for the company's development over time. The people who entered first took pride in their
special relationship with Bill, and in their pioneering efforts.
Newer people were both potential threats and outsiders who had
not shared the hard but commitment-generating pioneering. Later
arrivals were also more likely to have been hired because of special
skills, and sometimes did not reflect and share the "family" image.
They thought in more businesslike terms.

This contributed to a changing culture with which not all
members identified. There was a continuing shift likely in character: from family to business, from small to large, from loose
and unstructured to specific and defined, from shared learning
to reliance on expertise, and from relationships of friendship to
those of employment. As Andrews Winery continued to grow,
the tension between the reality and the remaining inappropriate images might also be expected to grow unless some of the
underlying issues were addressed directly and appropriate
structures developed.

TRANSITION TO MATURITY

During the next two years, Bill Andrews and the Andrews
Winery went through a series of major transitions. Enough
wine was available, though still from purchased grapes, to

begin to build a real market and, in effect, to "go public." Most particularly, with the critical acceptance that followed, the investors decided to go ahead and build a major winery facility that Andrews had been seeking. Typically, the architect selected was someone Bill had met at a local party—he had never designed a winery—and the project manager for Andrews was Skip, the young drop-in with an architectural background that he had never expected to use. With some reluctance, Skip agreed to stay on for this job, but was extremely unclear about his role after completing the construction. In fact, that was true for nearly everybody. The issue was: what will happen to Andrews and to us as the winery takes shape and is completed?

In a certain sense, the physical construction of the new winery forced the transition from a "company family," a loosely knit, relatively unstructured and informal organization, to a serious business with a more formal structure and a relatively defined organization. The very fact that the offices were now in an elegant—indeed, a prize-winning—structure, with all that that symbolizes, made people keenly aware that Andrews Winery had changed and that with it, they had to change as well. An equivalent process had taken place in Bill Andrews, for he was forced to make some things explicit, and to plan more concretely so that the new building could be built. Like it or not, there was a spacious president's office and even though Bill agreed to do it "only because people expect it," he grew very much accustomed to it.

Another major development coincident with the construction of the new winery was a much increased interface with the public. This was in part a reflection of the new marketing posture—Andrews began to have a steady series of important visitors—and in part the company's wish to have a visitor's center, a tasting room, and guides for taking tours through the winery. In addition, Andrews wanted to do something that was relatively unusual; namely, to start a full-fledged restaurant of sufficient quality to reflect the quality of Andrews' wines. It was to be a show piece, just as was the winery itself. Although there were many problems—zoning restrictions, the investors initial reluctance, and turnover among chefs, the restaurant was duly opened not many months after the winery.

Organizationally, however, all this created problems. The

addition of a tour guide staff and a restaurant staff not only added two new kinds of business to the several already noted, but it nearly tripled the size of the full-time staff (to about fifty). Bill found himself managing not only a very much larger and more complex organization but also one populated largely by people who had no sense whatever of the original excitement and character of the company, having instead taken a more or less conventional job in what looked like a perfectly conventional enterprise. The relationship between new and old hands, and the integration of all into a single organization, became the next challenge.

By the time the winery was completed, the investors were putting more pressure on Andrews to control costs and start making profits. Up to this point, expenses had been relatively modest. There had been only a small payroll, all of which was seen as start-up expense, and amply justified by production of just enough wine to demonstrate feasibility of the level of product desired. But the investment in the winery—some six million dollars—the switch to a major national marketing effort, and a large increase in payroll meant an enormously greater drain on resources. They accordingly started seeking faster returns than were visible, even though Andrews had warned them that it would take some time before income would be adequate to offset costs.

All together, these things forced a more conventionally businesslike posture on the company. Some people who had looked good earlier were fired when it became clear that they were not appropriate to the situation. Expertise was hired as necessary. The job of winery manager went to a new person with substantial experience and impressive credentials. Overall, however, a great many of the pioneers have stayed and grown, moving into more responsible, and more structured positions. Skip became manager of winery production, a job he had never anticipated nor desired—before he got it—but pleased when it developed. Louisa continued to become more important, finally as Director of Public Affairs, including public relations, publicity, and the visitor's center activities. John Carver and two other pioneers have become full-fledged vineyard managers in the several properties owned, so much so as to raise questions about the role that Phil North might play. Alice left before the winery was completed; her relationship with Bill was increasingly tense. Sam Harriman has proven nearly a perfect choice, supporting Bill yet increasingly professional in his own right.

The changing, yet continuing character of the winery is shown by some comments from the staff.

Jeanne (*a recent clerical addition*): "There's a breakdown between the office and the winery [before everyone moved to the new structure]; we don't have systems working yet. I still don't know what's going on, even when I'm supposed to. . . . This company is so much like a family that I really do feel left out when other people are doing something I can't join. . . . The job is getting more complicated; it was so easy when I came [six months earlier]. . . . Lots of people walk in looking for jobs. I send them to the winery."

John: "A year ago I just wanted to run my territory and play music, but now I see more. I don't want to be an expert in only a certain kind of vineyard. We need to get together more, learn to do more things. But I'm really proud of what I've done, creating a uniform stand of vines on a difficult piece of land. Now we need to get together more [the three vineyard managers], because we need to coordinate more and better."

Joe (*a worker in the winery*): "Bill had a very effective way of doing things. He did it himself. That was fine when we had only four people. Now he does something and doesn't tell anyone he's done it. We call it a "temporary situation" but it perpetuates itself. . . . I think it's a communication problem, but I may be wrong [He's so busy he doesn't go to the weekly meetings]. . . . Still, it's a good place to work and I feel good about it."

THE STATE OF THE WINERY: II

About this time, the consultants visited again, rather more briefly, but concluding their visit with a long meeting with Bill Andrews. The situation had changed.

—There was increasing interdependence among members and groups in the firm, which was to be expected. People and the winery could still have benefited from making it more explicit, however, and from supporting it explicitly.

—The tension between the "family" image and the business

was still present. Even people who had joined relatively recently continued to pick up the image of the family. However, that seemed to be truer of people working closely with pioneers. It seemed doubtful that the same would be true of the restaurant or tour guide groups.

—There was much more "managerial" language in general. People seemed in many ways much more businesslike and more aware of the needs of the organization. They also seemed much more prepared to accept more structured roles.

—There were clear signs of parochialism, with people paying more attention to the needs/demands of their unit than to the organization as a whole. In fact, there was less clear awareness of issues beyond people's own group. More integration, coordination and information flow would have helped. This was particularly true of the three main elements: vineyards, winery production, and office/administrative. The new restaurant/tour guide sections seemed likely to remain distinct as well.

—Concerns about equity were more visible. These were sparked by reductions of the collective commitment, replaced by more of a "this is just a job" image, and the absence of sufficiently clear policies.

In general, however, Bill Andrews had basically proven his point. It was unquestionably true that many people who would not normally have expected to do so had been able to take on roles and responsibilities involving substantial experience and skill. Most had started with little or no background, but were plainly effective in what was then a complex and difficult business. Applicable standards did not permit otherwise. Despite many problems, especially in retrospect, it is clear that if Andrews had erred on the side of too few policies and procedures, most organizations do the very opposite. But his approach also and unmistakably created greater opportunity, built better relationships and a more human climate than the traditional alternative. With continued growth would probably come more procedures, but perhaps never losing entirely the feelings and rewards of the pioneers.

SECTION FIVE

Life in Politicized Environments: Interdependence, Responsibility, and Skullduggery

ORGANIZATIONS do not stand alone; nor do their parts. Interdependence is a fact of life. We engage in transactions with other groups in the organization to get what we need or to get them to do what we need, and we also, if we are top leaders, engage in similar transactions with the world outside the organization. How we conduct these dealings, and how those others deal with us, is an important part of the organizational experience.

Because of numerous interdependences, there are also numerous "stakeholders" in every decision—people who will be affected by the outcome or can influence the results. They are the "environment" that must be taken into account, for they represent checks on unilateral authority, sources of needed materials or approval, or groups to which responsibility is owed. The clearest of such "environmental" constituencies are often top officials ("the boss"), owners and the government; but they also can include employees, members, students, consumers, political pressure groups, and average citizens.

When environments press or need to be managed, when stockholders are activated, when interests are strong but divergent—then we can talk about "politicized" organizations. These issues exist for all organizations, of course, but often in hidden, disguised, or latent form. But when political tensions are heightened, or when political dealings are particularly visible, then these issues rise to the surface and can be examined. In politicized organizations, we can see how people experience a variety of ways of handling interdependence with others inside or outside, and we can ask just how responsible and ethical political behavior in organizations really is, if it does not acknowledge all stakeholders and all interdependences.

The people who reside comfortably inside prosperous organizational groupings in quiet times when the outside environment is stable may never have to be troubled by organizational politics. But for those who live on organizational borders, as all managers and leaders do, then relating to their environments—whether this is other parts of the organization, other constituencies who feel they have a right to make claims, owners or directors, customers or consumers, governments and communities—is a critical part of their jobs.

And in times of crisis, when the environment "acts up" or change is rapid, nearly everyone's organizational life is touched by and affected by political issues. Indeed, internal and external political issues are intertwined with an organization's life stage, with matters of growth and decline, and so they make an appropriate bridge between them. Growing organizations must position themselves with respect to all of their environments. But if they fail to take into account political and environmental changes, they may find themselves decaying rapidly. Environmental change means organizational change.

Organizational politics represent attempts at control, at getting oneself or one's system in a more favorable bargaining position with respect to another entity, so that it is possible to make claims, gather resources, or have one's decision supported. One current social science perspective holds that organizations (or organizational units) *adapt* to their environments. But that view is very passive and misleading, especially in terms of human experience. People in boundary positions more often actively seek to *control* their environments. They do not always succeed, but that is because of some of the realities of political wheeling and dealing.

SOME POLITICAL LESSONS

Perspective is shaped by position.   In organizations, where people sit most often accounts for the positions they take. This is partly a matter of what resources and lines of action are open to them: what seems easy and what seems difficult. One well-known sociological theory about crime holds that deviant behavior has to do with the relative availability of legitimate versus illegitimate means. To extend this to choices about political action and ways to seek control over relevant environments, we have a clear analogy to "white collar crimes" in which businessmen or politicians (as in chapter 19, "The Bagman") use illegal tools such as bribery. Although the relative ease of illegal versus legal means does not justify illegal actions, it might be that large sums of money are more readily available than the means to produce better products, or that going directly to a politician seems easier than pleading one's cause before the public. Sometimes the most moral or the most reasonable action is also more difficult because of where one is in the system, and what pressures exist.

If tools for action differ with organizational situation, so do constituencies to which one feels responsive. Not all parts of an organization share the same environment. Delegation of different activities to different parts which then come into contact with quite different "stakeholders" means that they also end up with different perspectives about what is important, what goals predominate. Philip Selznick (1966) considered this a central source of organizational tensions. In San Francisco in the early 1970s, for example, as we see in chapter 16, the Public Works Department, because of historical connections, turns out to be auto-oriented, unlike the neighborhood-aesthetics-and-environmental-purity-oriented City Planning Department. No matter how hard Allan Jacobs, the planning director, tries to convince them, the Public Works people still see things in terms of "what's good or bad for the automobile." Yet, at the same time, Jacobs is aware of the strong commercial, pro-business stance of the Chamber of Commerce, and expects disagreement, to the extent that "when we did agree, I took a second look to see if we were on the wrong side."

Power is also shaped by position. There are predictable sources of bargaining power in organizations, also deriving from where one is located. In *Men and Women of the Corporation*, Rosabeth Kanter (1977) points to two sides of power accumulation that come out of one's position: jobs that permit risk and discretion, are highly visible, and appear relevant to pressing organizational issues, controlling important contingencies for others; or jobs that afford political connections with important power-holders (sponsors) or with teams of supporters. Power—meaning here an advantage in political bargaining which nets one the resources to get something done—is a matter of whether one is perceived by others to have it, others who then adjust their actions accordingly. For Jacobs in San Francisco, his influence with other city departments was based in part on the fact that he was seen to have something they needed (in this case, help) so that they were willing to support him, and in part on seeming to have the ear of the Mayor.

But when Jacobs refused to campaign for the Mayor's re-election, the relationship was lost, and so was much of his influence. The signs of loss of power were the same that we can look for in any organization:

—fewer meetings, harder to arrange;
—the word gets around of loss of favor;
—funds begin to disappear or go elsewhere;
—formal agreements don't work and informal agreements turn out to be illusory;
—an assistant is seduced away.

This shifting balance of power is solidified in organizational arrangements: Jacob's assistant is set up in a new office with overlapping functions, which reports directly to the Mayor and gradually takes over things the City Planning Department would normally do. In short, the formal, institutional side of power should not be ignored. The Public Works Department, Jacobs tells us, had power in San Francisco because of old connections, the fact that other departments were dependent on them for resources and official approvals, and their direct line reporting relationship to a senior official. Jacobs found it easier to stop them by forming other alliances (e.g., getting citizens together to testify) than by influencing their actions directly. Similarly, Warren Bennis' "campaign" for university president (chapter 17) relied on teams of supporters—on massing numbers—rather than changing stands to please the selection committee.

The alliances that build power are themselves, we can see, subject to change with circumstances: new issues forcing choices that may diverge, leaders turning over. The same sponsor, for example, that gave Bennis an initial advantage as a university vice president became a political handicap when Bennis decided to "run" for president. If nothing happens out there in the world, then alliances can be protected. But, of course, that never happens. There are always new events that force choices affecting one's political position, some built-in to the design of institutions (like periodic elections), others idiosyncratic or shaped by larger social changes: Mayor Alioto's call to Jacobs about a campaign picture, the student riots at Buffalo.

The "good guys" don't always win.   Finally, in organizations as in other political systems, the people who "fight fair" or show integrity do not always emerge with the edge in bargaining relationships. Times of crisis, as we see in "The Buffalo Search" (chapter 17), heighten political emotions, resulting in the invoking of slogans and stereotypes, rumors and innuendoes, and smear campaigns. The pressure to act with less than full integrity, to retaliate, to back down on controversial positions is there.

This is an unfortunate fact of organizational life. However, it is also true that leaders or managers who win not quite fairly also have a harder time leading or managing later. And it is also true that contentious internal fighting which disrupts cohesion and draws battle lines also makes the system much more vulnerable to outside intervention. We certainly saw this in the university crises of the late 1960s; student riots brought the police, the National Guard, or more control by trustees.

THE ROLE OF INTERPERSONAL COMMUNICATION: FACE-TO-FACE PERSUASION AND NEGOTIATION

Political issues are not the same as interpersonal issues. As much as it is appealing to many of us who have faith in the reasonableness of our fellow humans to believe that "if we only got together and talked it over, we could resolve this to everyone's satisfaction," organizational politics do not necessarily work that way. Face-to-face communication can sometimes worsen rather than improve relationships, as we see when Warren Bennis, candidate for the presidency of a university, finally meets with a leading member of the faction opposing him. Then the parties involved can see for themselves just how far apart they really are.

Furthermore, sometimes people leave a meeting or a bargaining session feeling good about the result, feeling that they have agreed or have been promised something, only to learn later that this was an illusion, and nothing has changed.

What used to be conventional wisdom in applied behavioral science—that communication increases trust—is now open to question, or at least we are aware that circumstances determine whether that formula holds or not (Brown, 1977). Decisions are shaped by more than the quality of interpersonal relationships; there are also real interests at stake. A public official like Jacobs in San Francisco might find relations with his board improved by socializing together at dinners and parties, but that still does not stop them from disagreeing when material interests diverge. Similarly, when Jacobs first encountered difficulty with the Public Works Department, he thought "it was just a matter of communication, not politics." Then he learned it was sheer politics.

Thus, it is important to look at the context. Persuasion and face-to-face negotiation are likely to work best when:

—The parties are genuinely unfamiliar with one another and are operating primarily on the basis of myths and stereotypes;
—The parties are not as far apart as they think, and communication allows them to explore areas of agreement as well as disagreement;
—The power positions are relatively equal, and trades are possible because each party has something the other wants;
—Not much is at stake in the decisions that will come out;
—Third parties (like the government) are forcing the parties to negotiate, insist on a concrete outcome, and will enforce the agreement;
—There are other parties that both would like to influence, and so there are benefits to getting together on this one issue or going into a meeting with prior agreements;
—There are overriding considerations or "superordinate goals" that both parties believe in and are willing to bend a little to achieve;
—There are additional costs to not going to see the other face-to-face, for even if the negotiation doesn't work, things would be worse if the other party felt ignored or was not forewarned.

REDUCING POLITICAL TENSIONS THROUGH PARTICIPATION

One way some organizations manage interdependence, diverging interests, and the co-existence of numerous stakeholders affected by decisions is to develop formal mechanisms for participation in decisions. Philip Selznick, in his classic study of the Tennessee Valley Authority, defined the term "co-optation" for the process by which power or the burdens of power are shared: "The process of absorbing new elements into the leadership or policy-determining structure of an organization as a means of averting threats to its stability or existence." (1966:259) For organizations with strong constituencies (and thus likely to be highly politicized), bringing in members of those constituencies and giving them a voice is a matter of protection against attack: "Failure to reflect the true balance of power will necessitate a realistic adjustment to those centers of institutional strength which are in a position to strike organized blows and thus to enforce concrete demands." (1966:260) Selznick pointed out, however, that it is possible to co-opt without actually sharing power, merely by creating a "front" that makes it look as though stakeholders have a voice.

Employees are a principal group of stakeholders. International Group Plans (IGP), a Washington, D.C. insurance company, is an example of what comes close to a complete system for giving employees a voice (chapter 18). Its 340 employees (whom Daniel Zwerdling finds quite typical corporate souls, not particularly left-leaning) own half the corporation and elect half the Board. Profits are divided equally rather than as a percentage of salary. Workers hire and have some say in firing. There are a variety of mechanisms for involvement in decisions: autonomous work groups, a worker-elected congress and court, and employee committees to make decisions that in other places would be managerial prerogatives. Like a handful of other U.S. companies such as Polaroid, IGP explicitly defines two goals: first, profits, and second, a model of humanness.

The atmosphere—the quality of life—in participatory organizations is clearly different from that in the kind of autocratic settings described in "Making a Life at the Bottom." It is not clear that we can define a "bottom" in participatory systems in quite the same way, even with respect to the lowest-paid employees or the most junior members. At IGP, for example, there is freedom to set one's own schedules, contact with top managers who listen, awareness of company possibilities and decisions, the chance to minimize boring routine by cooperatively spreading some of the least liked tasks. People drink coffee and chat at their desks and drop everything momentarily for a baby shower. Such climate changes are not the primary objectives of projects to enhance the quality of work life by broadening opportunity and power, but they do indicate how different the experience of the same job can be in settings that have taken different political stances.

The IGP successes are, however, only one side of the story. There are also a number of difficulties in trying to equalize power, to establish a thoroughly participatory-democratic organization. Many of these problems can be posed as natural human dilemmas; they are as much a part of life in participatory systems as the enhanced sense of freedom, control, and community. The existence of such difficulties is not confined to businesses with a profit motive trying to operate more cooperatively; they also run through the experience of cooperative communities trying simultaneously to operate a business, like the nineteenth century American utopian communities, the modern Israeli Kibbutzim, and the Yugoslavian self-managed enterprises (Kanter, 1972; Hunnius, 1971). But perhaps we see the dilemmas most sharply in businesses that try to improve the quality of work life by increasing participation in decisions and replacing much traditional management with self-management by work teams; the Gaines Pet Food plant in Topeka, Kansas, or Harmon Industries in Tennessee are well-known examples (Walton, 1974).

From the IGP case, along with other experiences, we can extract some of the central tensions around participation:

1. *The paradox of paternalism.* How does a participatory organization arise in the first place? Most organizations—especially businesses—are founded by a single entrepreneur or, at most, a very small group. Or else an ongoing business with a traditional leadership structure decides to become more participatory. In either case, as at IGP, democracy may be *imposed* on the employees by the leadership who then expect gratitude. "Like it or not, you're free"—what Zwerdling calls "liberating the masses by beneficent dictate."

2. *The problem of power.* Managers don't want to give it

up. And why should they? In many corporations, middle managers, as we have seen, feel sufficiently powerless anyway that they may be even more resistant to schemes which take away what limited authority they feel they have—and do not also give them something else to do to feel important and useful.

3. *Time.* Participation and involvement in decisions is time-consuming, and time is a finite resource. It generally takes longer to make decisions democratically rather than autocratically (Mansbridge, 1973), and there is no guarantee that the decisions that emerge will be of a higher quality, although the evidence is mixed, as we know from experiments contrasting "tall" organizations (many-layered hierarchical situations with chains of command) with "flat" ones (teams with shared responsibility). (See Kanter, 1977:276–77.) Perhaps not all decisions *should* be made democratically. But it is often hard, in such systems, to draw the line legitimately. Secondly, the extra time members or workers need to invest in meetings and in informing themselves may not always be worth it to them, particularly where they feel inadequately paid for the extra time. Worker apathy was a problem for some areas in IGP; teams shirked responsibility. Some psychologists have also argued that there are personality differences among people that make some "fit" better than others in participatory groups requiring responsibility and active involvement (Vroom, 1960).

4. *The knowledge gap.* Organization members do not always know *how* to exercise power once they get it. And the information and knowledge gap between workers and managers may be hard to budge, and it may mean that the better-informed (the managers) still have a greater voice in decisions. Indeed, Mauk Mulder (1971) has designed controlled experiments to demonstrate that participation does not always equalize power and may even increase discrepancies. If more poorly informed members, with less skill in analysis or leadership, sit with the more knowledgeable and skilled in meetings where they theoretically decide together, the less skilled may not only be "shown up" and keep quiet but are then also forced, in a de facto sense, to endorse the decisions they supposedly helped make. At other times, it may come to seem appropriate to leave them out of other decisions, not because *managers* should make them, but because the *most suitable* should make them; at IGP, for example, workers have little say in overall financial poli-

cies. Without training for those whose prior situation has meant they are less informed or less skilled at decision making, it is hard for them to be sufficiently involved, and the outcomes might be annoying to all concerned.

5. *The internal politics of teams.*   Declaring people a group does not automatically make them one, nor does requesting decisions in which everyone has a voice ensure that democratic procedures will always be followed. Teams can turn into oligarchies, with one or two dominant people taking over. The benign "tyranny" of peers can substitute for the benign "tyranny" of managers. Furthermore, historic tensions between members of the team can rise to greater importance in situations where they are thrown together and forced to interact and perhaps even to rely on one another. If the situation is also frustrating, as drawn-out committee meetings can be, emotions may rise to the surface. Tensions between workers and managers in meetings, for example, can result in driving them further apart if they engage in mutual blame for team problems.

6. *Social and emotional pressures: "It's hard to fire your friend."*   Participatory organizations that stress cooperation and overlay a feeling of community on a business make it hard to get rid of troublesome people, if a close working relationship has developed. It is often harder to level with people in more personal or intimate relationships for just this reason; too much else has been invested in them to allow complete honesty, if it would appear to jeopardize the relationship. Responsibilities to the person build up that extend beyond his or her usefulness for the business. So sometimes more impersonal decisions from the top save everyone's face.

7. *Great expectations.*   It is very easy for all of us to forget what the alternatives are when we evaluate our current situation. So new systems or relationships are often judged not in terms of how much better they are than others, but in terms of how far short of their promises they fall (Kanter and Zurcher, 1973). Organizations that appear to promise a great deal can also disappoint people more. There is more frustration and cynicism if expectations that are aroused are not fulfilled. We see some of this cynicism interwoven with the favorable reports in the IGP case. It is just this problem that managers often mention as a reason (or an excuse) not to try new programs that could expand opportunity and power: "Let's not arouse expec-

tations we can't meet and have them more troubled than before."

8. *Not all organizational problems disappear.* Participatory
systems are often painted as organizational Utopias that will
solve everything. But the IGP story also makes it clear that
results can be mixed and can vary from department to department. While profits were high, so was turnover, and there were
problems of absenteeism and backlogs and sloppy work in some
offices. It is unfortunate, however, that some people want to
judge the success of a participatory organization in terms of
whether or not it *does* produce results on every indicator,
rather than whether it manages to do well what it intended to
accomplish through participation. The greater involvement of
constituencies is a solution to some of the *political* dilemmas of
organizations, to issues of interdependency and conflict resolution; it is not addressed to every management problem.

ORGANIZATIONAL SKULLDUGGERY

The subject of how people in organizations handle their political dealings would not be complete if we ignored the hidden
side of organization-environment relations: those certainly secret and often shady means by which representatives of some
organizations have sought to gain an advantage: "skullduggery."

Organizational democracy is a style of operating which involves the open sharing of information and the inclusion of relevant constituencies in decisions affecting them (though, as we
have seen, there may be behind-the-scenes jockeying for position anyway). In contrast, organizational skullduggery is an
operating style defined by autocracy (the decisions of a few to
commit the organization to possibly illegal acts), secrecy, bribery (the use of organizational resources to buy decisions of constituents or controllers regardless of their merits or consequences), and collusion (the agreement of small coalitions to
maintain various pretenses). Such activities on the part of corporations and government units have increasingly been the
subject of investigation and sanctioning, especially in the last
decades. We learn about them in retrospect, often after one rev-

elation begins to shed light on other corrupt activities; investigation of the Watergate scandal also uncovered illegal corporate political contributions. Company and government officials now go to jail for these "white collar crimes," which formerly often were lightly punished by fine and without individual accountability for organization actions.

Between 1960 and 1973, John Brooks tells us in chapter 19, Gulf Oil distributed twelve million dollars in political contributions and payments, including to Nixon's CREEP (the Committee to Re-Elect the President); it was the Watergate-instigated investigation of CREEP that finally brought Gulf's illegal contributions under scrutiny. The story reads like fiction, a secret agent corporate thriller, but appalling because it was all too true. There were secret bank accounts to launder funds, records flushed down toilets, couriers carrying plain envelopes stuffed with cash, safes left conveniently open at night, packages changing hands behind barns on remote ranches, and executives slugging one another in a sedate upper-crust club. The major courier claimed he had no knowledge, asked no questions, and, presumably, must have thought no thoughts, since he actually saw the money. One executive, the administrative vice president, tried to pull out, but it appears that the architect of the bribes (the then-chief executive) wouldn't let him; one can only imagine the dialogue between them at that point: who might have threatened whom with what.

It is also clear in the Gulf case, as in other corporations in which some executives engage in skullduggery, that only a handful of people are involved. Part of the "secret agent" atmosphere in "The Bagman" stems from the fact that the plans had to be kept secret from the Mellon Family (the largest stockholders) and from just about everyone in the company, including those executives the bribers derisively called "Boy Scouts" (but who remain a repository of ethical conduct in corporations). The same thing emerges in the G.E. price-fixing cases; there were insiders trying desperately to stop any illegal activity.

It is a more difficult question to ask whether there are any built-in restraining mechanisms, if the activities remain secret and if collusion works. It was an almost accidental outside event—the Watergate break-in—that brought the attention resulting in thorough investigations. Otherwise, some of the secrets might have gone to the conspirators' graves with them; indeed, several were dead by the time of the investigations. A corporate Code of Ethics seems weak; G.E. had one that specifically mandated against price-fixing, and some executives seem to have passed it on to their subordinates with a wink. Brooks points out that we cannot expect market mechanisms to work either, because the Gulf revelations had no effect on profits or stock price. But there was one "corporate responsibility" device that ultimately, at least, built in some accountability at the end, after the activities came to light, and the Gulf Board of Directors had to decide the hard ethical questions involved. Many analysts currently argue that outside directors are essential ingredients in corporate responsibility (Dill, 1978). In the Gulf case, it was an outside director that cast the swing vote removing the current chief executive. Ironically, she was a nun and a college president.

But lest the impression be given that the stereotype of women as more virtuous and ethical is thereby confirmed, we can look at Dita Beard, the former ITT lobbyist who rose from a secretarial job to the position of the only registered ITT lobbyist in Washington, whose famous memo about Harold Geneen's $400,000 check to the Republican Party in 1971 was released by Jack Anderson in the newspapers, getting her fired and ITT a slap on the wrist.

Beard has been quoted as saying that there is "Nothing like a little action to pick up a girl's spirits. The next best thing to getting laid is a little political skullduggery." An ITT executive wrote:

> People who would normally have been rankled by man-talk from a woman didn't seem to mind it from Dita because it sounded natural. When Dita used her alliterative obscenities to describe people it fell hard on some ears, but it was always imaginative. Dita's success lay in her ability to play politics with men with no quarter asked or given. She swore like a man, drank like a man and felt like a man. Otherwise she could never have played Geneen's congressional court jester and private emissary; it simply wasn't a lady's role. [Burns, 1974:100]

> But while her battles and vendettas against the enemies of ITT weighed light on her mind, she was paranoid with respect to internal ITT politics. She feared and hated the "finks and spies" who were trying to do her in, get her job, embarrass her friends, or neutralize her influence with Geneen. [Burns, 1974:101]

Dita was candid about her role as a broker. She represented ITT in process of trading votes, favors and people. Her job was to head off situations adverse to ITT and Congress and the Administration before they turned into legislation or appointments. The coin of the realm was the tip-off, the payoff, and the introduction. A favor to Dita went into the record books for repayment on demand, from a bank called ITT. [Burns, 1974:111]

In 1971, Beard tried to make a deal on the ITT anti-trust case that ITT would keep Hartford, get rid of a "couple of losers like Avis and Canteen," and agree to an acquisition policy. In exchange, the Republican convention would be held in San Diego, where Congressman Wilson wanted it. It was this information on a scratch pad that journalist Anderson found.

ITT's internal response was interesting, especially in the light of the accountability and responsibility questions. ITT security people from New York went to her Washington office, took all the files, and shredded them in paper shredders. The office head wrote a memo renouncing responsibility for anything that had happened in the office in the last two years. The New York people made sure that Beard was gone, along with everything she owned. They took her pictures off the office wall—and one person joked that they might even be removing the wallpaper. Said another, "There's a hell of a lot more going on here than Dita's memo spells out. I'm just as glad they're shredding the files and plans in our office as well as the others. From now on I write on nothing but easily digested rice paper" (Burns, 1974:241–42).

Why some people fail to tell the truth in such situations, why people would often rather cover themselves than blow the whistle on skullduggery, is a complex question. "Why Should My Conscience Bother Me?"—the B. F. Goodrich case in chapter 9—shows the pressure put on ethical "Boy Scouts" in some organizations where the "I-only-work-here-I'm-just-a-hired-hand" prevails. Warren Bennis cited Nikita Krushchev's answer to an anonymous, written press conference question:

The question: What was he, an important figure, doing during all those crimes of Stalin he had retroactively exposed and denounced? Khrushchev was livid with rage. "Who asked that question?" he demanded. "Let him stand up!" Nobody did. "That's what I was doing," said Khrushchev. [1976:145]

THE SELECTIONS

The articles that follow look at examples of the handling of organizational interdependences and stakeholder claims in four different kinds of organizations: a local government, a university, a worker-owned business, and a large corporation. We see the official trying to balance responsibilities and manage relationships with varying constituencies, the leader "campaigning" for a higher organizational office, the founder turning over control to employees, the executive trying to short-circuit legal procedure. From both the insiders themselves and outsider reports, we learn about the experiences of people living in systems with different ways of responding to their constituencies and their environments. All four organizations are politicized, in that political dealings and dilemmas are a clear focus of action. We also have both good and bad examples. On the one side, we have Allan Jacobs, the ethical city official; Warren Bennis, the university vice president who doesn't compromise his beliefs just to impress decision-makers; and James Gibbons, the businessman who seeks humane goals and cares deeply about the workers. But the few Gulf Oil officials pose a striking contrast: lack of ethics and responsibility, willingness to lie.

"Running the San Francisco City Planning Department" is Allan B. Jacobs' first-hand account of his years (1967–74) as the professional Director of City Planning; he is perhaps one of the most widely-respected city planners in America. Now a professor at the University of California, Jacobs here reflects on the number of groups with which he had to manage relationships in order to do his professional work: his staff, the Civil Service Commission, the Public Works Department, the Chamber of Commerce, the elected Planning Commission, the Mayor, and neighborhood groups. The quality and kind of relationship with each, the potential barriers or roadblocks they represented—that is what made the difference in whether or not the City Planning Department could do its work.

Warren Bennis also provides an inside account in "The Buffalo Search." The State University of New York at Buffalo was in 1969, he writes, "everybody's political football." And, "university politics make other kinds seem as fierce as shuffleboard." In such a highly politicized environment, it is not surprising that daily administrative tasks are often sacrificed to the rigors of campaigning for one's own position; the article shows nicely how much time went into political rather than managerial tasks. "The Buffalo Search" also describes the atmosphere in such a system: rumors and innuendoes, smear campaigns and stereotypes, political fates resting on private decisions. We see at first hand the hard choices that in normal times hover below the surface and never need to be made. In crisis situations, it is impossible to escape being drawn into the battle; sides must be chosen.

At Buffalo, power ultimately resided in the hands of the University Council, which ignored most of the other constituencies with a stake in the presidential choice. As Bennis tells us, this undermined the legitimacy of the new president, even though it was still impossible to challenge the Council's power. "At IGP, It's Not Business as Usual," by Daniel Zwerdling, describes a very different system, in which the Decision Making Commandment is: No decision may be made until all the workers directly affected have been consulted. International Group Plans is an insurance company with 340 employees and over a million dollars in profit in 1976. It is one of the most successful ongoing experiments in worker self-management in America. If IGP is not a model for every company, because many problems remain, it is at least a source of learning. It *is* possible to share power more widely and handle interdependences democratically.

Finally, we turn to a very different issue: skullduggery. John Brooks, a well-known writer on financial and corporate affairs, produced "The Bagman" from material in the report of the Special Review Committee to investigate Gulf Oil's political contributions. The Committee was appointed under a consent decree with the Securities and Exchange Commission. A number of disturbing moral and ethical questions are posed by this article. If left alone, without accountability mechanisms or stakeholders pressing, some executives will resort to secret and illegal political dealings, then should the public demand more corporate responsibility? Should it demand that all stakeholders have a voice in organizational decisions affecting them? And, if the voice is deemed necessary, then how do we handle life in such politicized systems?

16 / Running the San Francisco City Planning Department

Allan B. Jacobs

MY FIRST RECOMMENDATION on a major city planning issue to the San Francisco City Planning Commission was a loser.

At a joint meeting of the Planning Commission and the San Francisco Redevelopment Agency in 1967, I recommended against some major changes in the plan for the Golden Gateway Redevelopment project. The Planning Commission, the same commission that had only recently hired me as Director, voted six to one for the same changes. The only holdout was a new commissioner, one that had not been involved in my hiring. He abstained.

A few days later I flew back to Philadelphia where I was still teaching at the University of Pennsylvania—I had agreed to spend ten days a month in San Francisco during the spring before taking over my duties as Director of City Planning full-time in May—and began to wonder why I had accepted the job in the first place. During the previous month's visit I had had my first tangle with the Redevelopment Agency and the architect-developer for the Embarcadero Center project. At that meeting, he allowed as how my views regarding his project were quite subjective and he didn't see why he should have to be concerned with them. My screaming reply, to the effect that as long as the project had to come before my department, for my recommendation, he'd better damned well be concerned with my opinion, was not considered friendly.

Then, too, on my first day in the city, I was greeted by a

Prepared especially for this book. Some of this material has been excerpted from Professor Jacobs' book, *Making City Planning Work*, scheduled for publication in 1978 by the American Society of Planning Officials, Chicago, Illinois.

headline announcing that my Department had just made public a report, without first informing the Planning Commission or its new Director, to the effect that we would oppose any future freeways in the city. The conclusion may have been reasonable, but the report was less than well-prepared and the timing left something to be desired for a new boy in town who was not looking for instant enemies among bureaucrats like the Director of Public Works or with the Chamber of Commerce. The staff, at first glance, seemed a mixed blessing in terms of quality and the caution with which they received me. I had met with the head of Civil Service and had been left with the impression that they were really serious about me not having any say over hiring and firing. Indeed, I was to find very shortly that I might not even be able to terminate an employee who was on probation, during which period I supposedly had absolute authority.

THE CIVIL SERVANTS

No one plans a city, runs a city planning department, or makes many day-to-day decisions on immediate issues alone. Staff—people—are required. In 1967, the staff of the San Francisco Department of City Planning, some sixty-two strong, was a mixed blessing. On the one hand, there were a few extremely bright, dedicated, experienced and well-trained professionals. They were underpaid, overworked and often abused by the public and even by their colleagues. They were augmented by four or five equally bright but untrained (in city planning) and inexperienced young people, full of social and environmental concerns and willing to try their hands at anything, and a drafting and graphic staff particularly worthy of note.

So much for quality. It was matched by mediocrity and some incompetence. There were basic problems in writing the English language and in adding columns of figures. More numerous were those that could not follow directions, could not complete assignments themselves, or could not direct subordinate staff. Among these were senior people, people who seemed to have been there forever and who had reached their high protected civil service slots by reason of their endurance, not because of merit. But by far the largest group was made up of those who might be termed neither good nor bad. Some simply suffered from inadequate education. Many, if they were once competent professionals, now showed the strains and insecurities that can come with time and unappreciated or unrecognized talent. One staff member, in earlier days, had proposed an underground freeway where now stands the monstrous, never-to-be-completed two-level Embarcadero freeway. Reportedly, he was publically chastised by his director with the words to the effect that, "How can I do my job when I have staff that proposes stuff like this?" And so, for this or other reasons, they came to work every day and simply did their jobs, but without spark or enthusiasm. Maybe it would be possible to light a few fires among them.

It seemed a top heavy staff in the sense that the highest levels of incompetence could be found among the most senior positions, positions from which they could not be removed. Civil service practices gave tenured employees an insurmountable advantage for most higher level positions and this, combined with a fear of other psychic inability to terminate unqualified younger staff during probation periods at entering levels, resulted in a largely locked-in staff, except for a few specialty and lower level positions.

Over time, about a dozen of the professional staff employed by the department would prove to be as competent as anyone might hope to find anywhere. But overall, in my early years in San Francisco, the staff was not up to the calibre I wanted, had too few people trained as specialists in one or another of the areas of expertise that city planning required; and contained too many people who looked at planning differently than I. It was critical, therefore, to attract, as rapidly as possible, people of high quality to fill unstaffed positions so that we could better establish a solid professional base in the community and get on with the work that needed to be accomplished.

There were two parts to attracting and hiring good city planners; one involved finding and persuading them that San Francisco would be a productive place to work and the other was in getting and keeping them on the staff despite the civil service system. That system was to prove a much more formidable hurdle to a high quality staff than would be attracting good people in the first place.

San Francisco's employees are supposed to obtain, hold and advance in their jobs by merit. With few exceptions, they are hired via competitive examinations, administered by staff of the Civil Service Commission. It is a bureaucratic nightmare. Qualifications for open positions have to be agreed upon, announced, and advertised. Since most examinations (especially in the late 1960s and well into the 1970s) were both written and oral, the written exams had to be prepared, usually by an unknown outside consultant. Written exams had to be graded, and, after an appeal period, preparations had to be made for an oral examination board, usually composed of city planners in the Bay Area. After the oral exam and another appeal period, a list of those who passed the exam is published and the top person is offered the job. Unlike other cities, the Planning Director (until the late 1970's) was not given a choice of the top three (or more) on the list. The top person got the job and served a probation period of up to six months after which he or she became a permanent employee if not terminated earlier by the Director. The system is similar for advancement to higher level positions except that, as long as they pass an exam, however poorly, existing employees almost always have priority for advancement over outside candidates.

The system was incredibly cumbersome and did nothing to attract top people. The best people already on the staff seemed to be there despite, not because of, the system. Employees' unions could and did protest the required minimum qualifications of entry level positions on grounds that they might later be used to prejudice minimum qualifications for promotive positions. These protests took time as did the protests and required hearings at each examination step along the way. Since exams were given in San Francisco, only people in the Bay area could take them unless an outsider were willing to spend the money necessary to travel to the city for that sole purpose or unless exams were coordinated with infrequent city planner's conferences. The time between the announcement of an opening and the appearance of a final list of those who passed was so long that most qualified applicants were likely to have found and taken other positions long before San Francisco concluded its process. The best people were gone. Since essay questions on written exams were open to judgment in grading and therefore to bias, all questions had to have single, factual answers or were multiple choice. Questions like "in which direction does the Seine River flow?" became famous but hardly tested for competency in city planning. Finally, city planning jobs in the late 1960s were plentiful, and applicants, especially the best ones, could pick and choose. The beginning salaries for planners in San Francisco ranged from $1000 to $3000 less than were being offered elsewhere.

Although our approach to overcoming Civil Service barriers was by no means original, our doggedness and perseverance may have been noteworthy. We hired people on what was called a "limited tenure" basis. This meant that with Civil Service permission, I could hire people, directly, on a temporary basis to fill positions which were open but for which exams were not yet announced or in progress. I would hire people, and we would try to get the exam postponed for as long as possible or until the new employees wanted them. Some exams would be postponed for years. We tried, with some success, to change the emphasis from written to strictly oral examinations. When exams were announced for positions already filled with top-notch but temporary professionals, we made efforts to have the filing period as little advertised and as brief as possible, so that only "our" candidates would be taking the tests. I tried to influence the choice of examiners, tried to create specialist positions to get the people I wanted, and tried to influence examining boards to see things my way. Attorneys for one employees' union accused me of cheating and lying.

On one or two occasions we requested and received Mayor Alioto's assistance in influencing the staff of the Civil Service Commission to do things our way. One of those times involved an exam for my administrative assistant. This was a professional position created when I arrived, at my behest, so that I could have a right-hand confidential assistant to help carry out the myriad details associated with being director. The person filling the position on a limited tenure basis was doing magnificently, and more than met the most important criteria of compatability and total trust. Ultimately, he had to take an examination, both written and oral. When that time came, he advised me that a lot of questions were irrelevant to the position and he was not sure he had passed the written part (he later proved wrong). On that possibility, I requested that the passing score be lowered by five or ten points; but it took the Mayor to influence the head of the Civil Service to do that, and it took still more influence to get an oral examination board that was likely to listen to my admonition that they should not pass anyone they thought would not be personally acceptable to me. He was the only person who was. These kinds of battles with Civil Service on testing, hiring, firing, promoting, setting qualifications, and determining proper salaries were continuous and enervating. The rules always seemed to change, and they rarely got easier.

I continued to have trouble with Civil Service, with the employees' union, and with those members of the staff who knew and cared about all the written and unwritten rules of the system, who seemed to spend hours and days studying and memorizing the regulations: the caucasian who could tell you why he should not have to work on the Chinese New Year or the veteran who could challenge and thereby hold up the establishment of a position requiring some special skill.

I once terminated an employee during his probation period, a time when I supposedly had absolute authority, was upheld by the Civil Service Commission after his appeal, but still found him back to work the next week because his name was returned to a civil service list from which only the Planning Department drew staff. I had to fire him again. Ultimately, I was represented by my own lawyer at Civil Service hearings because the City Attorney advised me that he would not send his staff to back me up because that Commission wouldn't listen to them.

Despite the problems, over time, we were becoming a top notch, active staff. The quality of our work in the early 1970s was good and getting better and we could be empathetic to real problems as well as hold our own with developers and other bureaucrats. Word was getting around, I think, that we had some smarts. There was an overall sense of purpose, an understanding of and general agreement as to the most important issues, and a willingness to take them on. This does not mean that everything was sweetness and light on substantive planning issues. Although I'm not sure that I overtly encouraged the strong advocacy of points of view different than my own, neither did I discourage them. My door was always open and a lot of staff came through it to discuss, advocate and argue.

Whatever the staff was or was becoming was due in part to the reality that many of us were friends as well as colleagues.

We spent a lot of time together socially. So there was a good spirit, overall, and we could share in each others' joys. We shared in personal grief and losses as well, some of which came with illnesses and deaths. From 1969 through 1973, several staff members and one commissioner died of cancer. My secretary also died and during her long, lingering illness I could not bring myself to fill her position. With increasing commitment, personal as well as professional, came greater joys and sadnesses.

OTHER CITY DEPARTMENTS

The nature of what we were doing and how we went about planning and addressing issues combined with the times and people to make the years from 1969 through most of 1972 ones of growing power for the Department.

We were becoming somewhat more influential with other city departments, although the record was spotty. Most local agencies seemed to recognize that we had some fairly intelligent people on the staff and that it might make sense for them to work with us. Our familiarity with neighborhood issues and our sense of what was or wasn't politically possible may have suggested that we could help them achieve their objectives. The fairly loose style (loose compared to them) that we displayed before elected officials may also have had an effect. Our abilities in a few areas to get programs funded, that could be helpful to other departments, such as in urban beautification and miniparks, did nothing to hurt our popularity. More significant, I suspect, is that key personnel in some other departments perceived us as having a fairly good rapport with and the ears of the decision makers, especially with the Mayor. Whether or not they were correct is less important than their perceptions. In any case and for whatever reasons we spent increasing amounts of time in joint efforts with the Police Department, the Municipal Railroad, the Recreation and Park Department, the Bureau of Building Inspection and, yes, even the Department of Public Works.

In truth, our relations with Public Works was less than outstanding. We saw things very differently. Automobile-oriented with a vengeance, they could find a hundred reasons for freeways, for more traffic lanes and for street widenings, but never one reason for narrowing a street. In cases before the Planning Commission, they could be counted on to testify that any given development would not cause undue congestion, regardless of the size of the proposal or the smallness of the street. The idea of public transit was fine, but not at the expense of autos. Downtown parking problems could be solved by more and more garages. There were twenty reasons against street trees in neighborhoods but damned few for them and fewer ways still to help achieve them. At first, I thought the problem was one of communication, that they were nice guys and we just didn't know how to communicate our ideas to them. Planners always think that's the problem. I was wrong. We really did differ and there was no way we could persuade them of the rightness of our positions. To me they were more neanderthal than nice.

But they had power. Public Works is an old and large department. They knew their way around City Hall. They let contracts and they built and maintained things. Other departments were highly dependent upon them. They were under the Chief Administrative Officer and as such had a better and continuous line to him in his role of Planning Commissioner than did the Director of Planning. A lot of money flowed their way. We tried to get through or around them time and time again with only modest success. We became fairly adept at stopping them through any manner of means, not the least of which was mobilizing citizen testimony and direct lines to sympathetic supervisors. We never had great success, however, at getting them to carry out planning policies, at least not the level of success that I wanted. If they didn't want to plant trees or narrow a street, or divert traffic from neighborhoods, or implement plans to favor public transit, they could and did find ways not to, regardless of whether the plans and policies were made by us or the Board of Supervisors. Too often, at best, we fought each other to a standstill.

However bad our relations with Public Works might be at any given moment, it would be hard to categorize them as out and out enemies. The Chamber of Commerce—they were enemies. I think the only times we ever agreed on anything was when we favored a development proposal or when they knew that some kind of plan or program was inevitable and that ours was the best they were likely to get. Development, development, development, that was the name of their game. Despite their protestations to the contrary, they wanted what they wanted with as few controls and as little city planning input as possible because that only hindered private development. Our direct contacts were usually gentlemanly but there was no question but that they were the enemy. When we did agree, I would look a second time at our position to see if we were on the wrong side.

THE PLANNING COMMISSION

Positive relations and mutual respect between the elected Planning Commission and its paid professional staff, particularly the Director, are obviously central to how well a Planning Department works, or does not work. They do, after all, appoint the Director, and they alone can fire one. They also set policy for the staff. Most of the time we got along just fine. There were times, however, when our relationship and our interaction resembled a fast-moving roller coaster, hitting peaks and troughs in rapid succession.

Generally speaking, we got along fine in setting the overall tone and direction of the Department and in making decisions on the myriad issues that had to come before them. In a somewhat simplistic but nonetheless real sense, our objectives were really similar; to "do right" in terms of what was best for the long range physical development of San Francisco in relation to its people, balanced by concern for more immediate needs and equity. Overall, I'm sure that the Commission's members wanted, as badly as I, to maintain and improve San Francisco as a fine place to live. For the most part the commissioners were available to me, and the staff were bright, knew the city, were prepared to listen and learn, advocated for us when that proved necessary, and all but one or two stayed out of the day-to-day running of the Department. They gave considerable weight to staff recommendations in most cases, especially to mine, and on issues where nothing personal or political was at stake their debate was often spirited and productive. Most important, they agreed with me more often than not. Mutual respect and affection existed to a high degree.

It was not all business. I gave and went to dinners and parties with commissioners. Jim Kearney knew where Julia Porter kept her liquor and long after dinner, when Julia had stopped serving, he would get it and we would drink and then sing late into the night. On other occasions Julia would fill me in on the histories and gossip of people of note, including fellow commisioners. After observing my propensity to shed clothes in meetings, tie, jacket, shoes, she opined that only when I had them all off would they know that I was really planning.

But there were conflicts, too, and some came close to being lethal. Any honeymoon period with the Commission had ended when they approved the Transamerica Building over my opposition. Soon after that, with prodding from the Mayor, they approved another project I felt to be ill-advised, the U.S. Steel proposal for another highrise development that would violate the city skyline. At an executive session during that period I told them that a few more decisions like those and I would quit. Publication and widespread acceptance of the Department's *Urban Design Plan* in 1971 brought us back together, with a new sense of consensus and purpose that would in time be shattered by fights over other development issues. In short, our relations went up and down.

THE MAYOR

No one was more positive or exuded as strong a "can do," "will do," and "by the way, things are not so bad" aura as Mayor Joseph Alioto when he took office in 1968. A bright, energetic, eminently successful lawyer and New Deal type Democrat with strong labor backing who could and would talk with enthusiasm, passion and compassion on just about any subject, Alioto appeared accessible to everyone. He seemed to listen and understand problems, and he gave promise of solutions. He had the ears of the Johnson administration, he was admired by local liberals who appeared to have established good ties with him; and his deep roots in the Italian community stood him in good stead with most ethnic groups. His enthusiasm was contagious. San Francisco might have problems but they were solvable, and there was no better place to be.

For some reason that I will never fully understand, I seemed to have had it "made" with the Mayor from the beginning. Perhaps he and his staff had been advised, I'm not sure by whom, that his city planner was among the top department heads around. It might have been that the Planning Department was quick to produce about 40 possible sites for mini parks when he needed them in a hurry, or that we had a sense of the issues in the city. My manner with him was different than that of other city officials. Respectful but not deferential, I assumed he wanted to hear my professional opinions, and so I gave them to him without mincing any words. My counsel was sought and I believe listened to on most public matters related to city planning. Our meetings were frequent and easy. We cooperated with and helped his staff when called upon. I kept him up to date on issues, concerns and pending projects. Most important, I felt little or no compulsion to hide my opinions on planning matters even though our views were diametrically opposed. I felt that as long as I didn't knock him there would be no cost to me for differences in opinion. Nevertheless, it had become clear early on that we were very different kinds of people with very different values. Under the circumstances, it was surprising that we got along so magnificently during his first term.

The bubble burst between the mayor and me during the election campaign of 1971. On Yom Kippur day, a holiday for me, I got word that the Mayor wanted to talk to me. I reached him late that afternoon to find that he would be shooting a TV ad for his campaign the next morning on a boat in the Bay and that he wanted me in it. He wanted to be talking to me against a background of San Francisco. It was an abrupt request, one that made me immediately uncomfortable, one that expected a quick, clear affirmative answer, and I said, "yes."

I was terribly bothered by that phone call and my reply. I didn't want to campaign for anyone. That was not the job of the Director of City Planning in San Francisco. Beside the question of propriety, it is also true that Mayor Alioto would not have been my choice in the forthcoming election and although I would campaign for no one else, neither would I feel comfortable putting my name out publicly for him.

So, after much soul searching, deliberation and hemming and hawing I called the Mayor back and advised him that I could not do what he had asked. It would be improper, I felt, for me to do so. I wished him luck. He was his usual courteous, understanding self.

There were no real problems or repercussions with either the Mayor or his staff until after his overwhelming election. Then the coolness and the aloofness set in. I got the word from old friends that my name wasn't too well received in the Mayor's offices and that my days were numbered. It was clear that I was on the outs. Fewer meetings were held with the Mayor, they were harder to arrange, and they were uncomfortable for me when we had them. I counted the votes on the Commission and concluded that they would not fire me. Maybe the Mayor counted them too. But those were uncomfortable months and even though I discussed the matter privately with Mayor Alioto in an attempt to clear the air, that incident colored all of our future relationships.

There was one most ominous and disconcerting note as we moved to the end of 1972 and beyond. During the early months of that year, I hadn't paid too much attention to what was going on in the Mayor's office, especially in relation to shifts in Federal policies and programs, leaving that largely to others on the staff. I was putting all my attention then into getting a major new ordinance passed that would go a long way toward carrying out the citywide Urban Design Play we produced in 1971. Jack Tolan, the Mayor's Deputy for Development, had at one point almost jokingly wondered about the possibility of one of my Assistant Directors joining their staff. It was asked in an off-hand, casual way and I was sure my negative response had ended the matter. I was wrong.

I was quite surprised, then, when I received a call from the Mayor during a meeting of the Planning Commission, one Thursday, and heard him ask how I would feel about my Assistant Director joining his staff, to serve under Tolan as the head of a new Office of Community Development to be funded by the Feds. My response was strongly negative and I told the Mayor that I had so advised Tolan earlier. The person in question was a key member of the staff and would be extremely hard to replace. If I had had troubles with the Mayor's office in the past, and if they had not been wholly supportive of planning, his office had at least never been all that sharp on planning matters either. Intuitively, I knew that power would begin to shift with such a change and that this new office would ultimately come into conflict with our Department. While I did not advise the Mayor of all my reasons, I felt I could stick with my position. One reason was that I felt sure that my key assistant would not want to work there.

I was wrong about that, too. Within a day I told him about the call and my reaction to it. To my surprise he said that he was indeed interested in the job and wanted to pursue it. I could not bring myself to stop that. Throughout the unfolding drama I had a sense that something had happened earlier, when I wasn't looking or paying attention, that a script unknown to me had been written and was being played out in some previously prescribed manner.

THE OFFICE OF COMMUNITY DEVELOPMENT

The federally funded Office of Community Development in the Mayor's office became reality in late 1972 with seven new professional positions. There were and would be other new city planning related positions moving to the Mayor's office from federally sponsored programs. Positions from the model cities program, for example, would move there. Moreover, that office was growing with other positions and activities related to matters like law enforcement and economic development, all with federal funds. At first the Board of Supervisors (the San Francisco version of a City Council) seemed to pay little or no attention to a growing executive branch. They approved applications for funds when that was required. After all, little or no local money was involved and no one seemed to be counting what staffs and what positions were going where. To me, the balance of power in the city seemed to be shifting, from a balance that favored no one or no group in particular, to one that favored the Mayor, at the expense of the Board and the departments. Most important, to me, I perceived beginnings of a competing city planning agency in the Mayor's office, one that could not bode well for my Department of City Planning.

From the start, I did not get along well with the new, budding bureaucracy in the Mayor's office. The fact that it was peopled with city planners told me that they would soon have their hands in some of the kind of work that had always been in our sole domain, or that the Mayor's city planners would be second guessing the Department's. Certainly my ego was involved. What had previously been requests were now more in the nature of directions, or at least they sounded that way to my ears, and I did not take kindly to them, particularly if they came from people who had recently been working for me. By the latter half of 1973 we were engaged in a quiet warfare with the Office of Community Development, the kind of battle where the combatants know what is going on and what is at stake but rarely confront each other directly for resolution and where the general public is not privy to the action. It was the kind of conflict that I did not handle well.

My apprehensions had proved well founded. By 1973 we were being cut out of a major source of federal planning funds that heretofore had been used solely by the Planning Department. The Mayor's office wanted just a part and then increasing amounts of the federal planning moneys. Since they worked together with the Feds and since we could no longer apply directly for those funds, we were in the process of being cut off at the pass. I could bellow in magnificent anger all I wanted and it would not get us those funds. In 1973, too, there had been at least one case of staff raiding although there had been an agreement not to do that. Attempts to come to agreements, in writing, that would clearly define our roles and minimize conflicts while respecting our charter-defined responsibilities were time consuming and not terribly productive. The mere fact that we were going through the exercise would tell any astute observer that a major conflict existed. Things got worse as time passed, and by 1974 one heard reports, some confirmed, some not, of intentions to move the city planning function into the Mayor's office, or the possibility of a November charter amendment that would leave the Planning Commission to deal only with zoning matters, and of assertions to my staff and others that "the Mayor's office is going to have a city planning staff whether we like it or not."

I did meet with Mayor Alioto more than once during this period to tell him of my concerns. On those few occasions when I could get his sole attention, without the almost ever-present Jack Tolan, he seemed to listen, understand, and even agree with me. No, he did not want to weaken the Planning Department. Yes, we should be able to meet and deal directly with federal agencies. Yes, we should have access to funds that had been "ours" in the past. Yes, we should continue in our role as planning representatives to the regional planning body. No, the Office of Community Development should not overlap or dupli-cate the Planning Department's physical planning capability. On one occasion I told him that with federal help power was becoming more and more centralized in his office, that I felt this would be bad for the city, and made references to conse-quences similar to those then so apparent in Washington under what would be the last hours of the Nixon administration.

The trouble with those meetings, regardless of how attentive and agreeable to my point of view he seemed to be, is that nothing came of them or that the damage was done by the time we could get together. I could walk out of one of those meetings feeling good, with a sense of progress, and then nothing would happen.

THE NEIGHBORHOOD MILITANTS

By early 1974 I had pretty well decided that it was only a matter of time before I would take another job. An evening meeting with neighborhood activists in their area helped con-firm that evolving position. We were being "mau-maued" by neighborhood activists for designation of a new subsidized code enforcement program in their area. That was a far cry from how people in San Francisco and across the country were re-sponding to some public programs at the time. Hell, it was my Department's program and nothing would have pleased me more than to see it used all over the city. But there were no funds available and I wasn't about to promise something I couldn't deliver. I was also not sure that the group that had been arriving unannounced at my office, filling the halls and demanding on-the-spot meetings represented all the people of the area. Sure enough, on the night of the meeting I was greeted by not one, but two militant groups. The second was opposed to a project and had managed to put out a cartoon flyer in two languages saying I was proposing all kinds of terri-ble things for the neighborhood.

Waiting to be called on (and for the first, well-prepared "have you stopped beating your wife" question), I was aware that at that moment I hated everyone in the room, even those few who "understood." At the same time I knew that feeling to be unreasonable, that they were doing what they were supposed to do, they were participating. I had been in situations like that a hundred times before and though my adrenalin might be going pretty good I had not felt anger. Then why did I hate them?

I felt sure I would raise hell that night, that I would lose my temper. But, as a middle-aged lady read that first terrible question that someone had prepared for her, something snapped and I knew I had the evening made. I got up, talked, and answered questions for over an hour. I laughingly told them everything that was on my mind and that we were all in a "no win" situation. There was some shouting, but some laughter, too. I explained my position and suggested some things they could do, if they wished. Positions may or may not have changed by the time I left, but I sensed there was a lot learned and lot more understanding than when we had started.

I thought about that night. What had happened? Prone to exaggeration, I concluded that maybe I was becoming like a punch drunk fighter, sitting in his corner. The bell had sounded and I came out and did my thing. It was time to do something else.

17 / The Buffalo Search

Warren Bennis

[In 1970, while I was vice president—second in command—the University of] Buffalo was also looking for a new president. For almost the entire duration of the Buffalo search, from late Feb-

Excerpted, with permission, from *The Leaning Ivory Tower,* by Warren Bennis, with the assistance of Patricia Ward Biederman, pp. 39–40, 43–48, 50–62, 64–66. Copyright © 1973 by Jossey-Bass, Inc., Publishers and The Twentieth Century Fund.

ruary until the end of the academic year, the campus was racked by upheaval after upheaval, including a student strike, sporadic violence, a police occupation, and a mass arrest of faculty. The search process did not gain real momentum until April. By that time, finding a president seemed far less important than keeping the strife-ridden campus from any further explosion. . . .

The official procedure for choosing a UB president is laid down in the *Policies of the State University Board of Trustees*, fleshed out by guidelines issued by the board in 1963. Final selection is to be made by the board, from a group of candidates winnowed down primarily by the university council—a body made up of leading townsmen—with only an *advisory* role being played by a faculty committee and *none* by students. Three or more candidates *must* be interviewed by both the council and the State University central administration in Albany before a final nomination is made.

With these guidelines in hand, the council and appropriate university bodies began mobilizing to find a president. Less than a week after President Meyerson's resignation in January 1970, the search hit its first snag. On February 4, 1970, the executive committee of the UB faculty senate announced that the faculty committee advisory to the council in the search would consist of five faculty chosen by the senate executive committee, an alumni representative, and three students—one to represent undergraduates, one to represent graduates, and one for night students. Students immediately cried "Tokenism!" They complained that this apportionment of search committee seats gave only *one* vote (and that merely an advisory one) to 12,000 undergraduates.

The student paper, *The Spectrum*, urged that students demand and get five seats—parity with faculty—or refuse to sit on the committee at all. At a meeting on February 9 of their polity, the town-meeting assembly that was then the basic unit of student governance at UB, the students voted overwhelmingly to reject the faculty senate plan and to form an alternative search committee of their own. As *The Spectrum* argued in support of this boycott, "All the student power slogans, the debates over university governance, the increase in student demands for self-determination of their academic futures are reduced to nothing but empty rhetoric if students are willing to submit to token representation in the decision of who will head the university."....

The crisis mood of the campus heightened the polarized atmosphere of the search. The local press and networks blared each defiant student act, each faculty protest, each broken window. The public was soon inflamed by such coverage. One morning the *Courier-Express* ran an entire page of more than thirty angry entries signed "a taxpayer." "Taxpayers" thanked Pennsylvania for taking Meyerson off their hands and urged that "in our war on pollution, perhaps we should first drain the cesspool of vice, drugs, and revolution on the UB campus." The university was everybody's political football. The mood was ugly. It was clear that the community itself wanted a hard-line, "law and order" president.

The academic community was not so sure what it wanted. Before the crisis began, the law faculty had publicly urged that an inside candidate be found in order to ensure continuity of the programs and policies of the Meyerson administration. By the end of March many faculty favored an outside candidate, fearing that an insider would be unable to reunify the campus because of animosities engendered by whatever stands he might have taken on the controversial issues of the strike. Toward the end of April, the *Buffalo Evening News* able education reporter Dan Hertzberg revealed that no decision could be reached in time for the April 29 target date. The faculty search committee, now with student representation at last, was considering more than seventy names, the *News* reported. One of them was my own.

By this time, I had reluctantly decided to become a candidate. Although an active and open campaign for office—any office—is infra dig on campus, academics who have spent time in business or public life invariably remark that university politics make other kinds seem as fierce as shuffleboard. During a period of presidential succession it achieves a secretiveness and subtlety that would have shocked the Byzantines.

Declaring for the UB presidency that April simply meant publicly admitting that I wanted the job, and saying, when asked, "I feel I can handle it, at least as well as any other inside candidate."

Before the crisis, I had been a strong backer of Acting President Peter Regan for the presidency. As his only visible possible rival, I felt that Regan was the more appropriate candidate for that particular time. It seemed to me that what the university most needed, following the spirited if spastic Meyerson years, was a "compleat bureaucrat" in the best sense: orderly, programmatic, practical, "savvy" about how to move large, complex human institutions. Regan had all these qualities. . . .

My own image for the job was not right for the times. I was seen as Meyerson's "prodigy" and protégé. His patina had rubbed off on me, for better or worse. Regan had been around before Meyerson, and many of the pre-Meyerson faculty saw him as one of them. For all these reasons, I saw Regan as the candidate whose hour had come. When a representative of the presidential search committee first questioned me about my possible interest in the job, I gave Regan my support.

The crisis changed my view. I was in fundamental disagreement with almost all of Regan's actions, and the massing of police on campus had clinched it.

Regan's actions caused others on campus to rethink their positions on the presidency. Early in April forty-nine members of an emergency-born University Survival Group, made up largely of senior faculty and department chairmen, urged Albany to hasten selection of a president who would have "the trust of both faculty and students as well as the outside community" and especially "the ability to act with even-handed restraint, sensitivity, and compassion in situations of crisis," a pointed reference to Regan's overreaction. The survival group also urged that adequate student participation in the selection procedure be guaranteed, and recommended that Albany obtain the advice and consent of a broad spectrum of faculty and students before making any final decision. "We are convinced," the statement concluded, "that it is vital for the peace of this campus and the success of the future presidency that faculty and students be extensively involved in the selection process." The statement could hardly have come at a time when Albany was less likely to listen nor did it enlarge the undemocratic selection process already prescribed. Albany did not respond. . . .

I knew that my chances were slim, and initiating my own campaign was uncongenial to me. What tilted my ambivalence toward running was the fear that all the progress made under Meyerson would be lost. I was afraid that anti-Meyerson forces, both within and without the university, would turn the clock back to the uninspired "good old days." These fears deepened when I learned that a conservative caucus of UB faculty, in co-operation with many prominent townspeople, was strongly backing a new possibility for president. It was the former vice president for facilities planning, Robert L. Ketter, who had re-signed abruptly in mid-1969—all but openly blaming Meyerson for building delays on the new campus site. Ketter had been playing a leading role in the conservative caucus. If no other in-side candidate materialized, and if the search committee could not come up with a distinguished outsider, then Ketter would be unopposed. If I still didn't have a call, at least I now per-ceived a mission. . . . Depending on which side of the "law and order" and/or Meyerson issue one stood, Ketter was "down to earth, sensible, straight-talking, strong, tough" *or* alternately, "rigid, anti-intellectual, vindictive, mediocre." Our audience could construct two equally polarized archetypes for me. My supporters depicted me as "liberal, humane, charismatic, a mediator, an administrator with some credibility with stu-dents, an idealist, a creative scholar." My detractors pictured me with equal ease as "permissive, disloyal, dreamy, effete, soft on standards." (The "effete" image seemed to arise from a Tyrolean cape I sometimes wore around campus.) Crisis has a way of reinforcing these archetypes. In crisis, one cannot easily get feedback or, rather, can too easily ignore feedback that might jeopardize one's strongly held beliefs.

The immediate response to my announcement of candidacy was a flood of mail. Friends sent notes of encouragement. Many friends and colleagues endorsed me to the search committee and later to the local council and state trustees. Foes—all nonuniversity people except for a few alumni—sent hate mail. Several "spawn of the devil" letters arrived every week. Some were pasted together like ransom notes with letters cut from newspapers and depicted me as a Communist or Soviet agent, or both.

By mid-April it seemed appropriate to organize some kind of informal campaign. I gathered at my home a dozen or so col-leagues and friends whose judgment I had relied on heavily as an administrator. They included faculty and administrators as well as townspeople I had become close to in my three years at Buffalo. Also Mark Huddleston, acting president of the student association, and his predecessor, a politically astute black student, Bill Austin. Bruce Jackson, a brilliant young professor of English and folklore who had come to Buffalo from Harvard, became my informal campaign manager. My supporters represented a diverse set of the university's constituencies and shared most of my values, particularly on educational reform.

The strategy we devised was simple: (1) Consult the only member of the faculty search committee known to favor me. (2) Identify as much faculty support as possible and ask individual faculty to write letters to the search committee and the council on my behalf. (3) Get to any friendly members of the community who were close to members of the council and SUNY trustees. I was supposed to take a leading hand in this. (4) Articulate honestly and forthrightly, whenever and wherever possible, my own views.

Over the next two months, my work in my continuing role as academic vice president was largely sacrificed to presidential ambition. My conscience is clear, however, since UB was all but non-functioning, administratively, during the crisis. One wag said the only life in Hayes Hall, the main administration building, was "The frightful specter of waddling administrators, all out of breath, searching for new jobs."

From mid-April to early May, I was on a round-the-clock political schedule. My first hurdle was clear: I had to get the faculty committee advising the search committee to forward my name to the council as an eligible candidate. My own advisors saw as many faculty, students, and community people as they could and urged each of them to write letters of support, or personally see or phone faculty search committee advisers. We began to take stock. It was difficult to determine how broad my support was among the university's 1,500 faculty—or even where it was. We figured on strong support from the faculties of arts and letters and of social sciences and administration. The two groups accounted for almost half the total university faculty and also accounted for many of the most politically active faculty members. . . .

Faculty members [of the search committee] were taking their oaths of confidentiality with admirable seriousness. There were numerous rumors, of course, so contradictory they canceled each other out. As far as I could tell, everyone was in the dark. Dan Hertzberg of the *Buffalo Evening News* stopped in at Hayes

Hall at least once a day, but there was little hard news to be had. We heard vague talk about the council: that almost to a man they preferred Ketter. Ketter had a routine administrative record and academic background. We reasoned that his only strength was with the educationally conservative members of the faculty, who saw him as a reliable plodder for the status quo. To many students and liberal faculty, his name had become a symbol of reaction. Since March 1, Ketter had served as head of the university's Temporary Hearing Commission on Campus Disruption, and his "Ketter Commission" had recommended the suspension of demonstrating students. Students regarded the Regan-named group as a "kangaroo court" usurping the authority of the student judiciary. Among the New Left on campus the Ketter Commission had about as much esteem as the Old Left had felt for Joe McCarthy's senate committee. Previously a rather neutral figure, Ketter was now high on the radicals' list of administrative bad guys. But clearly his involvement in the suspension of radical students won him high regard in the Buffalo community, and it was community sentiment through the community-oriented council that would decide the new president. We made the error of underestimating Ketter's strength. . . .

From a variety of sources it was learned that thirty-five letters had been sent by the council to potential outside candidates and that only one had shown enough interest to visit the campus. . . .

It did not take much imagination to figure out why no outside candidate wanted the job. No senior official in the SUNY system expected to be in ofice after the predicted Democratic sweep on Election Day. The state university's liberal chancellor, Samuel Gould, had already announced in mid-April his intention to resign. No one knew what the presumed new governor would have in mind in the way of appropriations for higher education. The Buffalo campus had a particularly indefinite future. Years after the target date, new campus construction was still not under way. After weeks of unrest, the campus looked less like the once-touted "jewel in the crown" of the state university system than a battered and harassed battleground. Green lumber covered every window in sight.

Rumors continued to fly that the names of from five to fifteen internal candidates had been forwarded to the search committee. Two names appeared on all these alleged lists: Ketter and Bennis.

Late in April, my media friend called to say there was going to be an announcement that day. Later a friend in the university's public relations office confirmed that the council was about to make its recommendation and that its choice was Ketter. No announcement actually came, but on the way to my Hayes Hall office that afternoon I saw the council members filing glumly out to their cars. Later I heard that they had been rebuffed that afternoon by Chancellor Gould in their bid to have Ketter named at once.

The final stage of the Buffalo search process coincided with the "seven days in May," the week when most of the nation's colleges were on "general strike" in reaction to the Cambodia–Kent State–Jackson State incursions. The effect of that week— including and perhaps especially Vice President Agnew's personal attack on Yale's Kingman Brewster, and the physical assaults by New York City "hardhats" on antiwar protesters— cannot be exaggerated. Many trustees, who in normal and more tranquil times could have expected to represent a moderate liberal to conservative attitude toward potential candidates and college matters in general, became "politicized" and rigidly hawkish. One prominent member of the SUNY board of trustees said during this period, "What the Buffalo campus needs is a General Patton." . . .

Whatever fragile hopes I had of winning plummeted during and just after the Cambodia–Kent State crisis. Anger at the news drove students off the campus and out into the streets of Buffalo. The Buffalo city police drove them back with sortie after sortie of tear and pepper gas. On one night during that long week, some one hundred Buffalo city and suburban Amherst police stood on the sidewalk on Buffalo's Main Street, a university boundary, lobbing canisters of tear gas toward campus. My wife opened the window to find out what direction those dull and repetitive noises (like wet tennis balls hitting concrete) were coming from, then slammed it to protect herself from the fumes that swept across campus, over the golf course which separated our house from the university, and into the bucolic town of Amherst.

A publisher friend from New York had an eerie experience that night. The film *Z* was playing at a theater immediately across from the campus. Half dazed from the movie's powerful portrayal of life in a police state, he walked out onto Main Street only to see a hundred policemen firing tear gas across the front lawn of the university. The scene was so like those in the movie that he was temporarily unnerved and dropped to the sidewalk. Actually, the gas wasn't too bad at the theater. The wind favored that side of the street. After he pulled himself together, he began to wonder if the whole thing was not a staged happening. When I saw him next morning, he was still shaken.

For five straight days and nights the student-police confrontation continued. . . .

The first week in May my twin preoccupations were the crisis and the campaign. My advisors now turned their attention almost exclusively to the community and the UB council. I was on the phone or in strategy meetings at least twelve hours a day. Evenings I spent at the medical station at the student union. I would leave the house at the first familiar pop of a gas canister. My wife would be watching by the door as I dashed out, usually with Bruce Jackson or Mark Huddleston, all of us dressed in combinations of ski clothes and army fatigues. It became a weird ritual, with Clurie passing each of us a treated cloth to protect our noses and eyes as we ran out the door.

I became a boarder in my own home, occasionally sleeping in. Clurie, my durable frontier wife, only once looked sad enough to cry. "Is anything wrong?" I asked her. "Am I too busy? Do you mind being left alone? Do you mind my spending so little time with the children?" "Oh, no, that's not it," she finally answered. "What is it then?" "I'm afraid you're enjoying this too much."

As university-community tensions mounted again, my campaign advisers expressed concern about my image with Buffalo's establishment. The wife of our family physician, an especially good friend of Clurie's, told her that "being seen in public with Warren is like being seen with Che Guevara." In normal times that remark would have been laughable to no one more than to radical students themselves. But in the public eye I was increasingly being cast as a "student lover," "power seeker," and even a "terrorist."

I went to see an esteemed and friendly member of the Buffalo community for guidance. Manly Fleischmann is senior partner of one of Buffalo's finer law firms and also one of western New York's two SUNY trustees. I didn't ask for nor did he offer me his support. He did provide friendly advice. He told me, as I was saying goodbye, that my qualifications, experience, and credentials made me the outstanding internal candidate. "But here," he said, and handed me a fistful of postcards. "These just arrived today. A batch of 75–100 come each week." There were about fifty cards and each of them contained the usual slurs, some bordering on anti-Semitism, most emphasizing my "permissive" and "radic-lib" tendencies. "We've all been getting them," he said, "All the members of the board and, I suspect, many others."

When I got back to the house, Manly was on the phone. He had meant to tell me earlier, but he had forgotten. "Look," he said, "If you want to be president of the university, you'd better not do anything publicly that links you to the Buffalo Forty-Five." Manly had just received an invitation to a lawn party Clurie and I were giving to raise money for the arrested faculty's defense fund. "We can't come," Manly said, "but whatever you do, avoid any publicity about your party. That'll kill your chances quicker than anything."

Social/fund-raising activities had been going on all spring for the defense of the forty-five faculty members indicted for occupying Hayes Hall in March in protest at the police occupation. Clurie and I planned a large party to precede another fund-raising activity for the forty-five, a concert of "Words and Music."

Even without Manly's warning, we had made no effort to publicize the party. But the next morning's Buffalo *Courier-Express* headlined it on the society page.

At least three hundred people attended that May 11 party. It was a social success and a political disaster. Almost all invitees from the university attended. Almost all invitees from the community were "going out of town" or "tied up." The airlines were oversold, judging from all the people "going out of town" that night. A surprising number of Buffalo friends phoned or wrote to say straightforwardly that (1) they did not want to be seen publicly supporting the forty-five but *would* send a check, or (2) they felt that by coming they would lend support to a dubious, most likely illegal, cause.

Weeks passed, and still no word came from the search committee. I was getting impatient, because of the possibility of [a] Northwestern job as well as another presidential possibility in New England. I was also growing concerned, as were my advisors, at the remarkable momentum building for Ketter. It was becoming clear that Gerald Saltarelli was going to be the "kingmaker" and that he wanted Ketter badly.

So I decided on the advice of a Buffalo friend to see Saltarelli [the newest and most powerful member of the council that made the final nominations]. I called him on a Sunday afternoon and he set up a meeting for the following Wednesday. I had met him a number of times during my three years at Buffalo. I have always enjoyed being with him: he is aggressive, boisterous, direct, self-made, strong-willed, yet a vulnerable person. I always felt that he was a determined and decent man, not really snug yet in his worldly achievements.

I hoped to accomplish at least two things in meeting with him. I wanted to get straight, once and for all, whether I was a serious candidate. Second, I thought that if I had a chance to talk with him at greater length than in our previous social encounters, he could determine for himself, unfiltered through the press or television or postcards, what I was like. I reasoned that even if he did not agree with me on every point, at least he would find out that I am a law-abiding, loyal, and responsible citizen, none of which simple virtues the opposition was willing to grant me.

The day before the meeting, he called to say that the chairman of the UB council, William Baird, would be joining us. I arrived at Saltarelli's office on time at 4:30. Chairman Baird was already there and seated. Saltarelli was on the phone in an anteroom and didn't join us until about 5. In the interim, Baird and I exchanged niceties. Our conversation was kept on the level of sanitary chit-chat. Baird is a man hard to dislike. He is thoughtful, quiet, and constructive, scarcely capable of anger or high passion of any kind.

When Saltarelli finally finished his phone call and took a seat opposite me, Chairman Baird and I were discussing the "Buffalo Forty-Five." On hearing those supercharged numbers, Saltarelli went into a rage. "Goddam stupid faculty. Serves 'em right! And people like you who condone that kind of anarchy are just as bad!" That was for openers.

I tried to reply quietly. When Saltarelli stopped talking, it seemed as if the air conditioners had just gone off. I said that the Buffalo Forty-Five would have their day in court, that I was interested in their getting a fair trial, that that depended on raising a lot of money, and I wanted to help do that in any way I could. I also said that whatever the court eventually decided, I thought that the overreaction of the university administration had been stupid and that it played right into the hands of "those anarchists you seem so concerned about." Somehow the possibility of imprisonment for a peaceful "sit-in" in an unoccupied university office on a quiet Sunday morning after almost thirty straight days of terror seemed a bit stiff to me, despite the fact that I wouldn't have joined the forty-five if I had been asked. "Would you," I asked him, "respond to a sit-in in your office the way the university administration did? Wouldn't you have come down to your office to talk to the people, if they were *your* employees?"

That's how the interview went. Saltarelli would make a charge; I would respond. Baird sat absolutely still, not even having to move his eyes from opponent to opponent because we were leaning over the coffee table with our heads no more than six inches apart, like two tennis players at the net with racquets at port arms.

The entire hour and a half continued like a David Susskind show on "law and order." Saltarelli and I talked past each other most of the time. Baird was a passive observer. I was charged up and didn't care, at this point, whether I blew it or not. At about the half-time mark, I asked the two men whether this was an official candidate's interview. I think they said yes. Then, to change the metaphor, Saltarelli and I touched gloves and started in again.

The only points we did *not* cover were all the things on my mind when I decided to call him in the first place. Nor did we discuss whether or not I was interested in the job, what my educational and managerial philosophy was, or for that matter anything of consequence.

I learned later from a friend of Saltarelli's that he thought the interview was "worthless" and was quoted as saying, "I knew as much about him before we started as I did when it ended."

What I learned was that "search" had little to do with the search committee's function in the eyes of the council. . . . The

UB appointment was made with *no* significant student involvement and with the faculty playing a narrow "secretarial" role, merely forwarding eligible names to the council. . . .

[I] suggest [an] iron law of crisis: The more crisis, the more presidential succession; the more succession, the more autonomy the local unit loses. What we can learn . . . from Buffalo is that *unchecked disruption leads to more external intervention at successively higher levels,* from council to trustees to governor. If at some future time our campuses again become violent, federal, even White House intervention is possible. The threat to a truly free university presented by this pattern is staggering.

Search processes need not succumb to panic in crisis. During 1970, Stanford University endured as serious a campus upheaval as Buffalo, possibly as serious as San Francisco State's earlier disruption. President Kenneth Pitzer, a noted chemist who had come to Stanford less than two years before from the presidency of Rice, resigned unexpectedly in late June 1970. Ironically, John Gardner, in his speech at Pitzer's inauguration, had said: "We have now proven beyond reasonable argument that a university community can make life unlivable for a president. We make him the scapegoat for every failure of society. . . . We can fight so savagely among ourselves that he is clawed to ribbons in the process. We have yet to prove that we can provide the kind of atmosphere in which a good man can survive."

With only three months to go until the beginning of the 1971 academic year, Stanford designed and implemented a truly monumental search process, which should be a model for all universities, certainly those concerned with academic freedom, due process, and broad participation. Serious candidates were interviewed by groups representing every important university constituency: faculty, students, alumni, trustees. Out of these interviews grew a consensus. Richard W. Lyman, Stanford's noted historian, was chosen as Pitzer's successor because many of the people whose lives would be touched by the new president wanted him. After the choice was announced, the faculty advisory committee on the Stanford presidency distributed to the entire academic community a six-page summary outlining each step of the selection process.

I think that President Lyman will have a successful tenure in office, that he will be in office far longer than his predecessor was, in spite of the impressive experience and credentials

Pitzer brought to the job. I am convinced that the new man starts from a firm footing *if the search process is effective.* Pitzer faced a student "sit-in" in his office on the second day of his term because student members of the search committee felt that their voice had not been given proper weight. While no one can know how important this factor was in the subsequent events at Stanford, it is my hunch that the effect was significant.

The Buffalo search ended without the strong sense of legitimacy and due process that marked Lyman's selection.

The April 29 target date had come and gone, and Buffalo was still without permanent leadership. The violence of the first week of May gave added urgency to finding a fulltime president. Weeks before, in mid-March, the faculty senate voted no confidence in Acting President Regan because of the police occupation. Many other administrators, including myself, had resigned university offices. Under considerable pressure, the state trustees were expected to name Meyerson's successor no later than their regularly scheduled meeting on June 24. Rumors grew that their choice would be Robert Ketter.

As that meeting approached, twenty of the university's deans and department chairmen signed a letter to Chancellor Gould protesting Ketter's rumored imminent appointment.

By mid-June the question was closed. The council announced that Ketter was its choice. *The Spectrum,* the student daily, promptly termed Ketter "unacceptable" to the students. Buffalo's conservative voice, the *Courier-Express,* endorsed Ketter on June 22, following a lengthy *New York Times* analysis of the controversial nomination, in which Ketter was reported as saying, "It is time to get back to some semblance of order on the Buffalo campus."

On Tuesday, June 23, the day before the trustees' meeting, a group of provosts and deans were invited to council chairman Baird's Statler Hilton suite to meet with Ketter. In a privately circulated memo, a faculty member at that meeting recounted what happened.

Ketter opened by saying that he had been approached by the council subcommittee about two months before and had been instructed at that time not to talk to anyone about the interview or any other aspect of the presidency. He had not heard from the council again until late the previous week, when official word arrived that his appointment had been recommended to the trustees. Over the weekend he had met with the executive committee of the faculty senate and others; at that time, the present meeting with the provosts and deans had been proposed.

He said that the day before, June 22, he had gone to Albany, met for three hours with retiring Chancellor Gould, and subsequently for more than an hour with Vice Chancellor (later Chancellor) Ernest Boyer. Apparently, Gould expressed regret that Ketter had been put in the middle between Albany and the council. Gould and Ketter agreed that the handling of the nomination had been unfortunate.

Ketter said that he had been told in Albany that UB had better straighten up or its budget would be jeopardized. This threat had apparently been transmitted to the state university central administration by leaders of the state legislature. Ketter said that Gould had advised him that when he became president he should appoint people to work with him whose absolute loyalty he could expect. A single policy should be pursued by his subordinates.

One of the deans and provosts asked Ketter how he would handle things differently from Regan. He answered that he would be visible and that he would have called the police a week earlier than Regan did.

When a few of the provosts suggested that he might not be the right man for the job, Ketter countered that others disagreed and said that he would do the best he could. He said that the trustees were meeting that night and that people who desired to do so should communicate their views to the board.

Afterward the provosts and deans met privately. The majority felt that the procedure by which Ketter had been chosen was not acceptable. . . .

More than a year after Ketter assumed office, many people were still angry. In mid-October 1970, the president appeared before the polity, the student assembly. Afterward *The Spectrum* reported on page 1:

Speaking with a double handicap of laryngitis and a hostile audience, President Robert Ketter attempted Monday to explain his position on various university matters to the student polity. . . .
In all, Dr. Ketter was called everything from a pig to a marshmallow. The meeting ended when his laryngitis became too bad to

continue speaking, and when most of the students left the
meeting. . . .

Students did not forget the tokenism of the original search
committee. In a November 1970 editorial, *The Spectrum* made
explicit the widely held feeling that Ketter was a president
without legitimacy:

> A search committee was formed at this university last spring to find
> a replacement for the departing president, Martin Meyerson. Student
> input was, however, totally ignored by that committee.
> The man subsequently elected to the position by the board of
> trustees has found that he has absolutely no student constituency with
> which to work. Dr. Ketter has admitted with admirable candor that
> the process by which he was chosen left something to be desired. . . .
> In any community it is the right of the governed to elect their own
> officials. It should be no different in a university community. This
> basic right must be extended to students.

What the students are saying is clear, and it speaks directly to
State University of New York, whose official presidential
search procedure still badly needs revision. It speaks to every
institution seeking a president.

If controlling bodies insist upon dictating university presidents, instead of selecting men by more democratic processes,
the campuses must expect resistance from all those excluded
from the selection process. The president forced on a reluctant
university accepts a job that is difficult in the best of times. If
students or faculty perceive his appointment as coercive, his
job becomes impossible. In these uncertain times, no president
has *time* to spend winning over sulky constituents. I am convinced that no university president, hard-line, soft-line, whatever his style, can overcome the handicap of a peremptory appointment. A selection process that is not broadly
representative hamstrings the man it settles on. . . .

POSTSCRIPT

Late in November of 1970, I received a call from Cincinnati.
The caller was M. R. Dodson, vice chairman of the board of
directors at the University of Cincinnati and chairman of the
committee searching for a successor to retiring president

Walter C. Langsam. "Would you," Dodson asked, "like to visit the University of Cincinnati as a presidential candidate?"

In the week before the winter break, I met on campus with members of the board of directors and with a few of the university's 35,000 students and 2,200 faculty. Four months later, on April 6, 1971, the board announced that I had been named the eighteenth president of the university.

18 / At IGP, It's Not Business as Usual

Daniel Zwerdling

FOR SHEER POLITICAL DRAMA, the board of directors elections last February at the Consumers United Group, Inc., beat the Carter-Ford election cold.

Consumers United—usually called International Group Plans, or IGP—is the $60 million worker-managed insurance corporation just ten blocks from the White House in the financial heart of Washington D.C. Its 340 secretaries, accountants, file clerks, salespeople, and other employees own half the corporation and elect half the board of directors.

The results of the national presidential campaign meant no more than minor political variations. But the outcome of the IGP elections promised a dramatic difference. For the incumbent board was staging a coup of sorts, trying to impose more traditional corporate work styles. Board members were proposing widespread layoffs in a company that forbids laying workers off. The board wanted to bring back worker attendance records in a company where keeping track of attendance is forbidden. And the board wanted to give management the power to fire workers in a company where firings are controlled by a worker court.

Excerpted, with permission, from *Working Papers for a New Society*, Spring 1977, pp. 68–73, 76–81. Copyright 1977 by Daniel Zwerdling.

But the entire board was ousted—and the workers elected a new board with "democratic" views. "It was a major show-down, a turning point," one insurance clerk told me. "The people—and democracy—won."

The board elections at IGP went unnoticed in the press. But in just five years this insurance corporation has developed the most important experiment in worker self-management in North America. It's an ongoing experiment, not a finished model; the democratic decision-making structure changes so often, as workers grapple for the "best" system, that by the time this article is printed some of the information may well be obsolete. . . .

IGP . . . is a modern white-collar company using advanced computer technologies in a competitive market. It's a success-ful corporation that earned about $1 million in profits last year. Workers at IGP aren't leftist college graduates like workers at so many collectives. Instead they are a typical assortment of middle and lower income office workers—46 percent white, 43 percent black, two-thirds female, and only a third with college degrees.

Most important, IGP is a firm where rank-and-file employees really do exert fundamental powers. For example, 85 percent of the workers turned out for the board of directors election, an enviable turnout in any political campaign. "Look, just say we are completely in charge of our own jobs from day to day," a claims clerk told me. "I mean that individuals like myself, mak-ing close to [IGP's] minimum wage, make decisions on our own that could affect a whole insurance plan, such as whether cer-tain people are eligible to receive claims or not—decisions which only a manager could make at any traditional insurance company."

The lessons IGP offers are not all about success. It faces some serious problems and has made some tactical mistakes from which self-management activists can also learn. The experience at IGP suggests that the road to self-management will be a dif-ficult and painful process—but then, so is any social change.

The self-management system remains wobbly and sometimes embattled, plagued by managers who resist giving up their traditional powers and by production clerks who don't know how to assert their newfound powers. And despite the dreams of some advocates of worker self-management to the contrary, there are employees at IGP who say they could not care less about making important decisions about their work lives.

"I would love to go back to a traditional company, punching time clocks and being told exactly what to do, when and how to do it," one clerical worker told me. "I just can't stand the confusion anymore."

James P. Gibbons, the current president, founded IGP in 1964 with three partners and an IBM 1401 computer. . . .

Gibbons says he considered business just a way to make a living while he pursued more cosmic visions of social and political change. He marched—and was twice arrested—in antiwar, antipoverty, and civil rights protests, and says, "I was marching for the power of people to control their own lives.

"I had always thought I'd sell the business and use the money to set up some sort of foundation, like the Stern Fund or something, and give money to political causes," Gibbons says. He's sitting at his desk, which is one among many in a large room; there are no executive offices at IGP. "But then I started thinking, 'What's the point? Set up another foundation that is trying to change the very people and system that gives us all our money?' It occurred to me what we really had to do was create an economic institution that was self-sufficient. And that," Gibbons says, "is when I became consciously committed to making this company a self-sustaining, living model of social change."

"What I've done," he says, "is to create the first corporate power structure in this country which the employees have the power to change as they want. I'm not talking anything short of a total revolution."

The birth of democracy at IGP was a paradox. Gibbons imposed self-management on the workers as the enlightened monarch of a tiny nation might liberate the masses by beneficent dictate. One day in spring 1972 he announced he was transferring half the company ownership to the employees in a nonsalable, profit-sharing trust. Six months later he announced that employees would begin electing half the board of directors (Gibbons appoints the other half). And then he began creating a network of employee committees which, he decreed, would gradually make the corporate decisions traditionally reserved for executives. . . .

In Gibbons' revolution, the business itself has become . . . [a]

tool for creating a radical society, "a utopian community," as he puts it. He has proclaimed his goals in a credo, emblazoned on a silver poster and taught to new employees on their first day on the job:

Goal I: To build a lasting economic institution which helps satisfy the real needs of our client organizations . . . and to provide quality service . . . [while] making enough profit to keep the corporation in existence. . . .

Goal II: To build this institution on a foundation which maximizes the humanness of everyone involved, and which creates a new ethic for economic institutions—an alternative model for business. . . .

WHO DECIDES

Gibbons and IGP employees have spent five years groping for a sensible decision-making structure. There have been so many committees created, modified, abolished, then resurrected again that even veteran employees can't remember them all. Today the basic structure at IGP is this:

The *worker teams* are autonomous work groups throughout the company, each with about six to a dozen employees who perform the same job. Clerks who pay claims to military clients, for instance, work on the military claims team. Although team power has never been defined on paper, in practice the teams are responsible for organizing and managing the company's day-to-day work, and for handling staff hiring and firing.

Each *department* is composed of several teams. Department-level decisions, such as staffing levels and budgets, long-range objectives, and coordinating the work of the teams, are made democratically by a *department operating committee*. The committee includes the *team leaders* (a worker representative elected from each team) and a *department coordinator* whom the team leaders help select. A department coordinator doesn't have the powers of a traditional corporate department head, but he or she is supposed to guide the staff and carry out the decisions of the operating committee.

Each *division* includes several departments. Division-level policies are made by the *division operating committee*, which includes the department coordinators, a representative elected by the workers, and a *division coordinator* elected by the department coordinators. The division coordinator—called a "center forward" in IGP's lingo—is supposed to carry out the decisions of the committee, not give orders like a boss.

The *corporate operating committee* is made up of the handful of top managers who run the corporate business from week to week. It's the least representative committee of all. Except for one member directly elected by the workers, the members are hired by the board. The corporate operating committee reviews all major policies and corporate operating strategies devised by the lower committees before sending them for approval to the board.

The *board of directors* is half chosen by Gibbons and half elected. The board is supposed to be the ultimate decision-making body, the final vote on major policies from investments to sick leave to wage scales.

I've left two of the most important committees until last, because they operate outside this chain of responsibility. The first is the *personal justice committee,* the worker-elected court. "All decisions of the Personal Justice Committee shall be final," company policy says, on disputes over pay, promotions, leave policy, job transfers, anything. The only exception is firings, which employees can appeal beyond the court to a special committee of three worker representatives and three managers.

The committee that created the court is the *community relations assembly* (CRA), the worker congress. Its twenty representatives are elected by popular vote. At least one CRA representative sits and votes on virtually every committee in IGP, which ensures that at least one direct representative of "the people" votes on every decision.

But the guts of the CRA's job is to formulate all the workplace policies that directly affect employees, from vacation rights to production standards, from hiring guidelines to wages. The CRA doesn't have final say, according to corporate policy, but sends its recommendations for "review" by the corporate operating committee and "approval" by the board.

When I first visited IGP in 1974, I began by asking the employees, "But does it *really* work?" It was a simplistic question that reduced the complex power relationships to an absurd yes or no. For instance, how much power can employees exert over their day-to-day work life? How much power over corporate finances and business? How much power can employees exert over financial questions that directly affect them, such as wages and benefits? And just as important: no matter how much or how little power the employees have available through formal voting, how much power do they actually assert?

When it comes to the day-to-day life in the "economic community," as Gibbons calls it, the rank-and-file employees have enormous power available—and they use it. File clerks making under $10,000 a year hold an impromptu meeting one morning and vote to revamp the entire central files system, the heart of the corporation. Clerks churning out new insurance policies take a break to decide who should answer the telephone; they vote to rotate the hated task. A team of researchers, who answer clients' questions about their insurance policies, vote to hire a job applicant they interviewed the day before. The department coordinator hasn't even met her. "A department head," one researcher says, "shouldn't stick his nose into team business."

The worker teams also wield effective control over firing fellow employees, although the power is slightly ambiguous since team leaders and department coordinators also have the power to fire; the company has never firmly resolved just whose power should take precedence. In practice though, the rank-and-file employees have made firing a rare event in this company. A small drama flared one day in the life insurance department, when the team leader tried to fire a worker he said "wasn't producing." He backed down when her teammates marched angrily to his desk and declared he had no right to dismiss a teammate without consulting the team first.

Some employees at IGP complain that it's becoming *too* hard to get rid of troublesome and unproductive employees—"it's kind of scary to stand up to someone you've been friends with and say, 'sorry, you're not working out, you've got to go,' " one claims clerk says. But workers do it. "We fired a dude last week," a mailroom clerk says. "When he didn't carry his load we had to do the extra work. We warned him, had meetings with him, put him on probation—he wouldn't listen." He appealed to the personal justice committee, but the court upheld the team's decision.

The clerks paying insurance claims and peering in the microfilm machines don't exert direct power over department and division-level policies, since they don't have a direct vote on the operating committees. But most employees I talked with say they aren't interested in worrying about long-term planning and budgeting.

They can, however, exert considerable informal power over department and division decisions when they feel the issues touch them directly. For one thing, there's a company commandment called the "IGP Decision-Making Model": it declares that no decisions may be made until all the workers directly affected have been consulted first. But more important, the workers exert power because there is an assumption at IGP that leaders are supposed to act on behalf of the employees and to watch out for the employees' interests.

"We don't assert ourselves very often by taking initiative," says one claims examiner, "but people resist because they know they have the right to resist." When one department announced it was installing a new computer system to keep track of claims, for instance, the claims team announced they didn't like the system and would refuse to use it. "The computer people were forced to sit down with us and design it the way we liked," one team member said.

Managers who don't respond to the rank and file don't survive in their positions very long. "We called our department head before a meeting of the entire department to air a lot of grievances," one researcher says, "and one of the big issues was, do the people have confidence in the top man? We were terribly, painfully honest with him. We gave him a vote of confidence only to give him another chance." . . .

Viewing IGP through descriptions of the CRA, the teams, and other committees misses the spirit of employee power and freedom there—a spirit that contrasts dramatically with employee feelings at traditional white-collar firms. A claims examiner at Geico, a major insurance company with headquarters in Washington, tells what it's like at her office. "A bell rings at 8:30 and if you're five minutes late they reprimand you," she says. . . .

At IGP clumps of workers sit on their desks, drinking coffee and chatting about a recent CRA vote to reimburse workers for meals, transportation, and even babysitting fees if they work after hours or on weekends. Work in one department comes to a noisy halt when the researcher team throws a baby shower for one of the teammates; the department coordinator doesn't scowl, he takes some wine and a piece of cake. There's no morning bell at IGP. "I've been coming to work at noon lately because I'm training some horses every morning at a stable," a researcher in the life insurance department says. "I stay and work until 8 o'clock."

My Geico acquaintance has "never even met the company president"—but Gibbons and three top managers take forty-five minutes one morning simply to meet with an angry IGP employee who has questions about disciplinary procedures "which just can't wait." And workers at Geico are afraid to speak out. I dropped by the IGP board of directors campaign assembly last year and heard one candidate, a twenty-four-year-old claims clerk, declare that "Gibbons has been feeding us a lot of bullshit and it's about time the people bring it to a halt." He received some healthy applause; then everyone adjourned to a conference room for a wine and cheese party and the vote.

UPS AND DOWNS

There's a sharp dichotomy at IGP between the daily world of work and the world of business. When it comes to making decisions about what insurance packages to market, what strategies to use, and what investments to make, the rank-and-file employees have little voice.

The theory behind the structure at IGP has been that "employees don't have any business making decisions about finances if they don't have financial expertise," one researcher explains. Instead, representatives accountable to the rank and file are supposed to make such decisions. Until a couple of years ago, financial decisions were handled by a finance committee, most of whose members were elected from each department. But it didn't work. For one thing, in the effort to be as democratic as possible, membership was rotated so often that individual representatives couldn't build up enough knowledge of the committee to play a meaningful part. To make matters worse, many of the representatives had little financial background, and the company made no effort to provide training.

"Frankly, the meetings were terribly frustrating," one elected representative told me. "Half the time I didn't know what they were talking about." Both these factors increased the tendency of the chief financial officer, the chairman of the committee, to "play the cards close to his chest," as one finance committee member recalls. "He controls the books, he controls the figures—so he'd make a recommendation and we had little choice but to nod our heads. We should have been more forceful, I know," the representative says, "but we were intimidated."

Since then the finance committee has faded away. Now most of the power to make financial and marketing decisions rest with the corporate operating committee, far from the rank and file, although there are still a few possibilities for direct worker involvement. The chairperson of the CRA votes on the committee, but so far none of the chairpersons have learned enough about the business to take an active part. And the board of directors, which is half elected by the employees, does have the power to reject operating committee decisions. A few years ago, the directors acted like a rubber stamp—"one year the Board hardly even met," recalls board member George Allen. Recently the board has been asserting itself more and more as the voice of "the people." When managers on the operating committee insisted that they should control wage scales, for example, the board insisted that it would make the final decisions. "The operating committee is mostly managers," one board member explained, "when the people should have a large say in deciding wages."

Workers at IGP do exert substantial power over financial issues that touch them directly. The CRA drafted the last major wage scale revision, after consulting with "the people"; it was changed little by the board. CRA representatives also selected the company-paid health insurance plan, one of the most generous packages at any company in Washington.

And when really crucial financial policies come up, the board turns over the decision to the entire work force for a vote. It was the rank and file who voted to establish the $9,450 minimum annual wage, and it was the workers who decided how to divvy the profits. Most managers, not surprisingly, wanted to apportion profits as a percentage of salaries. But the rank and file, the two-thirds earning under $11,000 a year, voted to split the profits equally, to president and mailroom clerk alike.

Now the caveat: despite the successes at IGP, the self-management system does not work as well as it might. For every team that asserts its autonomy and power, employees point to a team that shrinks from responsibility. For every decision that a committee reaches by democratic vote, workers point to a committee that waffles and submits to the decision of a self-styled boss. . . . This place," says Larry Bonner, a former member of the top operating committee "is a mass of contradictions."

And the contradictions are nourishing worker discontent. The corporation preaches trust, maximizing humanness, and a new quality of work, yet the absentee rate is increasing, turnover is high (up to 15 percent during the last few years), and some departments are mired in chronic backlogs and sloppy work. You can read the discontent in managerial memos that float around, talking about "tremendous tensions, anxieties, character assassination, and balkanization." . . .

While many employees feel overwhelmed and confused by their sudden rise to power, managers at IGP feel uncertain about their fall from it. Consider the qualities that mark a good manager in a self-managed enterprise—"Damn it, don't think of yourselves as managers, think of yourselves as leaders," Gibbons fumes at an operating committee meeting. "*Manager* implies control; *leader* implies government with equal rights." As self-management advocates emphasize, a good leader shares information with the rank-and-file employees, delegates power as much as possible, inspires and motivates workers rather than giving orders, and, most important, sees his or her role as working on behalf of the workers, not over them.

"Now you tell me," Gibbons says with a sigh one day, "where you can find leaders who have administrative and insurance experience who also believe in these democratic values? Right— nowhere."

"Managers are afraid and confused here because they lose the power of being the boss," says Del Clark, a former member of the corporate operating committee. More than a dozen top managers—*leaders*—have come and gone since I first visited IGP in 1974, largely because they couldn't handle democratic-style leadership. "At my last job if a secretary so much as talked back to me I could have said, 'Shazam, you're fired, finished,'" one department coordinator says. "But now at IGP if I try to boss someone around *I* could be fired, or at least deposed. After twenty years in the cutthroat business world, it's hard suddenly having to accept a secretary or mailroom clerk as equals."

And most leaders at IGP complain that group decision making takes too much time in a business that demands quick action; and unless all the members of a committee are doing their required part, they're right. Some leaders have become so afraid of crossing the line between providing leadership and imposing dictatorship that they shrink from exercising any initiative at all. "And then," one division center forward says, "inertia sets in."

"I'm telling you, it's absolutely impossible to make every decision democratically," says Del Clark, who used to be center forward of the largest division in the corporation, with 200 employees. "Our committee would take three weeks trying to solve a problem I could have solved like that"—he snaps his fingers—"in a couple days, and we'd get ninety-nine problems a week. The department heads on the committee would all agree to do certain jobs during the week, and then at the next meeting they'd say they didn't have time. So if I took action on my own I'd be accused of being a boss. If I didn't the work wouldn't get done and as division head I'd be blamed for it. I got so frustrated and confused," Clark says, "I just had to resign." Now Clark works in a nonleadership position, doing what he calls "busywork."

Put employees together with managers who are equally unprepared for self-management and you have a vicious circle. Teams, the CRA, and other committees don't meet their responsibilities, and the work falls behind. Tensions rise as people sense the system isn't working; instead of asking themselves how to solve it they blame their leaders for failing them. The leaders blame the rank and file for dragging their feet and withdraw in defensiveness and secrecy. The workers become more hostile . . . "and then we all ramble along in no real direction," one researcher says.

The stalemate inevitably ends when a strong leader, usually Gibbons—impatient and furious at the breakdown, frantic for the system to work—plunges into the power vacuum and imposes his own solutions. I watched Gibbons undercut his own carefully nurtured democratic structure many times, pleading, "This is a business, we've got to go on." He solves the immediate crisis but contributes to a more profound crisis in the long run: cynicism.

"We have no power to do anything, really," a team leader

scoffs after Gibbons has intervened in her department to solve a work backlog. "Uncle Jimmy tells us we have the freedom to do what we want, but then he just goes ahead and does what he wants anyway."

"I feel like I'm really suffocating here, we've got no influence over anything," a claims clerk told me. Then she paused— "well, I guess it depends on a person's initiative. I'm the type of person who doesn't ever do anything. I mean, they *say* you can do things here, but I don't believe they really feel you can do it."

"Lots of us come from such uptight work or school environments that it's hard to eye a less structured situation without suspicion," one employee wrote in the company newspaper. "Knowing only gross manipulation by employers or instructors, we expect it. . . . We look for the fine print, sure that we're being had. . . . At least the old system clearly defines the enemy. Are we strong enough to risk a system where there may not be an enemy, other than our own cynicism?"

Many employees do acknowledge that when the system doesn't work as it should, they are at least partly to blame. "The mechanisms are all here, the freedom and power are all here for us to really take control and run this company the way we want," a young claims examiner named Kurt Carr told me—before he became elected department coordinator. "Why don't we? I don't want to call it ignorance. Let's call it lack of education—lack of education in democracy."

LEARNING SELF-MANAGEMENT

Education in democracy is one area where IGP has neglected the employees. The transition to self-management is expected to be difficult, but Gibbons neglected to make it smoother by creating long-term training programs to teach employees self-management values and skills. True, IGP has made some attempts at education: new employees take orientation courses in the philosophy and finances of the business, and at one time the board of directors held seminars with workers to teach them how the employee trust works. Over the years the company has hired various consultants to help committees work more effectively—and now the company has its own in-house team of troubleshooters who float from crisis to crisis, attempting to teach employees how to tackle problems and solve them on their own.

But these sporadic attempts to spread a little democratic or financial knowledge among the work force haven't done the job, as Gibbons acknowledges: "I'm tired of these ad hoc, hit or miss, part-time efforts to solve problems. We need a long-term training program, and I want someone to get to work on it full time." But he adds in the same conversation: "People don't understand that we don't have the luxury of time for all this training. We're not an educational institution, we're a business, and we have economic problems that have to be solved." But that may be a deception. The time the workers would divert to self-management training, say a couple of hours each week, may be vastly outweighed by the time they now waste in ineffective committees and in complaining. . . .

What are the prospects for long-term education and training at IGP? The question is synonymous with a more fundamental one: What are the long-term prospects for self-management at IGP? For although the tensions are healthy—they indicate the corporation doesn't squelch people but nourishes intellectual and emotional ferment—they are reaching a stage where they will move people in one of two directions: toward a more stable and smoothly working self-management structure, or back to a more traditional corporate hierarchy.

"We're at a critical turning point in this community," Gibbons acknowledges, "where the experiment is up for grabs. The people here have the power to throw me out, throw out all the values I stand for, even piss on me if they want."

For a time last year it seemed as if Gibbons' values would be thrown out. The company, like the nation, is constantly swinging through varying political moods, and last year was the year of the conservatives. To begin with, IGP faced considerable financial pressures: after ten years of spectacular growth the company's income began leveling off, partly because of the national economy and partly because, after years of dominating the mail order health insurance market, IGP began to face some stiff competition.

Although the corporation was making a profit, some employees felt it wasn't making enough, especially at a time when some long-term debts were coming due. And employees were tiring of the constant changes in Gibbons' experiment. "People tend to be a lot more conservative when things keep changing," one researcher says. "They need something secure and stable to hold on to. And here," he laughs, "what you write about us today will be totally different six months from now."

The rank-and-file employees voted their mood in last year's board elections: they defeated the "liberal" candidates and elected a Washington bank president and an IGP manager known for his traditional, straight-line approach to business. Gibbons, who in the past had appointed such people as a Marxist economics professor and a civil liberties lawyer, picked three top managers with conservative fiscal reputations. "I figured it was time to put some financial knowledge on the board," he recalls.

To a point, most employees seemed to approve of the new climate. The CRA and the board revamped the election process so rank-and-file employees had far less power in selecting top leaders; and workers started putting more pressure on fellow employees who took too much advantage of liberal leave. "The place has the feel of a Republican administration," said Kurt Carr at the time. "The company is really cracking down now and become more conservative, and putting emphasis on the bottom line. But I think it's a healthy thing for democracy here in the long run. Things were getting too chaotic. We just have to be careful that it doesn't swing too far in a conservative direction."

But the climate did swing too far—as top managers began to argue that IGP's obsession with democratic vlaues and workplace freedoms was damaging the corporate profits. When a board resolution called for the end of some of IGP's basic workplace freedoms, however, the political mood swung back. The managers were ousted from the board, and now a new group of directors known for their "liberal" and democratic outlook sits in control of the corporation. . . .

Ironically, one of the major obstacles to full self-management at IGP will continue to be its most dynamic force—Jim Gibbons himself. The employees at IGP never asked for self-management. Most probably never even dreamed of it. Gibbons alone dreamed the self-management vision, imposed it on the employees, and with his charisma made it work.

But now Gibbons' role is starting to stunt self-management's growth, for the employees can't quite shake the notion of Gibbons as the beneficent monarch, themselves as grateful subjects.

"I know I've got to go," Gibbons says, "because this experiment won't really have worked until it can function without me." . . .

The system does work—better than any other self-managed enterprise in the country, and, I would argue, better than any other corporate system in America. Despite the problems and tensions at IGP, 340 rank and file workers and managers are operating a $60 million corporation—and making a profit—with a degree of freedom, democracy, and equality never before achieved by a major corporation in the United States. If they're facing problems, every corporation faces problems. The difference is that workers at IGP can shout their complaints and problems if they want, without fear of getting fired. More important, they've got the power to change the corporation.

19 / The Bagman

John Brooks

BETWEEN 1960 and 1973 the Gulf Oil Corporation distributed political contributions and payments in the United States and abroad aggregating over twelve million dollars.

The public disclosures about Gulf's political activities were made piecemeal, beginning on August 10, 1973, when the corporation issued a press release stating that in 1971 and 1972 it had made an illegal contribution of a hundred thousand dollars to the Finance Committee to Re-Elect the President, an adjunct of the Committee to Re-Elect the President, or CREEP. . . .

In October, 1974, the S.E.C. began an investigation to determine whether or not Gulf had violated the federal securities

From "Funds Gray and Black" in *The New Yorker*. Reprinted by permission; © 1976, The New Yorker Magazine, Inc. Issue of August 9, 1976, pp. 29–32, 37–38, 40 and 42–44.

laws. The investigation and attendant negotiations with Gulf led, on March 11, 1975, to a consent decree under which Gulf agreed to appoint a Special Review Committee with a mandate to get to the bottom of Gulf's political contributions, past and present. The committee—consisting of two members of the Gulf board of directors . . . and one outsider, the New York lawyer John J. McCloy, who served as chairman . . . issued its report and recommendations . . . December 30, 1975. . . .

The McCloy report (as the report of the Special Review Committee has come to be called), along with the other available evidence, gives a far more detailed account of the techniques and procedures of corporate political bribery than has so far become available regarding any other corporation. Since ethical matters are best examined in detail and in the context of their social and cultural setting, one may logically choose the Gulf situation for a study of the subject without implying that Gulf's activities have been more egregious than those of other corporations, even though Gulf's illegal domestic contributions appear to have been unusually extensive. In doing so, however, one must point out the dubious provenance of some of the . . . evidence—hearsay, perhaps, of the least unacceptable sort, but hearsay all the same—[on which] that part of the story as it is now known is based. . . .

Machinery by which corporate funds could be surreptitiously collected and illegal contributions made from them appears to have been set up in 1959. Late that year, Gulf hired [Claude] Wild as a Washington lobbyist, at an annual salary of twenty-five thousand dollars. According to Wild—a lawyer, then in his middle thirties, who had previously worked for the Mid-Continent Oil & Gas Association and had acquired a reputation as an effective lobbyist—two of the Gulf executives who hired him told him that his mission was to build an organization that would give Gulf more "muscle" in politics, and that for that purpose he would have a budget of about two hundred thousand dollars a year. (Later, the figure was doubled.) Nothing was said about where the funds would come from. Also in 1959, [Joseph E.] Bounds, then the administrative vice-president of Gulf, learned of plans to establish a political fund, in a series of meetings with William K. Whiteford, then the company's chief executive officer. Whiteford, according to Bounds, was convinced (incorrectly) that if funds for domestic political use were generated outside the United States and were handled by a foreign corporation, with no deductions on Gulf's United States tax returns, the arrangement would be legal. Whiteford also insisted, Bounds said, that he had learned from the top management of some of the other major oil companies that they had already set up schemes similar to the one he had in mind. (Up to now, no such setup has been shown to have existed at any other major oil company.) Nevertheless, Whiteford made it clear that his plans must be kept from the Mellon family, which held the single largest block of Gulf stock, and from certain other Gulf executives, whom he described as "Boy Scouts"—among them Dorsey, who was then a vice-president and was to become Gulf's chairman and chief executive officer in 1972.

In Bounds' account, Whiteford was the moving spirit in the establishment of means whereby Gulf could make political contributions both at home and abroad and keep them secret, from all but a few even within the company. . . . It was presumably under his direction that early in 1960 Gulf began channelling funds for political use through the Bahamas Exploration Company, Ltd., an oil-exploration subsidiary with headquarters in Nassau. Bahamas Ex., as it was called, was ideal for this purpose in several respects. For one, it was relatively dormant, its chief activity in 1960 being to hold licenses against the day when Gulf might decide to undertake oil-exploration work in the Bahamas. For another, it was not consolidated with its parent company, Gulf, for tax purposes, and it existed in a tax-haven country, so it was not required to reveal its annual income and disbursements in income-tax returns anywhere. On January 8, 1960, Gulf opened an account at the Bank of Nova Scotia in Nassau, in the name of Bahamas Ex., and on January 15 the company made an initial deposit of two hundred and fifty thousand dollars. The account was not recorded on the books of Bahamas Ex.; the Gulf executives authorizing deposits in it did so by handwritten notes, which were customarily destroyed; and the bank's statements and records of deposits and withdrawals were never placed in the files of Bahamas Ex. but, rather, were regularly torn up and flushed down a toilet by William C. Viglia, a former assistant comptroller of Gulf, who in July, 1959, had been assigned to Nassau to maintain the accounts of Bahamas Ex.

The secret Bank of Nova Scotia account was now ready to make disbursements. (Some time later, Whiteford, upon being appointed to a quasi-honorary post as a vice-president of the Bank of Nova Scotia, wrote in jocular vein to a working officer of the bank, "This is good news, especially to me, as the next time I have to make a confidential arrangement to secure political funds I can put the blame on the Bank should this great institution . . . fail to protect my anonymity." The recipient of the letter, who had no idea that the Bahamas Ex. account was for political purposes, assumed that the letter was an example of Whiteford's well-known sense of humor. In hindsight, it may be seen as evidence of a penchant of Whiteford's—quite extraordinary in the chief executive of a great corporation—for deliberately skating on the thinnest of ice, for no purpose other than to dare the Devil.)

Late in the winter of 1959–60, on instructions from Bounds, . . . Gulf's comptroller made several trips to Nassau and on each occasion withdrew amounts ranging from twenty thousand dollars to forty thousand dollars in cash from the Bahamas Ex. account and in each case subsequently delivered the money to Gulf executives in Pittsburgh. Such deliveries in the early months of the Bahamas Ex. arrangement were, as Bounds told it, handled as follows: the courier from Nassau would hand Bounds, in Pittsburgh, an envelope containing the cash; Bounds would lock it in a safe that, at Whiteford's request, Bounds had had installed in his own office; whereupon Whiteford would enter Bounds' office in his absence and remove the envelope from the safe, leaving the safe open until the next delivery from Nassau. What possible purpose this routine could have served, other than to gratify Whiteford's taste for the baroque, it is impossible to say.

By July 6, 1960, one hundred and fifty thousand dollars had been withdrawn from Nassau and delivered to Pittsburgh, and as early as that April the withdrawals had been large enough to cause a logistical problem: the Bank of Nova Scotia sometimes didn't have enough cash on hand in United States dollars to meet the demand. To solve this problem, another intricate routine was worked out. The Bank of Nova Scotia would systematically collect U.S. dollars, in exchange for local currency, from a local casino where visiting Americans were in the convenient habit of losing them; when a good supply of dollars had been assembled, the Bank would notify Viglia, the Bahamas Ex. man; and Viglia would then withdraw the dollars and put them in a safe-deposit box at another Nassau bank, ready for delivery to the mainland as required.

The ultimate destination of the dollars thus collected came, after the earliest days, to be the province of Wild, the lobbyist, who from 1960 on was generally in charge of selecting recipients of political contributions and making deliveries to them. In one of his first assignments along these lines, Wild, by his own account, delivered fifty thousand dollars in cash over a period of months to Walter Jenkins, an aide to Senator Lyndon B. Johnson. As time went on, an efficient standard operating procedure evolved in Pittsburgh, Nassau, and Washington. A Gulf official in Pittsburgh, usually someone in the comptroller's office, would authorize a transfer, usually of one or two hundred thousand dollars, to the Bahamas Ex. account in Nassau. Viglia, in Nassau, would deposit the money and wait for delivery instructions. When they came—usually from Wild, but occasionally from other Gulf executives—Viglia would put the required sum (usually twenty-five thousand dollars) in an envelope, buy an airline ticket (which he would later destroy), and fly to a prearranged destination in the United States—no longer Bounds' office in Pittsburgh but usually somewhere in Washington, Miami, or Houston. (According to Viglia, he became so friendly with the U.S. customs people that his baggage and his person were never examined.) Upon arriving, he would deliver the cash-filled envelope to Wild or another Gulf officer, and then he would fly right back to Nassau. Wild would pass the envelope on to the intended recipient, in Washington or elsewhere—sometimes in the recipient's office, but on other occasions, at the recipient's request, somewhere else.

By the beginning of 1966, some two and a half million dollars had been transferred from Gulf to the Bahamas Ex. account, of which almost two million had been carried by Viglia in cash to the United States for delivery to political figures—most often to national ones, but sometimes, according to Wild's statement to Wright, officials or candidates at the state and local levels. . . .

The entire arrangement suffered a temporary setback in 1961, when Bounds staged a revolt against it. Sometime that year, by his account, he told Whiteford that he did not like "the Bahamian setup." Whiteford told him he had better like it or

he would be fired. The matter came to a head with a confrontation between the two men that October at the Duquesne Club, a
favorite gathering place of Pittsburgh's business élite, where,
after a violent argument, Bounds, as he put it, "decked"
Whiteford. Whether or not, by so doing, Bounds violated the
bylaws of the Duquesne Club, he violated those of Whiteford,
who got up off the deck and shortly thereafter sent Bounds into
a sort of exile by assigning him to run a Gulf property in California. Bounds, nevertheless, continued from exile to write
requests for tranfers of corporate funds to Bahamas Ex., right
up to his early retirement, in 1964. So the revolt was quelled,
and the arrangement returned to smooth functioning.

Sometimes, Wild found that he needed help from others in
making deliveries of cash to political figures, because, he explained, it was "physically impossible for one man to handle
that kind of money." Such a helper was Frederick A. Myers,
who had been a Gulf employee for forty-seven years at the time
he retired, in 1975, and who for fifteen years had held positions
in Gulf's Washington office, reporting to Wild and another Gulf
official. In October, 1975, Myers, testifying before the S.E.C.
under a promise of immunity from prosecution, related that,
on orders from Wild, between March, 1961, and September,
1972, he had made twenty-two separate trips to various places
in the United States to deliver sealed envelopes to political figures, and, in addition, had made four to six such deliveries per
year in Washington to members of Congress or their staffs.

The picture that emerges from Myers' testimony is one of a
man forced by circumstances to reduce himself to pure mechanical function—to do what he was told while asking no questions
and, if possible, thinking no thoughts. In Washington, Wild
would give him a sealed envelope along with precise instructions about where and to whom it should be delivered. Myers
would board an airliner and proceed to the designated place.
The designated person would always be there. Myers would
greet him, and hand over the envelope. The recipient would say
"Thank you," and after an exchange of chitchat Myers would
fly back to Washington. Most often, the delivery would be at an
airport or at the recipient's office, but occasionally it would be
at a place suggestive of a desire for secrecy on the part of either
the donor or the recipient. In October of 1964, for example,
Myers went to Albuquerque, New Mexico, to deliver an enve-

lope to Edwin L. Mechem, who was then running for re-election as a senator from that state. At the Albuquerque airport, Myers was met by a man who conveyed him by private plane to a ranch, where Myers delivered the envelope to Mechem behind a barn, saying, as usual, "Mr. Wild asked me to give this to you." Again, in 1970, Myers said, he handed an envelope to Representative Richard L. Roudebush, of Indiana, at the latter's suggestion, in the men's washroom of a motel in Indianapolis.

In no instance did Wild, in giving Myers his instructions and a sealed envelope to deliver, tell Myers what the envelope contained, and in no instance did Myers ask. Nor did Wild ever explain why the delivery was to be made by hand rather than by mail. And in no instance, according to Myers' testimony, did he learn from the recipient what the envelope contained. Or, rather, in hardly any instance. On one of several occasions when he made deliveries to Herbert C. Manning, a Gulf attorney in Pittsburgh—presumably for distribution to local political figures—Manning opened the envelope in Myers' presence, revealing cash. On one other occasion—a 1970 delivery at a bank in a small town in Tennessee—the recipient similarly opened the envelope, and Myers saw that it contained cash. Did these two incidents suggest to Myers that his many other deliveries had also been of cash? Apparently not. Time and again, asked by S.E.C. counsel whether he knew what was in an envelope he had delivered, he replied, "I do not," or "I have no knowledge." A minor figure in the tragedy, Myers was apparently content to spin constantly by airliner above the cities, plains, and mountains of America, not knowing why, not wanting to know why—a man living in a moral void. . . .

At a Gulf management meeting in the fall of 1972, it was decided that, as a cost-cutting measure, all the company's offshore subsidiaries, including Bahamas Ex., should be consolidated into a single entity, Midcaribbean Investments, Ltd., with headquarters in Nassau. The move was approved by Gulf's corporate financial council early in December, and on the last day of the year the effective liquidation of Bahamas Ex. was completed. Thus the laundry for Gulf's illegal political money was put out of business—almost entirely, it appears, by executives merely anxious to save the company money, and innocent of any knowledge of the purpose that Bahamas Ex. had been so efficiently serving. Early in 1973, Wild began clamoring for more funds in Washington, and Viglia, in Nassau, had to reply that there were none, because the Bahamas Ex. account had been closed. Viglia then got authorization from ... the Gulf comptroller, in Pittsburgh, to borrow funds temporarily from Midcaribbean to meet Wild's need, and by April a whole new system, using Midcaribbean almost exactly as the previous system had used Bahamas Ex., was established and operating. On March 15, 1973, a new infusion of two hundred thousand dollars went from Pittsburgh to Nassau, and between April 26 and July 19 of that year Viglia made five cash deliveries to Wild totalling a hundred and twenty thousand dollars.

But time was running out. A delivery by Viglia of twenty thousand dollars to Wild on July 19th proved to be his last. A few weeks earlier—the exact date is not known—Wild, realizing that the court order to the Finance Committee of CREEP [the result of a suit brought by Common Cause] would force it to disclose Gulf's two fifty-thousand-dollar contributions, told Dorsey, by then the company's chief executive officer, about them. On July 19th (the same day that Wild—rather ruefully, one may imagine—was taking his last cash delivery from Viglia), Gulf engaged the Pittsburgh law firm of Eckert, Seamans, Cherin & Mellott to represent the corporation in the matter; a week later, lawyers of that firm met with lawyers for the Watergate Special Prosecutor's office, and the process of disclosure leading to the McCloy report began.

The McCloy committee concluded that Gulf's domestic political activities had been "shot through with illegality," and that the whole program, domestic and foreign, had "raised serious questions as to the policy and management of the company." ... [It also concluded] that "in the last analysis it will be in the tone and attitude of top management that the eradication [of improper political activities] will be ensured in the future."

The personnel, as well as the tone and attitude, of top management was the principal question at issue when the Gulf board of directors met in Pittsburgh in mid-January of this year, shortly after it had received the McCloy report. The meeting turned out to be a corporate thriller. Nearly all the Gulf executives who had been mentioned as accomplices in the testimony of Bounds, Wild, Viglia, and others were by this time either dead, like Whiteford, or retired, like Bounds, Wild, and

Viglia. But a few were not, and among these was Dorsey, the company's chairman and chief executive officer. The Gulf board, meeting for a total of more than twenty-three hours, in two sessions, between the afternoon of January 12 and the early morning of January 14, devoted its marathon deliberations almost entirely to the question of whether Dorsey and three other Gulf executives should be forced to resign.

The McCloy committee's conclusions about Dorsey's involvement had been equivocal. While Dorsey had freely admitted his personal negotiation and authorization of two Korean payments, totalling four million dollars, the committee concluded that he had apparently known nothing of the Bahamas Ex. secret account or its successor, and that the evidence fell short of demonstrating that he had known of Wild's unlawful political activities, but that concerning the latter he "was not sufficiently alert and should have known," and he "perhaps chose to shut his eyes to what was going on." With that judgment as a starting point, the board settled down, in closed session on the thirty-first floor of the Gulf Building, in Pittsburgh, to decide Dorsey's fate. According to Byron E. Calame, the *Wall Street Journal*'s man on the spot, it quickly developed that five directors who were considered representatives of the Mellons—the economic royalty of Gulf and of Pittsburgh itself—were bent on getting Dorsey's resignation, and were unwilling to have the blow softened by any face-saving compromise such as a "Ford-type pardon." With Dorsey and . . . another board member who had been mentioned by the McCloy committee as having been "involved," not participating in the deliberations for obvious reasons, the board consisted of twelve members, with the result that the Mellon block fell only two votes short of a majority. However, according to Calame, three other directors were equally adamant about keeping Dorsey in office; and Dorsey's lawyers were present to plead his case.

As the hours wore on, in an atmosphere described by participants as "brutal" and like that of a jury room, the Dorsey forces gradually gave ground, suggesting compromise plans under which Dorsey would remain in office with reduced authority until his normal retirement, in 1978. These plans were rejected. In the end, a key vote—if not, indeed, the swing vote—belonged to a director who, it seems safe to say, had been nominated with Dorsey's approval, and elected by Gulf stockholders the previous April, with no thought that nine months later she would all but hold the chairman's fate in her hands. She was Sister Jane Scully, president of Carlow College, a local liberal-arts institution for women, who had been elected in conformity with the current custom in corporate circles of putting a token, and presumably harmless, woman on the board. Sister Jane started out neutral, according to Calame, but eventually swung to the anti-Dorsey side. At last, at 1:15 A.M. on the fourteenth, the meeting was adjourned and the results were announced: Dorsey was to resign that same day as chief executive officer and from the board. . . .

With the forced resignation of Dorsey, and with a statement in March by Dorsey's successor, Jerry McAfee, that set forth a stiff new code of business principles to which "strict adherence" by all employees worldwide was described as "a condition of continued employment," Gulf's symbolic and substantive acts of contrition were accomplished, and there was reason to believe that the tone and attitude of top management would change notably in regard to political contributions. . . .

The disclosures and the attendant brouhaha do not appear to have caused much shock or outrage among investors or their professional advisers. Revelations of corporate bribery threaten a corporation's good name but not, apparently, its good profits or good prospects. The price of Gulf Oil common stock was not significantly depressed by any of the revelations, and [in the following months it rose] strongly. . . . Corporate bribery, it appears, has been for a decade and more a pervasive and accepted norm of conduct among many of the nation's largest and usually most respected enterprises. And there is no conclusive evidence that the practice has stopped and will not resume.

SECTION SIX

~~~~~~

Organizational Death Watch

ORGANIZATIONS rarely die gracefully. There is too much invested in their immortality for people to let go without conflict or tension, or for leaders to be perfectly honest about the possibility of system deaths.

Yet, there has been little attention to the question of how organizations die, and what constitutes a graceful death. Some analysts have commented on the importance of an organization knowing when to die, when to dissolve, when its purposes have been served and it would be more successful if it ended. Joyce Rothschild Whitt, in fact, has said (1976) that one way organizations manage to maintain democratic and participatory systems is by their willingness to dissolve when it is no longer possible to maintain democratic values, rather than holding on to survival as the ultimate good.

Perhaps it is true that organizations do need to "die," in whole or in part, when they are decaying. But practically no attention has been paid to the human side of organizational decay, decline, and death—the impact on the people living through them. People build enormous investments in organizations that go far beyond the stated purpose of the system, and these investments—concern for the job, connections with the people, meaningfulness as a part of the overall life of the individual—do not disappear just because decision-makers and power-holders have decided that the organization shall no longer exist or shall cut down, cut back, and reduce.

How does gradual decay or impending death affect the quality of life in organizations? How is decline experienced by—and handled by—the people inside? The experience differs in each organizational slice.

DEATH AND THE TOP

At the top there are the leaders, often far removed from the people struggling to keep their job and their part of the organization alive, and making decisions that appear sometimes as remote and unfeeling. Perhaps executives need to perform major surgery to keep an organization alive or to close it with minimum loss, but at least in the organizations represented here, these decisions seem unconnected to the reality experienced further down in a company's operating layers, yet disrupting it dramatically.

Top leaders are forced to make the tough decisions—indeed, this is the source of what we call their "power"—who goes and who stays, what business areas are viable, what parts should be cut out or rearranged to revive a declining organization, which jobs should be redesigned or eliminated. There are numerous cases, such as the Smithton National Bank (a pseudonym) in chapter 20, where it is clear that ineffective middle managers using outmoded practices are themselves a principal source of the organization's decay and that a new chief executive may need to fire people or close down operations in order to tighten up and save the organization. Yet, as sensible as this seems from the point of view of the top, the impact further down is often, predictably, different. In every case represented here, those below tend to see the top as insufficiently sensitive to their needs and concerns—or to their information and expertise—when it comes to decisions about cutting or closing.

Indeed, in the case of W. T. Grant's (chapter 21), central headquarters really did not always know what was going on or make the most appropriate decisions. For example, Ara Duclos, local store manager, was ordered to enter the credit card business even though he thought it would spell disaster. The pressure from headquarters was so intense that at one point the district credit manager called hourly to ask how many accounts had been opened. Then it turned out to be a disaster. New management undid the order, but it was now too late to save the company. Later, there was still another example of top executive ignorance of what local managers know. Paper towels had to be sold at a loss because they were not on the "approved list." Then it turned out that the list was incomplete and when a completed list was sent to each store, the manager had to reorder paper towels. It is easy to question the wisdom of central headquarters under such circumstances. The store manager helplessly watches disastrous central policies while he *knows* his customers and what they will buy. Orders and directives come from central headquarters but seem to have little relationship to what is actually going on at the store. They ask him to cut back when he's doing well, to add merchandise when things are bad, to spend money that will have to show up as additional costs for one year and therefore reduce profits. But the central office does not tap the wisdom of its local managers, and indeed, Duclos had never even been to headquarters until just before the company folded.

Furthermore, the same large organizational scope that constitutes the view from the top (the big financial picture, the demands of stockholders or trustees, the pressure from changing social conditions) prevents those at the top from seeing how their supposedly "rational" decisions for the sake of the organization set off "irrational" emotional reactions in the people who feel they give the organization life (by making policy real through daily activities) and thus feel threatened by any hint of death.

To the people at central headquarters and the bank, W. T. Grant's was merely a financial matter, an entity existing on paper in terms of the manipulation of assets and balance sheets. But to the people who invested their work lives at the store level, it meant a great deal more, that could never be expressed in mechanical, impersonal, financial terms.

There is a lesson for top leaders in this. First, decisions about change (shutting down a facility, letting people go) may be uninformed if they do not take into account the potential of the human resources of the organization. But more importantly, the responsibility of executives extends beyond merely making such decisions. Leaders must also gauge their impact on the people below. The process of gathering data relevant to the decision and of informing the organization and of easing people into the change with full recognition of their feelings, ought to be given equal weight to the actual decision itself.

"MIDDLEPERSONS"

The perspective of the managers in the middle is perhaps clearest: trying to mediate between remote central office decisions and the mass of employees. They are caught in a variety of dilemmas. They are expected to motivate people to produce until the very end even though rewards are about to be cut off, and no payoff for investment of effort can be promised. They are expected to exercise authority and make daily decisions when even they may be in the dark about what is going to happen. How can a manager, like Ara Duclos of W. T. Grant's Store 1192, have much credibility with his people when he must read about the company's closing in a newspaper rather than hear about it from his own management? And there he is getting the store reorganized and repainted—at headquarter's request.

In an unfortunately large number of instances, middle managers, as the top leaders' designated representatives, must act as though they have the information, must act as though everything is really fine, when they are themselves as threatened, insecure, and uninformed as the people below. A group manager at the Smithton Bank received a list of people he was to call that day to tell them they were being terminated; but he himself did not know if his name appeared on someone else's list. And he certainly could not reassure anyone else with any degree of confidence, despite being a boss.

Middle managers in local units, such as Grant's Duclos, can motivate the workers to put forth their best efforts only if there is a ray of hope of saving the store (or the factory or the office), but even if they demonstrate their own unit's viability, central management may close it anyway.

One of the tragedies is that even doing everything right (new colors, a jammed parking lot, sales up, etc.) may not stop the decay and decline. No single part of an organization stands alone—even when, perhaps, as in the case of Store 1192, it should. So where does that leave the middle-person's ability to promise and reward? Anger at the stupidity of decisions coming down from the top can be expressed—but there is no power to stop them.

THOSE WHO STAND BY

The mass of organization members, from those in other middle positions to those at the bottom, have no direct responsibility for decisions about organizational change or termination. They stand by as mere passive recipients of the decisions of others, watching decay or waiting for death.

The feelings of those watching things fall apart or waiting for the end of one's own operations cover a range, from emotional disengagement for those who have other options to depression and self-doubt to outright anger. A few with activist leanings might try to organize to prevent dissolution, as in the examples of organizational preservation tactics described below. But for the most part, emotions are expressed in erratic behavior, in suspicion and mistrust, in self-protective disinterest in the organization, and in departure from routine practice. The "rules" cease to have the same compelling meaning under conditions of extreme uncertainty. We also see this unravelling and defiance of convention in disasters, riots, and wars. Why, indeed, *should* traditional authority be obeyed if the end is imminent?

Thomas McCann, a former corporate vice president of United Fruit, described this experience as his company declined:

When a complex organization begins to fall apart, it doesn't all go at once: it isn't like a bomb in the cellar or a plane crash. It happens in bits and pieces, a fissure here, a missing part there.

The process starts with the people. They become angry. Or frightened. Or restless. They take longer lunches. They change their work habits; those who worked long hours now work less; those who took it easy begin to show up on time and leave later. They talk a lot about the man at the top.[1976:181]

It is not hard to see how the typical response of organization members to decay, and particularly to what appear to be arbitrary and autocratic decisions from the top about the management of decline through cutting, reinforce a process that promotes further decay. We see this in the Chapter 20 case of Farm Products Corporation (not its real name), a large midwestern company that will undoubtedly survive, but not before destroying significant parts of the company and, with it, morale.

A system in crisis—one where things are declining, one that does not openly face the decline and empower its members, is likely to create behavior responsive only to stress—but not the kind of behavior likely to put the system back on its feet. For example, people feel that they can't act because they don't know whether their decisions can be sustained. Nothing is secure. Things done for one purpose, such as performance appraisals to improve effectiveness, may be turned to another purpose, such as differentiating who stays and who leaves, and so people start fudging on the forms. When authority is exercised arbitrarily and decisions are countermanded, people are living in a state of ambiguity; that means they will do their best to preserve their own territory and their own job, but not to take risks that could possibly benefit the system. The situation resembles a game of musical chairs: everyone dancing madly to the music trying to promote the illusion of accomplishment and then looking around to see who is left out when the music stops for a moment.

When it is clear that they might be cut, some people feel the way they might about impending retirement: concerned that they won't be able to find another place for themselves, depressed at the thought that they are no longer needed. This is harder, of course, for those with fewest options who have been with the system longest. As one woman expressed her feelings about retiring from a factory job:

> I'm pretty mixed up now that I'm going. I've been here for more than 30 years. I'm going to be pretty lonely. When I work as a layout, I feel I am needed. A lot of time some of the girls come to me and confide in me with their problems. They ask for advice and you feel like you're needed and it's a good feeling. I'm going to miss that, because at home, nobody wants my ideas or help or anything . . . I've got to get myself into other projects . . . I just hope I won't be too lonely. . . . [Balzer, 1976: 231–32]

But despite the similarities, there are also clear differences between individual retirement and losing one's place because, to stretch the analogy, an entire organizational segment is being retired or a whole unit has come to its last stage of work life. While the people whose organization dissolves on them do not necessarily have to feel individually displaced, that everything will go on without them, they still may feel like failures and outcasts. And they cannot know in advance, as with the socially defined retirement age, that they must leave; therefore, confusion and ambiguity are heightened.

Anger is likely to be strongest, in fact, where there is the least honesty about the organization's and its people's futures. People resent being lied to. Sometimes, of course, the future is unknowable and the information is, by definition, unsharable. But in too many other cases, organizations try to hide their situation or their plans, pretending nothing is in jeopardy. They might do this through a variety of euphemisms for programs and policies that attempt to mask the human problems of decline: "outplacement," "overhead value analysis," "de-hiring." W. T. Grant's word for reduction in store space was "compaction."

Yet everyone knows anyway what the real intent is, and so they are angry at the implied insult to their intelligence as well as at the impending terminations. A satiric notice was circulated at the plant where Richard Balzer (1976) worked concerning an "early retirement program"—management's steps to reduce the work force in the light of a declining workload. The memo named two programs: Retire Aged Personnel Early (RAPE) and a Survey of Capabilities of Retired Early Workers (SCREW). There was also a third for all employees who had been "raped" and "screwed"; they could then apply for a final review, a Study by Higher Authority Following Termination (SHAFT). Said the mock memo, "Program policy dictates that employees may be raped once and screwed twice, but may get the shaft as many times as the company deems appropriate."

DEATH WITH DIGNITY

Is it possible for organizations, like individuals, to die with dignity? Can death (of pieces or the whole) be seen as a natural part of organizational life, so that it can be dealt with openly and supportively? Or must the threat of organizational death be handled defensively, as something to be avoided, just as Americans have traditionally turned away from the sight of dying individuals and wished to pretend that individual death did not exist?

If there is such a thing as organizational death with dignity, then Frank Robertson tried to make it happen at the Baker plant before its closing (chapter 22). He wanted the workers and managers at Baker, a manufacturer of auto finishes, to go out with their heads up. Faced with the dilemmas of keeping the plant going and terminating it at the same time, Robertson chose to be flexible and supportive of the people who had to live in such an ambiguous state of waiting to die. He argued with the manager who was being tight over a few hundred dollars in disability pay for one of the workers. He worked on keeping the maintenance team together. He understood and did not fire the employee caught taking a ladder out of the plant. Faced with still more stealing, Robertson decided to give some of the materials away. He supported and counseled the people concerned about their future security, and he participated in the nostalgic rituals that helped people say goodby to one another.

But like many managers in the middle, as we saw earlier in this book, Robertson was also handicapped by the contrast between his own style and inclinations—support, flexibility, and information sharing—and the actions of remote, central office company decision-makers. Among other things, the Baker plant, like W. T. Grant's Store 1192, was being killed off by the company at a time when it was patently profitable, a full warehouse and bottom line productivity. Like Ara Duclos, the Grant store manager, Robertson was not given all the information about when the plant might be closing and what central policy decisions were being made. He thus lacked some of the resources it would take to ease a part of an organization into its death with minimum traumas for the people involved.

We can identify at least three conditions that are necessary in order to support organizational death with dignity:

1. *Accurate information, so that it is possible for managers to level with people.* Just as with an individual's death, organization members are treated with more respect and dignity when they are given full information about what to expect. This stands in contrast to "protecting them" from the knowledge of

their system's imminent demise, a frequent justification for withholding painful facts. Such "protection," whether it is by a physician or a top manager, is a form of power maintenance in disguise that puts someone else in control of the individual's fate; not knowing the truth prevents the people involved from making their own choices based on complete and accurate information. Since they suspect the truth anyway, they feel more dignified—and are, indeed, more in control—when fully informed of the state of affairs. Open disclosure is even more important when the unit being shut down appears to its staff to be doing very well, because they are not only losing their organization, they are also losing faith in the people making the decisions.

2. *Tolerance for people's irrational or emotional responses.* Extra flexibility and generosity are required, along with understanding of the uncharacteristic things that people might do in the light of the anticipated end of the system in which they have invested so much. When significant change is about to descend, especially change that represents endings for at least some of the people—that is no time for organization leaders to become stingy and penny-conscious or to insist on unbending adherence to "the rules"; the savings are rarely worth it. Instead, leaders (who may be having their own traumatic moments) need to understand what drives people at such times, and, by being generous and sympathetic, may prevent some very serious and costly crises.

3. *Gradual disengagement, the chance to slow down by bits and pieces over time.* Perhaps contributing to some of the more disturbing outcomes of the Baker plant closing and Grant's company's dissolution was the pretense, fostered by central organizational decisions, that the plant and the store were in full operation until the moment of death. Abrupt endings are more difficult than gradual transitions, especially when the pretense of full operation prevents people from coming to terms with the system's end. In practical terms, people cannot take the time they might need to look for something else. In emotional terms, they have no chance to slowly disentangle their investments and place them elsewhere. (It is not surprising that, under such circumstances, a senior Baker plant manager committed suicide at the end.) A growing number of companies have retirement counseling programs, including systems that enable man-

agers who will retire in a year or two to go on reduced schedules and gradually ease themselves out. But it is usually only the highest-paid workers who have such options, and rarely do they extend to people who are the victims of organizational, rather than individual, terminations. Yet the need is clearly there.

THE STRUGGLE FOR ORGANIZATIONAL PRESERVATION

Organizations decline and must consider death for a variety of reasons. "Decay" can occur inevitably just because people age and environments change. Some organizations who succeed in gaining the commitment of their people, but do not expand enough to keep adding newer, younger people, may find themselves with an aging membership. Similarly, because social change in the wider environment is itself inevitable (particularly in twentieth century America), markets close, missions disappear, demands shift, technological innovations radically alter the character of life, and other rules of the game, such as government regulations, change. Indeed, as change speeds up, or, at least, as companies become more aware of the impact of changes on their internal capacity to be effective, some organizations are aware of an increasing need for long-range social forecasting.

In addition to these sources of decline, the very life cycle of organizations contributes to decay. Internal sluggishness cuts down on effectiveness. As organizations mature, they often lose potency. The analogy to human aging is often provocative and apt, as we saw in the section on "Growing Pains." Organizations, too, get older and perhaps automatically closer to death. McCann, the former United Fruit executive, saw it this way:

Companies, like people, have most of their energy when they are young, and as they age they lose their potency; they become more rigid, their vision becomes narrower, their prospects fewer and they resist the kind of originality that marked their beginnings. While they still have the vigor of youth, the most important part of life is opportunity. As they age, and as their early labors bear fruit, they gradually change their priorities: habit becomes more important than innovation, and how things get done takes precedent over why. When I joined United Fruit in 1952—as an eighteen-year-old office boy at pier

3 in New York—the company was already well into middle age and its arteries had started to harden. [1976:14]

Given such conditions, why don't organizations just die quietly or fade out of existence gradually with no fuss? Clearly, some do. But there are also forces acting upon organizations that seek to keep them alive. Regardless of the purposes for which an organization begins, people build up investments in the organization's continued operation that may have little to do with the system's primary goal. There are a variety of constituencies who build on-going relationships with the organizations, as we saw in the last section, and who do come to play a role, in many organizations, in shaping policy quite apart from the organization's founding purpose. An airline is formed as a profit-making corporation. But then passengers begin to count on it for transportation; the government, in giving the airline its routes, counts on it to use them; its suppliers count on it for orders; its employees count on it for jobs.

Philip Selznick wrote about such organizational commitments in his classic study of The Tennessee Valley Authority (1966). Organizations develop obligations over a period of time that may have nothing to do with their end goals but rather what they owe to other constituencies. For Selznick, the emergence of organizational commitments led to goal displacement and the disruption of the organization itself. But David Sills (1967) used the March of Dimes organization to show the opposite phenomenon: that displacement of goals could, in fact, insure the survival of the organization. He studied The Foundation for Infantile Paralysis, the organization that invented the March of Dimes, and was highly successful in terms of recruiting volunteers, in maintaining their active interest in the program, in raising funds, and, finally, in making progress towards its ultimate goal of eliminating the threat of polio. But by definition, this goal was a finite one. What happens when it is achieved? Sills addressed the issue of "succession of goals": how an organization decides to maintain itself even when its goals are met because the organization itself has value to its people, who have come to count on it for the satisfaction of needs quite apart from its ostensibly "larger purpose." Dissolution is not the only course of action open to an organization when its purposes are either achieved or become irrelevant because of change in the social environment. The March of

Dimes essentially chose a redefined goal and a new "market"; the elimination of other diseases. There are many other examples of organizations which have remained intact for the purpose of working toward new or sharply modified objectives. Dartmouth College was originally founded to educate and christianize the Indians of New England, but it transformed itself into a general liberal arts college (1967:257).

The YMCA is one of Sills' major examples of the process of organizational adaptation. Over time, the YMCA has devoted increasing attention to its physical and social goals and less attention to its religious and spiritual aims. One of the reasons for the March of Dimes' continued existence was that its membership developed a great deal of investment in its participation in this particular organization. Sills commented that "A considerable portion of the volunteer membership of the foundation has found its organizational characteristics sufficiently appealing, and its activities sufficiently rewarding, to be willing and anxious to take part in the organization should it seek to realize new goals" (1967:268). It is a case of commitment to *means*—to involvement in the organization, to working there—as well as to ends. And the membership perceives the organization as a "pacesetter" and thus, with the capacity as a collective body to attack other problems with as much vigor and success as they attacked the polio problem.

In short, the most important source of the pressure to preserve organizations comes from the people inside, the members and employees who build up investments over time, who are supplied with their livelihoods, regardless of other reasons the organization exists. In the case of W. T. Grant's Store 1192 in chapter 21, we can see the great enthusiasm, commitment, and dedication of those people for whom the store had been their entire life. The clerks wanted to get together to take the store over when it sounded as though the company might be going into bankruptcy; they were willing to invest their life savings in preserving the store. Indeed, there are a number of instances in which employees *have* taken over a plant that would otherwise close; the Vermont Asbestos Company is the major example.

Ought an organization have the right to die—to shut down units that may have value to the people in them and that may operate quite effectively, solely on financial grounds? This is a serious policy question today. At the time of this writing, there is a bill before Congress addressing this very question, the Voluntary Job Preservation and Community Stabilization Act. Congressman Kostmayer of Pennsylvania said in hearings on March 1, 1978:

> When businesses close their doors or move away, employees lose their jobs, and the economic dislocations can be devastating. Announcements of steel plant cutbacks have sent shock waves through Youngstown, Ohio, an industrial community of about 130,000 people. Last September, the Youngstown Sheet and Tube Co. decided to abandon a prominent mill and lay off up to 5,000 workers. Within a few months, United States Steel followed suit with plans to phase out another 5,000 jobs at two other Youngstown plants.
>
> Smaller towns and rural areas can be similarly affected by such disruptions. Zenith, hurt by competition from imports, decided last summer to phase out 1,000 jobs at its color television plant in Watsontown, Pennsylvania—and produce abroad instead. The move not only wiped out the main source of employment for Watsontown (population 5,000), but for a wide surrounding area as well.
>
> This act is essentially a response to the problems of Youngstowns and Watsontowns across the country. Where plants would otherwise be abandoned, it would encourage and assist interested groups of employees or community residents to purchase them and try to run them profitably. [Congressional Record, 1978]

It becomes clear, indeed, when organizations face death, that an organization is much more than its financial or paper existence, its material assets. It is also the capacity to do something, the connections between people, the source of their jobs (Stein, 1971). People's struggle against organizational death comes from the fact that they are *living* inside it.

THE NEED FOR RENEWAL PROCESSES

If goals or ownership cannot be changed, is organizational death inevitable? McCann, looking back at United Fruit, framed an answer this way:

> Companies have one great advantage over people: they can renew themselves. But they have to want renewal first, and that means that the men at the top have to recognize the signs of senility before the disease advances to the stage where it is incurable. . . . [But] many of the men who were running the company in the fifties learned their trade and methods from the men who had founded the company fifty years earlier. [1976:14]

United Fruit and the Smithton Bank demonstrated the possibility of preservation and the need to attend to the signs of decline early. This often means changing accepted procedures, learning new styles. But this kind of internal renewal is often very hard for the old hands. Trained in a different era, full of memories of the way it used to be in "the good old days," they are often barriers to renewal in three ways. First, they are likely to be blind to the changes going on around them; their very capacity is, as Thorstein Veblen put it, a "trained incapacity" to see things differently. Second, they themselves may be contributing to the decline by outmoded operating behaviors. And third, they may be extremely threatened by change, as at Smithton National Bank, if renewal for the organization means obsolescence for themselves. Those at upper levels of an organization who are "stuck," to use Rosabeth Kanter's term, and see no growth prospects for themselves, often become the conservative resistors who seem to prevent organizational progress. Thus, unless given new opportunities or the chance, at minimum, "to die with dignity," the old hands who may be a central source of the problem will also block its solution.

Internal transformations are one way organizations can struggle to stay alive: new technology, new people, new policies and procedures, new facilities and equipment, new education. In this sense, for most of today's organizations, the continual processes of addition and change ought also to be seen as processes of—and opportunities for—renewal (examination of effectiveness, evaluation of organizational "health," creation of new opportunities for old hands).

THE SELECTIONS

There are many reasons organizations begin to decline and, from a policy and practice standpoint, much that organizational leaders can learn about how to manage decline and, if necessary, promote "death with dignity." But our primary point in this section is to illustrate what impact decay or impending death have on the people experiencing them.

The first set of articles, "Organizations in Trouble," by Barry Stein, sketches the experiences of people in two different companies, both of which are under severe financial pressure. The first, a leading bank given the fictitious name of Smithton National Bank, shows the confusion of the old hands who remember how things used to be when times were better. The second, about a food processing company ("Farm Products"), looks forward, in the sense that people are functioning in a state of continual uncertainty, afraid they will be cut next, and angry that they are not given more information. Both companies are likely to pull out of their crisis, in Smithton's case because of good new top leadership, and in Farm Product's case because the company is financially well situated to weather decline. But in the meantime, some parts are dying, and some people are living under the shadow of death.

Rush Loving Jr.'s account of "W. T. Grant's Last Days—As Seen from Store 1192" is a journalist's portrait of how one local unit tries to adapt but eventually goes under through no fault of its own. The people's feelings about their store, the ways their lives revolve around it, are particularly poignant.

Finally, "Termination at Baker Plant" is told by Alfred Slote but also contains excerpts from the diary of Frank Robertson, plant manager. We can see events from the perspective of their key actors.

20 / Organizations in Trouble: Two Vignettes

Barry A. Stein

"The Good Old Days"

Not all the cities in the sunbelt are prospering. One of them, in the South, has been suffering a long slow process of urban decay with businesses and people moving out into the suburbs,

Prepared especially for this book.

and with taxes rising and services lagging within the city itself. This has been bad news for the Smithton National Bank.

There was a time, not many years ago, when Smithton's core banking business, which involved several dozen retail branches around the city, was prospering. Like most traditional banks, it counted on long-term customers, and, in turn, offered its employees long-term job security: regular promotions based on seniority and a good record of reliability and loyalty. Advertising was minimal, marketing was unheard of, and there was no formal management training. People moved up the ranks because they learned, were affable to customers, and fit the town's image of proper, civic-minded bankers.

As the city changed, however, both the branches and the bank itself suffered. Things came to a head approximately two years ago when the bank's earnings, which had been declining slowly for the preceding five or six years, suddenly fell to zero. The bank's management called in a nationally known consulting firm, a specialist in evaluating and cutting overhead costs, to look at the bank overall, and especially at the "retail" division, the unit responsible for operating the city branches. This study led to several branch closings and the layoff of roughly 15 percent of the retail division staff.

Two years later, these events are still fresh in the minds of the survivors. One of three vice presidents in charge of the branch banks remembers it this way:

"When the people to be let go came in that morning, I called them into my office one by one, told them what was happening, asked them to clear out their desks and be gone by the end of the day. This was how we were told to do it. We all had lists we were working from, but had no idea who was on the other lists. I wasn't sure whether or not I personally was on somebody else's list. By the end of the day, a number of our best people—the ones we wanted to keep—were cleaning out their own desks and starting to pack up to leave. When I asked them what they were doing, they said 'Well, we're obviously on our way out too, and we might as well get it over and done with.'

"I told them to stop. The decision about who was on the list was made by the president with very little advice from anybody else except the consultants. None of us knew what was happening until it was announced. It was terrible."

And then he hastily added: "Of course, it used to be different.

Before that, a career in the bank was secure. As long as you were doing your job reasonably well—as a matter of fact, as long as you weren't either stealing money or (if you were a manager) having a visible affair with your secretary—you could be sure of a job until the day you retired. We're trying to tell our people now that they don't have to worry; that as long as they're doing their job satisfactorily, they don't have to worry. But it's hard to convince them. They don't believe us anymore. They're suspicious and easily threatened."

Shortly after these events, the division was also reorganized. The president of the retail division was demoted to a staff position, the three group vice presidents were maintained with somewhat altered responsibilities, and a new president, John Anderson, was brought in—a Northerner. In fact, he had been in the banking business for only a few years, and then as a marketing expert who had done extremely well in helping banks more aggressively pursue business, but had no line experience managing banking operations. All in all, a most untraditional choice. It must have seemed to the old hands like the final blow.

President Anderson came to the conclusion that the division was still in very poor shape. No one seemed to be working very hard. Morale was low. The atmosphere was one of gloom and pessimism: "We're going under, and there's nothing that can be done to save us. There's no more business in this town." The mood showed up in the physical structures. Branch offices looked shabby, never seemed to get completely clean. Tellers were short-tempered and surly. And managers reacted to new ideas as though personally attacked, immediately finding all the reasons why something couldn't be done. Transfers and even some promotions were regarded with suspicion, not excitement: "Why are they trying to get rid of me?" "Is this the first step on the way out?" It was considered a *reward* to be placed in the more prosperous branches, where business went on regardless of the talents of employees, and it was possible to play it safe. It was considered a *punishment* to be put in charge of a declining area that management hoped could be improved, even though one's own actions could potentially make a big difference, and there was room for growth.

Anderson remembers his first days as president: "There were (and are) good people in the division but there was also a lot of apparent dead weight—people putting their time in but not much more. The group vice presidents simply were not doing what was necessary for the branches and the bank to function effectively. It's hard to believe how little contact the group vice presidents had even with their direct subordinates—the branch managers—let alone other people in the branches. Performance appraisals have virtually never been done; when I asked for specific information about branch managers and other people to see who might potentially be most valuable, I was met by blank stares and undiscriminating responses—'They're all fine,' they told me.

"One of the first things I did was merely to visit all the branches. Never before had the president (or nearly any other senior executive) actually visited the branches. The phones of the group vice presidents didn't stop ringing for days. Often it was the branch managers: 'How did I do?', 'Did I look all' right?', 'What did he think?' One poor branch manager I talked to was so nervous I thought he'd spill his coffee all over his suit. His hands almost literally couldn't stop shaking.

"But I wasn't there to appraise anybody. I simply wanted to get to know the people. I did it again at Christmas: I brought them all boxes of candy. But of course they didn't know how to take that either."

A year later, Anderson thinks, there are some signs of improvement: "Things are starting to change. I think I've had an impact on the system, and I think I've earned the respect of the more traditional members of the bank. For one thing, it became clear that some of the branch managers really could use help; others, it was equally clear, were less good and needed to be watched closely or perhaps even terminated. Originally, when I discussed them with the group vice presidents, I met strong argument. But in most cases I've been proven right, often to the surprise of the group vice president. To their credit, they've been able to admit it when I've been right, and in some cases they've shown me I was wrong. Overall, they are beginning to look harder at some of those issues.

"I'd also decided to implement a more systematic planning process. For the first time, we are looking to the branch managers to make formal plans and projections, and to present them to me and my staff. We *are* in a difficult environment, but that doesn't mean there's nothing we can do. To listen to many of my subordinates, you'd think there was nothing to do but sit back and wait for something to happen.

"Most of them also had a peculiarly frustrating habit of resisting decisions. It is almost impossible to get a straight answer out of some of them. One of them—not by any means the only one like this, but the one who most exemplifies it—had his college training in Greek. He takes five typed pages to respond to a question that could be answered with a simple yes or no. But we all have to get to work. Things are changing, the banking business is not the same as it was, and we all have to recognize it."

As a matter of fact, the group vice presidents and the other members of the president's staff, do understand that things are changing. The problem is that they are not yet sure what to do about it, or how to operate. There are also hints of a concern that they will lose their place, that they cannot be helpful in these circumstances; so different from the "good old days." All three of them and the demoted ex-president have been with the bank for over twenty-five years, the youngest of them is fifty-five, and all have spent their careers entirely in the banking business.

The oldest vice president remembers how it used to be: "When I was a young man here, and until recently, everyone came up the same way. You entered to train as a teller or a clerk and worked your way up through the ranks. You learned to be a manager by learning how to make good credit decisions. That's why we give people increasing credit responsibility, starting at a very early age. Responsibilities start with perhaps a hundred dollars, then $200 and then $500, and eventually thousands or more. Every step of the way, you're learning how to make decisions, how to make *better* decisions, and that makes better managers.

"But that was at a time when the bank was really benefiting from its retail activities and the branches were important. When we established our branches—some of them as many as fifty years ago—they were an important part of the community. They were located in real neighborhoods, and people participated in them, and the flow of cash from those branches and the business generated in loans were the keys to the bank's success. Those of us in the branches and in the branch banking business had a certain status and responsibility. We were able to make a real contribution.

"It's not like that anymore. The city is losing 5 percent of its population a year. Everybody is competing for the same business. The savings banks have 'NOW' accounts, so they take away some of our traditional business, and the neighborhoods are changing. We have branches that don't make any money at all, and there's no way they can. This bank doesn't look to its retail division for major income any more. It looks to corporate activities or credit cards or some other new financial service not related to the city branches. Let's face it. Branch banking is probably on its way out."

Another group vice president talks about the younger people, the ones coming up now: "We seem to have a hard time keeping the college people. We do college recruiting, like all the banks, and we get in as many good people as we can. But of the fifteen that I think came from our college recruiting programs in the last few years, all but one have left. The people that stay are still the people that come up through the ranks. But of course there isn't that much opportunity anymore. We have a lot of very good people in the branches, and fortunately many of them want to stay where they are. We have head tellers, assistant branch managers, and other people on the platform (management and loan staff) who like doing what they do, and aren't interested in other opportunities. And it's a good thing they feel that way because I don't know what we would do otherwise. We have one woman—a grandmother—who's the best head teller in the whole bank. She enjoys being a head teller and isn't interested in being anything else.

"For the few good people that we do see motivated to get ahead, we have to make room for them. So we find a way. We make a space or we create jobs for them. There is some opportunity here. After all, we're all relatively old, and our jobs will be opening up soon.

"We are also anxious to help. My door is always open, and that's just as true for my colleagues. If anybody needs help, if any of the branch managers want to ask a question or would like to discuss something, they have only to call or come in." But he later added, "Of course, one of the ways we evaluate our managers is to make sure that they can make decisions on their own. That's the important thing. If they come in too often, well, they just don't have it."

President Anderson's response to all of this is crisp and to the point. "Nonsense.

"There's plenty of opportunity, and there's plenty of room to make improvements in the bank. And for those people ready to try to do it, there's a great deal that we can do. We have figures that suggest we could handle our present business with fewer tellers than we have now, but we're not pushing. I understand it takes time. But it's important that people begin to come to grips with that situation. They just aren't trying hard enough.

"At one of my staff meetings recently, they were insisting that there was nothing more to be done. The situation in the city is such that if we want more buiness or more customers, we have to get them from another bank. There is no more business available. Period. To which I said, 'In that case, we don't need so many loan officers.' You should have seen their jaws drop."

In fact, the changes for the Smithton National Bank and for banking generally are serious. Not only is that city, like many, changing its character, but the nature of banking itself is becoming very different. Competition has changed, technology is changing. Electronic banking and transfer of funds, greater use of credit cards and other alternatives for cash, and a whole array of new financial services are all having a big impact on traditional banking. It *is* true that at Smithton, the retail division is much less a factor than it once was. There are other alternatives for the bank's use of its own assets. Three more branches were recently closed. Moreover, there are programs to appraise credit risk by computer; a change that would take away the single most important identity of the traditional banker; that is, the authority to make credit decisions and to loan money.

The new people succeeding in the banking business are also different; they are not like the group vice presidents and their colleagues who came up through the ranks and worked for twenty-five years to do it. Instead, they're college students or even more likely MBA's—"hot shots" full of new tools, techniques, motivations and manners. They don't behave the same way, and they don't even *look* like traditional bankers. There is pressure from equal employment opportunity and affirmative action regulations. Blacks and other minorities have already been entering the bank in increasing numbers; now women are following suit.

The effect of all this on the bank itself, and on the traditional employees like the group vice presidents is clear. They are, in their own view, obsolete. Their skills, developed and honed at a

different time and for different ends, seem no longer to be useful. They are, at best, operating a holding action. They, and the
traditional banking business represented by the retail division,
may fade out of the picture at the same time. Those people that
can survive the change and apply themselves to it will presumably prosper; those that cannot will be maintained in an increasingly precarious position until they too disappear. Why
would people still join the retail division, particularly with all
these problems?

A vice president replied, somewhat wistfully: "The answer is
simple. It's more interesting. The branches are relatively
small—our largest one has less than thirty people—and it's exciting to work with the public directly. We and the people in
the branches meet them all the time. The problems are always
changing. There's a chance to be identified and seen as an individual, and to do things that are direct and meaningful. And
particularly for those in the mainstream of the banking business, making credit decisions is important; it provides standing
in the community, and it gives pride to individuals. Those are
decisions that count, and most of us would rather do that, and
be in this position, than to be one of the dozens or hundreds of
people sitting in the inside offices at headquarters, rarely meeting anybody except others in the bank."

How much of this answer reflected Smithton's present reality—a dying bank unless it revives itself with new practices
and new human energy—and how much is merely nostalgia for
how things used to be? For the older bankers at Smithton, their
thoughts cannot help but keep returning to the "good old
days."

"We're Going to Make Sure This Never Happens Again"

November 6, 1971 was Black Tuesday for the Farm Products
Corporation (FPC), a major Chicago-based producer of agricultural intermediates and materials. On that day, approximately
one-fifth of the work force was laid off as a result of mounting financial pressures from the general economic recession. Until
that time, FPC, a large factor in a large industry, had been a

successful if somewhat stodgy firm with few striking market successes but equally important, no major failures. Black Tuesday was the day on which notices were received by the unfortunate employees of the company. FPC management swore that: "We're going to make sure this never happens again."

Six years later it happened again. This time it was most clearly the result of enormously increased costs for petroleum-based raw materials, coupled with considerable overcapacity in the industry. Between those increased costs and widespread soft markets, FPC found itself unable to raise prices enough to cover the extra cost margin. After trying a variety of less draconian measures, the company felt forced to again lay off a substantial fraction of the workforce. The whole cycle took only some three months.

There had been, for the better part of a year, comments and suggestions from those who watched the financial affairs of the company and its economic environment. There was nothing obvious, nothing marked, but rather a general feeling of softness noticed by businessmen, including many outside of Farm Products. As a result of this, managers and executives at FPC laid their plans modestly and tried to hedge their bets as much as possible. Despite that, by the end of the first quarter of 1977 it became clear that there were problems. Sales were up (indeed they were well above expectations for the quarter), but profits were down—disturbingly down. Increased costs were the reason. Some of the costs, such as those attributable to raw materials and long-term contracts, were essentially impossible to reduce. The solution in the short run seemed clear: cut overhead. That meant cutting people.

Signs of what was coming appeared first in the company through messages conveyed personally in memo form by corporate officers to their subordinates. Tighten up wherever possible, check carefully, watch every penny, and be prepared for stronger measures. By early summer it became necessary for one of the key members of the president's staff to send a formal announcement to all senior management. He first described the financial situation, took note of the reduced profits and the difficulty of controlling the costs of basic raw materials, and underlined the need to focus on overhead. He then said, "We do not wish to set quantitative targets for reducing overhead. We regard that as a last resort. On the contrary, we wish everyone in the company, and all of you in particular, to pay the closest possible attention to a new posture, in which the greatest pains are taken to make sure that every expenditure is justified in terms of our present situation and that their value can be assured." Finally, he noted that a number of high level task forces had been set up, and promised to keep everyone informed as time went along.

Although there were some results from this general exhortation, they were insufficiently satisfactory. People did pay attention and some expenses were pared. However, the situation facing the company became both more serious and more evident by the time another couple of months went by. At that point, despite FPC's stated reluctance to set quantitative targets, that was the next step. Several things happened in close succession toward the end of the summer. First, there was a cluster of new moves in a management reorganization that had been slowly taking place over the entire course of 1977. The new senior executives and officers were, to a man, (there were, of course, no women) known as hard boiled, extremely cost conscious, control minded, and very tough. They were men who very clearly would not hesitate to do whatever seemed required—and to do it fast.

The second step was a formal policy eliminating a considerable number of the small perquisites and traditions that FPC managers and professionals had long enjoyed. These included, for example, luncheons and small gifts for twenty-five-year employees, business lunches on a relatively casual basis, staff Christmas parties (all of which were immediately cancelled), and sales and staff meetings at off-site or out-of-town facilities. Also introduced were stringent new rules about expense accounts, arrangements to minimize corporate travel, a virtual freeze on staff transfers from one office or region to another, and extreme scrutiny of all part-time employment or use of consultants. These measures, more than any other single thing, made it clear how serious management was about cost-cutting to "save" the company. None of them could have been terribly important in terms of the actual amount of money saved— Christmas parties are not expensive—but their impact on the people working at Farm Products Corporation was immediate. There was general agreement that morale and productivity started to drop at once; simultaneously, anxiety and stress rose. People talked about "waiting for the other shoe to drop."

People's anticipatory concerns were well-founded. Very shortly after these control measures were instituted, all managers were asked to re-appraise their subordinates, particularly those holding the rating of satisfactory in the company's performance appraisal system. Although this had an ominous ring, those that asked the direct question were told that it was merely calculated to sharpen the effectiveness of that appraisal system and to prepare for more effective personnel decisions in the future.

It only took a month for that future to arrive. One of the first signs (at least in retrospect) concerned the company's director of personnel systems, who suddenly disappeared from his office for an entire day without a word said to anybody, and with no explanation given either to his secretary or to people expecting him at other meetings: behavior that was entirely uncharacteristic of him. It turned out that he had been called in secret by a committee of senior officers, to discuss a layoff plan that he would be asked to direct and implement on behalf of the corporation. The expected impact was clearest at headquarters where some 15 percent of the staff were expected to be phased out over a four-month period.

The new policy had three components. First, as many people as possible who were not absolutely essential were encouraged to resign or to take other jobs; the company made "outplacement" assistance available to help them. Second, FPC created a temporary mechanism whereby certain people who had accumulated an appropriate combination of tenure and salary (according to a detailed formula) could opt for early retirement with greater benefits than would normally be the case for those people. Third, and most important in its impact, people who had been re-appraised as "low" satisfactory in the new round of performance ratings, rather than "middle" or "high," were put on probation. (People appraised lower than satisfactory had, in principle, *already* been dismissed.) Technically, since the probation period was for three months, those on probation could theoretically be retained. But the instructions that went out simultaneously to the managers responsible for the interviews actually placing people on probation said, "Be pessimistic." The whole process was to be complete by the middle of February, 1978. In the meantime, people were allowed to maintain their offices and stay in their units, and outplacement help was made available. In reality, no one in management expected more than a trivial number of them to stay; the clear intent was to reduce staff.

The consequences on the organization were immediate and profound. Since this entire activity was carried out in secret, initial information for most people came from rumors. Even those people in relatively senior positions knew only a fraction of the total, and no one was encouraged to share what they knew or to ask for more. The only authoritative statement forthcoming from top management discussed the whole thing in rather vague terms, euphemistically labelling the changes part of a "management productivity improvement program"— MPIP, as it immediately became known.

Information rapidly started to leak out anyway, as it would in any organization with an efficient employee "rumor transmittal system." At one meeting of the management of a large department, a twenty-five-year veteran addressed his colleagues in a tone of complete disbelief. "You won't believe what I just heard. Sam Wilson has been put on probation! Sam has never been rated as low as 'satisfactory!' He's been here for years and he's highly valued. That really shakes me up. Who else is on the list?" Someone else responded, "I heard that Joe Duffy was already gone. And Marty Vincent told me personally that he had been put on probation." Then the meeting turned into a discussion about how it could happen that people long regarded as real contributors to the organization and well-known members of its professional or managerial staff could have been put on probation as part of the "management productivity improvement program."

On another occasion, the associate director of a personnel group asked some poignant rhetorical questions. "What's it going to feel like to be here in the building with all these people—God knows how many—on probation but still in their offices? What will it do to us? How will it feel to be here? I don't even know *who* they are. When I walk through the halls now, or go to the cafeteria, I don't know whether I'm looking at people who are staying or who are about to leave. I don't know what to say to people." After a long pause, a colleague added, "This isn't the end. The other shoe still hasn't dropped yet. Going about our job is like rearranging the deck chairs on the Titanic."

Throughout this period so little information was available and so many "decisions" were being reported and denied, the entire organization took on some of the character of *Alice in*

Wonderland. Decisions announced one day were counter-manded the next. Authoritative statements flatly rejecting the possibility of option A were no sooner stated or promulgated than option A was announced by someone else. At the beginning of a conversation, executives talked about the possibility of a certain action which, by the end of the same conversation, they utterly denied. The one thing that *was* clear was that another shoe was going to drop.

One of the characteristics of FPC, like most other large corporations, was a fairly diversified posture within its industry. It had tried to develop many new products, which varied widely in their market acceptance and profitability. Among the key decisions still to be made were those defining which of those businesses ought to be maintained, which closed, and which sold. But closing a business inevitably meant laying off the people associated with it, whether competent or not. For many people, that was a cruel joke. FPC, once again like most American corporations, had a policy of moving its exempt people fairly regularly from one area to another. Managers and other staff members currently in a business about to be closed might well be there for no reason except the good of the company and the promise and excitement held out at the time the new business was launched. But the number, scope, name, and shape of these potential decisions was not known, nor was the timing. There were others who felt that even this would not be the end: that still more shoes would be dropped even after these relatively short-term decisions, because of potentially permanent and long-term changes in the industry.

The atmosphere, of course, reflected these feelings very directly. One manager, who had taken a two-week vacation at the time people were being put on probation, was astonished at the change. Things, he said, had been bad when he left, but they seemed much worse after he got back. Rumors were rife, jokes were bitter or sardonic, and the most visible sign of activity was the endless scheduling and rescheduling of people as they rushed from one meeting to another, meetings at which, because too little information was available, plans were being made that were unlikely to be carried out because of subsequent decisions that would render them obsolete or inappropriate. Nor was there any great prospect of getting the kind of information that *would* enable serious planning.

Under the circumstances, the fact that the company was continuing to do business was in part a tribute to the ability of its managerial staff, and in part a reflection of the extent to which modern corporations are designed to operate even in the absence of direction. The enormous momentum built up over time could not be stopped suddenly any more than it could suddenly change direction. That, for the time being, was what was supporting Farm Product's ongoing effort.

This time, however, there was a difference. There were comments from top management. No one *is* promising to make sure this never happens again.

21 / W. T. Grant's Last Days —as Seen from Store 1192

Rush Loving, Jr.

AT 9:30 in the morning, February 10 [1976], lawyers for the creditors' committee of W. T. Grant Co. walked into a federal courtroom in New York with a surprising proposal. For months, Grant's had been trying to reorganize under the protection of a bankruptcy court, and the once vast retail chain had shrunk from 1,100 stores to 359, and from 75,000 employees to 30,000. With no warning, the creditors' lawyers declared that the seventy-year-old business should be liquidated at once.

Two days later Federal Bankruptcy Judge John J. Galgay granted the committee's request, and the company's stores were padlocked to await a closeout sale. It was the final chapter in the largest bankruptcy proceeding in the history of retailing—the company's debt totaled more than $800 million.

Reprinted from the April 1976 issue of Fortune Magazine by special permission; © 1976 Time Inc. Pp. 109–14.

FIGHTING FOR THEIR LIVELIHOOD

The liquidation of a multimillion-dollar enterprise is a poignant business drama even as it is played out where the public most often views it—at the level of the lawyers, the accountants, and the creditors' committees. But Grant's decline and fall takes on a different, more human perspective when it is perceived at store-level, so to speak, where men and women were fighting for their livelihood as well as the survival of the organization. The view from Store 1192, Grant's branch in Westerly, Rhode Island, also tells a good deal about what went wrong with the company and why it couldn't keep itself off the rocks.

The manager of Store 1192 was Albert J. Duclos (pronounced "du-close"), forty-one, a man whose hazel eyes sparkled with an enthusiasm that seemed almost unquenchable. He is methodical and, surprisingly for one so immersed in detail, articulate as well. His thoughts roll out decisively in a voice edged with the clipped, harsh accents of southeastern Massachusetts. His decisiveness helped to dispense confidence, and some small measure of comfort, among the eighty employees of Store 1192 during Grant's last uncertain hours.

Duclos spent nineteen years with Grant's, his entire working career, and over the past ten years he managed six Grant's stores in various New England towns. In that decade his annual income multiplied from $8,000 to $37,000, largely because of bonuses. He was so successful a manager that he led his district in sales and profits for six years.

Duclos took over the Westerly store in 1971. A seacoast town on the Connecticut border, Westerly is a marketing center for 140,000 families. Many shoppers come from across the state line, where the sales tax is a penny higher, and during the summer extra thousands from New York and central New England fill the shingled cottages that line the nearby beaches. Most of these people shop at the Franklin Plaza Shopping Center, a strip of sixteen stores just outside town. The largest of the stores was Grant's.

The year-round residents, many of whom work at the submarine yards of General Dynamics in Groton, Connecticut, shopped in Store 1192 for such staples as work clothes, cosmetics, and housewares. The vacationers, who knew the Grant's name from back home, came for fishing tackle, toothpaste, and similar traveling needs. And both groups patronized the Bradford Room, the store's restaurant. One of the most popular eating establishments in Westerly, the Bradford Room earned thirty cents on the dollar, making it the most profitable department in the store.

During his years in Westerly, Duclos played to this market well. Within two years after his arrival he had increased his store's sales by 19 percent, to more than $2.5 million, while doubling profits to $245,000. This 10 percent return on sales was about twice the average for all America's retailers. Under Duclos, 1192 became Grant's twenty-third most profitable store, and continued to make a little money even after the company had fallen into the red.

Every morning Duclos made the hour-long drive to Westerly from his home in Attleboro, Massachusetts. The commute was inconvenient, but not unusually long for that part of New England, and Duclos and his wife, Val, preferred Attleboro to Westerly as a place to bring up their two daughters. The store was open from 10:00 A.M. until 9:00 P.M., and Duclos was always there an hour or more before opening time. He rarely left before 6:30 or 7:00 P.M.

At the store Duclos was used to feeling like the captain of a ship—in charge of just about everything that went on. With the aid of his merchandise manager and two assistant managers, he oversaw all orders for new stock and plotted the mix of goods that Grant's offered Westerly's shoppers. He could raise or lower prices at will to beat the competition, and he had the power to concoct special promotions, even drawing up his own newspaper and radio ads. Once his bosses in New York City tried to keep him from stocking swimming pools, on the ground that pools wouldn't sell in a seaside community. Duclos went ahead anyway and ordered $5,000 worth, selling out in a week. Duclos had been in love with merchandising since the age of eleven, when he set up a Kool-Aid stand outside the neighborhood grocery in Fall River.

Duclos felt his first qualms about Grant's policies in the early 1970's. New York headquarters had ordered the stores to begin selling furniture and large appliances. To bolster those sales, the company had entered the hazardous credit-card business full steam ahead. Clerks were offered $1 bounties for each customer they signed up for a card, and Duclos was ordered to push the credit-card campaign above everything else. The pressure grew so intense that at one point his district credit manager called hourly asking how many accounts he had opened. "We hated the goddam things," says Duclos.

On New York's insistence, only cursory credit checks were conducted. When one manager insisted on making thorough inquiries, New York threatened to fire him. Meanwhile the new card holders were using their new credit to haul away hundreds of dollars worth of washing machines and beds. Duclos and virtually every other manager warned that the cards were brewing trouble, but New York didn't listen. By last year Grant's credit-card receivables totaled $500 million, and half of that was deemed uncollectible.

The day of reckoning finally came early last year when the company plunged into the red—$177 million for fiscal 1975. Despite the immensity of the loss, Duclos's hope still ran high; he'd heard rumors that the directors were already searching for a new president who could turn the company around. And, sure enough, one morning last April, Duclos's district manager called to say that the directors had found their man. His name was Robert H. Anderson; he was a merchandising vice president from Sears.

Through the summer Duclos thought Anderson really might be able to do the job. The new boss sent order after order from New York undoing disastrous policies of the old regime. The best news Duclos got was a bulletin from headquarters telling him to stop issuing credit cards; Anderson had ordered the entire operation to be phased out. At a meeting of managers came more good news: Duclos was ordered to close out appliances and furniture. These higher-priced stocks turned over too slowly and did not generate enough sales per square foot of floor space. His district manager told Duclos to rearrange the store so that the first thing customers saw when they entered was women's fashions. Someone in New York had finally discovered that 80 percent of Grant's customers were women.

Despite these favorable signs, Duclos kept hearing rumors that Grant's might go bankrupt. After his district manager informed him that there would be no semiannual bonus coming up in September, Duclos canceled plans for his family's annual vacation trip. He spent the three-week holiday in July on a ladder painting the house, because now he also could not afford to hire anyone for the job.

One morning several months later, a customer walked into the Westerly store and told a clerk that she had just heard on the radio that Grant's had gone bankrupt. The report spread rapidly across the sales floor. In the office Duclos and his immediate subordinates clustered around a portable radio on a secretary's desk as the 10:30 news came on. The news about Grant's was all they had feared—the company had indeed plunged into bankruptcy.

There had been no warning from New York, no word at all. Everyone stood there in stunned silence. Finally Duclos spoke up, trying to reassure his people. "This could be the best thing for this company that could happen to us," he said. He tried to explain that bankruptcy would permit them to get out of some bad contracts. "This may be the best way to save the company."

But for all his reassurances, the bankruptcy hit Duclos with a jolt. In Grant's better days he had invested more than $20,000 in company stock, drawing on most of his savings and borrowing from a bank to finance his purchases. Now his holdings were virtually worthless, and he still owed the bank $5,000.

Several days after the bankruptcy five clerks came to his office and announced that each of them would raise $10,000 and buy the store if he would run it for them. Duclos was moved, but he told them the idea would not work—they would need more backing than they could get. But Duclos was impressed by their morale.

Meanwhile, his own morale was being severely shaken. Hundreds of his fellow managers, many of them respected friends, were laid off as New York headquarters closed down their stores. Val Duclos, an outgoing and equally outspoken woman in her late thirties, kept telling him to quit, that the company was doomed. But Duclos was determined to stick it out.

Into the winter word kept coming down that Anderson was changing the chain's merchandise mix, orienting it more to a narrow line of items that sold the fastest. In November, just as Grant's biggest selling season got under way, Duclos was told to begin a series of clearance sales. He fretted about the timing. November and December are the months that can determine a chain's year-end profit, and when managers are ordered to slash prices at such times, profits can only suffer. The creditors' committee was watching the turnaround from the sidelines. Duclos feared that if Anderson misjudged the committee's mood, climbing losses might impel the creditors to push for liquidation.

A DAY IN "GRANT'S TOMB"

In mid-January Duclos and his fellow managers were summoned to New York for a special briefing. It was the only time he had ever been inside "Grant's Tomb," which is what employees called the fifty-three-story headquarters building on Times Square that had been completed only five years before. They assembled in a third-floor auditorium, one wall of which sported a banner proclaiming: "Best of the Stores . . . Best of the Items!" Remembering the many old friends who were not there because their stores had been closed, Duclos resented the insensitivity of the slogan.

In a marathon of speeches and slide shows, Anderson and his key executives outlined a bold new plan for creating a "New Grant's." First off, they said, all stores would be "fashionized," a term Anderson had coined; it meant emphasizing women's fashions. And, since they were discontinuing slow-selling items, the managers would have to put their stores through "compaction," another Anderson coinage meaning to squeeze the sales area into a smaller space. They must also "colorize" their stores, i.e., paint counters and walls a selection of bright colors, in shades and types of paint decreed by New York.

Anderson warned his managers that every store must be spotless. "If the windows are washed at nine o'clock, and it rains at ten, they'll be washed again at eleven," he snapped. "That's the way we're going to run our stores." Anderson said the New Grant's would be launched on February 1, the beginning of their new fiscal year. They would open with a "supersale," featuring drastic markdowns of such items as boots, toasters, and electric saws.

On the evening train back to Providence, Duclos pondered the day's events. He was elated by a promise that, come spring, he and the other managers would get those canceled bonuses after all. Of far more importance to company and career, he felt a sense of excitement about the New Grant's. Here at last was something definite and creative, a plan a real merchant could get enthusiastic about.

Yet, there were things that troubled Duclos. More than once during that day at Grant's Tomb, they had been told to charge all the costs of the transformation to the current fiscal year. Duclos worried that this would push the company's year-end losses higher than the creditors might stand for. On a more personal level, he and the other managers were rankled by the New York office's increasingly patronizing attitude, signalized by the excruciating detail of its edicts for paint hues and merchandise mixes. "We did something wrong, but we're not all stupid," Duclos had grumbled during a coffee break. As he and the other managers had reminded one another, it had not been they who had bankrupted Grant's, but the executives who sat in New York.

Within days, Duclos was well on his way toward creating a new store. His clerks and stockboys were painting the counters, and Duclos had "compacted" the sales floor from 60,000 square feet to 41,000. Over on one side, two dozen shoppers picked over the clearance sale, where everything not on New York's checklist of approved merchandise had been stacked and marked down 75 percent. The checklist had not included such popular items as paper towels and barbecue grills, meaning that Duclos had to put them in the sale. Then, it turned out that New York, incredibly, had sent out an incomplete list. So Duclos had to reorder paper towels to replace those that he had sold at a loss.

The carpenters arrived to rebuild some of the walls. A floor man showed up and began replacing cracked tiles. Duclos juggled his maintenance budget and hired a cleaning contractor to strip old wax and polish the floor. "I can feel it all coming together." he said happily.

But then the district manager, Paul Carlson, a jovial but nervous little man, called with the news that Anderson had decided to make an inspection tour of the area on February 4, just after the scheduled opening of the New Grant's. And the Westerly store would be his first stop. Duclos was unshaken. But Carlson was jittery; he began pushing Duclos hard to create a perfect store.

Carlson had good reason to worry, because on a previous visit to New England Anderson had been displeased with the stores he had seen and had abruptly dismissed Carlson's predecessor. "Come on now, Paul, calm down," Duclos joked. "If they fire me, they fire you first. It'll take them so long to get to me it'll be like having two weeks' notice."

Word of the president's visit spread through the store, and everyone seemed to work more feverishly. While they toiled, a clerk talked about Anderson's previous trip to Rhode Island. "Mr. Duclos and the others stood at the door waiting," she recalled. "Someone was on the telephone calling that he was forty minutes away, then thirty minutes away, but he never came."

By early afternoon five regional and district merchandising and display men had arrived; they had been dispatched urgently from Massachusetts. The regional office near Boston seemed to have been swallowed up by panic, but Duclos was philosophical: presidential inspections create panic in every corporation.

Duclos showed his visitors how low he was on stock and displays. His own people had called New York and the warehouses, pushing for shipments, only to be rebuffed. One display man looked around the fashions department and turned to Duclos in surprise: "You don't have any mannequins at all?" "Just toss-ups," said Duclos—meaning simple cardboard figures. The display man hurried off to call New York and round up some mannequins. All afternoon the store's two phone lines were tied up, as the five men made call after call, using their authority—and the imminence of Anderson's visit—to get quick deliveries of displays and goods.

While Duclos wandered about the sales floor checking on the progress of the stockboys and clerks, one of the regional men informed him that the bright yellow paint on the infant's-wear counters was the wrong shade. Together they called the display manager in New York, who confirmed that he had just changed the specifications. "A bulletin is in the mail to you," he said cheerily. Duclos hung up, disgusted. Now they had to paint the department all over again.

Soon the two regional men were back; one of them announced that his colleague did not like the layout of the candy counters. "It's not according to the plan from New York," he explained. The Westerly store had never received the candy-department plan.

It became obvious that what really troubled the regional men was the layout of the entire store. They thought it should have the broad aisles and affluent look of a department store. Duclos was happy to hear this, because he and his merchandise manager had proposed just that sort of layout when they had gone through their "compaction." The regional office had turned them down.

Duclos and his visitors tried out new counter arrangements, shifting one department and then another, but after each move a neighboring area would cry out for a change of its own. Into the evening a half dozen stockboys and the older men sweated and puffed and pushed and pulled counter after counter. Five of the stockboys were teenagers who had been off from school that day because of snow. Duclos had hired them part-time, and at nine o'clock they put on their jackets to leave.

"Al! You're letting the boys go?" called a display man.

"They have school tomorrow."

"Get God to make it snow! Hasn't He ever heard of Bob Anderson?"

Wherever possible, during the coming days, Duclos used Anderson's visit to help get his store remade. When the tape of background music began to drag, he called the Boston company that leased the equipment and asked for a new player. The man in Boston said it would take ten days. "My president is visiting next week," replied Duclos, "and if he hears that thing dragging he'll probably order your machines pulled out of all Grant's stores." The new machine arrived in two days.

Duclos worked ceaselessly, arriving at 8:00 A.M., leaving at 10:00 P.M. for the hour-long drive home. Sometimes he jotted down reminders for the next day on folded pieces of note paper while steering his Vega down Interstate 95 with his knees. After he got home he would sit for an hour or more making more notes and sipping a Seven and Seven (Seagram's 7 with 7-Up).

The thing that plagued him increasingly was the lack of merchandise. He even rented a truck and dispatched an assistant to a Grant's warehouse in Windsor Locks, Connecticut, to bring back a special load of auto accessories. Despite this effort at self-help, Duclos found himself trying to serve his customers from stockroom and shelves that remained too bare. The warehouses seemed unable to distribute fast enough; the flow of goods to all stores was so slow that Carlson called to say that New York had ordered the supersale delayed. Now the New Grant's would open on the very day of Anderson's visit.

As the big day loomed, the truckloads of merchandise began arriving at last, and the shelves and racks were filling with goods. But then Carlson called again: Anderson was not coming. He could not leave New York—something about a meeting with the creditors.

The New Grant's blossomed forth on schedule. Shoppers poured in. Some women asked if this were a new store; others commented on the fresh colors. Sales for the day reflected the customers' positive attitude: volume was up 60 percent from a normal Wednesday.

Sales were still running high in the next week. Monday two vice presidents visited and offered nothing but praise. But soon after he arrived at the store on Tuesday morning, Duclos received a severe jolt. The manager of another New England store telephoned to say that he had just called a New York buyer about some needed goods, and the buyer had told him that the creditors were going to court to ask that Grant's be liquidated. Duclos called his wife, who had planned a shopping trip that day. "Don't spend any money," he warned.

He was on the phone the rest of the day seeking information. A manager in Warren, Rhode Island, told him that the creditors had pulled the plug after discovering that the year's losses were running higher than they had been led to expect. Duclos had feared just that reaction. Another manager passed the word that the bonus was now dead.

Like the other managers, Duclos was growing increasingly bitter with each call, especially when he remembered that the same bankers who were now closing the company had guaranteed Anderson's salary for five years, to the tune altogether of $1,050,000. Through the entire day there was never any word from New York. "I figure we'll get notified when the guy is putting the lock on the door," Duclos grumbled.

Duclos kept hoping that the report of liquidation was merely another rumor. But late that afternoon a friend called to report that New York had put out a press release confirming everything. "What can I say?" Duclos said, his voice hollow. "It was a great company." He was close to tears.

But only as Duclos drove home that night did he finally realize what this all really meant: he had to find another job. "This is it, boy," he said to himself. "You'd better get moving." What kind of work should he seek? Did he want to stay in retailing and put up with the long hours? Duclos thought of the past two weeks: "I loved it," he thought. "That's the kind of thing I want to do."

That night the emotions and the shock kept thundering over him. He drank five Seven and Sevens, sitting in the family room. When he went to bed he could not sleep; he just lay there watching a Frankenstein movie on TV.

Wednesday morning Duclos performed the most heartrending task of his entire career. Although he still had heard nothing from New York, he broke the news to his clerks, calling them into a conference room that the carpenters had just finished paneling. "It's nothing official," he said. "I have nothing official, but it looks like the Grant Co. will go out of business." Several women wept.

Thursday afternoon the judge signed the order to liquidate. All stores were to be locked that night. Duclos received his instructions about 6:30. It was the first direct word he'd had from New York in all those three days.

FRIDAY THE THIRTEENTH

The next morning Duclos was sitting with his merchandise manager in the restaurant silently sipping coffee and staring out the window at the jammed parking lot. The other stores at Franklin Plaza were beginning their Washington's birthday sales. It was Friday the thirteenth. While they sat there one of the district display men came in.

"Sit down, and have a cup of coffee," Duclos said dejectedly. "It may be your last cup of coffee at Grant's."

"We were really up after Monday," said the merchandise manager.

"Yeah, we were 400 ahead in sales," said Duclos.

"Then someone zapped us."

Duclos looked out the window again. "Look at all those cars out there," he said wistfully.

After awhile they got up and went back to the sales floor. Most of the lights were out, and they wandered among the counters, thinking about how beautiful it looked and how the customers at the liquidation sale would ravage it. The floor seemed to gleam brighter than ever. All the merchandise sat in neat rows. The store was immaculate. "Now the animals will come," Duclos blurted out angrily.

"They'll tear the place up," said the display man, Bob DeBroisse. "You'll never recognize it by the first night."

The tape of background music was still running, and as they passed a counter of coffee makers and toasters that were about to be marked down for the liquidation, it blared gaily into "The Best Things in Life Are Free."

They walked on, and the display man began worrying aloud about being out of work. Duclos suddenly regained some of his old bounce and tried to cheer him up.

"You've known hard times before, Bob."

"Yeah, but I never had a big house to unload fast."

"They're not going to take your house." Duclos said, putting his hand on the man's shoulder. "The banks don't want your house."

But no sooner had the display man left than Duclos was somber again. Head down, thinking, he walked once more through the empty store with a friend who had come to commiserate with him. He walked very slowly in silence. Through the fashions, down the back row past the draperies, back up along the housewares and the toys, past the records and the jewelry. He stopped and leaned against a checkout stand and looked into the gloom of the unlighted store. He stayed there for some time thinking, remembering. Two customers came to the door, read the "Closed" sign and walked off to Fishers Big Wheel, the discount store down the way.

"I really think it would have worked," he spoke up at last. "But Anderson went about it the wrong way. He went too fast. You don't give away a quarter of a billion in merchandise in the last quarter of the year. If we'd come up with a better profit picture for last year I think the creditors would have gone along.

"This has always been a very tight company," Duclos went on, his voice rising, the words now tumbling out. "His idea of cleanliness has always been in my book, but . . . goddamit! . . .

you don't do it in a year when you're not making money. I don't mean leaving crud on the floor, but . . . goddam! . . . you don't paint the whole goddam store in a bad year! He said: 'Get it all done; get all the expenses in this year and get it clear before 1976.'" Duclos paused. His tired, black-rimmed eyes looked over the store once more, and he said bitterly: "There wasn't any 1976."

22 / Termination at Baker Plant

Alfred Slote

FROM THE RECOLLECTIONS OF FRANK R. ROBERTSON

3/28/63

Thursday. The big item today was a call from Merritt [Harley, Plant Manager, Baker Plant]. Called me into his office to say he just got a call from home office [in Pittsburgh] and we're both to go [there] tomorrow. . . .

"Sit down," Tom Frohman [VP-Manufacturing] said, and we all sat down around the round table by the bookcase. I put my briefcase on the table and Tom said, "You won't need that, Frank. Not yet anyway. A decision was made less than twenty-four hours ago about the Baker plant."

My heart skipped a beat. I knew what was coming.

"You all know about the 1958 product alignment study and we all know how obsolete the plant was twenty years ago. Well, a decision's finally been made to close the plant. We're going to build a new, completely automated plant. . . .

For some reason Tom kept looking at me. His voice was soft. "Our timetable is tentative at the moment, but the task force to engineer the new plant is being set up. It's too early to set target dates right now. Frank, are you with me?"

"Yes," I said.

"I've got something I know you'll be interested in. We want you to take over the plant as of Monday, April first."

I stared at him. After thirty-seven years at Baker, I was finally being offered the top job.

I don't know how long the silence lasted. Frohman was waiting for me to say something and my first instinct was to say, *No, I don't want it; you want to bury it. I won't do your dirty job for you. Merritt was good enough to bleed it. Get someone else to bury it.*

But I didn't say anything. I just sat there. And Tom went right on. Harley was being transferred back to General Office as a process engineer. Everyone agreed that I was the only man who could do it. He realized he was putting me on quite a spot. No one knew exactly how long it would take to finish the new plant. It would have to be no later than December 31, 1965, when the union contract at Detroit ran out. That was about two and one-half years from now. In these two and one-half years I had to keep Baker going, lay off people, terminate and bury, and show a profit too. I knew the Baker people, he was saying. There were men there I'd started work with thirty-seven years ago. They trusted me.

"I know I'm putting you on quite a spot, Frank," Tom repeated.

I nodded. "It's a spot," I said.

"Do you want to think about it? Take a moment and think about it?"

Take a moment? I didn't even think I needed that. I believed in growth, the future. I was no undertaker. That plant was everything to me. The men in it were everything to me. I'd seen plants close before, even within our own company. I'd seen things fall apart, seen the chaos. As I thought about that—I knew suddenly I'd accept the job. Someone was going to have to do it; and it ought to be someone who loved the plant and the men. You don't want to be buried by people who don't know you. In the single moment that I rejected the assignment, I accepted it.

I heard myself saying: "It's a poor thing, Tom, but if you feel I can do it, I'll consider it. But I'd like to ask a few questions."

Tom said: "I'd be surprised if you didn't have any questions."

"This first question might surprise you even more. Do you

want, does the company want to keep the original finish business? It's just that simple."

Tom said: "Oh, my God, yes. Everybody down here wants that original finish business."

And I said: "Well, would you want to fight for it? Work for it? We're on our way out right now as a major supplier. We've gone way down from No. 1 in Chrysler ratings and way down in Ford ratings till we're almost out of sight. Will you help me get those ratings up?"

"Yes," Tom said, "I'll help you get the ratings up." Then I knew I'd get the $140,000 for the ball mills and the grinding equipment.

But what madness. To accept a job to terminate a plant, and. then fight to get more money to make the plant productive again before it dies. . . .

I got my briefcase out and we went over plant improvements. Tom agreed to them all. Also a new salary program, freedom to move certain people. It was good to get lost in details. I almost forgot that I was hired to terminate the plant. About 3 P.M. the phone rang. It was Wysse Allen, Tom's boss, the vice-president in charge of all operations of the coatings and resin division. He wanted to see me. . . .

When I got into his office he motioned me to a chair without saying anything and just looked at me for a few minutes. Then said: "Robbie, you don't know how happy I am you've taken it on. This is the dirtiest, toughest job I ever handed a man. I know you're the only man who can do it. And I can understand your emotions. All I can say is thanks. And tell you that any facility, anything you need out of General Office is yours."

I didn't say anything.

"Robbie," he said, "you're going to walk alone."

He swiveled around and looked out the window. "This is one of the biggest moves we've ever made. There are dangers in it. It could be a fiasco, and we could pay for it with our stockholders. But Baker is and always has been a high cost plant. If we're going to survive in the automotive paint business we've got to start somewhere."

He looked at me.

I didn't say anything. I was thinking, *You bastard, you could have started ten years ago by putting some money in as well as taking it out. You let it get cancer and now you're curing it by killing it.*

"How do you feel, Robbie?" he asked.

I shrugged. "Scared as hell," I said, though at that moment there was a kind of peace inside me. He was a big man, Allen, and I was doing something for him and the company that no one else could do. I was a little proud even, God help me.

"Lots of things are going to happen, Robbie. Lots of things we haven't thought of. We don't know what we're getting into. A lot of it will have to be played by ear. But I'm here to help you. Whatever you need, just pick up the phone or come down to see me." . . .

IT WAS GOOD BUSINESS TO BE DECENT

Baker in the Fall and Winter of 1964

Between the time of the first [plant] announcement of the closing, in November, 1963, and . . . August, 1964, more than sixty new people had been hired to replace those (mostly transients) who had quit. After . . . [August] those who quit were not replaced. In addition some jobs concerned only with the production of original finish were terminated. . . . Robertson urged men to leave at this time, urged them to use their vacation time to try out new jobs, but the rebuilding of the boiler house had convinced many that the company had changed its mind about closing the plant. Still others believed it would close but they were going to "stick it out to the very end, going out like Frank Robertson said, with our heads up."

One group of workers Frank Robertson did not seek to relocate was the maintenance crews. They would be needed to keep the plant going to the very end and then to close her down properly. Robertson worked hard on keeping the morale of the maintenance boys high.

During this period Robertson wore two hats: that of factory manager concerned with production, and that of industrial relations manager concerned with morale, for he neither liked nor trusted his industrial relations manager, Lee Jones, popularly known among the men as "The Commander." Jones, tactless, brusque, egocentric, had antagonized almost every employee in the plant—hourly and salaried alike. Robertson had long felt that a stupid move on Jones's part could wreck the strange but very real harmony that existed in the dying plant.

Towards the end of December, Jones made his stupid move.
It concerned a man named Hicks, . . . a man who had reached
the point where they were terminating him. Hicks had signed a
severance pay application on which his length of time at Baker
was listed. There was an error, an error the company made.
Hicks had been out ill for four months and they should have
counted him as him being on the payroll during this time. It affected Hicks's severance pay somehow, though not much; what
it did make a difference on was the sickness and accident pay
he'd receive and on any unemployment compensation he was
entitled to receive after the plant closed. The error wasn't discovered until after the statement from the sickness and accident people arrived. Then it was realized that Hicks's record
had been dated wrongly on the severance pay form.

"The point was," says Robertson, "that the man had signed
his severance pay form, accepting the amount as binding. And
Lee Jones figured he could stick by the original dates because
the man had signed it, and thereby he could save the company
a few hundred dollars in sickness and accident pay.

"It was Paul Tilyard, our safety engineer who had originally
pointed out the error to Lee and Lee refused to change it. Paul
came into my office one day—and mind you, Paul's a quiet one,
not a squawker; he doesn't see trouble where there is none, but
he knows a whole lot. He's an old-timer and what you'd call a
kind of father-confessor to the whole plant. He came to see me
and said: 'Frank, we're going to get a grievance on the Hicks
termination and I want you to know, Frank, in my opinion
they're right, not us.' "

"Well," I said, "I don't want any grievances, not at this stage
of things. We're doing well, everything's going smoothly. We've
all got things to do besides mess with grievances. If we're wrong
let's correct it. Why don't you talk to Lee Jones about it?"

Paul looks at me kind of funny but doesn't say a thing and I
get busy on other things. A few days go by and Lee Jones pops
into my office. "Frank," he says, "we got a grievance on this
Hicks business." And he started telling me the whole story.

"Look, Lee," I say, "are we right or wrong?"

"In my opinion, Frank, we're right."

"Now wait a minute. What makes you think we're right? Go
get the records and we'll look at them together."

"Well, maybe technically they got a point."

"Look, Lee, let's give this man what he's got coming to him. Let's quit fooling with this. We're talking about two hundred bucks at the most."

"OK, Frank," he says and leaves.

I thought the whole thing was settled. You tell a man to do something and you assume he's going to do it. A few days later I'm crossing the yard and Ned Rockwell [chairman, union plant committee] falls in step with me. His face is twisted up in fury and I know then he's been looking for me.

"What's the matter, Ned?" I ask.

"Are you going to back up that son of a bitch?" he asks.

"Which son of a bitch are you speaking of?"

"Lee Jones. Holding out on that money to Fred Hicks."

"Oh, that's all settled."

"The hell it's all settled."

"It certainly is, Ned."

He stops and looks at me. "I got news for you, *Mister* Robertson. This is one thing we'll take to arbitration."

"You will like hell," I say, "because you don't have any case."

"Well, we'll see whether or not we got a case," he says angrily and stomps off. . . .

I thought about it all for a moment and then instead of going back to my office I went down to the industrial relations office. Lee was at his desk.

"Lee," I said to him, "did you or did you not do what I asked you to do on the Hicks case?"

"Frank," he says to me, "I swear to you they don't have a case. We'll beat them in any grievance. Hicks signed that form. I got his signature right here."

I could hardly believe my ears. I exploded. I called him every name I could think of and I told him to change that figure on Hicks' form right away and get on the phone to Rockwell and tell him it was changed. We're not going to cheat that guy out of a couple of hundred bucks no matter what form he signed. Sure we could fight it out in arbitration and maybe win. I know that. We could go to court and maybe win but what on God's earth would we be winning? Nothing. We'd have hurt a man unnecessarily. A human being was involved here. It would have been cruel, sticky, and if it was legal, it would also have been unfair. We're too big to be trying to feather our nest at one man's expense.

And you know what else going to arbitration would mean? It would mean breaking the harmony, breaking up the pattern these men had, men working to the very end, going out with their heads up, men who loved this plant in a way Lee Jones could never understand.

Here I was skating on thin ice trying to keep a plant going and terminate it at the same time, trying to meet moral obligations to a man and do business too, and this rotten son of a bitch was going to throw a monkey wrench into the works.

I called General Office and spoke to Howard Green [director, industrial relations] and told him Jones had to go. I wasn't going to put this plant to bed with Jones as my industrial relations manager. I wanted Tom Morgan back [Tom was the previous industrial relations manager.].

Howard didn't like Tom. He said Tom was too soft on the men and maybe he was right. But we were done negotiating, done bargaining; we were trying to stay in business and terminate, trying to transfer without losing a customer—we had to coddle the men now. It was good business to be decent.

Green understood. He called me back a few days later and said they found a spot in industrial relations for Jones in the Springdale plant. . . .

FRIDAYS WERE SAD DAYS

The Baker Plant, May–June, 1965

In February, General Office had informed [Robertson] that the York plant would be ready to open in July, and so he had adjusted the production schedules accordingly. In May, he began laying off some of the seniority men. "We'd let them know on Monday that Friday would be their last day," Robertson explain[ed]. "Some of them had a hard time believing it; others just nodded. Fridays became sad days around the plant. There would be a lot of handshaking with the man leaving, perhaps a drink or two at the bar across the street. Men worked right up till noon on their day to go home. Then I'd go over to their department and shake their hand and thank them for being so loyal. Some of them I'd get jobs for, others I'd written or telephoned recommendations, still others just weren't sure what they were going to do. There were tears from time to time. It was easiest on those men who could cry, I always thought."

Then, suddenly, in June, General Office dropped a bombshell. . . . Robertson [was] told . . . that the York plant was having unexpected problems and it was going to be delayed about five months. They wouldn't be able to open till December. Robertson just had to keep Baker going and producing another four or five months.

The news floored Robertson. To transfer operations, to keep producing so as not to lose a single customer (and, in one case, to take on a new and big customer), to keep men happy, help them find new jobs while making sure key people stayed on the old job, to terminate some and not others—and now not to know when it was going to end. It was an impossible mental and physical juggling act.

The situation at the Fitzwarren warehouse finally broke the logjam. More and more stock was being put into the rented warehouse on Fitzwarren until it was overflowing. Stealing was on an alarming increase at the warehouse. In February, Robertson signed a contract with Pinkertons to keep the warehouse under surveillance. But even as this was happening more and more stock was being placed in there. The situation had become intolerable.

Robertson made a phone call to General Office to tell them he was coming down there. The next morning he flew to Pittsburgh and met with Frohman and Wysse Allen in Allen's office.

"You've got to let me start this thing," he told them angrily. "It's going to be a marathon if I can get the help to keep it. I have one hundred and forty truckloads of stock of all colors and types that has got to get down to York. I can't keep it any longer. I will not be responsible for it. This has been horsed around and played with till I'm sick."

Frohman and Allen looked at him. What had happened was that no one had been prepared for the miracle Robertson had wrought. The high production, the high efficiency, and now proof of this—a warehouse filled to overflowing. They had been caught out in their miscalculation.

Frohman said: "Frank, the truth is you're making us all here at General Office look kind of funny."

"It's not me. It's my people," Robertson said bitterly. "They been making you look funny. And would you like to know why?"

"Shoot."

"You won't like it."

"Shoot anyway."

"You wrote us off. You let us alone. You let me take advantage of the psychological reactions of people. And it could have gone otherwise."

Wysse Allen spoke quietly. "You walked alone, Frank. You walked alone."

"I was used," Robertson snapped at him too.

They were silent. Then Tom Frohman said: "Frank, why don't you go down to York and get them moving on this stock matter? I think that's got to be the answer."

And so Robertson flew from Pittsburgh down to York, Ohio, where he could see that no progress had been made since he'd been down there a month or so before. He talked to the factory manager, a man named Donald Lockhart, and for a half hour Robertson listened to *his* complaints. Finally, he said: "Now look, Donald, I was down here a month ago and things are still setting in the same places. So I'm going to have to break our friendship. I've tried everything I know how to help down here. I've pleaded, I've begged, I've threatened. Nothing's been done. Not much, anyway. When I go back to Detroit I'm calling in trucks. And I'm concentrating my people. And we're going to start shipping it to you, at the rate of seven trucks a day."

"We can't take care of it," Lockhart said.

"Get on that phone and tell someone you can because I'm going to start shipping the minute I get back to Detroit."

"You can't do that."

"The hell I can't. Wysse Allen told me to close that plant and, Mister, I'm going to close it."

"We won't know what to do with it."

"Months ago I asked you to get some rented space down here."

"We don't have authorization for it."

"Damn it, whose responsibility is it?"

"I guess it's mine."

"Then get the authorization and start renting space because those trucks will be rolling the day I get back."

Lockhart got on the phone to Pittsburgh, got authorization.

Robertson returned to Detroit. The next day trucks started rolling out of the Fitzwarren warehouse. . . .

FROM THE RECOLLECTIONS OF FRANK R. ROBERTSON

July–August, 1965

Thursday. "A bird in the hand is worth two in the bush, Charley," I told Charley Hazzard this morning. Charley had been offered a job at United Paint and was wondering what he should do. Should he give up his severance pay to take it? With his fourteen years his severance pay would come to about $400. Not much compared to a good job now. But Charley, a steam fitter, wasn't sure. He wants that severance pay. That's *his* bird in the hand.

Making phone calls for two boys from the resin department. Both good workers being terminated tomorrow. They came in and asked me for letters. I'll give them letters but a phone call sometimes works better.

Finished the second call when Harold Peterson [sales manager] came in. A shipment of astro-blue paint for a Plymouth Valiant had been sent back from Atlanta. It hadn't matched. He'd gone over to the lab with it to ask them to do a test, but no one was there.

"Well, Harold," I said, "they're probably out on a coffee break. Try them again in ten minutes."

During those ten minutes Harold sat in my office cracking his knuckles and telling me that this was what it was going to be like when the plant moved. No lab at all. One enormous coffee break. "That's foolish thinking, Harold," I said. "All you do is call York and your salesmen send the paint back to York. If anything it will be a lot easier to telephone York than to keep running over to Building 2."

Harold nodded, but I could tell he wasn't hearing a thing. He started talking about his boy.

I listened, but my mind was elsewhere. A note on my desk saying Johnny Johnson wanted to see me. I had an idea what it was about. Some of my maintenance boys I'd heard were beginning to get job offers. This was one group of people we could not afford to lose until we shut the whole plant down. I wanted to keep this bunch together no matter how little work there was for them at times. These were my own boys. The elite of the plant. They'd never have trouble getting new jobs. I'd raised them myself. They could repair every machine in the plant as well as run it. I was determined not to let them bust up until it was all over. Each week I had to send General Office lists of men to be terminated and it was Ike Kraeger [general manager, production] who noticed that not one maintenance person was being laid off. He telephoned me about it and wanted to know if it was my intention to keep the maintenance boys together till the end.

"That's right," I told him.

Ike, a goddamn jug head if there ever was one, wanted to know what in hell I was doing that for. Did I need *all* of them?

"Yup," I said trying to restrain my temper.

"What for?"

I said to Kraeger. "Did you ever put a plant to bed? Did you ever handle people? The answer to that is no. If you're not perfectly happy—and I've told you this twice before—you get yourself a new boy and get him here tonight."

"Now, now, Robbie," he started.

"Then lay off me, damn it," I said, and slammed the phone down on him and all of General Office.

Harold Peterson said he was going to give the lab a call. I picked up the phone and called the lab. The men were back. "Harold." I said, "why don't you send someone over with the paint and you go home and take a nap? I know how hard you've been driving yourself lately, and the sales charts show it."

Harold shook his head. His old energy was flowing back in him. It was incredible what a few supporting words could do for him. "I don't need a nap, Robbie. I'll straighten this thing out: I've got to fly down to Nashville tomorrow. I'm firing our man down there, and I've got a red-hot salesman from Technico going to take his place. This closing has thrown things out of whack; we've had more complaints from distributors than ever before but I'm going to rattle the dead wood hard."

We hadn't had any more complaints than before. It was just that Harold was magnifying them more during the closing. It was him the closing was hard on, not the Nashville salesman. I suppose I should be more patient with him. He is a magnificent sales manager when all is said and done. He drives himself hard, and if I could only take away his worries about the closing, a closing that shouldn't really affect his job anyway. . . . Perhaps I should try not to let my mind wander while he rattles on. But you can pay so much attention to one man and then another needs your time. . . .

Friday. Handshakes with twelve employees, but the big event of the day took place at 4 P.M. at the main gate when, believe it or not, Austin Wagle who works in the grinding department and has twenty-two years seniority tried to walk out of the plant carrying a ladder. The guard called me and John Franklin the super of the grinding department, and John and the guard brought Wagle and the ladder over to my office. It was a five-foot aluminum step ladder. I couldn't believe it. . . .

"Austin?" I asked Wagle gently, "just what did you think you were doing with that ladder?"

"I don't know, Mr. Robertson. I honestly don't know."

"Did you know you were carrying it out the main gate?"

"I don't know," he repeated. "I don't know." . . .

"There isn't a ladder in the world worth all the severance pay and pension money you can lose." He nodded, looking down at his knees. "We can fire you for just cause, you know that?"

"Yes, sir."

"But I'm going to give you a break. We're going to pretend it was an honest mistake on your part. You thought you were taking the ladder over to Building 1 and got mixed up and walked out the gate."

That did it. He burst into tears. . . .

In the wake of the Wagle incident, I've done a lot of thinking about stealing. More and more of it is going on. Mueller tells me he saw two colored boys hoisting paint over the fence. An inventory from the warehouse shows that a lot of stuff is missing there. We've already caught two men stealing paint there and fired them both. Yet, I didn't fire Wagle. Why not? Because he'd been a good worker. Because it was a kind of temporary insanity, a striking back at General Office. People are just not themselves these days.

Friday. Stan Powaluk came in to say goodbye to me. I wrote him a job recommendation and asked him what his plans were. He said he had none but was thinking of maybe going into a handyman business. Helping old ladies, general house maintenance and window cleaning. I asked him if he needed tools. He said sure, so I wrote a note to Johnny Johnson over at maintenance to give Stan some secondhand tools, hammers, a saw if we had an old one, any old wrenches, squeejees, sponges. After I did this I realized this was one way I could cut down the stealing. Give the stuff away. There are hundreds of items York wouldn't be needing and it would cost the company hundreds of dollars to auction them off when the time came to sell the machinery—why not give the old stuff away now?

Tuesday. Yesterday I gave three old Stilson wrenches to an old-timer from shipping and receiving and Tom Morgan reported to me today that he stole a fourth before he checked out for good. Maybe it's not the things they want but some kind of revenge. Maybe it's simply that some people would rather steal things than ask for them. I'm still telling them to ask me for things.

Thursday. We've got a Pinkerton guard on full time at the warehouse. Starting today.

Monday. I've been averaging two hours a day writing, telephoning, and sometimes going on visits to help people get jobs. Tom Morgan's been working too. He's not so keen on making trips to other plants, but I've told him it's part of his job. . . .

Thursday. How lost you get in details. How much you thrive on problems. And when the biggest problem of all is staring you in the face, you don't even see it. Maybe because you know all along there isn't anything you can do about it.

Twice last week Harold Peterson asked me to have lunch with him and both times I couldn't make it. Thank God, I somehow had the sense to eat with him yesterday and today. Yesterday we talked over some of the methods of handling distribution from York and I had Harold pretty well convinced that basically things wouldn't change without the lab and the plant production in the same city with him. Today, he was in my office again and said he wanted to buy me lunch and I said all right, and we went over to the Terrace Lounge on Greenfield, a pleasant place. I bought Harold a scotch and soda and I had a bourbon old-fashioned. I was pleased to note that Harold was not acting jumpy or nervous. Perhaps that should have warned me. He complimented me on how well I was doing that impossible job of mine.

"That's to your credit, Harold, not mine," I said sincerely.

But Harold told me that this plant wouldn't be closing if they'd made me plant manager five or ten years ago. And he knew how hard it must have been for me to have incompetent men, one after the other, put in over my head. People who had no real feeling for Baker, for the men, for the product. He was very flattering. I had never really heard him talk this way. He usually just talked about himself and his problems. But he seemed to have reached a kind of serenity and I enjoyed listening to him. Then he quietly apologized for his behavior the past year or so. "I know I've been a pest to you, Frank, all these months."

"That's not so, Harold."

"Yes," he said, and smiled. "I know how much I've hung myself around your neck. But no more. Everything's going to be all right. I was bothered that the factory was leaving us, but I can see the sense of it now."

And on he went, assuring me that everything was going to be all right. And as he talked his nervousness really seemed gone. I actually believed him. He told me Jim Sweeney, his assistant was doing a fine job, and that things were never better in distributor sales. This afternoon he was going to do a little more work and go home early.

I told him I thought that was a fine idea, and then the food came and when we finished eating we went back to work. Harold left, as he said he would, about 3 P.M.

At 5 P.M. Jim Sweeney, Harold's assistant, came into my office and shut the door. He had just got a call from Mrs. Peterson. Harold had gone home early and his wife had to go out to Hudson's in Northland and wanted him to come with her. Harold said no, he had some work to do. And then he kissed her which he rarely did, told her to drive carefully. She had her own little car. He waved her out of the driveway and she went off to Hudson's. When she came back, he was dead. In the garage. He was fifty-nine years old. Making over twenty-one thousand dollars a year. He wasn't going to have to relocate; nothing much would have changed for him except he'd have to telephone the plant in York rather than walk over to the plant across the yard. He had a history of psychiatric care, which no one but Tom Morgan and I knew about.

I called Tom and he came right up and I told him what happened, and I told him and Jim Sweeney that not a word about this was to get out. It was going to be a heart attack. Then Tom and I drove to the Peterson home. It was hard to believe that Harold and I had just had lunch a few hours ago. He had seemed so calm, so above the storm. I should have been warned. But I'm glad I at least had lunch with him. It would have been awful if I'd turned him down.

Right now I've got to consider Harold Peterson a casualty of this awful closing.

Friday. The news that Harold had a heart attack is all over the plant. Everyone is very quiet about it.

At noon I shook hands with ten men being terminated today. One of them wept. I told him it was only a matter of time before we all joined him and I wished him luck. . . .

FINAL DAYS

[The] last weeks . . . Robertson was less concerned with the hourly people than with his salaried personnel. "The hourly had the union looking after them," Robertson [said] "the salaried had no one but me. And this brings up one of the most degrading experiences of the closing for me. Because General Office was always responding to union pressures, they didn't have time for the salaried people. The [thirty-odd] salary people who were being terminated didn't know till way late in the game what their annuities or severance pay were going to be. It made them very uneasy, to say the least. I tried time after time to get answers from General Office and they gave me one excuse after another. The actuarial figures weren't ready, and so forth. I kept after them about this and finally in the last few weeks [before the closing on December 30, 1960] I got the answers. . . . Well, twice the company informed me that the figures they had given me and which I had passed on to two people were wrong—too much money was being given to them—and each time I had to go back and call these people in and tell them their amounts were to be reduced. It was humiliating and degrading. And it made all of the salaried people suspect me and suspect all the figures I'd given out. . . . Twice I had to call people back in. Now those people ought to hate me. They just all ought to hate me, don't you think? . . .

"And then there came a third case. They wrote me and told me a third mistake had been made and I was to call another person back in and tell him he was going to get less money than he thought. That was it. I called Wysse Allen in Pittsburgh and told him no more. I told him that unless he personally assured me that this was it, I was not going to go back to that third person. That all the [figures] were now in and that they were final.

"Allen apologized. He said he was wrong in approving those sets of figures and if it was any comfort to me, the man who drew them up was no longer with the company. But it didn't matter because it wasn't any comfort. I'll have a deep-seated resentment as long as I live for what they put me through. Those moments at the end when I had to go back and tell people they were going to get less money than I said they were, those moments were even worse than the lie I lived at the beginning of the closing when everyone was congratulating me on becoming plant manager and none of them knew that I'd been picked plant manager to bury our plant. It was a nightmare at the beginning and the end, but especially at the end." . . .

All that were left of the hourly on their last day—December 10, 1965—were maintenance people, the members of the union committee, and a few old-timers. At 11 A.M. Robertson walked over to the maintenance department to say goodbye to his favorites. "They *were* my favorites too," he said. "They knew every inch of the plant, every pipe, every electric line, every tunnel, every machine. They knew this plant as only men who build and repair things can know them."

They were waiting for him too. About fifteen of them—old-timers, each with more than twenty years' seniority, standing in a semi-circle, waiting to shake his hand. "Well, boys, this is it," he said. "There's no more work to do this afternoon. We're taking the afternoon off.". . .

He paused. Words came hard. "I want to thank you boys for your loyalty and hard work through the years and especially during this long and hard closing."

He'd got through it and everything would have been all right then if suddenly one of the maintenance boys, a tough little Italian who'd worked there for more than twenty-five years, hadn't suddenly burst into tears. Tears ran down his face.

"He grabbed my hand. 'Now, Tony,' I said, and I couldn't talk either. I patted his hand, shook hands with the others, and turned and walked out before I broke down too. I went over to the cafeteria. And there was Ned Rockwell and the members of his union committee sitting there drinking coffee. Some things never change, I thought, smiling.

" 'Well,' Ned says, 'there you are. We were wondering when the hell you were going to show up here.'

"I laughed. They laughed too. I told them I'd come to say goodbye and to tell them they could take the afternoon off.

" 'We know about that too,' Ned said. And he grinned. 'And we got an invitation for you too. We're all going across the street, us, the maintenance gang, whatever old-timers want to come along, and we're going to get good and drunk and cuss this rotten old place out, and we want you to come along and have a drink with us.'

"I stood there a second, I hadn't expected this, and I didn't know whether I could take it. But they were all there looking at me, men I'd hired, fought with, praised and punished.

" 'I'll be privileged to come along,' I said.

"So after lunch we went solemnly across the street, and they bought me a drink, a bourbon old-fashioned, and then I bought them all drinks and we fell to talking, to remembering things, sometimes how they were and more often how they weren't. Everyone told his own story, the funny things, the angry things, stories about guys who'd left fifteen to twenty years ago, and what happened to old so-and-so who had worked in S and R and used to pitch horseshoes behind the boiler room, incidents out of the past came tumbling out, fights, ball games. . . . old Christmas parties; old secretaries; rush orders from Chrysler that had kept them hopping week-end nights; the big snow-storm in 1952, and the time Ramsey and Paddleford backed a truck into forty drums and the drums went rolling every which way and Ramsey laughed and laughed; and the time the trucks got stuck in the yard during an ice storm and the drums started rolling off; Steve Toucek's fight with what's-his-name. . . . And on it went like that, stories that were partly true, maybe even mostly true. I knew then, watching the men drink and listening to each man tell his tale, that each of them had his own Baker, each had his own plant, and each had his own memories to last him the rest of his life. It had been a good place to work—for all of us.

"I stayed about an hour and then I got hold of the manager in the corner and told him to let them stay as long as they wanted and to put the bill on my name. Then I ducked out. No one saw me go."

REFERENCES

Balzer, Richard. 1967. *Clockwork: Life In and Outside an American Factory.* Garden City, New York: Doubleday.

Barnes, Louis B., and Hershon, Simon. 1976. "Transferring Power in the Family Business." *Harvard Business Review* 54 (July–August):105–114.

Bennis, Warren. 1976. *The Unconscious Conspiracy: Why Leaders Can't Lead.* New York: AMACOM.

Blau, Peter M., and Schoenherr, Richard A. 1971. *The Structure of Organizations.* New York: Basic Books.

Blauner, Robert. 1964. *Alienation and Freedom.* Chicago: University of Chicago Press.

Brown, L. Dave. 1977. "Can 'Haves' and 'Have-Nots' Cooperate? Two Efforts to Bridge a Social Gap." *Journal of Applied Behavioral Science* 13:211–224.

Burns, Thomas S. 1974. *Tales of ITT: An Insider's Report.* Boston: Houghton-Mifflin.

Chandler, Alfred D., Jr. 1962. *Strategy and Structure: Chapters in the History of the Industrial Enterprise.* Cambridge, Mass.: MIT Press.

Chinoy, Eli. 1955. *Automobile Workers and the American Dream.* Garden City, New York: Doubleday.

Cohen, Lawrence B. 1976. "The Structure of Workers' Decisions." *Journal of Economic Issues* 10:524–537.

Congressional Record. Wednesday, March 1, 1978: No. 27. Washington.

Downing, George. 1967. "The Changing Structure of a Great Corporation." In W. Lloyd Warner et al., eds., *The Emergent American Society: Large Scale Organizations.* Vol. 1. New Haven: Yale University Press. Pp. 158–240.

Dill, William. 1978. *Running the American Corporation.* Englewood Cliffs, N.J.: Prentice-Hall.

Ephron, Nora. 1976. "The Bennington Affair." *Esquire* 86 (September): 53–58, 142–51.

Gardner, B. B., and Whyte, W. F. 1945. "The Man in the Middle: Position and Problems of the Foreman." *Applied Anthropology (Human Organization)* 2:1–28.

Greiner, Larry E. 1972. "Evolution and Revolution as Organizations Grow." *Harvard Business Review* 50 (July–August):37–46.

Gyllenhammer, Pehr. 1975. *People at Work.* Reading, Mass.: Addison-Wesley.

Hackman, J. Richard. 1977. "Work Design." In J. R. Hackman and J. L. Suttle, eds., *Improving Life at Work: Behavioral Science Approaches to Organizational Change.* Santa Monica, Cal.: Goodyear. Pp. 96–162.

Hall, Richard H. 1968. "Professionalization and Bureaucratization." *American Sociological Review* 33:92–104.

Heydebrand, Wolf V., ed. 1973. *Comparative Organizations: The Results of Empirical Research.* Englewood Cliffs, N.J.: Prentice-Hall.

Haden-Guest, Anthony. 1973. *The Paradise Program.* New York: William Morrow and Company.

Hollander, Samuel. 1965. *The Sources of Increased Efficiency: A Study of DuPont Rayon Plants.* Cambridge, Mass.: MIT Press.

Hughes, Everett C. 1945. "Dilemmas and Contradictions of Status." *American Journal of Sociology* 50:353–59.

Hunnius, Gerry. 1971. "The Yugoslav System of Decentralization and Self-Management," in G. Benello and D. Roussopolous, eds., *The Case for Participatory Democracy: The Case for the Radical Society.* New York: Grossman, Pp. 140–77.

"Industrial Psychology on the Line." 1978. *Psychology Today* 12:66–76.

Kanter, Rosabeth Moss. 1972. *Commitment and Community.* Cambridge, Mass.: Harvard University Press.

Kanter, Rosabeth Moss. 1977. *Men and Women of the Corporation.* New York: Basic Books.

Kanter, Rosabeth Moss. 1978a. "Powerlessness." *New York Times*, April 6.

Kanter, Rosabeth Moss. 1978b. "Work in a New America." *Daedalus* 107:47–78.

Kanter, Rosabeth Moss, and Zurcher, Louis. 1973. "Evaluating Alternatives and Alternative Valuing." *Journal of Applied Behavioral Science* 9:381–97.

Katzell, Raymond A., and Yankelovich, Daniel. 1975. *Work, Productivity, and Job Satisfaction.* New York: Psychological Corporation.

Kissinger, Henry A. 1968. "The White Revolutionary: Reflections on Bismarck." *Daedalus* 97:888–924.

Lawrence, Paul R., and Lorsch, Jay. 1967. *Organizations and Environment.* Boston: Division of Research, Graduate School of Business, Harvard University.

Lieberman, Seymour. 1956. "The Effects of Changes in Roles on the Attitudes of Role Occupants." *Human Relations* 9:385–402.

McCann, Thomas. 1976. *An American Company: The Tragedy of United Fruit.* New York: Crown. P. 181.

McKinley, Donald Gilbert. 1964. *Social Class and Family Life.* New York: Free Press.

Mansbridge, Jane. 1973. "Time, Emotion, and Inequality: Three Problems of Participatory Groups." *Journal of Applied Behavioral Science* 9:351–68.

Mechanic, David. 1962. "Sources of Power of Lower Participants in Complex Organizations." *Administrative Science Quarterly* 7 (December):349–64.

Merton, Robert K. 1961. "Bureaucratic Structure and Personality." In A. Etzioni, ed., *Complex Organizations: A Sociological Reader.* New York: Holt, Rinehart.

Michels, Robert. 1949. *First Lectures in Political Sociology.* Minneapolis: University of Minnesota Press.

Mulder, Mauk. 1971. "Power Equalization Through Participation?" *Administrative Science Quarterly* 16:31–40.

Parsons, Talcott, et al. 1961. *Theories of Society.* Vol. 1. New York: Free Press.

Rosenbaum, James. 1978. Personal communication, Yale University.

Rothschild-Whitt, Joyce. 1976. "Problems of Democracy." *Working Papers for a New Society* 4 (Fall):41–45.

Schrank, Robert. 1978. *Ten Thousand Working Days.* Cambridge, Mass.: MIT Press.

Seeman, Melvin. 1975. "Alienation Studies." *Annual Review of Sociology* 1:91–124.

Selznick, Philip. 1966. *TVA and the Grass Roots.* New York: Harper & Row.

Sills, David L. 1967. *The Volunteers: Means and Ends in a National Organization.* Glencoe, Illinois: The Free Press.

Silverman, David, and Jones, Jill. 1973. "Getting In: The Managed Accomplishment of 'Correct' Selection Outcomes." In J. Child, ed., *Man and Organization.* New York: Wiley. Pp. 63–106.

Smith, Richard Austin. 1963. *Corporations in Crisis.* Garden City, New York: Doubleday, 1963; Anchor edition, 1966.

Srivastva, Suresh, et al. 1975. *Job Satisfaction and Productivity.* Cleveland: Department of Organization Behavior, Case Western Reserve University.

Starbuck, William H. 1965. "Organizational Growth and Development." In J. G. March, ed., *Handbook of Organizations.* Chicago: Rand McNally. Pp. 451–533.

Stein, Barry A. 1971. *The Community Context of Economic Conversion.* Cambridge, Mass.: Center for Community Economic Development.

Stein, Barry A. 1976. "Getting There: Patterns in Managerial Success." Cambridge, Mass.: Goodmeasure.

Stein, Barry A. 1974. *Size, Efficiency and Community Enterprise.* Cambridge, Mass.: Center for Community Economic Development.

Steinmetz, Lawrence L. 1969. "Critical Stages of Small Business Growth." *Business Horizons* 12 (February):29–36.

Stinchcombe, Arthur L. 1965. "Social Structure and Organizations." In J. G. March, ed., *Handbook of Organizations.* Chicago: Rand McNally. Pp. 142–93.

Strauss, George. 1974. "Adolescence in Organizations' Growth." *Organizational Dynamics* 2 (Spring):2–17.

Torbert, William R. 1974/75. "Pre-Bureaucratic and Post-Bureaucratic Stages of Organizational Development." *Interpersonal Development* 5:1–25.

Torbert, William R., with Rogers, Malcolm P. 1973. *Being for the Most Part Puppets: The Interaction of Men's Labor, Leisure, and Politics.* Cambridge, Mass.: Schenkman.

References

Vroom, Victor H. 1960. *Some Personality Determinants of the Effects of Participation.* Englewood Cliffs, New Jersey: Prentice-Hall.

Walton, Richard E. 1974. "Innovative Restructuring of Work." In J. Rosow, ed., *The Worker and the Job: Coping with Change.* Englewood Cliffs, N.J.: Prentice-Hall.

Wolff, Kurt H., ed. 1950. *The Sociology of Georg Simmel.* Part 3: "Superordination and Subordination." New York: Free Press.

INDEX

Index   441

up and, 220–23; Lordstown strike and, 209–12, 216, 219; and worker control, 188
Professionals, 106–15; as experts, 96; knowledge specialists as, 116; as part of middle management, 80, 85, 89, 90
Promotions, see Advancement
Proxmire, William, 174
Public Affairs, Bureau of, 55, 59
Publicness/privateness issue: facing top executives, 30–34

Ramon, Simon, 119
Ramsey (Baker plant employee), 428
Rationality: purpose served by organizational, 88
Readers's Digest plant, 179, 180, 183, 227–28, 233, 236–38
Reese, Jack (pseudonym), 114·
Regan, Peter, 335–36, 346, 347
Reingold, Edwin, 207
Renda, Dominic P., 69, 71–72
Renewal: closings and need for, 385–86
Retail sales workers, 239–51; birth of, 241–43; in coats departments, 243–45; lunch hour of, 245–47; personnel policies affecting, 248–51; quarters for, 247–48
Retirement: being fired vs., 378–79
Reuther, Walter, 210
Revson, Charles, 8
Rice (Stanford University president), 345
Risk-taking attitude: play-it-safe vs., in middle management, 92–93
Rituals: fighting boredom of factory work with, 182, 190–202
Robertson, Frank, 380, 387, 412–28
Rockwell, Ned, 417, 427–28
Rodgers, Malcolm P., 184
Roosevelt, Franklin D., 46
Rosenbaum, James, 84
Roth, Philip, 38
Roudebush, Richard L., 369
Routine: in bottom positions, 81–82, 177; as destroyer of creativity, 37; of factory work, 197 (see also Assembly line work); interference of, with exercise of power, 9–10; powerlessness of middle management and, 94; see also Boredom
Roy, Donald, 177, 179, 181, 182, 191–205

Sabotage, 183, 185, 206, 215
Safety issues: in factories, 217
Saint-Exupery, Antoine de, 7
Sales careers, see Career women
Salinger, Pierre, 67
Saltarelli, Gerald, 343, 344
San Francisco Bureau of Building Inspection, 324
San Francisco Chamber of Commerce, 304, 319, 325
San Francisco City Planning Commission, 316, 318–19, 325–37, 329
San Francisco City Planning Department, xiii, 304, 316, 318–33; civil servants at, 319–24; Mayor Alioto and, xiii, 306, 322, 327–31; neighborhood militants and, 332–33; Office of Community Development and, 329–32; other city departments relations with, 324–26; Planning Commission and, 316, 318–19, 325–27, 329
San Francisco Municipal Railroad, 324
San Francisco Police Department, 324
San Francisco Public Works Department, 304, 305, 307, 316, 319, 324–25
San Francisco Recreation and Park Department, 324
San Francisco Redevelopment Agency, 318
Schoenherr, Richard A., 267
Schrank, Robert, 183
Scientific management, 178
Scully, Jane, 372
Seagram's Distillers Company, 18
Secrecy, 9; in dissolution process, 398–99; in foreign policy-making, 63; skullduggery and, 312; Watergate scandal, 10, 44, 48, 313
Secretaries, 21; career women as bosses of female, 150; as status symbol, 22–23
Securities and Exchange Commission (SEC), 317, 363, 369
Seeman, Melvin, 187
Self-assertion: to handle identity confusion problems of career women, 145–46
Self-estrangement: alienation and, 181
Self-management (worker control), 15, 187–90, 217; see also International Group Plans; Participation
Selznick, Philip, 304, 308, 383
Seniority: status and, in factories, 195
Sex discrimination: in bottom positions, 179; in retail work, 250–51

10 3 4 9 *A*

Date Due

SEP 8	1987		
OCT 2 5	1987		
MAR 1 3	1989		
NOV 3	1989		
MAY 9	1990		
NOV 0 2	1992		